Feature
Writing

Feature
Writing
Telling the Story

Third Edition

Stephen Tanner

Nick Richardson

Molly Kasinger

OXFORD
UNIVERSITY PRESS
AUSTRALIA & NEW ZEALAND

OXFORD
UNIVERSITY PRESS

Oxford University Press is a department of the University of Oxford.
It furthers the University's objective of excellence in research,
scholarship, and education by publishing worldwide. Oxford is a registered
trademark of Oxford University Press in the UK and in certain other countries.

Published in Australia by
Oxford University Press
253 Normanby Road, South Melbourne, Victoria 3205, Australia
© Stephen Tanner, Nick Richardson, Molly Kasinger 2017

The moral rights of the author/s have been asserted.

First edition published 2009

Second edition published 2012

Third edition published 2017

National Library of Australia Cataloguing-in-Publication entry

Creator: Tanner, Stephen, author.

Title: Feature writing: telling the story/Stephen Tanner; Nick Richardson; Molly Kasinger.

Edition: Third edition

ISBN: 9780190304881 (paperback)

Notes: Includes index.

Subjects: Feature writing–Technique.
Journalism–Research.
Authorship.
Digital media.
Online journalism.

Other Creators/Contributors:
Richardson, Nick, author.
Kasinger, Molly, author.

Reproduction and communication for educational purposes

Edited by Liz Filleul
Typeset by Newgen KnowledgeWorks Pvt. Ltd., Chennai, India
Proofread by Philip Bryan
Indexed by Russell Brooks
Printed in China by Leo Paper Products Ltd.

Contents

Acknowledgments

Journalism is a wonderful profession. Depending on how you view it, it can provide either a window on the world or a mirror that reflects the world. How we see that world, perhaps even interpret it, depends on the skills of the journalists whose words dominate the pages of newspapers and magazines, radio and television bulletins, or online sites. As such, journalism is multidimensional.

News reporting provides the first dimension. In news parlance it seeks to answer the 'who, what, when, where, how and why' questions. And while good news reporting answers these questions competently, it can often leave readers, viewers or listeners seeking more information. That is where the second dimension emerges.

This dimension is provided by feature writers, producers and columnists. Whereas news reporting is expected to be fair, perhaps neutral, feature writing is not governed by the same conventions. Feature writers, producers and columnists are permitted to give their personal opinions; in some instances they are expected to do so.

Features and columns offer considerable challenges for writers, particularly for young journalists who are seeking to establish their own identities and credentials, both among their peers and with a wider audience. We believe that this book will help you to develop the confidence to experiment across a number of different styles.

The book builds on our collective experiences as journalists and academics. It also draws on the experiences of other journalists and people whose work impacts on the responsibilities of journalism. It is obviously a joint effort and we've tried to present a single voice throughout, although just occasionally hints might emerge as to the interests of the author who wrote a particular chapter or shared a personal anecdote.

In this, our third edition, the work has been undertaken by Richardson and Tanner. Molly Kasinger, our colleague for the first two editions, was unable to contribute due to ill health. However, in recognition of Molly's contributions to the first and second editions, much of which has been retained for this new edition, we have continued to acknowledge her involvement.

As with the two previous editions, we're proud of the finished product, but we won't claim all the credit, recognising that many others have shared in the trials, tribulations and pleasures along the way.

Nick Richardson would like to thank a number of journalists who, over the years, have been wise mentors and great role models: John Kiely, Andrew Rule, Damien Murphy, Mark Gardy and Sybil Nolan among them. A special thanks to Steve, who has helped hatch and nurture a number of ventures—including this one—that have drawn on our shared (journalistic) past and our mutual commitment to a closer fit between journalism theory and practice. It's always been great fun. And, as always, thanks to Sue and Patrick, for taking care of the back story.

Stephen Tanner would like to thank Nick for his friendship and support across their various publishing ventures. At a time when universities seem to be losing sight of their primary responsibility—namely to educate and train future generations of professionals—it is a pleasure to have a colleague and friend who shares such a belief and who is a rare combination of academic and practitioner, one who understands the importance of collaboration between the academy and industry. Thanks also to his colleagues—journalistic and academic—who have taught him so much about this wonderful profession over nearly four decades. It has been an enjoyable learning experience. Finally, but most importantly, thanks as always to Kath, Millie, Lucy and Hamish, who provide the little sparks that inspire and motivate him to do more.

To the feature writers, all of them wonderful exponents of the craft, who contributed their time, thoughts, experience and work for this publication—Trent Dalton, Melissa Field, Michael Gleeson, Mike Grenby, Lee Gutkind, Patrick Carlyon, Andrew Rule, Huw Parkinson, Joshua Robertson, Wendy Tuohy, Rebecca Skloot, Leanne Edmistone, Alexandra Fisher, and Annika Smethurst—thank you all.

To the academic practitioners who contributed the professional review sheets—Shady Cosgrove, Tim Maddock, David Vance and Diana Wood Conroy—thank you for shedding light on your respective disciplines.

Finally, thank you to our colleagues at Oxford for the faith they have shown in this project—to Karen Hildebrandt who has championed our work, including the three editions of this book, and our other book (*Journalism Investigation and Research in a Digital World*) and Shari Serjeant, who managed this edition, almost to the end. Thank you both for your patience and forbearance. To Alex Chambers, who managed the production process and Liz Filleul, who has come on board as editor, thank you for your contributions; especially your kind words, Liz.

Nick and Stephen, 2017

The authors and the publisher wish to thank the following copyright holders for reproduction of their material.

Amy, P. (2008) 'Honour for cricket great', Mordialloc Chelsea Leader, 12 March, licensed with Copyright Agency Australia; Carlyon, L. (1997) 'On Her Majesty's service', The Sunday Age, 19 October, licensed with Copyright Agency Australia; Carlyon, Patrick for 'Yep, wait, we definitely have a...Medic! Medic! Medic! Medic!' Sunday Herald Sun, March 17, 2013; Dalton, Trent for Orange crush by Trent Dalton, The Courier-Mail, Q Weekend magazine, 9 July 2011.; Edmistone, Leanne 'If there were a magic pill to suddenly be tall would I take it? No.' by Leanne Edmistone, Q Weekend magazine, 2 April, 2016, licensed with Copyright Agency Australis; Field, Melissa for 'If celebrities can adopt children from overseas ... why can't we?', Marie Claire, March 2008; Gleeson, Michael 'Who gets hit by a tram?', The Age, 22 November 2008, licensed with Copyright Agency Australia; Grenby, Mike for 'Dainty plates eatery all the rage in London', by Mike Grenby, Calgary Herald, 30 June 2010; Copyright Guardian News & Media Ltd 2017 for 'George Christensen on poverty, priesthood and a flirtation with One Nation' by Joshua Robertson, published The Guardian (online) September 26, 2016; Parkinson, Huw for the case study 'Huw Parkinson, ABC Insiders, 2015 Walkley Award for multimedia storytelling, talks about how he makes video mash-ups that comment on the week's news'; Rule, Andrew 'Saving Lynny: The ultimate love story', Herald Sun, 25 June 2011, p. 1 and pp. 23–6, licensed with Copyright Agency Australis; Skloot, Rebecca for 'Fixing Nemo', The New York Times, 2 May 2004; Tuohy, Wendy 'Rougher, harder, violent: how porn is warping the male mind", by Wendy Tuohy, RendezView website, published July 24, 2015, licensed with Copyright Agency Australia; MISTER TANNER, Words and Music by HARRY CHAPIN, © 1973 (Renewed) STORY SONGS, LTD, All Rights Administered by WB MUSIC CORP, All Rights Reserved.

Every effort has been made to trace the original source of copyright material contained in this book. The publisher will be pleased to hear from copyright holders to rectify any errors or omissions.

Introduction

> Begin at the beginning and go on till you come to the end; then stop.
>
> Lewis Carroll, *Alice's Adventures in Wonderland*

Since prehistoric times, when exploits were recorded on rock faces using simple drawings, humans have communicated through storytelling. These stories have detailed the exploits of hunters and gatherers, generals and kings, martyrs and local heroes. They have covered wars, plagues and fires, new discoveries, and sporting and political victories. They have covered the good and the bad, the hopeful and the hopeless. In short, they have informed society about itself and, in so doing, they have provided history's first draft.

If you read some of the earliest journalistic accounts, such as those documented in the *Faber Book of Reportage* (Carey, 2003), you will see a wide range of writing. Some reflect standardised news writing models, with a distinct emphasis on the '5Ws and H' (*who, what, when, where, why* and *how*). Others, however, reveal a more literary style, which is reflective of the so-called 'New Journalism' that emerged in the 1960s. Today, this style has established an important following among writers, particularly those who seek to immerse themselves in the story. More recently, technological change has seen the ranks of journalism embrace other creative types—those whose forte is humour and satire, as well as those who have the capacity to add to a story through the ever-increasing range of software programs that add sound, movement and analysis to the written or spoken word.

Journalism has faced some extraordinary challenges during the past 25 years, not just from the pace of technological change and the collapse of newspapers' revenue model. In fact, there have been plenty of issues about the craft of journalism—whether it was the revelations from WikiLeaks and the Panama Papers, or the tawdry revelations of the Leveson Inquiry—that have reaffirmed the need for journalists, wherever they are, to adopt an ethical and scrupulous approach to hold authority to account. And to do that effectively, we must be armed with a set of skills that enable us to go below the surface news and to tell a compelling story.

Throughout this text we use the term 'writer' or 'writers' when referring to people who produce feature articles. Occasionally we use other terms too, such as 'producer' to reflect the fact that feature articles are not confined to the written word. Although, having said that, the word—be it oral or written—does tend to underpin much of what we call features. And there is evidence that despite all the technological challenges facing print, many of us are still heavily engaged with the so-called 'legacy' product. A 2016 study found that the overwhelming majority of British newspaper readers spent far more time with a print edition of their 11 national mastheads and hardly any time with the papers' websites. The study revealed readers spent on average 40 minutes with their preferred print title but less than 30 seconds a day for each online visit to a newspaper's website (Shafer, 2017). Nonetheless, recent technological developments have meant that much of what is produced no longer appears on a static page. Much appears in a multi-platform format. It can appear in print in a hardcopy form. But that is becoming increasingly rare. Today, much of what we call features is appearing online in a mix of formats. The word is still central, but it no longer needs to be written down. It may be spoken (such as in longer form interviews and audio documentaries), or it may be presented as a video-based documentary where interviews are complemented by outstanding vision. Audio and video have taken feature-writing to a new level of engagement, in which emotion can be captured and presented with an immediacy or harshness, that in the past words alone or words in combination with stills photography struggled to portray. At a time when many people within the industry are bemoaning the death of traditional journalism, the reality is that technology is creating many opportunities for people who want to produce feature-length journalism.

Underpinning all forms of journalism is the desire to tell a story and a wish to tell it accurately. But to do so we need access to the people we want to write and talk about. Again, there are challenges here for journalists. The election of Donald Trump as US President highlights this. Trump has become president at a time when technological change, particularly the development of social media, gives newsmakers the capacity to speak directly to their constituents and, in the process, bypass the mainstream media. Political figures like Trump have also used social media to question the motives and integrity of media organisations that are critical of them, leading to the emergence of new terms such as 'post truth', 'alternative facts', and 'fake news', the latter being named *Macquarie Dictionary's* word of the year for 2016.

But what do they mean and what are the implications for journalism? 'Fake news', according to the *Macquarie Dictionary*, refers to the 'creation of deceptive content', such as the claim that Donald Trump had been endorsed by Pope Francis (Guardian Australia, 2017). It further defines 'fake news' as 'disinformation and hoaxes published on websites for political purposes or to drive web traffic' as well as 'incorrect information being passed along by social media.' The key words and phrases are 'disinformation', 'hoaxes' and 'for political purposes'.

Journalists have always been wary of the motives of people they write about, particularly high profile political and business figures who generally have a particular agenda in mind when they speak to the media. But the need to be wary has taken on a new significance in the aftermath of Trump's inauguration, particularly given the emergence of the phrase 'alternative facts', coined by Trump counsellor Kellyanne Conway, who was defending White House spokesman Sean Spicer for attacking the media over claims that the crowds attending the ceremony were significantly lower than those for Barack Obama's inauguration. Spicer wasn't convinced by photographs or television footage, choosing to play semantics, telling the media during a briefing: 'I think sometimes we can disagree with the facts'.

The concern for us is that while social media can be an important form of communication, there is a risk that because it is subject to such blatant manipulation, people are becoming increasingly vulnerable to 'fake news', be that news manufactured by people with a particular political agenda, or information produced by like-minded people, with the truth being sidelined in the process. One of the challenges for mainstream journalism is to reassert its credentials, be that in a watchdog role, or simply by ensuring that all critical voices involved in an issue are represented in a story. Journalism's role has rarely been more important. Of course, there are forms of feature writing that are not contentious. But that doesn't mean that there aren't challenges attached to those as well, including working within—and to—the new technologies that journalism has embraced. This book is designed to help you tap into those opportunities by developing the skills that will enable you to work as a feature writer or even to delve into the area of creative non-fiction.

Beyond writing the news

If you have ever sat in a local council meeting taking notes on a four-hour discussion about whether the dog park's hours should be 8 am to 5 pm or 9 am to 6 pm, and wondered if this is all there is to journalism, this book has the answer. Here, you will be shown how to step out of the hard news world and into the realm of journalists such as Alexandra Fisher, Andrew Rule and Leanne Edmistone.

Perhaps you are a journalism student or a fiction writer and you want to try something new and challenging. This book will show you how to research, structure and write stories, how to navigate legal and ethical issues, and how to market your work. You will learn how to tackle different styles of writing, from profiles to issues-based stories, columns, biographies and reviews. The book offers you a chance to change the way you see journalism, or to start a new career that can pay the bills and fulfil your passion, whether that passion is to see the truth on the page, reveal new worlds to readers or spend every day doing what you love—writing. Feature writing offers enormous possibilities—as a staff writer on a newspaper, a columnist in a magazine, or a freelancer with a laptop as your office. It also opens doors for people who don't want to work in mainstream media, but have an interest in a particular area, be that fashion, motor vehicles, technology, travel or fine dining, to give just a few examples, and want to turn that into a career by establishing a blog or vlog.

Why write feature stories?

Feature writing is for journalists who find traditional news formats too limiting. It appeals to writers who find the 'he said, she said' approach to reporting too stilted; who can't engage with the inverted pyramid structure for telling a story—where the 'who, what, when, where, how and why' questions are answered at the beginning of the story—or who find pitching their stories at an audience with an average reading age of between 12 and 14 too mundane. Feature writing is for people who have a creative streak, but nonetheless recognise that journalism is still about conveying the truth.

Feature writing can take many forms, and while we tend to refer to it as longer-form writing, it need not be. Some effective features can be short and punchy, running to perhaps a few hundred words. Newspaper features, for example, can range from as few as 400 words to as many as five or six thousand if they are dealing with a complex issue. Specialist magazines such as *The New Yorker* or *The Atlantic Monthly* may give writers space for a 10,000-word piece. However, feature articles are not really distinguished by their length, but by what they do and how they do it.

Feature writers have more freedom, both in the topics they tackle and the approach they take, though they still seek to answer the 'who, what, when, where, how and why' questions that underpin news reporting.

Obviously the degree of autonomy they enjoy will depend on the nature of the writing they undertake. Political or business journalists, for example, will often be asked to write issues-based features that seek to explain a complex announcement or event. They will be expected to work within fairly predictable parameters; cover the major arguments for or against a proposal; interview the key stakeholders; and conduct sufficient research to ensure that the readers, viewers or listeners who engage with the feature are sufficiently informed to be able to make their own assessment of the issue being debated.

But feature writing is not only about providing explanations of complex political, social or economic events and issues. Feature writing is versatile; in fact its scope is limitless. Feature writing techniques are also widely used to produce profiles, obituaries, reviews and columns. Whereas the issues-based feature embraces traditional journalistic practices, including balance and fairness, other forms invite (even expect, on occasions) writers to immerse themselves in the story. Some, including reviews and opinion columns, are, by their very nature, opinionated.

Powerful writing can reduce readers to tears at one turn and have them laughing until it hurts at the next. It has the capacity to engage or offend. But above all, it 'aims to inform, persuade or entertain a large audience in a purposeful way' (Hennessy, 1989, p. 7). The key phrase here is 'in a purposeful way'. Feature writing is never tackled lightly, even if the outcome is intended to be a light-hearted piece that is designed to entertain rather than inform or persuade the audience.

Underpinning all forms of feature writing are the following fundamental ingredients: strong research, strong 'talent' (journalistic jargon for sources), strong writing and a strong structure. If one of these is missing then the article is not likely to meet its goals. Strong writing will not make up for underdeveloped or inaccurate research. Poor sources will limit the capacity of a writer to develop key themes, particularly if coupled with poor research. Finally, strong research is wasted if the writing is undisciplined or the story thrown together in a way that does not permit the argument, commentary or narrative to flow logically.

From feature writing to creative non-fiction

Some journalists, having experienced the freedom feature writing offers, want to take their writing to the next level. For many, that means creative non-fiction. This is not, as the term suggests, a hybrid between journalism and fiction. Although some journalists have become successful novelists, creative non-fiction is firmly rooted in journalistic traditions.

The differences between feature writing as the traditionalists understand it and creative non-fiction in its various guises boil down to three elements. The first is style. Creative non-fiction or literary journalism makes greater use of narrative technique than traditional journalism features. The second is immersion. Traditional journalism encourages the writer to stand apart from the story. Creative non-fiction, on the other hand, encourages immersion. The journalist becomes part of the story, a participant-observer. The third is length. As we discussed earlier, feature articles can range from a few hundred to a few thousand words (generally fewer than 6000). Creative non-fiction, on the other hand, is often book-length. Such pieces may range from 50,000 words to 150,000 words, depending on the subject matter.

Students of journalism may argue that narrative technique has been used in journalism throughout history. Though this is true, for much of the modern era literary styles were discouraged and the inverted pyramid reigned supreme. It was not until the 1960s that a number of American journalists began to question the merits of traditional journalism, embracing narrative forms and becoming known as members of a movement called 'New Journalism'.

Journalists such as Tom Wolfe, Truman Capote and Hunter S. Thompson wanted to emulate the style of journalism favoured by the likes of Ernest Hemingway, George Orwell, Lillian Ross, Joseph Mitchell, A.J. Liebling and John Hersey. The style of journalism embraced by Wolfe and his contemporaries rattled the traditionalists, who believed in a journalism that was built around objectivity and unbiased factual reporting. The New Journalists, on the other hand, were advocating a style of journalism infused with literary techniques.

New Journalism, as described by Wolfe, involved 'scene-by-scene construction', recording dialogue 'in full' and 'presenting every scene to the reader through the eyes of a particular character' (Taylor, 2002, p. 29). But you should remember that while the journalist may aim to produce work that reads like a novel, this work should never stray from the truth. It is clearly non-fiction and, as such, should never include fabricated facts, composite characters or invented scenarios (that bag of tricks is for the fiction writer).

Wolfe became a staff writer for *New York* magazine and used his literary journalism techniques to provide deep insight into a wide range of topics, including the world of hippies, the Black Panther movement, *Playboy* founder Hugh Hefner, rocket pilots and artists. The keys to his work and success were in-depth reporting, characterisation and detail.

One of Wolfe's contemporaries was Truman Capote, author of *In Cold Blood* (1966), the first novel-length piece of reportage. *In Cold Blood* is a 360-page account of the brutal murder of an American farming family. Capote spent years researching the murders and reconstructing them in the book, which was subsequently turned into an Oscar-winning film. Of the experience, he said:

> While writing it, I realized I just might have found a solution to what had always been my greatest creative quandary. I wanted to produce a journalistic novel, something on a large scale that would have the credibility of fact, the immediacy of film, the depth and freedom of prose, and the precision of poetry.
>
> PBS.org, 2006

New Journalism also struck a chord with other journalists, including Australian author Evan Whitton. In 1967, Whitton, a journalist for a not-so-reputable Melbourne newspaper, *Truth*, set out to write a feature story on the life of a pensioner. His editor had asked for as much detail as possible, so Whitton believed there was only one way to cover the story—to live as a pensioner. He dressed in old clothes, lived on the equivalent of a government hand-out, was fed by charities and slept in a Fitzroy doss house, spending his days as a down-and-out pensioner, looking in shop windows and lounging in public libraries to stave off the boredom and the cold.

One afternoon in the State Library, Whitton came across an old copy of *Encounter* magazine. Inside, he found correspondence between Tom Wolfe and Frank Kermode on New Journalism. This was writing that covered intimate detail, delved into character, called for immersion in the subject matter and reported on the 'status life' of people—their customs, clothing, relationships and social standing. Whitton had found his medium. He then wrote a diarised description of life on $15 a week and won a Walkley Award for the Best Feature Story (Hurst, 1988, pp. 117–20).

This type of approach has also been adopted by a number of contemporary Australian writers, including Sarah MacDonald (*Holy Cow!* 2002), Estelle Blackburn (*Broken Lives*, 2002), Helen Garner (*Joe Cinque's Consolation*, 2004) and David Leser (*To Begin to Know*, 2014). If you are serious about journalism and longer-form writing, these writers all warrant your scrutiny.

Many such works have grown out of shorter pieces written for magazines or newspapers. A good example is Mark Bowden's *Black Hawk Down* (1999), which was originally written for *The Philadelphia Inquirer* and published as a series in 1997. The full text of the story, including photographs, audio and video, can be found at <http://inquirer.philly.com/packages/somalia>. Sometimes such writing is based on the individual writer's own particular situation, as was the case with *Girl, Interrupted* (1995), a memoir by American writer Susanna Kaysen, which talks about her mental illness. Both these books are excellent examples—as is Blackburn's *Broken Lives*—of how creative non-fiction can be used to tell a journalistic story.

A number of colleagues have questioned why we included a discussion about creative non-fiction in a book intended to teach the skills of feature writing. We feel that because experienced journalists have made the transition to this genre, a chapter that introduces this topic would be useful.

However, you shouldn't expect to produce book-length exposés immediately you walk into a newsroom. For a start, you won't be allocated the stories that lend themselves to such treatment. In addition, you won't have the skills—or the wherewithal—to attempt such a story. In fact, you'll probably have to wait five, 10 or 15 years before you either get the opportunity or have the confidence in your own abilities to attempt such a challenge.

What we are saying is that creative non-fiction is a viable option for experienced writers and, increasingly, it is being included as a subject in journalism programs to give students an insight into its possibilities. But the reality is that it will take time before you are in a position to give it a go. First, you need to be confident in your ability as a writer, and second, you need to have a story—and the reputation—that will attract a publisher. But it should not be beyond the reach of those who believe in their abilities and are prepared to work hard to realise a dream.

What this book is about

This is a book about writing, about craft, about how to hone your skills to the point where you are ready to send your stories to a publisher or editor. It will even help you deal with your first rejection, because you will *know* that you can write a feature story.

Given our backgrounds, the focus tends to be on the written word. But a lot of what we discuss in this book can also be applied to writing features for radio, television and online. The fact is that many of today's best feature stories are being published or broadcast electronically—via radio, television and, increasingly, the internet. We acknowledge this by starting the book with a new chapter on digital journalism. To be able to write successfully for these platforms you will need some additional skills that are generally learned outside a traditional feature-writing course, but increasingly are being incorporated into the core of degree programs. These are the technical skills that will enable you to edit your interview material so that the sound grabs can be interlaced with your own commentary, or that of another narrator, and perhaps even with some effects, such as music (in the case of radio). Television requires an additional suite of skills, as you will be expected to provide vision that not only complements the storyline but often steers it. While many radio journalists work solo, television journalists, particularly documentary makers, may work as part of a team that includes a journalist, a camera operator and a sound person. Writing for online publication often requires a multiple skill set that draws from print, radio and television. It may sound daunting, but the reality is that it provides tremendous opportunities for journalists who possess a creative bent that cannot necessarily be satisfied by the more traditional media.

Technological advancements have meant that journalists can now work on their own, juggling the responsibilities of script, video and sound. Increasingly, media organisations expect their journalists—staff and freelance—to perform many roles and there are now many opportunities for multi-skilled people to work on quality documentaries. These are broadcast by channels such as SBS, and on the growing number of independent websites. The new environment provides many opportunities for journalists—freelance and staff—to develop their work to suit a niche market, both in the mainstream and developing media. Having said this, however, the future of journalism (particularly multi-media journalism) appears to be with teams. This is highlighted by some of the examples we refer to, particularly in Chapter 1, which discusses the award-winning 2012 *New York Times* piece 'Snow Fall,' or the more recent 'Phoebe's Fall,' a six-part podcast produced by Fairfax. These superbly crafted pieces highlight the skills of a range of people.

Structure of the book

This is a practical guide. It utilises the work of professionals and the hard lessons they have learned from their experience as writers to help you understand feature writing and to develop your skills. Step-by-step descriptions of styles and techniques, discussions of real articles, and interviews with working journalists who reveal all the behind-the-scenes action of how they write their stories will help you develop your own feature-writing skills.

This book also asks you to critically evaluate not just your own work, but also that of more established journalists. It takes hard work to develop a writing and presentational style that you can proudly call your own. Initially you will be influenced by some of the writers, broadcasters and bloggers you admire—and even some you dislike intensely. You may borrow from the former and learn from the latter, seeking to avoid what you consider to be the weaknesses in their writing styles—considering the words or phrases they use, and the methods they adopt to develop an argument or introduce an opinion.

Your writing will mature over time. We believe, as do many other experienced journalists, that feature writing is not a skill you can pick up overnight but is acquired with experience. Young reporters can be trained quickly to produce news stories. But feature writing in its various forms requires specialist skills. The first is the ability to write in an engaging manner, in a style that people feel comfortable with. They might not agree with what you say—in fact they might read you specifically because they disagree with you. But they are unlikely to read your stories or listen to you on radio, television or online at all if your style is clumsy or tortuous, and your argument inconsistent.

In five years' time you'll look back at some of your early pieces, perhaps bearing your byline, proudly stuck into your scrapbook and say: 'How could I have written that?' In 10 years' time, hopefully, you'll look back on your first decade as a feature writer and say: 'Gee, my writing has matured. It has taken time, but I can see how it has developed and I understand why it has improved.'

Feature writing involves more than throwing together some facts and making sure that the most important information is at the top. It offers the opportunity to delve deeper, to paint a picture of what you have witnessed, and to focus on drawing in and engaging the reader right to the end. This is your chance to express yourself, to develop a personal voice that the world will want to hear. You *can* put your own ideas on the page and help to influence the lives of others through telling true stories (which could even be your own).

How to use this book

This book has been significantly re-worked since the first edition (2009) and the second edition (2013). We've added two new chapters, one on digital journalism to highlight the advances in journalism that have taken place in recent years, and the corresponding challenges and opportunities this has created for journalists and the organisations they work for. The second new chapter looks at investigative journalism. We've added this because we feel that all journalists can benefit from a basic grounding in investigative journalism: the skills that investigative journalists apply to their craft have a home in everyday journalism, be that feature-writing or news gathering. We've also re-worked many of the chapters to make the book more accessible, and we've added some new writing samples to reflect the outstanding work of the practitioners who have so willingly agreed to discuss their work with us (and you) in an attempt to demystify feature writing.

The first part of this book (chapters 1 to 11) provides all the background information necessary to start your feature-writing career. It explains how to find a story, how to research it, how to conduct interviews and how to use creative techniques. It also deals with ethical and legal issues, and the business of editing and polishing your work, then pitching it to a prospective publisher. You will discover that while feature writing can be an art form, it is not beyond your reach.

The second part (chapters 12 to 17) gives practical advice on different styles of non-fiction storytelling, including profiles, sports features, issues-based analysis, investigations, opinion pieces, columns, and creative non-fiction. You will discover the scope of this genre of writing and the myriad opportunities it offers. Many chapters include a case study featuring an author who has been where you are—at the beginning of life as a feature writer—showing how they have mastered the craft and offering strategies to help you tackle the tests and trials you may encounter when you sit down to write an article.

The third part (chapters 18 to 26) is devoted to reviews. In the previous editions we bundled a number of types of reviews into vaguely associated groupings. This time we decided to let them stand alone. In part this is in recognition of the fact that they are often produced by specialists. It also reflects their importance, particularly in a digital world.

You'll also notice that there are 26 chapters, though most university programs are limited to 12 or 13 weeks. We didn't want to limit ourselves, and we believe the structure of this book allows students and staff to choose what they want to learn, or teach, according to their own purpose.

At the end of every chapter there are questions that will help you to recall and examine key points about the topic at hand. There are also tasks to help you hone your skills and put what you have learned onto the page.

Storytelling is like playing the piano or any sport—the more you do it, the better you get. If you read this book, answer the questions and write every single day, you are on your way to a career in feature writing. But a word of warning. To become a great feature writer, you need to read widely (hence the inclusion of writing samples in many chapters). But ideally you should look beyond those samples. You need to broaden your horizons: investigate what other people are writing about and how they are doing it. It is amazing what you can learn from others. With any luck, by the time you finish, your perspective on the world will have changed, just a little. Your daily chores will no longer give you a sense of dread—instead they are ideas for articles. Your friends, teachers, family and co-workers are no longer just people in your life—they are sources for stories. Your hopes, your dreams and your ambitions are all fodder for your new life as a writer. Look around you—the world is an inspiration—learn the techniques of the feature writer and put the world on the page. Let the journey begin, and as Lewis Carroll so rightly points out, stick with it to the end.

References and additional reading

Blackburn, E. (2002). *Broken Lives,* Melbourne: Hardie Grant.

Blackburn, E. (2007). *The End of Innocence: The Remarkable True Story of One Woman's Fight for Justice,* Melbourne: Hardie Grant.

Bowden, M. (1999). *Black Hawk Down,* London: Transworld Publishers.

Capote, T. (1966). *In Cold Blood: A True Account of a Multiple Murder and its Consequences,* New York: Random House.

Carey, J. (ed.) (2003). *Faber Book of Reportage,* London: Faber & Faber.

Garner, H. (2004). *Joe Cinque's Consolation,* Sydney: Pan Macmillan.

Guardian Australia (2017). January 25. '"Fake news" named word of the year by Macquarie Dictionary', 25 January: https://www.theguardian.com/australia-news/2017/jan/25/fake-news-named-word-of-the-year-by-macquarie-dictionary.

Hennessey, B. (1989). *Writing Feature Articles: A Practical Guide to Methods and Markets,* Oxford: Heinemann Professional Publishing Ltd.

Hurst, J. (1988). *The Walkley Awards: Australia's Best Journalists in Action,* Melbourne: John Kerr Pty Ltd.

Kaysen, S. (1995). *Girl, Interrupted,* London: Virago Press.

Leser, D (2014). *To Begin to Know: Walking in the Shadows of my Father,* Sydney: Allen & Unwin.

MacDonald, S. (2002). *Holy Cow! An Indian Adventure*, Sydney: Bantam Books.

PBS.org (2006). *American Masters: Truman Capote*, 28 July: www.pbs.org/wnet/americanmasters/episodes/truman-capote/introduction/58/.

Shafer, J. (2017). 'Newspapers may be challenged, but readers refuse to let them die,' *The Australian*, 6 February, p. 25.

Taylor, P. (2002). 'Creative nonfiction', *Writer*, 115(2), pp. 29–33.

Part A

Mastering the Techniques

1
Digital Features

'[Blogging] is not a real job. Construction is a real job … Blogging is something you get to do. It is a quirky form of daily journalism, falling somewhere between live TV news and magazine writing, calling for sharp news judgement, and irrational taste for argument, and a complete absence of high standards.'

Hamilton Nolan, former Gawker blogger (Preston, 2016)

Objectives

In this chapter, you will learn about the range of options available for digital journalists who want to craft longer pieces. It will canvass blogging, podcasts and multimedia approaches. The chapter also emphasises the vital role audience occupies in the digital news environment. You are asked to look at:

o the prevalence of blogging

o the adoption of podcasts by mainstream media as a particular form of storytelling

o the need for collaboration to create meaningful multimedia journalism

o the opportunities to develop digital commentary and stories into satire and humour

o a Case study—Walkley Award-winning video mash-up man Huw Parkinson explains how he works and where he gets inspiration.

Introduction

In the early days of the internet, mainstream media outlets often saw their websites as just vehicles for longer versions of stories outside the time and space restrictions of the daily news cycle. Digital journalism was something that existed separately to the daily media, not as a rival or companion to it. Video was shot and audio recorded and then uploaded to news sites, often more from a sense of obligation to the digital environment than an understanding of how quality multimedia adds richness to news coverage. But as with many elements of the digital age, change has been rapid: there is an acceptance within mainstream media that those making engaging digital journalism have added a significant layer to the reader experience. Digital journalism that is thoughtful, considered and compelling—in a visual and audio sense—is now an effective measure of how evolved media has become. And that means digital journalism has become an exciting form of storytelling.

That is only part of the digital journalism story. For many older news consumers, reared on the (ideally) impartiality of newspapers, the modern version of journalism that embraces personal opinions and experiences, plus dialogue with readers, is somehow less than credible. It is as if the arrival of the perpendicular pronoun ('I') instantly disqualifies the content of authority and objectivity. Putting aside the ever-present tensions surrounding those two words, the reality is that journalists—and those who consume their content—now have a vastly expanded repertoire of informational experiences available to them. Digital media has created a range of opportunities that have given journalists a new playground to show off their skills. It has also provided them with new ways to promote their work—through Twitter and Facebook—that helps access audiences that previously had been less interested in conventional news and features. Whether it is blogging, podcasting, video or multimedia storytelling, there is a proliferation of ways to craft stories. Audience engagement is the key—how many and for how long can now be measured with such accuracy that feature writers can come away from a podcast they've created and know for the first time the size of the audience they've reached and what they think of their work. Some of the outlets—the lost and sometimes-lamented website Gawker, or Huffington Post or BuzzFeed—have a style (and content) that suits different journalistic tastes and priorities. But it has ever been thus. And all of these digital iterations represent the next stage in feature writing's evolution.

Let's look at some of the key examples.

Blogging

Blogging has, in some ways, passed most efficiently into the more mainstream of traditional media than some of its digital counterparts. And as a result, it is increasingly difficult to get reader attention without a particular perspective or gimmick. Nowadays it is not enough to have a rudimentary blog, shorn of embedded video and audio. The audience has quickly become more sophisticated and demands a digital presence that is instantly appealing, high on functionality and offers a range of diverting elements. Yet you will still find blogging in many mainstream media sites. One of the key reasons for this is arguably because blogging, in essence, is not radically different from opinion pieces or a personal column (see Chapter 16). Where blogs differentiate from columns is that they can be more instant—write when you are moved to do so or in the case of News Corp columnist Andrew Bolt, every day (often just several paragraphs) on a range of topics. It shouldn't be underestimated how difficult it is to have an opinion—and try to explain it or justify it—across a range of issues on a daily basis. Or in some cases, at various times during the day. Most people care passionately about a few things in their life—their family, their living standards, perhaps homelessness, poverty or mental health. Mainstream bloggers seem to be passionate about so many things. But what sustains them is audience engagement—without that constant stream of feedback, provoking, supporting, poking and prodding, the bloggers would have a hard time justifying their existence. Engagement is the bloggers' life source and the most high-profile mainstream bloggers—including Bolt and his News Corp colleagues such as Miranda Devine and Rita Panahi—have a loyal following that keeps echoing the bloggers' views and perspectives. Bear in mind though that these bloggers also have the weight of a newspaper behind them—their work usually appears in a newspaper and on the paper's website, providing a platform for interaction as well as a hosting point for the blog itself. Other bloggers don't have such a privileged position to develop their profile and audience, even if the dynamics of their work and engagement are similar. For those bloggers—whether they are using video (vloggers) and working in a specialised area—fashion, a particular sport, economics, military history etc.—there is a dedicated and knowledgeable audience that helps foster and preserve the niche offering. And in an era when the cost of producing information in traditional formats is increasingly uneconomic, a blog can be a cheap and easy way to find an audience that thinks like you do.

For all of that, there is an acknowledgment that blogging has morphed into something else that is part of the bigger social media environment of news and information. The international picture shows that the big international websites, such as BuzzFeed and Huffington Post (also with Australian presences), owe much to the philosophy of blogging and audience engagement. Professional networking sites such as LinkedIn also include blogging as part of their interactivity. One of the US's long-standing bloggers, Jason Kottke, wrote: '[T]he blog format has evolved, had social [media] grafted onto it, and mutated into Facebook, Twitter, and Pinterest and those new species have now taken over. No biggie, that's how technology and culture work' (Kottke, 2013).

Kottke's 'no biggie' comment perhaps underestimates the influence of social media. This was highlighted during the 2016 US presidential election campaign, when the 'fake news' controversy first broke. At the time, Facebook founder Mark Zuckerberg was forced to outline how his company would seek to combat fake news. Zuckerberg said that more than 99 per cent of Facebook's content was 'authentic' and introducing checks and balances was not designed to discourage sharing opinions. However this debate has taken on added importance following the election of Donald Trump as president. Trump's ongoing commentary about 'fake news', and his willingness to use social media as his main conduit to voters, has raised serious ethical questions about the capacity of the mainstream media to operate in such an environment (see discussion in chapters 8, 13 and 16). Questions about the veracity of content on a social media site's newsfeed will inevitably raise questions about the authenticity of the author: no serious journalist wants to have their credibility questioned or seen to be part of a discredited campaign by getting caught up in such shabby partisan exercises.

Podcasting

Australian radio, and the ABC in particular, has long been a champion of podcasting, following the lead of US and British public radio to help give listeners the opportunity to catch up on what they'd missed on air and sometimes offer unique content. It has only been recently that Australian newspapers and websites have followed that lead and crafted outstanding podcasts that were like true crime serials, weighted with first-hand testimony. The elements of a podcast have been around for a long time but these kinds of podcasts actually bring together several elements that result in something new. 'Podcasting has the raw intimacy of radio at its best, and it also has radio's advantage of informality,' one commentator noted. 'To listeners, it can feel as if the person is in their presence ... Podcasting ... like a novel or "binge" TV series [can] take as long as it likes to tell the story' (McCausland, 2016).

Mainstream media's embrace of the podcast is, in some ways, recognition that the format is now widely accepted and used. But it also shows an understanding of podcast's unique capacity to make personal connections with its audience. The choices of subject and storytelling are impressive: so too is the standard. As one US public radio reporter said of his podcasting business:

> We take more time, we spend more money, and we try to hone and craft more than 95 percent of the podcasts out there ... I think podcasting still has an association with something that two dudes make in their basement. There's a *Wayne's World* connotation to it. But I think of them as shows: sleek, produced, where you have people who are good at it doing it.
>
> Benton, 2015

The commitment to such a high standard is admirable but the reality of the technology is that a podcast—like blogging—can be done easily. The cost comes in the editing and production values that can transform a scratchy audio file into something compelling.

But like all good journalism, a podcast starts with a great story. Dan Box, a crime reporter with *The Australian*, covered the murder of three Aboriginal children in Bowraville in rural NSW in 1990 but the case was rarely given prominence in print media. In December 2015, 25 years after he first covered the story, Box decided to turn it into a podcast. The result was a compelling retelling of a true crime and an insight in to the racism that let three Aboriginal families down. It won numerous awards, but most importantly, finally gained the level of public attention that ranged from debate in the NSW Parliament to the NSW Police Commissioner pledging to meet the victims' families. It was a piece of intensive work for Box and his producer Eric George—17 interviews in four days at Bowraville, and then, once the first four episodes were released, a separate interview with the prime suspect who contacted Box after hearing the podcast. 'I have never done anything with this level of reaction,' Box told *The Guardian* (Walhquist, 2016).

Fairfax subsequently released a podcast, another true crime story, this time about the contentious death of Melbourne woman Phoebe Handsjuk, who died after falling down a construction chute from an apartment block. One of the senior journalists working on the podcast, Michael Bachelard, explained the difference between an extended print feature or series and a podcast: 'We knew if we did this story as a news story or feature, which is traditionally what we've done, there was the chance we'd leave too much out,' he said. 'We aren't the only media organisation dabbling in the format because podcasts have the ability to convey depth and complexity in an engaging way' (Bennett, 2016).

Both Box and Fairfax's podcasts have more than a passing association with the ground-breaking US true crime podcast *Serial*, first broadcast in 2014, about a man's murder of his former high school girlfriend. What all of the podcasts have in common is the capacity to provide elements of a story that a simple print feature cannot—the sounds from Bowraville, a bird's cry, the pauses as a relative contemplates their loss and the sense a listener has of actually being there. In all instances, the filter of the journalist at work is less obvious—a journalist or a producer working on a podcast will inevitably have to make choices about what to put in the story or leave out, but audio will enable them to add elements that words cannot. It is this kind of 'texture' that helps transform the storytelling. In addition, podcasts such as the two Australian examples can be presented as a serial—providing continuity but also suspense in a way that print features cannot.

It remains improbably difficult for newspapers and magazines to run serials these days—audiences do not have that habit of following stories over an extended time with printed material. But podcasts can achieve that, and their portability means the opportunity for their audience to listen becomes greater—when they are out walking the dog, on the train to work or eating breakfast. And then there is the virtue of social media discussion in the episode's aftermath to help the debate and promote the next episodes. From a journalist's point of view, podcasts provide a unique challenge—the capacity to tell stories through a compelling script, but with others' words and sounds, to a length that few publications can find space for. It is, in essence, a radio documentary that listeners can consume when and where they want. And from that aspect, the podcast is just another part of the broader multi-platform storytelling.

The multimedia route

From the text-based blog to the audio and scripted podcast, comes the multimedia piece of journalism, which adds the visual element to the mix. This is, in many ways, the most demanding of the digital expressions of feature journalism because it involves the visual, audio and a script. It will take time—in research and preparation let alone editing the final product—and require a collaborative approach, unless you have sophisticated video or photographic skills, in addition to your journalistic flair. An outstanding example of the long-form multimedia piece is the Pulitzer Prize-winning Snow Fall, produced by *The New York Times* (New York Times, 2012). It was a six-part story about an avalanche, with interactive graphics, video and short biographies of the skiers and snowboarders who confronted the avalanche. Its complexity is highlighted by the credits on the title page, which point to the team effort involved: 'Video by Catherine Spangler with Eric Miller. Reported by John Branch. Graphics by Jeremy White, Graham Roberts.' For some years, it was considered the prototype for digital long-form journalism.

Another example closer to home is Fatal Extraction, which is about the social and environmental impact of Australia's mining interests in Africa. The story involved journalists from the Centre for Public Integrity and International Consortium of Investigative Journalists (which subsequently revealed the Panama Papers), in harness with more than a dozen reporters on the ground in Africa. It took more than 18 months and featured data, documents, video and interviews. Multimedia editor Eleanor Bell explained exactly how it worked:

> [We had] uncovered a mountain of primary source documents and recordings. We also had a powerful data story, hundreds of hours of footage and multiple memory cards of images from some of the most visually stunning places on earth. These artefacts could be coerced into a video timeline or added as sound files, video stories and documents to a traditional text piece. But with so much unique material, there was an opportunity to allow the content to tell the story.
>
> Bell & Zubak-Skees, 2015

The outcome was a multimedia project that portrayed a complex picture of the impact of Australian mining companies on 33 African countries. The real challenge, according to Zubak-Skees, was to make the multimedia feel more than 'a slideshow or PowerPoint presentation'. The result was making a virtue out of each of the mediums they had at their disposal. 'If we had good video, we used video, if we had a quote we made it a quote, if we had data, we turned it in to a graphic,' Bell explained.

The conclusion from such an approach is that the best multimedia still demands a rigorous use of journalistic skills and an understanding of which medium works best to communicate the story. Journalists who embark on the multimedia path will face different kinds of problems to those feature writers working as freelancers for websites and magazines—they will need to consider how their story will look on different devices, from phones to tablets. They need to ensure the quality of their work—textually, audio or visually—is not compromised by the technology that carries it. You may not have those skills but it will be important to convene a team that includes someone who can think about and resolve such issues. This is the nub of multimedia storytelling—mastering the technological requirements to ensure all the story elements are available to the reader. One weak link—a video that won't load or a graphic that takes forever to appear—will be an incentive for the reader to move on to something else. The competition for eyeballs remains the priority.

Other (maybe more surprising) forms of digital journalism

In early 2017, *The Washington Post* placed a job ad seeking a producer with 'experience producing and writing comedy and will hire and manage a team of high-performing producers, writers and directors with a proven ability to deliver tightly produced, short, comedic segments on news-driven deadlines'. It was part of a plan to add 30 jobs to *The Post*'s video team. What made the ad intriguing was that it was about producing comedy, driven from the daily news. Not surprisingly, the new project would sit under *The Post*'s Opinion section. 'In the Opinion space, we see an opportunity to experiment with scripted programming that will bring to life key issues in smart, humorous ways,' the job ad said. 'We fully understand the difficulty of success in this area and we seek candidates who are comfortable trying new things and then iterating on them.' The premise, according to *The Post*, was to create video content that stood alone from the traditional text-based reporting. 'We are creating content ... that people come to and say: "Let's see what *The Washington Post* has today in video",' *The Post* executive said. 'It's reimagining what *Washington Post* journalism looks like in the future' (Lichterman, 2017)

This 're-imagining' has actually been going on outside the mainstream print outlets for some time with the proliferation of alternative sources of news and opinion. Plenty of it is digitally distributed in one form or another, and there are other examples on television and radio. These alternatives, in many ways, hold something of a mirror up to journalism and journalists—most particularly, they use satire and humour to make observations that journalists do not have either the scope or time, and in some cases, the licence, to make. These alternative sources include *The Daily Show*, Colbert and John Oliver in the US, all of which have (or had) a particular (usually ideological) point to make about the political and media environment. What transforms these programs beyond the satire boom that occurred in Britain in the 1960s and the US some years later, is that these alternative commentaries often become the viewers' main source of information about news and events, and not supplementary to their mainstream news consumption. This is the area where *The Washington Post* wants to pitch its new product. As such, these programs—and web presences—occupy an important place in the broader journalistic landscape.

This is where something that looks like entertainment is actually information, delivered with barbs and attitude that transforms it from basic reporting. Australia has its own, perhaps gentler, versions of this— ranging from *The Project*, to *The Weekly* with Charlie Pickering and Shaun Micallef's *Mad as Hell* (although Micallef admits he's not pretending to be doing political commentary. 'We never push a particular agenda or point of view. Any message is incidental to getting a laugh') (Vickery, 2016, p. 40). While these are TV offerings, they are, in essence, part of the broader journalistic environment (Micallef calls the three programs mentioned above 'the lighter news pool') and they inevitably become part of the digital timetabling of the ABC in Australia or any of the US networks. As an indicator of how efficiently these kinds of approaches have been integrated into the mainstream, the 2015 Walkley for multimedia storytelling in Australia was awarded to Huw Parkinson, for his satirical political mash-up videos that were screened on ABC TV's *Insiders* and also on YouTube. (See the Case study later in this chapter.)

Once again, many of the people who make up the production teams on these programs are journalists and their skills of being able to locate a story and then help shape it make them vital to the end result. These are longer stories—not documentary length—but they still spend more time on framing a story than news bulletins. Inevitably, those journalistic resources will have to work with production crews who have different skill sets well before the final package is delivered by the program hosts and debated by a nightly panel of shock jocks, comedians and overseas stars. It is material crafted for two audiences—one for television hosts to springboard ideas from and debate, and the other to trigger audience engagement and reaction. These priorities are perfectly aligned with digital journalism's priorities.

But it is clear that newspaper websites, such as *The Washington Post*, have an enormous challenge to rival the success of the digital distribution, television (or radio) manifestation of news commentary. A 20-minute John Oliver *Last Week Tonight* program in 2016 garnered 59 million Facebook video views and a further 19 million on YouTube (Klein, 2016). (Oliver won the 2016 Emmy Award for best variety talk show.)

In comparison, a Reuters Institute for the Study of Journalism study of 30 news outlets across four countries found that while 6.5 per cent of news site webpages had video, users spent just 2.5 per cent of average visit time on pages that had video and '97.5 percent of time is still spent with text' (Lichterman, 2017).

It suggests that news website consumers still have a priority for words over pictures. That may mean that they are not interested in video, or perhaps that news websites' videos are not sufficiently good enough in quality or content to turn readers into viewers. Depending on your perspective, that represents either an opportunity or a challenge.

What do I need to do to become a digital (features) journalist?

In many ways, it is significantly easier to be a digital journalist working on features than it is trying to report news for a digital outlet—news coverage is still dictated by newsroom structures and hierarchies. It can be hard to find your place and generate your own news. But if you want to look for longer stories, there are many opportunities. You will need a multimedia skill set—the capacity to shoot video, audio and edit. A photographer's eye and the technical understanding to get the image will help, and fundamentally, the journalist's skill in identifying the story and then being able to tell it. It sounds challenging but many people already do it, usually with their phones, every other day. The trick is to turn it in to a story rather than just a grab of a social event, and most importantly, make it look better than most amateur footage shot on a mobile phone.

And this is where the capacity to collaborate becomes vital. Good digital storytelling demands quality words, powerful images, telling graphics and video that provide nuance and clarity. Taken together, such a skilful multimedia package represents an exciting incentive for a reader to engage with the content. Assembling a team of people with those expert and specialised skills is the step that will potentially elevate your story idea into something special. A story in Fairfax's *Good Weekend* magazine in 2017 demonstrates the point. The magazine story on the first women's Australian football league was a conventional piece of journalism from a writer, with the mandatory display pictures. But there was also a multimedia package attached to the story that provided video and a stunning selection of images with some graphics on a clean and accessible design. The package took one journalist, images from seven photographers, one video producer, one overall producer and a multimedia story (Marshall, 2017, p. 104). It takes time, talent and special skills to bring that together.

But begin with the story. And from there, consider where you want to put the story—what platform—and what elements will add to that story. This is critical—don't assume that using all the bells and whistles of the digital toolbox will work for your story. It may not. Sometimes in digital journalism, less is indeed more. In other instances, it's entirely appropriate to bring every element of multimedia in to the mix. Think about a feature on the redevelopment of the city market. You know the market has been an integral part of the city's shopping for generations. It's a tourist haven but locals love it too—it's a foodie mecca. Now there are plans to move the market to the city fringe, where there is room for the market to grow. But it will mean that many of the small businesses around the current site will suffer. And many of the market stall holders feel they will lose business because patrons won't be bothered travelling that little bit further for their produce. There are also quite a few residents who live near the market who are relieved that they won't be losing their parking spots to market visitors. This is a story that works perfectly as a multimedia package—you can have the basic story that outlines the issues and serves as an anchor for your other digital elements: a photographic gallery of images of the market across the years; audio interviews with market stall holders and residents; a video of a chef walking through the market, identifying the best produce and how he would use them in particular dishes; and an interactive graphic about the old market site and the new site, comparing floor space, number of stall holders, and visitor car parking. There is something in that digital package for everyone, and most importantly, it represents everyone's interests and adds depth and layers of information to the story.

Compare that to a story about safety on a particular train line in and out of the city. You know several people who have had bad experiences on that train line—they have been intimidated by drinkers, instances of drug taking and passengers with mental health issues. You know that there have been police reports but nothing seems to have been done. Police won't officially confirm anything, and don't want to make a comment. The rail operator won't appear on camera and offers an anodyne response about 'doing its best to provide a secure travel environment for all passengers'. You're unable to secure CCTV footage from the stations' platforms and several of the travellers you've spoken to are nervous about appearing on camera or on audio because they don't want to be identified. There is clearly a story to be told but the opportunity to tell it with a full multimedia package is constrained. You could try to alter the travellers' voices to make them more anonymous, but visually there's no arresting image or video to carry the package—generic footage of trains and train platforms just won't cut it. In this instance, the story may well become a text-based story, with some accompanying images. But it won't be as powerful—or possibly reach the widest audience—without those other elements.

All of this is made more difficult if you are working outside organisations that have their own multimedia platforms. Nonetheless, there are still some accessible platforms, such as Storehouse, Creativist or Shadow Puppett that can help. (Some others are here: http://uncubed.com/daily/11-favorite-multimedia-storytelling-platforms/). Some will be subscription based, others are free. You will work out quickly which one suits your needs.

But for many journalists and other writers searching for a personal platform, it will be Facebook, Twitter and Instagram that will provide you with the best 'front door' to your work. Promoting your work—and your skills—through social media will enable you to identify like-minded people who may become part of the collaboration at the heart of your multimedia story.

One more thing ...

Katharine Murphy comes from a legacy media background; she learnt to be a journalist when print was still the cornerstone of news coverage in Australia. She worked for *The Australian Financial Review*, *The Age* and then became deputy political editor at *The Guardian* Australia. For that website, Murphy blogs, delivers podcasts, tweets and videos. There is one thing she knows more than anything else—the reader is now at the centre of the discussion. And that means ensuring journalists deliver for their audience.

> From my perspective, the consequential professional response to the rise of the reader should be to deliver better, richer, more informed, more collaborative journalism because there are ample opportunities to do just that ... Our collective ambition should not be to dish up breaking fluff with an over-egged headline in the desperate hope that audiences will fail to grasp the difference.
>
> Murphy, 2016

And multimedia storytelling is an ideal way to deliver that richer, better informed, more collaborative journalism.

Summary

o   Digital journalism offers a range of opportunities for feature writers.

o   A range of skills, beginning with being able to tell a story, is at the heart of quality digital journalism. Understanding how to use video, audio and graphic elements are vital.

o   If you don't have all those skills, find people who do and collaborate and go on collaborating.

o Digital journalism still observes the basic premise of storytelling—find a good story.

o Audience—who they are and how to engage them—is at the heart of digital journalism. If no one watches and listens, there's no point.

Questions

1 Podcasts are like what other form of electronic media storytelling?
2 What does the 'rise of the reader' mean?
3 Blogs, podcasts, multimedia ... what's another form of digital journalism?
4 What was a key example of the long-form multimedia piece that helped establish the extraordinary potential for digital storytelling?

Activities

1 Go to a mainstream media publication, e.g., *Good Weekend*, *The Weekend Australian* magazine, and find a feature story that has added online features—what are the differences? How many other people are involved in producing the web-based element? Does it add anything to the print story? Why? Why not?
2 Find three niche blogs that reflect your interests or hobbies, e.g., fashion, politics, football, kite sailing. How are they supported commercially? Look at the comment thread—is it a dedicated small audience of fans or a broader group of followers?
3 Pick a local news issue that you're interested in. Plan a multimedia package around it. How will you tell the story? What elements do you need? Think about what's achievable—can you actually get footage of the taggers at the railway station after dark? If you can't, think of alternative footage that will still help your story. Is there a graphic you could commission? Still images? You decide.

References and additional reading

Bell, E. & Zubak-Skees, C. (2015). 'How we used multimedia to tell the fatal extraction story.' https://www.icij.org/blog/2015/08/how-we-used-multimedia-tell-fatal-extraction-story. 19 August.

Bennett, L. (2016). 'Fairfax brings podcasts to newsroom with investigative series inspired by Serial.' www.adnews.com.au/news/fairfax-brings-podcasts-to-newsroom-with-investigative-series-inspired-by-serial#. 23 September.

Benton, J. (2015). 'Podcasting in 2015 feels a bit like blogging circa 2004.' http://www.niemanlab.org/2015/11/podcasting-in-2015-feels-a-lot-like-blogging-circa-2004-exciting-evolving-and-trouble-for-incumbents/. 18 November.

Klein, J. (2016). 'John Oliver shattered his own traffic record with Trump takedown.' http://variety.com/2016/more/news/john-oliver-shatters-his-own-traffic-record-with-trump-takedown-1201724139/. 5 March.

Kottke, J. (2013). 'The blog is dead.' http://www.niemanlab.org/2013/12/the-blog-is-dead/. 19 December.

Lichterman, J. (2017). 'The Washington Post is putting a big bet on video and trying to break in to Daily Show-style comedy.' http://www.niemanlab.org/2017/01/the-washington-post-is-putting-a-big-bet-on-video-and-trying-to-break-into-daily-show-style-comedy/.

Marshall, K. (2017). 'In a league of their own', *Good Weekend,* 28 January, pp. 10–12: http://www.smh.com.au/interactive/2017/their-own-league.

McCausland, S. (2016). 'The new golden age of Australian crime.' http://insidestory.org.au/the-new-golden-age-of-australian-true-crime. 20 December.

Murphy, K. (2016). 'How to be a political reporter: know your beat, respect the reader, hold your nerve.' https://www.theguardian.com/media/2016/feb/01/how-to-be-a-political-reporter-know-your-beat-respect-the-reader-hold-your-nerve. 31 January.

New York Times (2012). 'Snow fall.' http://www.nytimes.com/projects/2012/snow-fall/video/

Preston, P. (2016). 'Gawker is gone. We can't just look the other way.' https://www.theguardian.com/media/2016/aug/28/gawker-gone-cant-look-other-way-press-freedom. 28 August.

Vickery, C. (2016) 'Shaun Micallef,' *Herald Sun*. 11 May, p. 40.

Walhquist, C. (2016). 'Australia's Serial: Dan Box on the making of true crime podcast Bowraville.' https://www.theguardian.com/media/2016/may/23/australias-serial-dan-box-on-the-making-of-true-podcast-bowraville. 23 May.

Case study

Huw Parkinson, ABC *Insiders*, 2015 Walkley Award for multimedia storytelling, talks about how he makes video mash-ups that comment on the week's news

What the Walkley judges said:

> Huw Parkinson's satirical and highly shareable videos showcase how the craft and consumption of news are driving multimedia reporting. These mash-ups are both journalism and entertainment, taking hard-hitting news and creatively repositioning the characters and issues into satirical videos that amuse and inform. Parkinson's work wholly embraces the shareable power of the internet, with his clips being uploaded to multiple platforms and spreading across the web like wildfire.

1 What degree did you do (and where)? Did you always play around with videos like this?

It was a Bachelor of Arts, Communication Studies at Newcastle University. I was always making videos and experimenting with animation and at that stage I was just teaching myself computer-based animations after having played around with stop motion and hand-drawn animations as a kid.

2 How did you end up doing this work for ABC *Insiders*? Were you spotted by someone?

Well, I actually was working casual as a video editor at ABC News at the time. I would usually end up making these in my spare time at home just for fun. Eventually a few of my early videos had received a bit of attention and even *Insiders* had run clips from a couple of them as their light closer moment a few times. It wasn't long after that when Barrie Cassidy and the Executive Producer at *Insiders*, Kellie Mayo, approached me with the idea of bringing the videos onto the show. Having been a fan of the show from well before I ever worked at ABC it wasn't exactly a difficult decision for me.

3 Let's reflect on the body of work that won you the Walkley— please take us through the inspiration for each film, the moment when you realised the political event, e.g., 'The Fixer' (Christopher Pyne) fitted in with a *Star Wars* scene.

Woah, big question.

It is honestly different most times—and usually goes through a number of identities before it becomes the monster that finally emerges.

With Star Wars Fixed, the idea was purely of trying to play with the original interview between Christopher Pyne and [Sky's] David Speers. That two- to three-minute exchange where he repeatedly deflects every question with 'I fixed it' was really quite ridiculous, and that laugh Pyne gives at the end I think shows just how much he knew it. So I originally just started thinking about the types of scenes where someone saying that repeatedly would be funny. So I started to go with the idea of a classic crisis meeting scene. I tried a few different ones first, *Dr Strangelove*, *The Rock* ... and eventually I remembered that scene from the first *Star Wars* and how they're even discussing a troublesome senate (as was the case with Pyne himself at the time). So once I started to play around with the idea it just clicked into place—and was basically unchanged from the first draft edit I made.

With Breakfast Clubbing Season, the idea was a little more simple. I, like a lot of Australia, had been thoroughly enjoying [ABC TV's] *The Killing Season* on TV. Watching that show talk about all the gossiping behind the scenes and childish antics really brought home to me how much the whole Rudd/Gillard/Rudd saga in Australia's political history played out like a high school drama. It didn't take long for me to imagine that Rudd and Gillard were actually talking to their school principal instead of Sarah Ferguson. Then I just started getting the *Breakfast Club* soundtrack into my head and next thing I know I had decided to send two former prime ministers to detention.

Bronwyn Bishop's Arrested Development was a tough one. I had started about three different versions of a video around the Choppergate scandal over the weeks prior (one I was really hoping to do involved splicing Bishop onto Tom Cruise's body from the first *Mission Impossible* movie) but I just couldn't get enough together that made any sense. But the story dragged on for a few weeks and gave me plenty of chances to try something else instead. I had originally resisted *Arrested Development* as I had already used it in an earlier video with Clive Palmer and didn't really want to use it again. But once I started considering just how many ways Bronwyn Bishop seemed to embody Lucille Bluth (at least in her public persona) and how her predicament was feeling like a subplot from an episode of that show, the temptation became too good to resist. I was also happy to include a little moment with Clive Palmer in it, sort of as a cheeky acknowledgment of my first video with that show. Probably a bit too narcissistic but thankfully no one else knew that was why it was there [glances over to your readers].

4 How long does it take, once you've got the idea? What's your priority—a seamless head and body and OK video grabs of the pollies, or great grabs and a little less finesse around the head/shoulders etc?

It can range from only a couple of days to several weeks. The priority for me has always been to have an edit that works. So for me that means the right grabs in the moments of the film. The right soundtrack, the right pacing and structure. Otherwise I feel it's just showing off the technical side. If there isn't any point or if the scene doesn't make sense then I don't think it's as enjoyable. Likewise though, I've had plenty of times where I've been able to edit together what I think is a really strong scene, however for one reason or another, the FX side might not work out (i.e. they're not looking enough in the right direction in the frame—there's usually a bit of wiggle room with that but if the body is facing front on and the politician's head is almost entirely side on it really doesn't work). But in those cases I might be able to find another moment in the film, or even fake up a cutaway that never existed in the original film using elements from other shots. So ultimately I tend to work from a raw edit of the entire piece and then go, 'OK ... how on earth am I going to do this?'

I find there's usually more flexible options that way.

5 Why politics?

I've always had a morbid fascination with the world of politics and the people who inhabit it.

And I've loved movies and films my whole life.

But regarding the decision to blend these two things together ... I wasn't really thinking too much about that at the time. When I started to make these videos it was after a couple of months back in 2014 when almost every week a different MP was caught on camera making a gaffe—and it was as much a cathartic process to vent my own frustration at the time.

But I guess it's worked for as long as it has because there is just a lot of theatre in politics. With the 24/7 news cycle a politician needs to be in front of the public from dusk till dawn selling their ideas against a wide range of scrutiny. It's a tough gig and I certainly would never be able to do it. I think putting them into films and TV shows helps emphasise the theatrics a bit and I guess that sort of clashes in a nice absurd way to the otherwise mundane environment politics is usually presented in.

6 What does this format enable you to do that perhaps political journalists in the Press Gallery can't do?

a   I get to use some of the great movie soundtracks to help drive the emotion.

b   Not being in the Press Gallery means it's harder for a politician to chase me down if they're not happy with something I've done.

c   Honestly, though, I don't really know.

I'm obviously not making straight presented news stories, so our briefs are quite different in that respect. I think I get a lot of luxuries to just have fun which obviously isn't normally a priority for political news coverage. I don't take that for granted either. It can get quite gruelling having to cover very serious topics in an equally serious manner—the fact that I can slip in a line from Bill Murray to help ease the tension is a wonderful privilege.

7 What do you think the audience gets from your work that consumers of conventional media may not get?

This one is extremely tough for me to answer as I've always been surprised by the response my videos get. I only know why they work for me and what I get from them. I'm not sure I really see them as that comparable to a conventional media's presentation on the same story. My work is a little more reactionary after the story has already been well covered by the conventional outlets. (Trust me, I need their footage to work with.) I try to focus more on the personality and the way they're handling a story that's happening around them, whereas a more traditional piece would likely (and rightly) focus on the story first.

8 How long can you keep doing this? Do you think it really has a limited shelf life?

I've always only wanted to do this so long as I'm having fun with it. I now make these more formally for *Insiders*, but that approach has never changed. It takes a lot of work to get some of these together on time and I simply just won't put myself through any of that if I didn't enjoy the end result. But I'm also learning a lot about the process as I do this. Each video presents its own problems I hadn't encountered before. In working on the solutions I end up learning more and more tricks with the programs. which can speed things up next time I come across the same problem and can often open up a wider range of possibilities on what can be done, which always keeps me excited about future ideas.

In terms of a shelf life, I don't really know. I never expected the response I have received so I think it would be naive of me to pretend like I know when and how this will all end. I think there are probably a lot of people who might've seen one or two for the first time and then moved on. There are definitely ways the format could evolve to keep itself fresh. Ultimately, though, if the content is strong then I don't see a reason the format itself would die off. There's plenty of good films and I'm sure there'll be plenty of future political gaffes and scandals out there. If my work becomes stale it's probably more because I'm repeating the same jokes over and over again.

9 There is an argument that, although your cultural references are contemporary (*Game of Thrones*), there's also a lot of 'older' audience references, e.g. *Seinfeld*. Who is your audience for this material? Do you have a particular demographic in mind? Or is it driven largely by the audience of *Insiders*?

Since making these for a TV show on a Sunday morning I've taken more consideration in choosing films and shows that are at least a little well known and I've made more considerations to language, violence etc. (I wasn't really pushing those boundaries beforehand but I wasn't thinking too much about that angle either) but otherwise I just choose a film or show that I think I can work with.

So I work with films and shows that I know and usually ones I love (it helps when I can already remember several lines and scenes to begin with). I grew up in the '80s and '90s and I watched *a lot* of movies and shows back then so it is definitely easier for me to draw from that era—I do want to one day work with a great old all-time classic like *Casablanca* or *Wizard of Oz*—but I'm waiting for the right moment to present itself. I'd hate to spoil such a rich cultural classic with a subpar pairing.

However, I don't target any specific demographic when I choose a film. If I personally like the idea then that's usually all it takes.

10 Which generates the most audience engagement—*Insiders* or YouTube?

It's changed a lot along the way. These days it'll usually be *Insiders* and their online copies. However every once in a while if other outlets have also jumped on the video, the YouTube copy will take on a life of its own.

11 What else can you use this form for, other than politics? Will you do that?

I'm sure you can use this for just about anything. The more I learn about what can be done with these programs the more I find out just what is possible for future videos. It wouldn't need to be a politician, but any public figure. So long as the context fits I'm sure it's bound to get a reaction. Politics works for me because it's something I'm interested in, but also the people in that world often spend long times with their head in front of a camera without moving around too much so that makes things easier on a technical level. I reckon it'd be harder to find that good still raw footage of people in other fields.

12 Has conventional media lost its way with covering news and information for a younger audience? Does it require more work like yours to keep itself fresh? Does it matter—people will watch something if it's funny anyway?

I don't know if it's lost its way. I don't think conventional media has ever been that appealing to younger audiences. At least not in large numbers. But I don't think that's its failing, it just used to be all we had. With the modern media landscape as it is, there are now just so many other options out there to choose from. All with their own blend of information and humour to help keep its audience engaged. In addition to that we can all access the internet from devices we carry in our pockets and these devices can pool news from just about any source there is, not just the six or so options that were available at the post office on your way to work.

But in many cases, these great contemporary formats that we all love can only exist because of all the hard work done by the conventional outlets. Without it they would have very little to build their own presentations on.

It might be that over time, things like the evening news bulletin may take less of a priority in broadcasting interests as things shift to a more online focus, but I'm sure there will always a place for the straight, sensible, objective, uncomplicated news outlets. It's where the meat and potatoes are.

2
Preliminary Work

'As a journalist you are finally in the storytelling business … It's the oldest form of human communication … Goldilocks wakes up from her nap and sees three bears at the foot of her bed. What's that all about? What happens next? We want to know and we always will … Never forget to tell us what's up with the bears.'

William Zinsser, *The Writer Who Stayed,* 2012, p. 5

Objectives

This chapter explains how writers start to think about stories, where they can source their ideas and how they can develop those ideas into features that are professionally and commercially successful. It focuses on the need for writers to be curious and surround themselves with information from a range of sources that can stimulate their thinking and provide examples of how, and how not, to write. It covers:

o   deciding what the story is
o   where you get your ideas and find inspiration
o   who your audience is
o   pitching the story to a potential publisher
o   a Case study: Andrew Rule explains how a lifelong obsession led to an exclusive story that became a cause célèbre
o   a Writing sample: 'Saving Lynny: The ultimate love story' by Andrew Rule, *Herald Sun*, 25 June 2011.

Write what you want to know

Every writer is given the same advice—write what you know. The theory behind this well-intentioned (and largely correct) homily is that the end result will seem credible and honest. It will also be easier to write, because the material is familiar to the author. However, the usefulness of applying this to writing features for newspapers, magazines and websites is limited, simply because it is the nature of journalism to inform and enlighten.

Therefore, to write journalism purely from personal experience limits the range of subjects a writer can tackle, however broad their experience. Rather, feature writers should write what they are curious about.

This curiosity impulse is the most potent guide to evaluating what makes a story. If something interests the writer, it will interest other people too, and it will provide the writer with a constant source of motivation to explore a subject. Curiosity is, therefore, central to conceiving, preparing and pitching a feature for publication.

It also takes curiosity to tell a story, and feature writing is all about the story and how it is told. A good feature will be a compelling story that informs, engages and stimulates the reader intellectually and emotionally. It will represent the combination of a fine idea and diligent and intuitive research and interviewing skills with a precise storytelling technique. The first steps in a feature's conception are critical to its success. Let us consider some central preliminary tasks for all feature writers.

What's the story?

Countless times each day in a metropolitan newsroom, one question will be at the forefront of exchanges between journalists: 'What's the story?' It is the conversational shorthand that provides journalists with the opportunity to impart to a colleague what they have learned about a particular event, person or occurrence. The prosaic reason for this question is often to ensure that the (usually more senior) colleague can pass on those details, through the newsroom hierarchy, so that the prominence of the story in the next day's publication can be determined. But it also serves a more critical purpose for the writer. Put simply, having to articulate the essence of a story in a brief conversation helps clarify its importance, relevance and themes. And although, superficially, this seems to apply only to news reporters, it is a skill that is fundamental to feature writing.

A clear view of what you want to write about is essential. Writers who fail to formulate a brief and clear explanation of what their story is about will fail to convince anyone—least of all themselves—that it is worth pursuing. If it does not engage or stimulate the writer, then it will have no chance of engaging the reader. Writers need to feel comfortable and confident in their expectation of the story's outcome. You don't have to complete a two-decade apprenticeship to be able to establish the nub of a story.

The key is to have a realistic understanding of what is possible, in terms of time, resources and the media outlet for which the story is intended. Many journalists would love to have six months to research a four-part story on, for example, police corruption; but there is no media organisation in Australia that is likely to spare the resources, or the time and space in paper or on air, to run that kind of dedicated enquiry. So, approaching a story with a modest appreciation of its scope is valuable to help establish the parameters of the story before you can decide what the story might be about. But before the writer gets too far down the track, they need to arrive at a suitable idea.

If the writer cannot succinctly sum up the story, then they are struggling to understand what the story is about. If the writer is confused, so will be the editor, not to mention the reader, and it is highly unlikely that an editor is going to allow a malformed idea to appear in print or online. Clarity is all.

Generating ideas

No-one gets anywhere in journalism without ideas for stories.

News Ltd training manual

There is an abundance of ideas for features because features can be longer and more complex than news stories and they do not always have to be anchored in current events. But this range of inspiration also makes features harder to write (Hicks, 1999). They are often built on a range of diverse sources and demand the assembling of complicated material.

Consequently, features are usually more challenging than news stories, so every writer needs to be *prepared*, and to be constantly thinking about ideas. The easiest and most appropriate way to do this is to expose oneself to stories (news, features, gossip) from other media, whether they appear in mainstream newspapers, magazines, on television or radio, in specialist publications on news-stands, or online. The more information a writer consumes, the more they are likely to generate ideas (Evans, 1988, p. 25). Even then, it's not enough to have a broad idea. For example, a story idea about the proliferation of generic medicines is just a starting point—it needs more thinking to refine the idea into something more compelling. That could be a story on who buys generic drugs or the effectiveness of generic drugs compared to other medicines. The important element is to ensure you have an idea that is interesting and achievable—a vague notion for a story is impossible to realise. How do you focus your research, let alone your writing? The trick is to keep thinking and keep reading.

This vast range of stimuli should be a source of excitement for any writer, although many find it intimidating and are often overwhelmed and don't know where to start. The first rule in such circumstances is to think 'small', rather than try to conceive of every angle and exhaust every source. No reader expects a feature on how to achieve world peace, but they may be interested in how best to find peace in Iraq.

Feature writers who can find their own story ideas—rather than rely on a commissioning features editor or chief of staff to give them inspiration—are invaluable. A features editor is a busy individual. Daily duties may include weighing up commercial and advertising pressures, analysing contributors' budgets, trying to work out why the picture in the arts pages also appeared in yesterday's paper or replacing a feature writer who has called in sick and will have to miss the scheduled interview with a visiting international politician or Hollywood star. So, creative energy from a feature writer who confidently declares that they have an idea for their editor is welcomed.

But where does this energy come from? Where does a writer find inspiration? The truth is that there are very few new ideas; many of them are variations on themes that are constants in all our lives—triumphs and tragedies and the quest for understanding. What helps distinguish a good feature from a run-of-the-mill feature is how well the writer develops the brief behind the idea (Hicks, 1999, p. 51).

The presentation, the angle, the unique elements of the feature, all help the writer pursue the story and make the editor want to publish it (Evans, 1988, p. 28). A specific idea will always trump a general idea, even if the specifics are anchored in a general context. For example, a feature about the shortage of medical services in rural Australia is made more interesting if the writer suggests exploring the issue by spending a week with a country doctor.

William Blundell, author of *The Art and Craft of Feature Writing*, has identified five key techniques to help develop an idea: extrapolation, synthesis, localisation, projection and viewpoint switching (Blundell, 1988). These are helpful categories that can be applied to a range of features.

Extrapolation involves taking a small incident and magnifying it, by either consequence or implication, and seeing in sharper detail what has happened. Consider, for example, a story about a predatory older man who has attacked passengers on a suburban train. The news story tells the reader the basic details. The feature will go further, elaborating on the circumstances that occur in the lead-up to the attacks and their aftermath. The writer needs to think clearly about this extrapolation because they are trying to extract more information from the circumstances to help readers empathise with the passengers' predicament.

The questions a feature writer might ask in preparing for this approach to a feature would be: What are the common elements of these attacks? At what time of day did they happen? In what carriage? What seat did the attacker choose? Do the victims have anything in common: age? height? dress? Did the attacker look unusual? Was there anything he said or did before the attacks that made him memorable? These are fundamental questions that will help generate detailed answers.

It is the detail that will help drive the feature and keep the reader interested. But the element that transforms this feature from being just a long news story will be contemplation of the slightly larger picture. Ask, for example: Has this happened anywhere else? Are there other attacks occurring on other rail lines or other tram lines? If so, why? Is it because rising petrol prices have pushed people who would normally drive their car to work onto public transport? Some of these questions might seem fanciful, but they are of paramount importance if you want to convert a news event into a feature story with context and consequence.

Synthesis is an equally simple but potentially powerful technique, which involves a writer unifying what might normally be considered unrelated elements to make an informative whole. There is a strong tradition of synthesis in Australian features, largely because of the nation's state-based constituencies, the strength of the cities' papers and the existence of only one national general newspaper. Among the best contemporary illustrations of this have been features written about Australian water conservation in the face of climate change and enervating drought. The states have responded to these problems with different water strategies, and part of the political debate about these strategies has been underpinned by features that synthesise information from the various states about those divergent conservation strategies.

Blundell's third key technique for approaching a feature, *localisation*, is arguably the simplest. It involves thinking small—for example, bringing a national or international event or development back to the city or suburban level. To use the earlier water example in reverse, when the federal government announced a $10 billion program to save the Murray–Darling river system, the questions from features editors in Adelaide, Melbourne, Sydney and Brisbane to their feature writers were: What does this mean for us? What impact will this money have on our own river system?

Projection is a more complex and potentially more speculative approach to generating feature ideas. It involves looking beyond current events and trying to focus on what might eventually be the consequence and impact of these events, and the reaction to them. In this case the questions a feature writer would pursue about the railway predator mentioned earlier would concern the impact such behaviour would have on other rail travellers: Will patronage decrease? Will transit police increase their surveillance? What other precautions are being taken? And, critically, what will commuters think of these changes? Will the changes make life easier or harder for them?

The final technique is *viewpoint switching*. To some feature writers, attempting to look at something from various points of view is akin to professional perversity, but that does not deny its value in ventilating alternative opinions. The feature idea that involves switching a viewpoint is most likely to be wedded to a contentious or divisive issue. In the early months of 2007, nothing was more divisive than the battle over industrial relations reforms. Some publications were supportive of the ALP's proposal for a new policy that, it claimed, was more worker-friendly than the federal government's industrial relations regime. The alternative voice, of scepticism, was expressed through a series of interviews with leading Australian businessmen and women, indicating a shift in viewpoint from those who supported the ALP's policy. This approach is suitable for a feature that is based on ideas, issues and philosophies. Where loud voices representing particular sets of interest shout across the public divide, viewpoint shifting is an entirely legitimate feature idea.

No matter what subject a feature writer fastens on, there is one element that they must not ignore—timeliness. Features that have no connection to current events or personalities are common enough in mainstream media, but they lack the urgency and topicality of features anchored in the here and now. When embarking on a feature idea, it behoves the writer to consider its currency. The former Editor-in-Chief of *The Australian,* Paul Kelly, was fond of telling his reporters that 'good features grow out of hard news'. He was right in acknowledging the provenance of many fine features. A feature writer cannot ignore news events as their primary source of ideas.

Old ideas make tired features that never appear, but ideas that reflect recent events look fresh and relevant. Consider the revival of Pauline Hanson's One Nation party in the 2016 federal election. Hanson had been in the political wilderness for a decade, and her party marginalised. But in the internationally changed mood that also saw British voters support leaving the European Union and US voters put Donald Trump in the White House, there were plenty of Australians who embraced Ms Hanson and her party at the ballot box. All those factors made Senator Hanson newsworthy—her revival connected her to a worldwide embrace of deep conservatism. Feature writers and columnists tried to explain how that had occurred. Australian newspapers, magazines and websites were overrun with feature material on Senator Hanson, her party, her staff and the change in political mood. This development gave feature writers a fresh chance to revisit an old topic.

Having identified some techniques for generating feature ideas, we need to consider how the broad-subject type of feature can provide the writer with inspiration. Such broad subjects may seem, on the face of it, to be obvious areas for writing, and a quick scan of any magazine or news feature supplement will reveal how common they are. But they offer a file of potential story ideas for any writer to dip into with alacrity.

1 Social trends-based features (includes lifestyle)

These trends-based features are driven by new and observed social patterns. They usually focus on an expert source or sources who have studied the trend or have data to support the trend.

Alternatively, a writer with a specialist understanding of demographic information, science or health, for example, could build a feature by extracting the information base from a range of material. This is exactly what will happen with the results of the 2016 Census which the Australian Bureau of Statistics will progressively release in the years to come. This applies to other data sets as well, including the results of ongoing studies conducted by the Australian Institute of Criminology, or even polling organisations, such as Roy Morgan Research.

These features are not necessarily linked to a particular event or timely development. But they do reflect societal trends that are overt enough and, theoretically, occur with enough frequency to invite a feature-length story. The benefit of choosing a trends-based feature that is largely based on anecdotal evidence is that the writer has the scope to speculate about the extent of the trend, with the possibility of finding sources who support the trend's demise or its resurgence.

2   Anniversaries and milestones

There are also plenty of features that are built around anniversaries and milestones, such as the anniversary of a government's electoral triumph or defeat, the anniversary of a major event (for example, the Port Arthur massacre), milestone birthdays for iconic figures (for example, Jimmy Barnes turning 60) or the return of an important personality with an international profile to their home city (for example, Barry Humphries returning to Melbourne). Such features might also be written about institutions—80 years of the High Court, the centenary of the ALP, 50 years since the first Holden rolled off the assembly line, Ford Australia's 90th anniversary, and the pending closure of its local manufacturing plant, along with Holden's, the 100th test at the SCG. The features are linked by the idea of reflection – what happened then and what has changed? Could this event happen again? What did we learn from that? What did Jimmy Barnes learn from turning 60? What did he reflect on as the lessons of his life? Was turning 60 more important than turning 50? What did Barry Humphries lament about modern Melbourne? What did he love about the Melbourne he used to know? What were the highlights of Ford's (and Holden's) time in Australia? Did it cement our place as leading manufacturers of motor vehicles? What does the future now hold? Those are the sorts of questions that can drive these features.

3   Promotional features (including interviews/profiles)

Features can also be generated by interviewing an author, film director, performer or artist about their latest project. Such interviews are becoming increasingly common because they are ideal promotional opportunities for the person being interviewed.

A keen eye and access to a variety of publications (newspapers, magazines and online sites) or programs will enable you to see how journalists from different organisations have presented a 20-minute meeting with a star actor as a unique encounter.

4   Background/context features

These are designed to provide a 'back story' to an unfolding news event, such as Hurricane Katrina in the United States, which generated many weekend newspaper features that examined how prepared

New Orleans was for such a disaster, the impact on the city's infrastructure, and the political agendas that helped to shape the city's response. These are the common elements of the coverage of human tragedies, such as the five deaths that occurred in Melbourne's CBD in 2017 when a man drove his car through the Bourke Street Mall. The background features were on the alleged perpetrator, the human survival stories and the instinctive urge to help demonstrated by the city's workers and visitors at the height of the mayhem. These background features help readers understand the news at the front of the newspaper. In many ways, they are an attempt to answer the perennial question: 'Why did this happen?'

Identifying the potential market

The critical question for every feature writer, after they have progressed past the idea, is: Who is the audience? If the audience for the feature is too specific and therefore small, the feature is unlikely to be accepted by a general, broader publication. For example, a feature on the employment rate of graduating engineers will be of no interest to *The Australian*'s colour magazine or *Good Weekend*, but it may be of interest to *The Australian*'s Higher Education section.

However, if a writer wishes to specialise in a particular area, there are specialist magazines that would be delighted to accept features from those who know the subject area. For example, there are even titles, such as *Hazardous Cargo Bulletin*, that cater for those with a penchant for information about dangerous goods transportation.

Nevertheless, the reality is that most feature writers want to have the broadest audience for their work, which means that a new writer who does not wish to specialise enters a very competitive marketplace. Most of Australia's best features are conceived, shaped and published for a general audience by a small stable of highly talented staff writers and longstanding freelance contributors. The mainstream newspapers and magazines in this country know the audience they want to reach: for the weekend magazines, it is the high-end of the reading public—those readers who have a high disposable income and a comfortable lifestyle and are therefore attractive to advertisers.

Any writer trying to generate an income from their features needs to understand their audience. An idea that has no audience is no use to writer, editor or publisher.

There have been some notable changes in content in many Australian mainstream publications during the past 20 years, as writers and publishers have become much more aware of the diversity of their audience. A compelling example of this is how editorial content has increasingly shifted to include more news and features about parenting, mothering, families and children. This is partly the result of the introduction of paid maternity leave, which has encouraged female journalists to return to work after having a family. Thus the change in their own social and workplace environments helped these journalists to connect with that broad, fundamental audience—families. A similar change has occurred in the treatment of environmental issues, which are now regarded as mainstream areas of interest rather than fringe political or social movements, and thus a vital part of feature coverage.

Pitching your story

When pitching a story to a potential publisher, a writer needs to draw all the key elements of feature preparation together—the idea, the audience, the sources and the research. A more detailed analysis of the requirements for a pitch is given in Chapter 11, but here is a quick introduction to the basics. Every pitch should contain the basic elements of research—the names of contacts, reports (published or unpublished) etc.—to demonstrate to an editor that you are familiar with your proposed topic.

Editors are busy. They value their time and will give short shrift to a writer trying to pitch a story about which the editor has only the vaguest understanding. So the simplest approach is to contact the editor of the publication you feel is the most appropriate outlet for the story with an email. Make sure you know the editor's name and spell it correctly. Potential contributors often get this critical detail wrong. The email should contain the basic idea, the audience (why the story would suit that publication) and how you would treat the story (who you would talk to and a sentence explaining why they would be valuable for your story). Also, tell the editor you will contact them within 48 hours to discuss the idea. Don't be alarmed if you don't hear from the editor in that time. Editors will often use your call as the point of contact and discussion.

The other important part of the pitch is consideration of the visual or interactive element. A writer who can visualise and communicate ideas for graphic illustrations—such as an interactive map (see the BBC example in Online resources), table of data, a map or a breakout box with quotes from the story—can help an editor see how the story can look on the page or online, and that will also help the writer make a successful pitch.

Summary

o It takes curiosity to find a story.

o Good ideas are like gold—valuable and rare.

o Read, listen, watch and think to help generate feature ideas.

o Think of specific examples to reveal a larger, general idea.

o Timeliness is vital. Features have to tell us something about 'now'.

o Think carefully about who your audience is—it is not homogenous.

Questions

1 What is the fundamental tool for every feature writer?

2 What helps make a feature writer valuable to a busy editor?

3 What are Blundell's five ways of developing feature ideas?

Activities

1 Carefully read the news sections of a daily newspaper (including the domestic news, foreign news, business news and sport sections). Try to find at least three feature ideas from those sections.

2 Now look at a weekend newspaper—the news features sections, the review section and the magazine. How many features in those sections interest you? Why? Are there some features that could have been more interesting? What would it have taken to make you read those features? What was it about the engaging features that kept you reading?

3 Do you have an idea for a feature? Where did the idea come from? How would you pitch it to an editor? (Think about what makes the story interesting and how you would illustrate it with pictures, graphics and a breakout box.)

References and additional reading

Blundell, W. (1988). *The Art and Craft of Feature Writing*, New York: Penguin.

Evans, G. (ed.) (1988). *The Complete Guide to Writing Non-Fiction*, New York: Harper & Row.

Hicks, W. (ed.) (1999). *Writing for Journalists*, London: Routledge.

King, S. (2000). *On Writing*, London: Hodder & Stoughton.

Lee, C. (2004). *Power Prose*, Melbourne: Hardie Grant.

Remnick, D. (1996). *The Devil Problem and Other True Stories*, New York: Random House.

Ricketson, M. (2004). *Writing Feature Stories*, Sydney: Allen & Unwin.

Zinsser, W. (2012). *The Writer Who Stayed*, Philadelphia: Paul Dry Books.

Online resources

Australian Bureau of Statistics: http://www.abs.gov.au

Australian Institute of Criminology: http://www.aic.gov.au/

BBC (2011). 'Every death on every road in Great Britain 1999–2010': http://www.bbc.com/news/uk-15975720

Roy Morgan Research: http://www.roymorgan.com/morganpoll

Case study

Andrew Rule explains how a lifelong obsession led him to an exclusive story that became a cause célèbre

Publication details:

'Saving Lynny: The ultimate love story', *Herald Sun*, 25 June 2011, p. 1 and pp. 23–6.

The author:

In a distinguished career that started on Victorian country newspapers, Andrew Rule has worked at *The Sun*, *The Herald*, *The Age* and the *Herald Sun*. He has written numerous crime books, including co-writing the *Underbelly* series with John Silvester. Rule has won eight Quill awards from the Melbourne Press Club, two coveted Graham Perkin awards for the Australian Journalist of the Year and a Gold Walkley award.

The story:

The story behind the woman born with no arms and legs in suburban Melbourne had actually been years in the making for journalist Andrew Rule.

Rule, a multi-award-winning journalist and author, grew up in East Gippsland with a girl who had no arms and who had feet where her knees should have been. Rule's mother always claimed that it was the morning sickness drug thalidomide that was behind the girl's disability, even though the official line was that the drug was not officially available in Australia when the girl was born.

Rule remained intrigued by thalidomide, a story that had been one of the UK *Sunday Times'* biggest exposés in the 1960s when the link between birth defects and the drug was front-page news.

Years later Rule profiled Melbourne lawyer Peter Gordon for Fairfax's *Good Weekend* magazine in what was the first step in a journey that would lead him to Lyn Rowe.

Gordon is an incisive and aggressive lawyer who ran a Melbourne law firm built on cases that often involved unfashionable causes. Rule felt some affinity with Gordon's approach. 'He's an aggressive fighter for the underdog and I see some similarity between what he does and what investigative journalism does,' Rule said. Over the course of researching the story, Rule and Gordon became acquaintances and, when Gordon moved house and found himself close to Rule and his family, the two men spent time together, walking and talking.

During one conversation Gordon relayed how he became involved in taking a case against the makers of thalidomide, the German pharmaceutical company, Grunenthal. This was a new area of litigation because previous legal action had been against the drug's UK distributors, Distillers and Diageo. The German company had never been legally challenged on thalidomide outside its own country after developing the drug in 1954.

Gordon told Rule that there was a woman only 10 kms from where they lived who had been born without arms and legs, and was being cared for by her elderly parents. The couple, who had three other children, never complained about their situation. But they were confronting the sad truth of who would look after their daughter when they were gone.

Rule realised that the personal story was a potentially compelling insight into a problem that could have significant international repercussions. That was one element. The other important factor was the Rowe family.

When Rule met Wendy and Ian Rowe, he was struck by their decency and amazing good humour in the face of Lyn's predicament.

One of the elements of their story that stayed with him was 77-year-old Wendy's commitment to attending strengthening gym classes three times a week so that she could still turn Lyn over three times a night, as she had done every night of Lyn's 49 years.

'Lyn's parents were so generous, so unpretentious,' Rule recalled. 'It was the unsung heroism of the ordinary people ... It's a story that's human and local.'

Lyn comes through the piece with her own distinct sense of humour, which adds another dimension that engaged many readers across the nation.

Rule spent time interviewing the Rowe family before he went overseas and researched some of the thalidomide cases in the UK, and also Grunenthal's corporate history.

Yet when the time came to run the story in the Saturday edition of the *Herald Sun*, it was decided to put Lyn's story first and then follow it two days later with the corporate story. The reasoning, proved correct, was that readers would respond more to Lyn's story for its humanity than the more conventional and drier corporate investigation.

'It's one family's story, so in that instance it's a straightforward story to tell,' Rule said. 'But it was never a public relations piece for any impending court case. It sinks or swims on its content.'

Rule quickly worked out the story had to start with the moment of Lyn's birth. It was the most confronting element of the story, but in Wendy's initial reaction to Lyn is the basis of the couple's lifelong commitment to their daughter. And such an introduction also helped shape the rest of the story.

The upshot was that Lyn and her family went to court and won the right to fight their case in Melbourne, rather than travel to Germany as Grunenthal had argued to the Victorian Supreme Court.

Lyn Rowe became the standard-bearer for dozens of other potential cases from around the globe, including many in the United States.

Writing sample

Saving Lynny: The ultimate love story

By Andrew Rule, *Herald Sun*, **25 June 2011**

LYN Rowe was born with no arms or legs nearly 50 years ago. Doctors said let her die but her parents refused and took their tiny gumnut baby home. They have loved her every day since.

WENDY Rowe can't remember much about the birth except the dead silence in the delivery room and the look on the doctor's face.

He had delivered her baby. Now, as stricken nurses avoided Wendy's gaze, he braced himself to deliver the bad news.

Her daughter had no arms and no legs.

Wendy looked at him calmly and said: 'We'll just have to look after her very carefully then, won't we?'

With those words, the 26-year-old mother of three began the first hour of the first day of the rest of her life.

Her little family had been struck by lightning.

It was March 2, 1962. A Friday.

A lifetime later, Wendy Rowe admits she can't remember what she said to the doctor that day because they sedated her later and everything became a blur.

But the doctor never forgot her grace under pressure.

Dr Ron Dickinson is in his 80s now and long retired, but when a stranger recently came to ask him about delivering Lynette Rowe in 1962, he recalled it clearly.

Mrs Rowe was the patient of another partner in their Nunawading medical practice, Dr Hugh Indian. But Dr Indian had already been called out before Mrs Rowe's contractions started, so Dr Dickinson stepped in to deliver the baby at Box Hill Hospital.

Time has not erased the shock of delivering that tiny limbless girl. But it was the mother's bravery and unconditional love that touched him.

Not that Wendy Rowe felt brave, then or now. Neither did her husband Ian, who was at work in the city when he got the call that changed his life. The caller bluntly told him his baby had no arms and legs. Wendy still wonders if he ever completely recovered.

He ran to the station and caught a train to Box Hill. 'But by then they had drugged me and I was out of my tree,' she says.

Wendy can remember just one thing from the following hours: a doctor telling her she should put the baby in a home and forget about her 'because she'll be dead in six months'.

The suggestion repulsed her. But she agreed to leave the baby at the hospital for a few days so she could talk to her husband.

They drove their old Hillman station wagon to Mt Beauty and slept in the back. Not that they did much sleeping. There was a lot to talk about, but no argument; they knew what they would do.

A week later they went back to the hospital, picked up their little girl and took her home. One look at her face was enough, Wendy says, pretending to make light of the biggest decision in their lives.

'Lucky you had such a cute little face,' she teases, looking at her grown-up daughter strapped in her motorised chair, and they all laugh. What makes these ordinary people extraordinary is that capacity to smile in the face of heartbreak, to look after each other and to get on with it.

But positive thinking does not make it easy. Nothing is easy when your child has no arms or legs. Not even baby clothes.

The week baby Lynette got home, neighbour Edna Porritt made tiny sleeping bags to fit that little round body, not much longer than a man's hand. She was the gumnut baby of Nunawading.

As the baby grew, Mrs Porritt made more special clothes, for a little girl who would never dress herself. 'They've been good neighbours,' murmurs Wendy.

It's now 49 years and three months since they came home from hospital and Wendy, Ian and their Lynny are still doing what they did in that first traumatic 24 hours: coping a day at a time.

They live in the same unpretentious weatherboard house they moved into as newlyweds in 1957, when Nunawading was all gum trees, building blocks and unmade roads. The liquidambar in the front yard has grown huge, they have a little white van specially built to carry Lynny, and the house needs re-stumping, but little has changed in five decades.

Lynny still eats from the ingenious multi-spoon gadget her grandfather created when she was little: a dozen spoons fan out from a rotating hub so she can take a pre-loaded spoonful and then nudge it aside, ready for the next.

The front door screen has no snib in case there is a fire and Lynny has to barge through it in her well-worn electric wheelchair.

To visit is a rare privilege and a bittersweet pleasure. It is a first-hand insight into how the worst medical disaster in history made Lynette Rowe one of the most profoundly disabled thalidomide survivors on the planet.

But her story is more than another tragic postscript to the tragedy of thalidomide, the drug that killed so many thousands and crippled thousands more.

It is a story of ordinary people's heroism; a love story that brings a lump to a stranger's throat.

IAN Rowe met Wendy Tudor in Brighton at the Male St Methodist church youth club in 1951. He was 18 and she was 15.

They played tennis and badminton and went square dancing. She watched him bowl well and bat badly for a local cricket team. He'd taken it up at school and would keep playing until he was 48, a Nunawading Cricket Club legend.

He worked at a city insurance office while she trained as a kindergarten teacher. Engaged at Christmas, 1955, they married in January 1957 at the church where they met, honeymooned in Tasmania and moved into the house in Morden St, Nunawading, on Australia Day.

The house was £4200. 'We had the £200, borrowed the rest,' Ian reminisces. They started out with an old table and fruit boxes to sit on—no curtains, no blinds, no refrigerator.

The Porritts next door—Stan was a returned Rat of Tobruk and Edna a superstar housewife—let them keep milk and butter in their fridge until they saved up the deposit for their own.

Wendy worked at a kindergarten for a year but stopped when she had Merrilyn in April, 1959. Two years later, Alison was born. There were no plans to have a third so quickly, but two months later Wendy was pregnant again.

This time Wendy was so ill with morning sickness she could hardly bend over to pick up baby Alison without being sick. And she noticed something odd as the baby inside her grew: it rolled around in her stomach, like a ball.

Dr Indian's practice was only a couple of streets away. He had a young family himself and was generous with his time, making house visits and offering samples that drug companies handed out. He had been in the air force in the war and his father had been a Methodist clergyman. The Rowes liked that.

Dr Indian came around to the house and gave Wendy medicine: tablets and an injection. Later in the pregnancy, he gave her the drug Debendox.

None of this medication, as it turned out, was recorded at the surgery, which suggests he was using the drug samples handed to doctors by pharmaceutical company 'reps' doing the rounds to push new products from Europe and America.

At that time, and for years afterwards, there was nothing to stop salesmen from handing out drugs at random—and little to stop doctors passing them on. Some doctors, such as Ron Dickinson, were more cautious than others about what they gave pregnant women. Dr Indian wasn't one of them.

Wendy Rowe did not know at the time exactly which drugs she had been given. And nobody knew about 'thalidomide'—the sinister ingredient in products like Distaval, Contergan and Valgil, widely used before the Australian obstetrician Dr William McBride sounded the alarm in late 1961, just as overseas doctors were realising the same thing.

The revelation came a few months too late for the Rowes, and years too late for thousands of others around the world.

After Lynette was born, Dr Indian treated the Rowes with great kindness—and what his own family would see as an enduring sorrow. He was their devoted family doctor for decades until his death in the 1980s.

Although he initially tried to explain the cause of the birth defects as a 'virus', it was never convincing. It became increasingly clear to the Rowes' medical advisers over the years, including Dr Indian and his colleagues such as Dr Dickinson, that thalidomide was the logical cause. The timing was damning—the drug was named as the cause of a worldwide birth-defect epidemic just three months before Lynette's birth, although it took a shamefully long time for word to spread.

DR Indian's oldest daughter, Sue, remembers how anguished her father was about the Rowes' little girl.

'I remember he said he'd given the mother drugs and that he was distressed because he felt pretty responsible,' she says.

Sue remembers the Rowes were kind to her father, with no hint of blame or complaint. 'That little girl used to come and visit. She and dad got on very well.'

She can remember Lynette 'coming down our driveway to show off her new wheelchair'.

The Rowes still don't hold a grudge. At least not against Dr Indian, even if he gently steered them away from seeking legal advice and was evasive about the likely causes. He need not have been wary: they never blamed him. Instead, they made the most of the hand they had been dealt.

It hasn't been easy. For the first 12 months Lynny was 'a bright little button', says her mother. Then, when she was teething, she got a temperature that could have been fatal—108F (42.2C). Without limbs to radiate heat, she burned up. The fever almost killed Lynny and left her with brain damage that affected her speech and learning. Wendy and Ian wondered what else could happen.

Meanwhile, they had two other little girls to look after. Seven years later, reassured that the drug would not strike twice, they had another baby.

Andrea was another sporty and beautiful daughter who made them proud but who grew up in the shadow of all the extra care Lynette needed.

These are the things that can, and do, tear apart the families of those with severe disabilities.

All over the world, parents of thalidomide children separated, or worse. Some had breakdowns. Some suicided. Some ran away, abandoning their babies to the care of the state, church or charity.

But the Rowes endured, decade after decade. Eventually their other daughters grew up and married and moved on.

Three generations of children have grown up in the street knowing Lynny. A plumber who still lives down the road told them he didn't realise until he was eight that she was different because he'd seen her all his life.

'To me, she was just Lynny,' he said. Ian and Wendy still laugh about that. So does Lynny. They're as comfortable with each other as any three people you've ever met.

At first, she went to a special kindergarten in Burwood, then for 11 years to Yooralla, in Balwyn. For 31 years since she has gone regularly to Knox Combined Industries.

When she started, she propagated plants for sale at a nursery, using secateurs in her mouth. But a change in policy ended that. Even though she can answer telephones with a headset and use a computer, stick in mouth, these days she mostly sits in the passage to greet arrivals at the centre.

'I'm the bouncer!' she says, with the signature family laugh.

THE Rowes tackle life with humour and see the best in people, but it isn't always a two-way street.

Once, in a supermarket, a boy followed Lynny's wheelchair, making rude comments, until her sister Alison hissed at the boy: 'If you don't shut up, my dad will cut off your arms and legs too, just like he did to her!'

Problem solved.

Recently, a carer who was shopping with Lynny had to go to the lavatory. She left her in her wheelchair briefly in a waiting room outside. A mother with a toddler came in, took one look, clasped her hands over her child's eyes and raced out.

'Don't worry!' Lynny called out. 'It's not catching!'

How her parents laughed when she told them that tale. They have to. Crying doesn't work.

There have been times when Wendy felt like it. Once, when their youngest girl was at Nunawading High, Wendy was on canteen duty when another mother said to her about Lynny: 'They should put down people like that. Give them a needle.'

Nearly 30 years later, Wendy is still astounded one mother could say that to another.

Lynny is 50 next birthday, and her parents are heading for 80. Over them hangs the unspeakable prospect: what will happen when they can no longer look after her, let alone when they aren't around any more?

Ian Rowe is still as determined as ever, but he has a crook neck and other aches and pains. They are living on the pension and admit having not much in reserve.

They are pleased they took Lynny overseas a couple of times, years ago, because it gave them shared experiences to look back on, but there will be no more. Unless, maybe, the lawyers who came to see them last year win a landmark action against the German company that made thalidomide and sold it to a trusting world.

If that happens, Lynny Rowe from Nunawading will be known far beyond the street where she grew up. She will be the poster girl for an action that could help hundreds of people like her around the world.

For the Rowes, a win would mean they could re-stump the house and guarantee Lynny proper care and attention for the rest of her days. And Lynny could buy an iPad or a Kindle to read with. It's hard to read books when you don't have any arms.

Meanwhile, the Rowes keep on doing what they've done since lightning struck them on that Friday long ago.

Three times a week Wendy goes to a gym class to stay strong enough to help look after Lynny. She has to be strong because three times a night she gets up and rolls her girl over in bed, the way she has almost every night for 49 years and three months.

Friday's child is loving and giving, goes the old rhyme. This one gets it from mum and dad.

ONE awful question hangs over Ian and Wendy Rowe ...

Who will care for Lynny when they can't.

3
Researching the Story

'I always say the heart of any good story is good research.'

Chris Masters, award-winning journalist, in Fogg, 1994, p. 5

Objectives

This chapter will introduce the basic components of research, indicating research priorities and some efficient ways of using a variety of resources to provide the vital detail that will shape a feature. It covers:

○ introducing research

○ how to research

○ going online: upsides and downsides

○ exploring archives and library stacks

○ other options

○ a Case study: Patrick Carlyon explains what was required to identify, locate and convince a reluctant interview subject to become the focal point of a feature

○ a Writing sample: 'Medic! Medic! Medic!' by Patrick Carlyon, *Sunday Herald Sun*, 17 March 2013.

Building the bridge

Many enthusiastic writers embark on their first substantial article imagining their primary task is to turn their fine idea into a great piece of writing. What they forget is that vital element that builds the bridge between the idea and the writing—the research. The point about research is that no writer knows everything, which is a compelling reason for reading, watching, talking and thinking about your subject. Yet research is often overlooked as a foundation of good feature writing. It is essential to making sense of your subject—if the writer doesn't understand what they are writing about it, what hope does the reader have?

Writers compiling features will usually have to find facts, views and opinions about issues they are neither familiar with nor naturally inclined towards. Writers learn from all this and then disseminate the information to their readers.

Thorough and well-planned research can transform an ordinary feature into a good feature. Extra research can elevate a good feature into an outstanding one. Research underpins every part of the writing process, from preparation for the interviews that drive the narrative and provide information in the feature, to relating the background and context that are vital to issues-based features.

Many inexperienced writers are so keen to start the writing process that they neglect the research component. And there are plenty of experienced writers who find writing so challenging that they will go on researching in the vain hope of putting off that inevitable moment when they have to write their story. The ideal is somewhere between the two extremes. But the important rule is that good research makes the writer's life so much easier. There are significant time constraints on journalists in modern newsrooms, so it is tempting to reduce the amount of research carried out for each story. Where possible, avoid that temptation. That also applies to those who are freelancers or working as contributors for websites: there are hardly any occasions when you can, as a writer, make a virtue out of ignorance. Good research is part of a writer's preparation for the task of writing—and every interview subject will be more cooperative if they know the writer has taken the time to acquaint themselves with the subject. This chapter will explain research's important role in good writing and how best to complete good research.

Introducing research—why is it important?

Every well-constructed feature will involve a mixture of broad research sources. It will contain documentary material (from a library or newspaper stories), interviews (with the relevant people, by phone, email or face to face) and a writer's insights (gleaned from studying key individuals in the story or making some connections and conclusions from the material the writer has assembled).

These are the building blocks, but identifying these components does not actually tell us why they are important. For that, we have to understand more about research itself.

There are three critical uses for research. One is as a revelatory tool that is fundamental to investigative journalism. (The application of specific research techniques, especially database and internet enquiries in investigative journalism, is covered more thoroughly in Tanner, 2002; and Tanner & Richardson, 2013.)

The second use of research is to provide the facts or the information—the fundamentals upon which all the writer's observations and insights can be built. The third use of research is to give authority and credibility to what is written (Evans, 1988, pp. 30–1). Readers (and critics) are more likely to trust and therefore believe the contents of a story that is well researched. Whether the writer is searching through a screed of documents in pursuit of evidence to point to a government cover-up, or tracking the travails of a celebrity marriage, the nature of research is the same—it needs to be thorough and it needs to help the writer understand what the story is about.

Once the writer has the basic idea for his or her feature, the next step is to accumulate the information that will constitute the feature. This may involve preparing for interviews or becoming acquainted with an unfamiliar topic or area. Research can be the most rewarding or tedious activity, depending on the writer's perspective. It should be regarded as the writer's vital tool in helping shape and sharpen the idea behind the feature. Many feature ideas arrive only half-formed; if they are not the writer's idea, they may come from a features editor who has spotted a personality, an issue or a development in a news story and asks, in the most general terms, that the writer 'have a look at it'. Embarking on research with such an open brief will feel intimidating at first, but gradually the cloud will start to lift and the writer will gain a clearer sense of what the feature could be about.

This is just one of the values of research—it helps the writer work out what is important by identifying what has been the predominant element or angle in previous stories about the topic. For example, the research for a general feature on the health of the Australian film industry will reveal numerous stories that, depending on the year, will be anchored to a boom or a bust in local film-making. These stories, in total, tell the writer that there is clearly a cyclical pattern to the industry and provide a possible new line of enquiry: Will the local industry ever be able to sufficiently sustain itself to become immune to its own fluctuating fortunes? How will it overcome this cyclical pattern? From these questions follow a range of more specific and useful questions: How vulnerable is the local industry to overseas trends? Is more government investment the key? How do we develop talent within the industry and then keep it in Australia? Is it realistic to expect that talent will want to stay here?

Once those questions emerge, the writer can begin to tailor his or her research accordingly. This research will also narrow the list of potential interviewees. Rather than confronting a long list of film industry people who can talk about a variety of issues relevant to the broad topic, the writer can now draw up a list of target sources: those who have particular expertise, such as those, perhaps, in charge of film schools; those involved in the industry when it was linked to heavy government subsidies; and actors or production crew who have decided to stay in Australia rather than join the industry overseas.

This reveals what researching actually does for the writer—it is a process of elimination and enlightenment. So, while research appears to be primarily about acquiring information and preparing the writer for the feature, it plays a fundamental role in helping the writer shape the final direction of the story. Each piece of a writer's research needs to be tested against the idea behind the story to help establish what is important, what information needs to be kept and what can be jettisoned. As former Fairfax journalist turned journalism academic David McKnight notes: 'To research successfully ... you must know what your story is really about and, during the research, constantly make decisions about priorities on that basis' (McKnight, in Fogg, 2005, p. 1).

What McKnight is actually saying is that good research skills will leave the writer with 1) a solid body of knowledge that is central to their feature topic and 2) a clear idea of the topic itself, formed by the acquisition and disposal of information according to its relevance.

How to research

American author Alden Todd claims that a good researcher has the skills of a reference librarian, a university scholar, an investigative reporter and a detective (Todd, in Evans, 1988, p. 32). What he is talking about is a mindset that enables the researcher to find the relevant facts. This means harnessing the curiosity every writer needs, together with knowledge about which person or what institution would be able to provide the answers needed for the story.

But relevant information might be found in something as banal as a train timetable that can help trace the journey of a missing person or, more tellingly, a document that confirms a secret funding arrangement between a multinational company and a political party. Whatever it is, researchers will need to acquaint themselves with primary sources (interviews and first-person documentation, such as letters, diaries or even records of births, deaths and marriages) and secondary sources (such as reports and newspaper clippings: see Kirkpatrick, in Tanner, 2002; Tanner & Richardson, 2013).

Finding the right source is often the key to research. Once you know what it is you want, you have to then consider who or what has it (whether it is information from an interview, a document or a set of documents). Todd (in Evans, 1988, p. 32) identified three questions that are central in this quest:

- Who would know?

- Who would care?

- Who would care enough to publish it?

Any good detective work requires knowledge and motive. And though most research is not as exciting (or time-consuming) as solving a crime, Todd's questions are sound and every researcher should remember them as they work their way through the accumulated information. The answers to the question of 'Who cares?' can be various. Your research might involve a partner who has drawn up a document in a dodgy business deal, believing that writing down the details of the transaction will help make them less vulnerable to being ripped off. Or you might find a library that, because it believes that its civic duty is to manage a diverse archive, has kept certain historical documents relevant to a story about asbestos in an old city building.

How much research is enough? The simple answer is that you have done enough when you have the answers you need. So the most efficient method of research involves finding the right source that will best enable access to the information you need.

Experienced writers will have a list of contacts in the right institutions, agencies and organisations that will be able to access the information necessary to expedite the research process. Inexperienced writers will not have those contacts, and researching will therefore be a more time-consuming process. This is when the tyranny of the deadline can be useful. If you have only three weeks to research, interview and write a story, it would be counter-productive to spend two weeks on research. There would be no time for interviewing or writing. But in such circumstances, it would be fair to spend at least several days, and ideally a week, on the research. That would then allow a week for interviews (depending on the subjects' availability) and the transcribing of any recorded material, and a week to write.

A useful rule of thumb in such circumstances is that if the writer has lost sight of what the story is about and cannot explain it to a friend or the features editor in a couple of sentences, then the writer has probably become hostage to the research. Under-researching and over-researching are both problematic. But having too much information is less likely to cause hiccups in interviews than being ignorant and not attempting to understand the position or perspective of the interviewee. The other advantage of having too much information is that it allows the writer to construct a credible and thorough feature, by picking the strongest material to use for a compelling read.

Going online

One of the writer's allies is the internet, which offers many convenient and potentially time-saving research tools. However, the downside is that the vast, often untrammelled, universe of online information poses some unique challenges to every writer embarking on preliminary research.

There is a simple rule to be followed when it comes to internet research. Ask yourself: Is the internet the best place to look? Simple facts, definitions and spellings can take more time to find via the internet than by making a quick check of an encyclopaedia or dictionary. Some writers believe that the internet is a foolproof research tool. It is not; because not every document or every piece of information you require is there, and also because the information that is there may not be reliable (which we discuss further later). The internet is no replacement for the observations a writer can make and the rich information that can be obtained from a face-to-face interview. However, the internet remains a wonderful aid to research. It is, along with the telephone, one of the feature writer's best friends.

As Weaver notes, computer-assisted research (CAR) enables journalists to 'transcend the limitations of geography, time zones or limited inhouse resources' (Weaver, in Tanner, 2002, p. 58). This is particularly true for freelance writers, who do not have access to in-house libraries because they are working offsite.

There are simple steps involved in rudimentary CAR. Google, or whichever search engine the writer chooses, provides an easy way to access information. However, search engines are not only vast resources; they also mix the credible with the subjective, and can demand that you spend a good deal of time just to find the best source for your needs. University libraries have excellent internet tutorials on how to use search engines and how to take advantage of the libraries' online databases; they are a great starting point for writers. The trick to getting the most out of search engines is to be as specific as possible in the terminology you use for the search.

Many users will prefer to cast their search wide at the start and then narrow it down by slowly adding search terms. This can be time-consuming and unproductive, largely because of the internet's almost infinite capacity to embrace generalities. A specific search might not return many hits, but it is easy to eliminate words and phrases. For instance, a name is always easier to find than a phrase—a feature on 'Australian international models' could begin with an internet search for that phrase, but it will be more effective if the writer has names of Australian international models to feed into the search engine. The writer is likely to find more personal perspectives on Australian international modelling with such an approach, which will help shape the approach to the story.

Once the search engine has delivered a small and negotiable range of options, the writer needs to prioritise the sources, starting with the most credible. The best guides to these credible options are other publications or institutional sources, such as those published by the National Museum or the Australian Parliament. There is also a great deal of personal reflection and reaction on the internet, whether it is Twitter or blogs. These snap opinions may be helpful if a writer is canvassing opinions or reactions to a particular issue (for example, the conflicts across the Middle East, teenage drug use, the new Amy Schumer routine), but they can be of limited value for factual research. Just because a comment has been retweeted by many people, doesn't mean that it is truthful; you have to consider the motives of the person who originally made the claim and those who were prepared to accept or endorse it. In fact there are resources you can use to check the veracity of some claims, including Snopes.com. Equally, journalists should be careful with sites such as Wikipedia, which can be edited by anyone to present a particular slant—one that might reflect personal bias, rather than objectivity. Increasingly, Wikipedia entries contain a detailed list of sources and these should be more reliable than unsourced entries.

Perhaps one of the best ways, initially, to view the internet is as a virtual replacement for a newspaper library, albeit with a fair bit of rubbish strewn through it. The first step most journalists used to make when they embarked on a writing assignment was to head to the library to find the necessary background information on their topic. They would search old newspaper clippings, filed under subject headings (for example, 'assassinations—political') or individuals (for example, 'Gosling, Ryan, actor'). Nowadays, the internet fulfils that function. It contains several newspaper clippings databases, such as Factiva, which has access to 8000 magazines and newspapers from around the world. The bonus of such newspaper search engines is that they can include material from overseas publications. Individual newspapers' websites, such as that of *The Guardian* in the UK, also have their own online archives that anyone can search.

The only warning we should attach to using information from newspaper or magazine-related databases is that there is a risk that you will perpetuate another writer's error (McKnight, in Fogg, 2005, p. 29). This is not inevitable, but it is possible that the original published material contains a name spelt wrongly, an incorrect address or another factual error, such as a date, that could pose problems for the researcher trying to locate that person or test the veracity of the research contained in the original article. August publications such as *The New Yorker* employ fact-checkers, whose job it is to re-check the writer's submitted feature before publication. So, while newspaper and magazine databases can be wonderful assets, they need to be used with caution, scepticism and fact-checking when using some secondary material.

Internet search engines are, however, just one element of CAR. The sheer range of internet materials means there is potential for writers to access information they would usually never see. Facebook can be a useful tool for writers trying to find information about individuals who are not well-known. But it is vitally important to conduct Facebook research with integrity and that means respecting the privacy settings.

Exploring archives and library stacks

The best non-interview sources for a researcher are the ones that combine institutional credibility with speed and convenience. There are a range of internet sites that contain a host of official and contemporary material, from *Hansard*—the official recordings of debate in every state parliament and the Federal Parliament—to the online version of one of the nation's finest and most useful reference works, the *Australian Dictionary of Biography*.

The satisfaction of accessing the richness of historical and reference material available to writers is only matched by the thrill of actually discovering something of importance during your research. There are offices of the National Archives of Australia (NAA)—which keeps historical records of government departments and agencies—in every state. Most of the material is, however, kept in the national offices in Canberra. Each state library also holds large stores of archives about a vast range of topics relating to the settlement and development of the state, and the establishment of the capital city, whether it is Hobart, Adelaide, Brisbane, Perth, Melbourne or Sydney. There are documents, photographs, maps, drawings and posters that can help complete the resource. University archives are also useful research tools, especially the holdings of the older universities, such as the University of Melbourne, which has accumulated useful material from its alumni over more than a century.

While it is true that a lot of archival material is available online, this is often just the starting point for further, offline research. For example, the NAA each year releases the minutes of Cabinet meetings and decisions from 30 years before (the 1987 papers, for example, were released at the start of 2017). Much of this material is put on the NAA website (see <www.naa.gov.au>), but to understand the Cabinet decisions of the day usually requires a strong understanding of the political environment of the time, therefore biographies of the relevant prime minister (in this instance, Malcolm Fraser) might be helpful in providing that necessary background information.

The essential point about archives is that they contain historical material. An archive will help the writer find first-hand recollections of colonial life in Tasmania or the early drawings of the Brisbane Town Hall, but it will not provide thematic, contextual or synthesised information that is the strength of the information to be found on the library shelves.

The library is not only a writer's resource; it can also provide a wonderful sense of shared purpose: there will be other researchers and writers there, doing many of the things that you are doing. The first priority for everyone involved in researching at a library—whether it be the council-run library, the university library or a state library—should be the reference section, with its dictionaries, thesauruses and grammatical guides, vital to clear expression, and its encyclopaedias, which can help a writer find instant facts on many topics.

The library stacks are, however, where the real research is done. In the same way that smart use of an internet search engine will yield the best results for the researcher, shrewd use of a library catalogue will provide a similar outcome. Sadly, some universities are rationalising their holdings and the random discovery of a title that could contain some research gold on a library shelf has become harder. So it is important to have a clear idea about what you are looking for in a library: a writer researching the history of the Australian car industry will be able to find several titles in a library's business section about the topic. But those books will not necessarily give the writer the kind of colour, insights and anecdotes that they need. The trick is to search more widely, in this case by looking in biographies. Sporting biographies could reveal which motor racing identities have included their views about the car industry in their life stories (for example, the late Peter Brock, Sir Jack Brabham, Mark Skaife); business biographies—such as that of Australian Jac Nasser, who became head of Ford in the United States—might also reveal relevant information. Such personal reflections are vital to any feature. In this particular instance, it would be worth contacting the two major manufacturers, Ford and Holden, both of whom are closing their Australian manufacturing plants, to see if you could access their in-house archives.

Finally, for this topic, the researcher should also look at the politics and current affairs section of the library, to explore the debate about motor vehicle industry policy in Australia. The researcher will emerge from the library with probably six to eight books and may finish up finding a relevant paragraph from one, two pages from another, and deciding that a third is too dry and incomprehensible. Nonetheless, in the process of finding these books, the writer will have engaged with the feature subject to a level that will enable them to embark with some confidence on the task of building up relevant information. The writer will have started to shape the direction of the feature.

Other options, especially the best option

The one central research tool that involves the writer walking away from the computer and the telephone is the face-to-face interview. The interview can give the writer a vast range of information—facts, figures, anecdotes, perspectives, nuances and observations. No other research technique can match it. As experienced journalist Pilita Clark says:

> For me, the most successful research tool by far has been the face-to-face interview … when I think about the journalists whose stories I have admired most over the years, they are almost always people who have taken the time to sit down and talk with other people.
>
> Clark, in Fogg, 2005, p. 32

It is vital to actually engage with people as sources of research information. Documents and the internet will provide only certain details—usually what, when and who—but it takes the face-to-face interview to provide the answers to those most critical of questions: the how and the why. For example, an internet search on the Hillsong Pentecostal Church in Sydney will provide certain basic details about the movement and its membership. But a face-to-face interview with the people who run Hillsong and with members of their congregation will provide personal insight into why their faith is so important to them.

The central consideration here is not that an interview takes place—if that were the case, all interviews could happen over the telephone or via email. No, a face-to-face interview provides the basis for a more intimate exchange. Interview subjects are usually more candid face to face than over the telephone. You will also be able to ascertain more about the subject in research terms if you meet them in person—you will see how they look, how they react to topics you raise, what they wear and, if the interview takes place in their home or office, how those places reflect their personality. These subjects may not be the central figures in the story. They may, in fact, be 'bit' players, who can only offer part of the picture you are trying to assemble. But a personal meeting can help provide the winning detail and crucial information that can transform your piece of writing.

It may take several phone calls to find the right source, but once you have tracked them down, a personal interview signals to them how important they are to your story. This can be a powerful incentive for them to cooperate and talk honestly.

The inescapable fact of research is that if a writer wants to do scant research, they should not expect anything other than a superficial story at the end of the process. Good research takes time, skill and patience. But it also demands a willingness to think laterally to ensure the writer finds the best sources for the necessary information. Outstanding features wear their research lightly, but outstanding features are actually built on such research. Good research remains an essential tool for every writer.

Summary

o The point of research is that no writer knows everything.

o The three critical uses for research are:

    a   to drive central elements of the story

    b   to provide the foundations of the feature—that is, facts

    c   to give the feature authority and credibility.

o Research is a process of elimination and enlightenment.

o You have done enough research when you have the answers you need.

o The first question to ask when embarking on internet research is whether the internet is the best place to find the information you require.

o Face-to-face interviews are often the best form of research because they provide information, observation, anecdotes and insights.

Questions

1   What is the range of general source areas that a well-constructed feature will contain?

2   A good researcher needs to develop and employ a range of skills. What are they?

3   What are the advantages and disadvantages of internet-based research?

Activities

1   Pick a feature from your favourite newspaper, online site, television or radio program. List the number of sources in the feature. How many of them could be found on the internet or the library shelves, or generated from interviews?

2   Think about a feature you want to write (it could be anything, such as a feature on the future of pub bands, the end of celebrity, or problem gambling). Draw up a research list. Include primary and secondary sources, online and offline sources.

3   Pick a story from the day's newspapers, online site, radio or television programs that you believe did not tell you everything you wanted to know. What was missing in the story? Now try to find at least three sources on the internet that could help answer your questions about the particular story.

References and additional reading

Evans, G. (ed.) (1988). *The Complete Guide to Writing Nonfiction*, New York: Harper & Row.

Fogg, C. (1994). *Mastering the Maze*, Sydney: Australian Centre for Independent Journalism.

Fogg, C. (ed.) (2005). *Release the Hounds: A Guide to Research for Journalists and Writers*, Sydney: Allen & Unwin.

Hamilton, J. (2004). *Goodbye Cobber, God Bless You*, Sydney: Pan Macmillan.

Masters, C. (2002). *Not for Publication*, Sydney: ABC Books.

Tanner, S.J. (ed.) (2002). *Journalism: Investigation and Research*, Sydney: Pearson Education.

Tanner, S.J. & Richardson, N. (eds) (2013). *Investigative Journalism in the Digital Age*, Melbourne: Oxford University Press.

Online resources

National Archives of Australia: www.naa.gov.au

Snopes.com

Case study

Patrick Carlyon explains how persistence and commitment led to an extraordinary story about how a fateful moment affected one Australian soldier on duty in Afghanistan

Publication details:

'Yep, wait, we definitely have a ... Medic! Medic! Medic! Medic!', *Sunday Herald Sun*, 17 March 2013.

The author:

Patrick Carlyon was already an experienced feature writer when he wrote this story for Melbourne's mass-market *Sunday Herald Sun*. Carlyon had worked for the *Sydney Morning Herald* and *The Bulletin* magazine before joining *The Herald Sun* staff. This story won the 2013 Walkley Award for the best feature under 4000 words.

The story:

The story emerged from a joint research task Patrick Carlyon and colleague Ruth Lamperd had started on the high number of suicides among Australian army veterans. The sad truth was that many of the suicides were linked to post-traumatic stress disorder (PTSD), an increasingly identifiable consequence of warfare. What compounded the problem for soldiers diagnosed with the problem—and the families of those soldiers who had taken their own lives—was the perceived lack of support from the federal government.

From the start, Carlyon was looking for a story that would illustrate the issues. 'Let's dig down into the hidden price of being in a conflict and look at the shabby treatment of returned diggers,' Carlyon explained.

Importantly, he wanted to also make it clear that PTSD and the issues of treatment and support were neither a uniquely Australian problem nor a recent issue: war's horrible impact on combatants was a sad constant around the world and through history.

One of Carlyon's goals was to go beyond the official commemoration of the lost lives, which often featured the prime minister of the day at the funeral, and the Defence Force's formal farewell to its fallen colleague.

Carlyon's first step was to read the autobiography of the former Australian Army major-general John Cantwell, *Exit Wounds*. The book includes details of the 10 soldiers who died while Cantwell was in charge of an Australian contingent in Afghanistan in 2010. Carlyon also spoke to Cantwell, and a journalist friend who had helped Cantwell write the book. From those conversations Carlyon started to narrow down the subject of his story. It was a reference to the medic Lance Corporal Mark Hughes-Brown that appealed to Carlyon—especially the notion of the carer who as Sebastian Junger described it, suffered from 'a terror of failing to save the lives of their friends'. Hughes-Brown left the Australian Defence Force after an incident in which two of his colleagues—Jacob Moerland and Darren Smith—were killed by an improvised explosive device (IED). Hughes-Brown had PTSD. His military career was over. 'The story is about this bloke who in trying to save his mates' lives inadvertently ruins his own,' Carlyon said.

Once Carlyon had his subject, he then had to find him. Hughes-Brown was hard to track down. Carlyon finally found him but had to leave a message with Hughes-Brown's father. It took Hughes-Brown two weeks to respond. The former medic was suspicious of cooperating—there had been the standard military enquiries into the incident and he was wary of revisiting it. And as Carlyon noted, journalists often find themselves as de-facto therapists in such stories: Hughes-Brown had gone through plenty of therapy and didn't feel the need to explain, confess or reflect on the circumstances surrounding the death of his two mates again. He was vulnerable and uncertain.

But Carlyon persisted and kept talking to Hughes-Brown. He estimated that he finished up with 25 hours of taped conversation, spread over four months and two visits to where Hughes-Brown was living. Like every journalist working in mainstream media, Carlyon was also working on other stories while he was working on this feature. Carlyon also spoke to relatives of the two soldiers who died—Moerland's father Robert and Smith's wife Angela—and some of the soldiers who were on the same patrol.

Even after Carlyon had Hughes-Brown's cooperation, he had another significant issue: the fatal explosion and its consequence was barely two seconds in time. There were witnesses, other than Hughes-Brown, but there were various recollections about some of the detail. Carlyon wanted to tell the powerful story as a narrative, so he needed to be sure the detail was correct. That meant often asking Hughes-Brown to clarify details, expand on others, and try to explain discrepancies in others' recall. 'At the start, you don't know. You're open to all the information but after a time, you are mining for glitters of gold in the interview, the little facts and observations,' Carlyon said.

It was a delicate and patient task. 'I'm very comfortable with the final version of what happened [that day] because it was confirmed and reconfirmed. No one has questioned it factually,' he said.

And Hughes-Brown was pleased with the end result. Carlyon has kept in touch with the former medic, but as the story reveals, the level of support Hughes-Brown receives from the government still leaves a lot to be desired.

Writing sample

'Yep, wait, we definitely have a … Medic! Medic! Medic! Medic!'

Sunday Herald Sun, **17 March 2013**

Alpha Company medic Lance Corporal Mark Hughes-Brown knew it was bad. The blast 200 metres ahead threw up much more than dirt. But he didn't know who was hit or how many. One? Ten? PATRICK CARLYON reports on the blast that killed two Australian Diggers and the ripples that have torn lives apart ever since.

THE Australians huddled in a lane way of an Afghanistan village, tired and hungry.

The soldiers had spent a long morning uncovering enemy stashes of weapons and supplies. They joked about the nearness of death, their silent stalker on each of these patrols.

Well, they tried to. They'd been here so long, perhaps too long, in part because Sappers Darren Smith and Jacob Moerland were so damned good at their jobs. Smith came with his kelpie cross, Moerland with his metal detector.

Smith was 25 and pining for his wife and little boy. His other love, Herbie, was the bomb detection dog conscripted from an animal rescue shelter. Moerland, 21 and soon to be married, was the blond with the cheesy grin. Back home, he frocked up for parties: in combat, where in the words of a loved one he sought to 'blow up s---', he found blokier ways to get noticed.

The patrol radios had chirped with the pair's delight at each new find.

The village hollows, as a patrol member puts it, served 'like a K-Mart for insurgents'. The patrol had emptied them of ammunition, grenades and mortars. That was the worry, that success would invite retaliation.

The village lay in the 'dead ground' west of Patrol Base Wali, in the Mirabad Valley in the country's south, marked by a rock feature that resembled a shark fin. Any sortie in the zone called 'the box' could without warning become the 'nastiest day of your life'.

The patrol had piled the haul in preparation to blowing it up. The soldiers couldn't carry it all back to base. A warning countdown was set to begin.

Smith and Moerland mulled with the patrol's medic, Lance Corporal Mark Hughes-Brown, then 30, a dedicated smoker who shook out a Camel, one of his last in the pack.

He'd had 20 minutes sleep the night before. In recent months Hughes-Brown had been stabbed by Afghan patients and had treated rag dolls who once were children. He'd forgotten how to laugh.

'How many of those you got left?' Smith asked him.

Hughes-Brown gave his friend a cigarette.

The medic opened a can of tuna. Smith said that Herbie was hungry. Hughes-Brown's stomach was rumbling. But he threw the can to the dog.

Smith cupped Herbie's ears for the controlled explosion, but the dog barked in panic at the bang. Moerland wondered why Smith couldn't better control his dog. The team bickered.

Such tension was contagious. The duo had fossicked together for four or five hours, each in body armour that doubled as a microwave. They had been here so long, they now expected the village's exits to be booby-trapped with improvised explosive devices (IEDs). There might be an ambush as well.

You better not go and get yourself hurt.

The order to move out was issued. Smith had a final request for Hughes-Brown. He was out of water. Hughes-Brown gave him water—and another kind of mouthful. As Hughes-Brown recalls, the exchange went something like this:

'You better not go and get yourself hurt.'

'Why?'

'Because I've already given you enough stuff today. I don't want to give you anything else.'

'Yeah, whatever.'

'Seriously, switch the f--- on, I don't want you getting blown up and I don't want anyone else getting blown up.'

'Yeah, whatever.'

'I'm seriously going to kick your a--- if you do.'

'Yeah, whatever.'

> The combat medic's first job is to get to the wounded as fast as possible, which often means running through gunfire while everyone else is taking cover. Medics are renowned for their bravery, but the ones I knew described it more as a terror of failing to save the lives of their friends.
>
> Sebastian Junger, *War* (2010)

THE AUSTRALIANS had found a medical bag in one of the caches. Hughes-Brown spent time trying unsuccessfully to tape this to the medical pack on his back. The delay may have saved his life.

Normally, Hughes-Brown, known as HB, trailed Smith on patrols, which often string out and divide. This time, he was still trying to secure the medical bag when he heard a blast about 200 metres ahead.

He recalls a voice on the internal comms: 'Yep, wait, we definitely have a ... '

Then, shouts: 'Medic! Medic! Medic! Medic! Medic! ... '

Then, his own rasp: 'No, no, no, no, no ... '

Smith and Moerland were Smithy and Snowy to their mates. They had a yin and yang quality. A quiet front masked Smithy's wit. Snowy was loud and outrageous.

Smithy had been with Alpha Company for less than two months. Everyone knew Snowy: he donned a local hat with Afghan soldiers at evening chai sessions at Patrol Base Wali.

Former ABC correspondent Chris Masters bunked next to him until Snowy rose at about 3am. 'Snowy was a genuine wild man character,' he says, with affection. 'He liked to shock.'

As usual, the bomb detecting pair had led the patrol along a path out of the village, known as Sorkh Lez. Snowy, with blue eyes that jump out of photos, scanned the wheat fields and mud brick compounds. Smithy clicked and whistled to Herbie, who was off his leash.

It was just after 11.10 am on June 7, 2010.

Perhaps the sappers spotted a telltale wire or a clod of mud turned fresh in the pan of wet earth. Whatever the case, the bomb lay next to an aqueduct in a spot that amounted to a bottleneck. IEDs had been planted in every exit of the village: the patrol was doomed to encounter one.

Smithy had called Herbie. The pair stood together beside or behind Snowy, who was crouching. Children laughed and squealed nearby.

Meanwhile, back in Brisbane, Smithy's two-year-old boy, Mason, was having his afternoon sleep. He didn't normally sleep this late.

Before now, Snowy had furnished his father Rob with tales: after a letter about an IED blast in the morning and another IED blast the same afternoon, Rob only hoped his son wasn't telling his mother the same stories. Snowy's parents had separated years earlier.

HB had survived three IED explosions himself. The insurgents had got better at making booby traps. Earlier on, their homemade bombs tended to be buried too deep, or didn't detonate.

This blast sounded louder than the previous ones. The cloud ballooned bigger. This blast threw up more than dirt. Chris Masters, on another patrol kilometres away, heard a 'sickening thud' and saw 'a column of white smoke (lift) through the clear air.'

'Medic! Medic! Medic! Medic! Medic! ...'

'No, no, no, no, no ... '

HB stumbled towards the smoke in a direct line through an empty field. Training overrode self-preservation: it always did. He had to be 'over' his patients.

But his route had not been cleared of IEDs. HB became aware of shouts ordering him to stop. He paused, panting and shaking, and waited for searchers to clear the ground ahead. Step. Scan. Step. Scan.

He knew it was bad. But he didn't know who was hit and how many. One? 10?

A senior soldier at the crater site pointed and shook his head. Snowy was probably dead, a witness now says, 'before he hit the ground'.

The patrol consisted of about 35 men. At least one had been blown off his feet. Frag—shrapnel—had whizzed past others.

Jangled by the blast, the soldiers tensed for the tat-tat of an enemy machine gun or the whine of rockets. They braced for an ambush that would never come.

HB didn't want panic. He noted the children edging forward, the local men gathering in silence. Sergeant John Craig would follow HB's suggestion and clasp Snowy's hand, even though Snowy was clearly dead.

Herbie was missing. His body was later found riddled with frag. Smithy was missing, too: it took time to register he was in the aqueduct.

His mates had pulled him from the silty shallows by the time HB arrived. Smithy was blinded, disoriented and hit in the legs, abdomen, chest and head. HB didn't know who he was, not until he spotted the dog lead hitched to Smithy's pants. Here was a patient. But here, too, was his mate.

Smithy fought HB and his two combat first aiders in his confusion. Bandages and needles splashed into the mud: a cannula spiked HB's arm.

Smithy not only wanted to live—HB had had patients give up on life with lesser injuries—he wanted to return to work. He asked after Herbie: HB told him Herbie was searching for secondary bombs.

A 'fallen angel' dispatch had been issued for a medivac helicopter. 'The bird's coming, the bird's coming,' HB told Smithy. He checked his watch. He scanned the haze on the hills. He plundered his medical pack.

Ten minutes. Fifteen minutes. Twenty minutes. Out of Smithy's earshot, HB shrieked at Warrant Officer Kev Dolan, again and again: 'Where the f--- is my chopper?'

According to HB, a despondent Dolan told him that he had called Tarin Kowt base 'a thousand times'.

Two days earlier, HB and Smithy had chatted at Patrol Base Wali. They often talked about 'everything and nothing' over a smoke while HB played with Herbie.

It followed a gallows humour group discussion about combat injuries. The group drifted off: HB recalls Snowy leaving to play Call of Duty, a combat computer game.

The mood shifted. Smithy asked the medic to tell him if he was ever about to die of wounds. Smithy wanted a last chance to say some final words.

That last chance was now. HB had already revived him, with CPR, out of sight of the men. It was 30 minutes or more since the blast. HB leaned in close to Smithy's face.

Smithy apologised for making HB work on him. He had two breaths left. He said he loved his family.

At about the same moment, the two-year-old Mason Smith woke up in Brisbane, screaming: 'No Daddy, no Daddy, don't go, no Daddy.'

HB was still trying CPR when the Blackhawk landed. After it took off, HB bumped into an infantry soldier who recoiled at the sight of him. Blood clogged HB's mouth and nose.

HB shoved the private in the face and stomped back to the wheat field where he had lost Smithy. At some point, he threw down his helmet.

He pocketed Smithy's Leatherman all-purpose tool, which Smithy cherished. HB figured it now belonged to Mason, the little boy now being comforted by his mother.

HB steadied himself on the shoulder of Corporal Jeremy Pahl, Snowy and Smithy's section commander, and vomited blood ingested from the CPR.

In the wheat field, shielded from the other men, HB's manic burst dissolved. He and another soldier leant on one another and wept.

'I've just lost two of my best mates,' the soldier said.

'I know you have, I've lost two of my good mates, too,' HB replied. 'There's nothing we can do about it, the job's on, we still have to get back home.'

If he sounded sensible, it was a front. HB was falling into a daze of guilt that would not pass, even though outsiders would see no grounds for guilt.

More than two-and-a-half-years later, HB is resigned. His brain may always be stuck in overdrive. He didn't know that then.

The next day, the same men—down two mates—would head 'outside the wire' on another patrol.

HB WOULD lose 16 patients on his Afghanistan deployment. He is reconciled with 15 of these deaths. Some were Afghan children who faded slowly. Some were less banged up than Smithy.

He recalls that morning at Sorkh Lez like a slow motion sequence, as though describing a movie scene to a blind person. His actions passed every official measure and every unofficial medic peer review.

HB now smokes too much and won't remove the black metal wrist band—*Always Besides You*—that someone ordered to commemorate Smithy and Snowy. Dozens of people around Australia sport the same bracelet.

Some of the bereaved, jammed into a vortex of loss, are set to be friends for life. Some will never meet. Some have fallen out. Yet they are united. They won't forget. HB wears the band with a sad twist—he won't forget that he 'f---ed up', even if he didn't.

Lives have edged forward without Snowy and Smithy. They must, somehow. Snowy's fiancée Kezia was due to marry him in November, 2010.

She now has a child to a new love. Smithy's widow, Angela, was a bridesmaid at her wedding. They are close friends, as are Angela and Snowy's mother, Sandy. Angela herself got engaged late last year.

She wasn't expecting to find a new partner. Certainly, she didn't seek to. Her partner had met Smithy and he was close friends with Snowy. The three of them served together at Patrol Base Wali. He is close to Mason, who comes home from school each day to a house filled with photos of Smithy.

Angela and Smithy had 'the chat they had to have' before he left for Afghanistan. If he didn't return, he told her, he wanted Mason to have a father figure. He didn't want her to be lonely. 'I know you'd pick the right person because you picked me,' Smithy said.

HB hasn't embraced the future by accepting the past, not yet, anyway. He looks too boyish to be 33. But being raised in old-world manners, coupled with his lapses into army slang, makes him sound older.

He has just bought a house—he doesn't want the world to know where—to 'fallback, regroup and recover'. He wants to work, and has done contract paramedic jobs, but finds being honest about his state of mind muddles his job prospects.

HB doesn't often booze or invent slights to rage against. But he is stuck in a moment, or in a time, really, when being at war became the closest thing to being at peace, and being at home is being at war with yourself.

His June 7, 2010 patrol preparation didn't adhere to his methodical approach. He didn't recheck his kit that morning, as he always did. No time. Mind you, he had everything, the packing gauze, tourniquets and needles to reinflate collapsed lungs. With Smithy, he just ran out of options.

Afterwards, when vehicles arrived to whisk the men back to Wali, a senior soldier sat HB down in an empty field. HB was out of breath and out of tears. His commander had comforting words, or so HB thinks: he didn't hear a word.

HB remembers the deaths being announced at base. Then his hearing went again, along with his memory. Apparently, he wandered away midway through the address.

He was found in the Regiment Aid Post (RAP)—poised to smash the heart-starter paddles. He'd already trashed the beds and trays and benches.

That night, he was sitting alone in the RAP when a man's voice called out for help, HB's help. It was Smithy.

HB closed his eyes. Smithy was dead. His logical brain knew this. Yet this was real. This was happening.

The next night, HB did open his eyes. Smithy appeared at the door and manoeuvred himself onto the bed. HB backed into a corner, pinching himself. If HB went to him, he was convinced, he could touch Smithy. They started to talk.

'Hey, Doc, how you doing today?'

'Nnnnnnnot bad, Smithy. Yourself?'

'Yeah, good.'

Was HB going crazy? He thought so. He confided in a commanding officer and the padre. Psychologists were called in. They recommended more sessions. Only later would the 'encounters' be explained.

HB's guilt over his friend's death, and the trauma, had conspired with fatigue. HB had suffered 'day terrors', another version of 'night terrors', when a dream-like state pervaded his waking thoughts. It was a rude introduction for the visions that now rouse him and sentence him to a zombie-like state for the day ahead.

Major-General John Cantwell visited Camp Wali a few days later. Like a child, HB studied his own boots when he was pointed out to Cantwell, an unusual study in military leadership, in part for his absence of bluster. Don't come over here, HB thought.

Cantwell praised HB's actions as he gazed at the top of HB's head. Pushing aside self-loathing, HB looked up at the Australian Forces Commander in Afghanistan.

'All I want is my two mates back,' he told Cantwell. 'If you can do that, I'd be the happiest man in the world. But you can't do that. So I'm the unhappiest man in the world.'

HB trudged away, ending a meeting between a soldier in the first throes of post-traumatic stress disorder (PTSD) and a general who'd been hiding his PTSD for two decades.

Cantwell was awash in guilt, too. As he recounted in his book, *Exit Wounds*, he wept over Snowy and Smithy's caskets. He identified the bodies at a military morgue.

Cantwell went off script when he announced he would say goodbye to them. He put a hand, in turn, on Snowy and Smithy's shoulders and felt the chill of their bodies through his plastic glove.

'It feels perfectly natural to be speaking aloud to the dead,' Cantwell wrote. 'After a moment of contemplation, I say "Goodbye Jacob". Then I pause and say, "Goodbye Darren".'

Cantwell now speaks of the 10 Australian deaths under his command as HB speaks of Smithy's death. They both say they 'failed'.

HER HUSBAND hadn't called: he always called. Angela Smith sent him a Facebook message at about 7 pm: 'No phone call'. The padre came to her Brisbane door a few hours later with the 'worst possible news'. Smithy had been killed.

There is no textbook for such moments. Angela Smith laughed, in disbelief, then 'screamed the street down': to this day, she believes her husband shielded Mason so he did not stir, despite the racket.

Jacob Moerland was dead nine hours when his father Rob, in Brisbane, answered the phone from his ex-wife, Sandy. His son hadn't named Rob on his enlistment papers. Rob didn't qualify for a knock on the door. He officially didn't exist.

Rob Moerland turned 52 on the day Jacob's body arrived home. He couldn't see his son's remains—they were deemed unfit for viewing. Rob would have settled for seeing his son's hand.

Angela did view her husband. She twirled his hair—he was always playing with it. He 'wasn't there' anymore, not the man filled with the love and laughter she knew.

Yet the friend who drove her to the mortuary later said he could feel Smithy's presence in the car on the way home. He sensed Smithy thanking him for helping Angela.

There will always be pieces in the puzzle missing.

The notion that Smithy has, from the grave, guided others to help his family has consoled her. The lights flickered on and off at home at every mention of Darren's name as she readied his dress uniform a few days later. 'Yes, Darren, we know you're here,' a friend said, looking upwards.

Rob Moerland plots a tortured path. Last December, he met Cantwell, who plans to meet the families of all the men who died under his command. The two discussed details of the IED blast.

'I wanted to talk to him but I didn't want to talk to him,' Rob says. 'There will always be pieces in the puzzle missing. I don't think anything will set me free.'

After Father's Day, 2010, Rob stopped working as an orthopaedic nurse. He couldn't tend to patients in his blur.

'If you ask what I did for three months, I couldn't tell you,' he says. 'I existed. I functioned. Dysfunctionally.'

> We were back in the community, a part of it and yet apart. There was a gap we couldn't forget and others couldn't bridge.
>
> —Sapper Harry Dadswell, Military Medal, Australian Imperial Force 1915–1919

HB WOULD spook himself in his sleep as a child. He dreamt of dying alone, in the middle of nowhere. Even then, he thought this a bit odd. Psychologists have explained that he had a heightened grasp of his mortality at a young age.

Suicidal thoughts are entwined in PTSD. HB has had them. As in his dreams, he thought he would go off alone, where no one would suffer the trauma of discovering him. Unlike the dreams, he would not die an old man. He just needed the guilt to stop.

The guilt hasn't faded, but the urge to end things has. He finds a 'happy thought' and clings to it. He listens to music or watches TV. It doesn't always work. His unconscious mind breaches the walls built by his conscious mind.

HB finds himself researching combat treatment articles online. He compares medical advents with Smithy's injuries and ponders what he may have done differently. He has bombarded doctors with hypotheticals. 'My brain goes into overload, playing the what-if game,' he says. 'I'd love to turn it off. But I can't.'

The night terrors, as with the panic attacks, have eased, but they can be set off by random triggers. The whiff of a dead animal. Footage of a chopper crash on the TV news.

Fishing on the river near his home, HB might 'scan' an Aboriginal boy or girl wrapping a wet T-shirt around their head. He loses track of his surrounds. He's not in rural NSW, but in Afghanistan, wondering if the kid is the bomber in a plot.

HB, a 13-year army veteran, didn't quite finish his 2010 deployment. He couldn't: on the last four patrols, he was prone to panic attacks, which he says endangered other men. His emotional spiral wasn't just about

Smithy: he has photos of an IED roadside blast that killed 10, and close-ups of dying US soldiers. But he goes back to *that* morning in his mind. Again and again.

He says everyone who served on an Australian patrol base in Afghanistan might be liable to PTSD, which often doesn't appear until soldiers are back in civilian life and deprived of their outlets for shared experiences. 'Every single one of us saw s--- that I don't think anyone should see,' he says.

HB is not unusual. PTSD numbers are rubbery, but it's estimated that between one in five and one in 10 deployed diggers will suffer from a form of it. The true number from Afghanistan deployments may take decades to determine. Many sufferers will long deny it to themselves.

As the medic, HB was the first stop for ailments on a patrol base. The role carried over back home, he says, to men who couldn't bridge the disconnect between here and there, who drank and yelled and threw things because their wives and army colleagues couldn't grasp the chaos of their thinking.

He caught up with a friend, he says, for a chat. They shared a friendly secret and said a light goodbye before the friend tried to kill himself. The friend, who survived an IED attack, was released from hospital and told HB he would try again, as soon as he got a chance.

HB himself was told to 'harden up'. After his medical discharge, he faced a hurdle that all troubled ex-service people confront—the Department of Veterans' Affairs (DVA).

Queensland psychiatrist Dr Andrew Khoo, who treats veteran patients almost daily, says DVA is known for rejecting claims, for insensitive commentaries, for piling up paper work and for clouding already confused thoughts.

'A lot of guys like myself have just given up,' says HB. 'I walked in to the military in perfect health and I've walked out not so well.'

MASON SMITH is an intuitive boy. He seems to know when his mother needs him. Sometimes, Mason says he chats with his father 'protecting us from the skies'. He speaks of taking a space rocket to visit him. Sometimes, Mason asks when Daddy is coming home.

Angela is only now confronting her grief—for a long time, she tried to keep up a smile for her son. She's a 'completely different person' because of Darren's loss, she says, and perhaps a wiser one: 'It makes me cherish everything I do have—here and now—a lot more than I used to.'

Yet grief does not wash away. 'Closure' belongs in text books. It has no place in the human heart.

Rob Moerland put his son's ashes in a vial. He got some Afghan sand, Jacob's medals, badges and a commemorative box. He wanted the ashes with him everywhere.

Then he had a better idea.

He slogged the Kokoda Track last July. Rob scattered the ashes along the way, like little outpourings of liberation. This was the farewell he had to have, in the jungles of another country, commemorated for battles fought by another generation of men. It was two years too late and it felt just right.

Before last Christmas, Rob bought Call of Duty, the computer game that Jacob loved. Rob found he had no flair for shooting baddies.

A few weeks later, Rob and Kate, his second wife, laid a concrete slab. It was the start of their house redevelopment. The finish date, January 14, 2015, is the day that Jacob Moerland would have turned 26.

HB WAS tricked into attending a barbeque in Brisbane. He thought he was going to the house of a mate of a mate.

He didn't know that someone wanted to meet him. He twigged only when he walked through the front door, when he saw the family photos.

'Oh my f---ing God,' he thought. 'I'm in his house'.

When Angela Smith appeared, she hugged him and started to cry. HB didn't know what to do or say. So he recited the loop that played in his head.

I failed my job. I failed you. I failed your son. I failed Darren.

No, Smithy's widow told him. You didn't fail. You gave him more time than he otherwise could have had. You got his last message to me. Thank you.

HB started to cry, too.

4
Interviewing

'Are we promoting a movie?' asked Robert Downey Jr, clearly puzzled by how the interview was going. 'You are, but I'm not,' is what I perhaps should have said to clear up the confusion.

Krishnan Guru-Murthy, *The Guardian*, 27 April 2015

Objectives

This chapter deals with the central information-gathering tool of non-fiction writing—the interview. The emphasis is on doing the groundwork for interviews, choosing the questions that will draw out interesting and stimulating responses, and trying to develop strategies to cope with the many challenges that face interviewers. This chapter builds on our previous discussion about research techniques, and covers:

o   preparation: history, scope, reasons etc.

o   types of interview: personal, informative, investigative

o   the setting

o   what to do once you're there

o   asking the right questions

o   troubleshooting: 'I think I'm in love with my interview subject' and other problem areas

o   a Case study: Trent Dalton shows how he came to grips with interviewing one of the world's most important religious figures

o   a Writing sample: 'Orange crush' by Trent Dalton, *The Courier-Mail*, *QWeekend* magazine, 9 July 2011.

Flirtation, seduction, betrayal

The interview provides the basic and essential elements of a story, so it is important to understand how to conduct one. It can be intimidating and confronting, even for experienced writers, but there are several strategies that can help maximise the return on an interview.

But before we address those, we need to deal with the ambiguity at the heart of the interview—the often vexed relationship between interviewer and interviewee. For American author and academic Janet Malcolm, the interview—the centrepiece of the exchange between most non-fiction writers and their subject—is 'morally indefensible' (Malcolm, 1990, p. 3). This view is shared by British journalist Andrew

Billen, who specialises in interviews. He describes the process thus: 'The three stages of a successful interview are flirtation, seduction and betrayal' (Billen, in Farndale, 2002, p. 3).

Maybe there is a strong element of truth in these observations by Malcolm and Billen, but they presuppose a level of malice, even cynicism, from the interviewer and a degree of naiveté from the subject that rarely match reality. The interview process may be philosophically challenging, but it is usually elevated above these dilemmas by the interviewer's genuine curiosity and the interviewee's willingness to volunteer information. In other words, in these circumstances it can be regarded as a fair exchange. The value in considering these observations lies in the fact that it will alert us to the importance of being open and honest with everyone we interview. We cannot expect honesty from our interview subject unless we as writers are prepared to be clear from the start of the interviewing process about why we are talking to the subject and how we will be using the information gleaned from the interview. It is a simple rule that is central to the interview exchange.

The best interviews feel like conversations. That does not mean that the interview subject is suddenly the interviewer's new best friend. Rather, a good interview reflects the fact that the interviewer has made a connection with the subject. And to do that, good preparation, curiosity and a willingness to engage with the interviewee are required. When an interview works, it is a truly satisfying experience for both interviewer and interviewee.

The interviewer always has one advantage—very few people do not want to spend time talking about what they do, why they do it and what they will do next. That willingness instantly clears many possible barriers between the interviewer and his or her subject. That knowledge should comfort many inexperienced interviewers, who will find that, for many of their subjects, the mere act of being interviewed is flattering. And that usually guarantees a pleasant experience for everyone.

Bad interviews happen for a variety of reasons—inadequate preparation on the interviewer's behalf, lack of time for the interview, the interviewee's unwillingness to take part, or inexperience.

The quotation at the start of the chapter is an insight in to how an interview can go horribly wrong. Hollywood actor Robert Downey Jr was promoting an Avengers movie in which he appeared as the Marvel character Iron Man. The British journalist—Krishnan Guru-Murthy—is an experienced interviewer with Channel 4 television news. (See it at <https://www.youtube.com/watch?v=ALBwaO-rAsE>.) Guru-Murthy meets his obligations inherent in the transaction with Downey and the Hollywood studio by asking a series of questions about Downey's *Iron Man* and then raises personal questions about the actor's previous drug addiction and relationship with his father. The interviewer does, however, give Downey Jr the opportunity to not answer or avoid the question if he wishes. Downey Jr's eyes keep flicking to the studio publicist and then the actor decides he has had enough and walks out of the interview. Downey Jr later called the journalist a 'bottom-feeding muckraker' and said he wished he had left the interview earlier. 'There's an assumption that … because you've sat down there [in the interviewee's chair], you're going to be scrutinized like a kiddie fiddler who's running for mayor,' Downey Jr said (Needham, 2015).

Guru-Murthy, not surprisingly, had a different perspective. 'An interview with a movie star isn't intended to be "news",' he wrote. 'We do it to add texture to the normal diet of politics, foreign affairs and investigations ... Some [actors] are happy to engage, and seem quite relieved to escape the junket monotony engineered by the PRs ... . But when I've asked movie stars what they would like to talk about, to see if they have a nugget they would like to drop on Channel 4 News, the response is usually along the lines "not really, I hate all this"' (Guru-Murthy, 2015). The end result poses some interesting questions about whether celebrities—who have their fame or a product to promote—have irreconcilable expectations to journalists about the outcomes of the interview process.

And then there is the more profound challenge about how close an interview will get the journalist to the truth, of either events or the individual. Walkley Award-winning ABC journalist Sarah Ferguson reflected on the 144 hours of interviews with 55 people that went into the three-part documentary on the Rudd–Gillard Labor leadership changes, *The Killing Season*: 'A narrative emerged of Rudd's unravelling and Gillard's ascendancy, but no single truth. As Finance Minister Lindsay Tanner observed, "the truth is always conditional in politics"' (Ferguson & Drum, 2016, p. 139). These examples—of Hollywood and Canberra—might represent the high-end of the interviewing craft, but the issues they capture are still worthy of consideration, regardless of who is the interview subject—what is their agenda, how reliable are they as witnesses to events or participants in the everyday dramas that are often the basis of a strong feature.

So here is a quick list of DOs and DON'Ts for the scheduled interview:

- Do—be prepared.
- Do—look (and sound) confident and enthusiastic.
- Do—dress appropriately.
- Do—try to connect with the interview subject (find out where they live, their previous project, whether you went to the same school, if you share relatives or friends).
- Do—be firm in seeking answers to your important questions.
- Don't—talk over the interview subject.
- Don't—be aggressive.
- Don't—be frightened of asking one more question, especially a tough one.

Preparation

The best way to guarantee a good outcome from an interview is to have done the research (see Chapter 2), drawn up some potential questions and given some thought to what you need to get from the interview. The research is the raw material that provides the interviewer with the platform for devising the list of questions. Research will often lead to the same material being obtained from several sources. This is usually because the interviewee has been interviewed many times. In such instances, the interviewer needs to evaluate the information. For example, is there a way of getting a fresh perspective on the anecdote that the actor always uses about the first time he saw his girlfriend? Is there another way of getting the career academic to talk about her work on gene therapy? What will it take to get the politician to express his view about tolled roads in a new way?

Broadly speaking, the interviewer's preparation for personal interviews will fall into three broad areas: 1) job/career, 2) family/school/relationships, and 3) the rest of the world (perspectives on the issues the interviewee is not directly involved with). Questions will flow from those areas. For other interviews, which are predominantly for information rather than personal insights, the preparation is often more complex because it will necessitate researching topics the interviewer may find to be more abstract. An article, for example, on the impact of workplace relations reforms on trade union membership will require an understanding of the industrial relations environment, as well as current union membership, before you embark on the interviews.

In such instances, it is helpful to follow Blundell's prescribed approach. He sorts the areas of interest into:

- history: How much of what is happening now is rooted in the past?
- scope: What is the extent or intensity of the issue or event?
- reasons: Why is it happening? For example, is it happening for economic, political or social motivations?
- impacts: What are the consequences? For whom?
- counter-moves: What action is being taken in response to the issue?
- future: What could happen?

Blundell, 1988, pp. 71–5

There is another vitally important part of the preparation for interviews—the writer's appearance and manner. Writers should always aim to be neat and tidy for an interview. First impressions count. Turning up for an interview with an older professional person while wearing jeans with frayed cuffs, an unironed shirt and a three-day growth will not be a good start. Writers need to communicate a seriousness and engagement with their interview subject—appearing not to care is guaranteed to make the interview subject feel disinclined to be forthcoming.

Interviewers should also try to be confident in their approach. This is easier said than done. The authors remember feeling wracked with anxiety about interviews with 'important' subjects (for example, prime ministers and premiers) or heroes (for example, sporting or artistic figures). The thing to remember is that such people have been interviewed many times. They are comfortable with the process. They are usually forgiving and understanding. One of the authors recalls how, in his entire career in journalism, he has witnessed only a handful of instances where the interview has gone so badly that the subject—or the interviewer—has wanted to wrap up. The most likely outcome is that you will come away wishing you had asked more questions and had more time. As long as you have prepared well and asked the key questions, that is no bad outcome.

Types of interview

Interviews can be divided into three broad areas: the personal interview, the information interview and the investigative interview. The type of interview required to research and write a feature depends on the kind of feature being written.

1   The personal interview

As a rule of thumb, a profile will not only focus on the subject—politician, actor, musician or philanthropist, for example—but also on people who know the subject or have a view about the subject. A profile of author and journalist Stan Grant, for example, would not only involve an interview with him, but interviews with his partner Tracey Holmes, some of those who share Grant's indigenous heritage, those who have worked with Grant or known him for some time. So whether the interview is with the subject or with their friends and enemies, it will be personal, reflective, insightful and, ideally, revealing.

2   The information interview

A feature that seeks, for example, to look at drug codes and penalties in Australian sport will need a range of interviews that draw out information and opinions. The writer, in this instance, would interview the chief executive officers of the major national sports—cricket, Australian Rules football, soccer, rugby league and rugby union, swimming and netball—and the drug-testing authorities, as well as the federal minister for sport and perhaps some current or retired sportsmen or women. It is a big list, but the task could be made easier by asking each of them the same set of questions about drugs in sport in general and about drugs in their particular sport. Whatever the framework, the main aim of the interview is to elicit information rather than personal revelations (although relevant anecdotes will certainly help the feature, especially with such compelling examples as the Essendon drugs scandal in the AFL and the Cronulla Sharks in the NRL).

3   The investigative interview

This is often the central interview for a piece of investigative journalism. It is really characterised by the style of interview, which has the potential to be confrontational and aggressive, and involve an uncooperative subject. This interview will usually take place at the end of the research process—and sometimes towards the end of the writing process—when the writer is seeking a response to information, gained from other sources, which is potentially damaging to the interviewee. While these interviews can often be unpleasant experiences for both the interviewer and the interviewee, basic fairness requires that the subject be allowed to address any claims against them.

This type of interview is unlike the personal and information interview because it is fundamentally reactive. It is essential to the balance of the story and it can, in some circumstances, actually transform a feature from a series of untested allegations into something more substantial. But often this style of interview, with characters as diverse as corrupt police officers, dodgy businessmen, or architects of scams, will draw spirited denials or curt silence. In these instances, it is often legally and ethically desirable that the interview takes place, regardless of the outcome.

The setting

A writer should always seek a face-to-face interview. There is so much more to observe if you share the same room, or indeed the same table, as the interview subject. Sarah Ferguson found that former Labor prime ministers Julia Gillard and Kevin Rudd revealed something of themselves in the way they reacted and engaged during the interviews for *The Killing Season* documentary. But it took time for Ferguson to read the signals—early on, the TV crew 'were novices'. Later, after watching the two Labor leaders closely on video and then interviewing them, 'we were expert at watching her [Gillard] and Rudd for small gestures that revealed truths …' (Ferguson & Drum, 2016, p. 10). It is not always possible, however, to have the luxury of that amount of time, the frequency of engagement with your interview subject or a neutral location: interviews can take place in a variety of places. Legendary *Washington Post* journalist Bob Woodward had to go to the darkened recesses of a car park to get some vital facts about the Watergate conspiracy from his source, known as Deep Throat (later revealed to be FBI Deputy Director Mark Felt).

Interviews can often take place in strange circumstances—on ships, in the middle of sports grounds, on trains, in police stations and on military expeditions. Such interview environments are nothing like the cosy exchange in a grand hotel room, with a range of refreshments on hand. They can be taxing situations and the writer will usually need to be adaptable and resourceful. For example, one of the authors remembers interviewing a former New Zealand finance minister during a trip to Australia. The minister had agreed to the interview, but was running out of time after an engagement ran late, so told the author that he would need to conduct the interview in the bathroom while he changed clothes. Though most interviewees do not try to be difficult, such situations may provide the only opportunity for the interview to take place.

The reality is that because the interviewee is central to the story, it is the interviewee who usually determines where and when an interview will take place. For example, a train driver might insist that the interview take place at the train depot, and a doctor may choose their surgery. An interview with a cricketer will probably take place at the oval or the team hotel, usually in a private part of the lobby.

Decisions about the location for an interview with a person with a disability need to take into account their disability or impairment: Do they use a wheelchair? Are they hearing- or vision-impaired? Hearing-impaired people, for example, would usually prefer a quiet environment; someone with a vision impairment would probably feel more comfortable being interviewed in a setting they're familiar with; and someone who uses a wheelchair would prefer the interview to be conducted in a building with wheelchair access.

The writer then needs to think about how the setting will affect the interview, and try to minimise discomfort and anxiety for both parties. This may simply involve asking for the interview to be moved to a part of the location where one party feels more comfortable. If, for example, a swimmer wants to be interviewed on the pool deck, but it is so noisy that the tape recorder cannot pick up the swimmer's answers, then the interviewer should ask soon after arriving if they can move to a quieter part of the pool. By making such a request the interviewer will show that they are serious about the task at hand, and will feel more in control of the situation. Such a request should only be made, however, if the interviewer has a legitimate reason for such a change.

The most common interview setting is usually at the interviewer's desk, with telephone to one ear and pen in hand. The telephone interview can be challenging for young writers, who often find the concept of cold-calling an interview subject difficult. The best way to overcome any sense of intimidation is to be adequately prepared. If the research has been done, then there is no reason to fear a telephone interview, even if it involves asking difficult questions.

The advantage of the telephone interview is that it can be done in comfort and with the research materials on hand. In addition, because on such occasions the interviewer is confronted with few external distractions—no view out of the hotel room window, no publicist hovering over their shoulder and no photographer trying to butt in—it is easier to concentrate on the information. Because you can't see the person being interviewed, however, one of the disadvantages is that there are no non-verbal cues to pick up on, such as tugging at hair, ears or nose, crossing and uncrossing of legs, or looking away during personal questions. During telephone interviews, the interviewer needs to develop an acute appreciation of change of tone and emphasis from the interviewee, which can indicate that the conversation has moved past the pleasantries and is developing into an exchange that will reveal the kind of information that can be transformed into a valuable piece of writing.

The downside of telephone interviews is the exact obverse of its advantages—they can be unsatisfying precisely because they may not produce many personal details and insights. A telephone is not often the medium for an intimate and revealing exchange. It can also be hard to read the mood and sometimes even to interpret correctly the words a person uses in a telephone conversation. One of the authors recalls that for one of his first feature stories, he was attempting to personalise Anzac Day with an interview with an old Anzac. The digger lived some distance out of town so the interview had to be conducted by phone. The reporter rang his house and asked to speak to Mr Smith. The elderly female voice on the other end of the line responded: 'I'm sorry, he's no longer with us.' The reporter asked if the woman knew when Mr Smith would be home, but the woman, Mrs Smith as it turned out, reiterated that her husband 'was no longer with us'. The reporter politely persisted in the mistaken belief that Mrs Smith's husband had moved out of the family home. When he asked for the man's phone number and his new address, the woman, clearly upset, blurted out that her husband was, in fact, dead. The reporter's mistake was that he was unfamiliar with the phrase 'no longer with us'; such misunderstandings are more likely to happen on the telephone than in face-to-face interviews, when the physical or emotional triggers are clear to see.

The telephone interview can be useful, however, for the basic transmission of information. In this sense, telephone interviews are like smash-and-grab raids: the interviewer makes the call, asks the questions, gets the answers they need, and then hangs up. It is an entirely functional exchange between interviewer and interviewee.

The rising prevalence of the email interview is an unfortunate development because this type of interview has the potential to alienate the interviewer from the subject. More problematic still is the fact that in the email interview, the interviewer cedes the initiative to the interviewee, supplying questions and then having to wait for the replies. These types of interview also give limited opportunities for the sorts of follow-up questions possible in a face-to-face or telephone interview. They usually involve no small talk, no chance to make a connection with the interviewee and no chance to clarify meanings or misunderstandings. An email interview makes it possible for interviewees to respond to the questions in their own time, or even to ignore questions or choose to answer them in their own way. They may have more time to think about answers, but such a situation will not usually provide the freshness of material that comes from a real-time interview. You can usually pick up on the fact that an interview has been done by email—the quotations in the article are usually polished and often sterile as a consequence. For those reasons, the email interview should be the last resort.

Yet no interview will amount to anything unless the interviewer actually listens to the exchange in which they are engaged. The interview is not about the interviewer; it is about the other person in the room or on the other end of the phone. The interviewer must shrink their personality to enlarge their receptivity. Seasoned journalist Mike Munro explained it like this: 'It doesn't matter how thorough your preparation is, you have to be able to shift and weave and follow the conversational leads' (*The Weekend Australian*, 1–2 September 2007).

Once you're there

The first thing for every writer to do is to write down the broad path they want the interview to take. For example, an interview with the new mayor for the local newspaper may cover three broad areas—the mayor's personal path to the job (family, work history, involvement in local politics), their understanding of their local community (How long have they lived in the area? What is their view of the council and the important local issues?) and, finally, their hopes for the job (What do they want to achieve in their term? What are the challenges and goals?). Those broad areas provide a road map for the interview. When the interviewer feels that the interview is losing its way, perhaps because the subject is waffling or isn't saying much, then the writer has something to return to for guidance and, perhaps, inspiration.

Try this method. Use a spiral-bound notebook and, on the right-hand page, write down the broad areas you wish to cover in the interview. Allow enough space under each heading to write down specific questions—mostly open questions (that is, those that demand more than a yes or no response)—that fit into those areas. Try to prioritise. As the interviewer, you need to ask the basic questions, such as age and how to spell names, but if, for example, you know the local mayor has been a champion of childcare, then ask what arrangements they have made for their own children. Rank the priorities according to what you need to know most; that way, if the interview is cut short, you will still emerge with the most important information.

Keep the left-hand page of your notebook free until the interview is under way. If something comes up during the interview and you think it is valuable, interesting or fresh, write it down on the left-hand page as a reminder to ask the interviewee about it later.

Asking the right questions

The first thing to know about questions is that there are no wrong ones. There are silly, nonsensical, ridiculous, insensitive, provocative and wacky questions, but they will have done their job if they generate a genuine answer. Simon Hattenstone, a journalist with *The Guardian* in the UK, came up with a key question for his interview with American film director Woody Allen by asking a friend what he would want to know from

Allen. The friend urged Hattenstone to ask Allen why someone as plain as he had had so many beautiful girlfriends.

> When I finally worked up the courage to ask Allen ... [he] answered with terrific enthusiasm that he grew up with women so he knew how to talk to them, that as a filmmaker he could influence careers and that he had spent years working on his technique. It turned out this was the same question he had obsessed over for most of his adult life.

The Guardian, 7 September 2007

Of course, interviewers don't know the answer until they ask the question. And that is why the basic rule of every interview is: to get unusual answers, you have to ask unusual questions. How does the interviewer do that?

The first thing the interviewer must do is understand the difference between closed and open questions. Open questions—for example, 'Why did you decide to become a farmer?'—invite an expansive response. Closed questions are the opposite. For example, if you ask, 'Do you enjoy being a farmer?' you run the risk of provoking the interviewee to provide a monosyllabic reply.

Open questions are the most valuable tools for an interview because they go to the heart of motivation: how, why and what. Given the opportunity to think about the reasons behind their career choice, the farmer is likely to provide a more detailed response, such as: 'Oh, Dad was a farmer and it was in my blood. Love the land.' Closed questions are useful when you want to know when, where and who. The best interviews will feature both kinds of questions.

Troubleshooting

There are several potential problem areas in interviewing, no matter how well prepared or experienced the interviewer is. It is important to be resilient and resourceful, and, most importantly, not to take these problems personally, as they are often outside your control. However, there are several strategies that can be followed to reduce the impact of impediments to a good interview.

Let us take a look at each of the problems and potential solutions.

1   Deadline, but for whom?

This is the most basic of all problems. Some interview subjects, whether in government (all levels), bureaucracy or the corporate world, will utilise the time a writer gives them between requesting information and an interview to their advantage. Rather than be seen as unhelpful, the media adviser or personal assistant will initially make some attempt at cooperation, but they may also soak up the time as a delaying tactic. This is effectively 'no comment', because these people have made an assessment that for whatever political or corporate reason, it is not in their boss's best interests to be part of the writer's story.

The writer's best response in this situation is, at first, to ensure the subject is given sufficient time to respond. This can be a problem when the writer has taken time to collect material and, when finally it has all been gathered, needs a comment from the protagonist as soon as possible to be able to finish the story. News websites often want to source comments as soon as possible—time is vital in digital news and many interview subjects will respond accordingly to ensure their voice or their business is part of the debate. While feature stories have the luxury of providing the writer with more time, asking for a feature story can also send a signal to the interview subject that they don't need to deal with the writer's request with the same urgency as a news story.

Often, the best way to deal with the issue of the deadline is to keep reminding the media adviser or personal assistant that it is approaching. The legitimate ethical course of action in this situation is to remind the person that the story needs input from their boss to ensure that the story will be balanced and will provide an alternative perspective. This tactic won't always work, but it is important to remind people of their importance to the story.

2   Someone keeps getting in the way

As previously noted, there is often a 'gatekeeper' who will prevent the writer getting to the person they need to speak to. The former corporate heavyweight John Elliott had a personal assistant who was famous in media circles for her icy politeness, thorough professionalism and, ultimately, unhelpfulness on even the most banal of entreaties. It is worth remembering that such people are representing their employer's interests, and if you can convince them of the value of their boss being part of your project, then you are more than halfway to securing the interview.

The other form of gatekeeper is the publicist—the person deputised by the film company, record company or publisher to organise the artist's media commitments that usually coincide with the release of a new film, CD or book. The publicist's first task is to organise the media schedule, but their professional responsibility is to ensure the artist's message about their new product is the focus of the media interview. This leads to publicists occasionally issuing instructions to writers about what topics are considered 'off limits' during an interview. For example, Hollywood actors often specify that they will not talk about recent 'non-movie' issues (divorce, drugs, custody battles, financial troubles, religious beliefs). Seasoned writers try to work both angles and will start the interview talking about the new product and then, when the interview is nearly over, ask questions about the areas they have been asked not to raise. The theory is that by the latter stage of the interview, the transgressions will not matter. But it clearly did for Channel 4's Guru-Murthy (as revealed earlier in this chapter).

The more appropriate way to handle this dilemma is not to get into that situation. If there are conditions attached to the interview—such as certain topics being deemed inappropriate—the writer should not agree to the interview. It is a more transparent and ethical response to the situation than trying to eke out an outraged response from the interview subject at the end of the interview when discussion turns to the taboo topics. Everyone knows where they stand if the writer is candid from the start of the interview process, and that starts with negotiating the terms of the interview.

Gatekeepers will often want to be in the room while the interview is conducted. There is nothing wrong with this, but it can inhibit some interviewers. It is, however, rare for the gatekeepers to intervene in interviews in order to protect the subject or clarify their remarks. But if the interviewer does find the gatekeeper's presence intimidating, it is best to try to find a seating arrangement in the room where the gatekeeper is behind the interviewer, or at least out of sight. That way, the interview still feels as if it is between two, not three, people.

3 I'm not big enough

This can be an issue for young writers and freelancers. The problem is that many large organisations or governments will not be very interested in speaking to someone who represents a small or niche media outlet. It can also be a problem for freelancers and university journalism students. This is simply an issue of size and influence. While this will always be an issue for young writers, they can get around it if they work for a reputable local or metropolitan publication. The organisation or individual is more likely to know the publication and its audience.

However, it is harder for a writer to secure an interview with someone if they do not already have an outlet for their story. So it is important for the freelance writer to have already secured the commission for the article before requesting the interview. The way to enhance your appeal is to understand the publication's market and audience so you can tell the interview subject who will be likely to read the interview and why that audience is relevant to them and their business or profession. For example, a writer conducting interviews for a freelance story in *Marie Claire* on migrant detention in Australia needs to make it clear to Department of Immigration and Citizenship officials, migration lawyers and detainees that the magazine has a long history of publishing stories on national social issues, and that it treats such issues seriously and at length.

Another element to consider in this area is that the writer should not overreach when seeking an interview. For instance, a story about the demolition of a local school will need an interview with someone from the state Department of Education, but it will not require a comment from the federal government, as the matter is not under federal jurisdiction. Writers who try to seek comment beyond the parameters of their story are bound for disappointment.

4 What do I say next?

The interviewer's great fear is that they will reach a yawning chasm in their interview where they have either run out of questions or forgotten where they were taking the interview. It is a particular kind of feeling—a mixture of panic and numbness. But good preparation can minimise the potential for this to occur.

A good interview will cover all the broad areas and some new questions too. Interviewers should take heart if they are provoking new thoughts in their subject. It is the questions on the left-hand page of the notebook that may contain the seeds of a new perspective on an old topic. You should not be disheartened if you do not manage to get every question answered. Your first priority is to find out what you most need to know and ideally, something fresh and new.

5   I think I'm in love with my interview subject

It is one of the easiest—and most problematic—elements of interviewing to find yourself talking to someone you have admired for some time. Two outcomes are possible in this circumstance—one is that the subject will disappoint you and leave you with a sour taste of disillusionment. The other is that the interview will increase your regard for the subject. Both outcomes are fraught with problems. Disillusionment breeds cynicism and an article that could have a sneering or sarcastic tone; not many readers will be interested in that kind of story. The other article will be gushy and uncritical and do the interviewer—and their subject—no favours because of its breathless approach.

The best way to avoid such outcomes is to be as fair as possible; strive to ask penetrating questions, rather than obvious questions. If you are interviewing an author whose work you know intimately, phrase the questions from a different perspective. For example, 'I know your work very well, but how would you describe your writing style to a stranger? What would you say to get them to read your work?' In all instances, the interviewer must strive to be objective. It is not only an ethical requirement, but the best way to write a story that is not an amplification of the interviewer's devotion to their subject. No reader wants to read an interview that runs in only one direction. Leave the love at the door.

6   Haven't I heard this somewhere before and other drawn-out tales (waffling, stonewalling, silence)

Increasingly, interviews with certain groups of people—celebrities, politicians or performers—take place in a group environment, or occur during a day of interviews. A staple of the Hollywood journalism circuit is the regular press conferences organised by the Hollywood film studios to promote new films. Seven or eight (and sometimes more) writers are seated at several tables, while the stars of a particular film move between tables, spending perhaps 20 minutes at each, usually answering the same types of questions from writers with vastly different international audiences, from Japanese to Mexican to Australian. It is efficient for the Hollywood operation, but it does little to help the writer produce fresh or new copy.

The other problem interview occurs during the publicity tours arranged to push 'a talking head' before radio, television and press in order to promote a new book, CD or DVD. It is just a variation on the earlier theme; the chance for the writer to get something fresh in this circumstance is minimal. If you combine that problem with certain groups of interview subjects who have a propensity to waffle, obfuscate or just talk in complex sentences, there are many potential traps for the interviewer here.

The final—and most frustrating—type of interview block is silence or monosyllabic answers. This can be an outcome of an interview with someone who does not want to cooperate. It may not be because they have something they are trying to hide. It could simply be that they are frightened of the consequences of saying too much or are unfamiliar with talking about themselves. The worst-case situation is that for whatever reason— it's a bad day, they have a hangover, they just want to be mischievous—it feels like every question provokes not only an extended silence and a one-word grunt, but all of it delivered with an attitude that says: 'I'd rather stick sharpened pencils in my eyes than answer these questions.' A notable—and cringeworthy—example of this is a Michael Hann interview with legendary, but prickly, Cream and Blind Faith drummer Ginger Baker, who was trying to promote his documentary 'Beware of Mr Baker'. During the Q & A, Hann tried to canvass a number of topics that Baker either simply ignored, or agreed that 'they were stupid', a proposition put to him by Hann, who was clearly frustrated at Baker's refusal to engage with him (Hann, 2013). The interviewer needs to remember in such circumstances that is appropriate to be assertive, but not aggressive: for the interviewer to persist firmly in search of an answer. There is no justification for an interviewer becoming rude or allowing their frustration to show. Interviewers need to remain measured and patient in the face of such responses. Otherwise, there will be no opportunity to get any engagement with the reluctant interviewee.

One of the best tactics in these circumstances is to strive for original questions, ones that provoke fresh thoughts or at least slightly different reactions. This is particularly helpful when trying to elicit information from politicians, who are used to offering the same kind of response to the same kinds of questions. Even a moment of insight, glimpsed through an interview subject's second thoughts, will provide the interviewer with something fresh. As Walkley Award-winning journalist and ABC broadcaster Virginia Trioli says: 'I'm a great fan of the dumb question, like: "What do you mean?" or "Explain more … "That's not being coy, nor [is it] an affectation. It's simply listening' (*The Weekend Australian*, 1–2 September 2007).

The interviewer's goal when dealing with these seasoned interview subjects is to provoke the response: 'No one's ever asked me that before …' as was the case with Hattenstone's question to Woody Allen. And that can be achieved by thorough research and a willingness to ask interesting and fresh questions. It is worth remembering that a well-rehearsed, even jaded, interviewee is likely to be particularly happy to be challenged and stimulated in the interview process. That does not mean an adversarial approach; it can be as simple as asking an unexpected question. It can be worth it.

7   My tape recorder didn't work

Technology can be a difficult servant. The key to minimising its hazards is to test it before you use it, particularly the batteries. Many reporters use two recorders, just to be sure. There is nothing worse than conducting a great interview, only to find that for some reason the audio did not record, or cut out midway through. It is always good to take notes, anyway, during an interview. It helps your recall and gives you the opportunity to note the environment—details about the hotel room, the bar, the change rooms etc.—and the physical manifestations of the personality of the subject displayed during the interview. So test the recorder, but don't trust it completely. Always work with a notebook as the safety net.

Summary

o   Interviewing should be fun.

o   The best interviews are like conversations.

o   The priority in an interview is to ask the questions you want answered.

o   Good preparation will ensure most interviews are productive.

o   Email interviews are the interviews of last resort.

o   To get an unusual answer, ask an unusual question.

o   Aim to ask questions that will have the subject saying: 'No one's ever asked me that before.'

Questions

1   What are the three types of interviews?
2   What is the difference between a closed question and an open question? What kinds of information does the interviewer glean from closed and open questions?
3   Name the five broad areas that Blundell identifies as being central to the preparation of some interview-based features.

Activities

1   Interview someone you know very well (it could be a friend or a relative). Talk to them about their life. Try to learn something from the interview that you did not know about that person before you sat down with them. How were you able to find that out? What did you think of the experience? Ask them what they thought of the interview.
2   Pick a current issue in the news that you think warrants in-depth treatment. Identify what you don't know about the issue from the elements that are not being covered in the mainstream media. Draw up a list of people who could help address those elements. Then do some research, and draft the questions you would need to ask them.
3   Choose a program transcript from *Australian Story* (see <www.abc.net.au/austory>), the ABC interview program where the interviewer is never seen or heard. Look at what appears in the transcript and try to work out what the questions were to get that response from the subject of the program.
4   Have a listen to the Ginger Baker interview (<https://www.theguardian.com/music/video/2013/may/15/beware-mr-baker-qa-ginger-baker-video>). What lessons does this hold for journalists in relation to: (1) the use of open and closed questions; and (2) dealing with a prickly interviewee?

References and additional reading

Blundell, W. (1988). *The Art and Craft of Feature Writing*, New York: Penguin.

Farndale, N. (2002). *Flirtation, Seduction, Betrayal*, London: Constable.

Ferguson, S, & Drum, P. (2016). *The Killing Season Uncut,* Melbourne: Melbourne University Publishing.

Guru-Murthy, K. (2015). 'Krishnan Guru-Murthy: do stars and news need to go their separate ways?', *The Guardian* online, 27 April.

Grobel, L. (2004). *The Art of the Interview*, New York: Three Rivers Press.

Hann, M. (2013). 'Beware of Mr Baker: Q&A with Ginger Baker – video', *Guardian* (UK), 15 May: https://www.theguardian.com/music/video/2013/may/15/beware-mr-baker-qa-ginger-baker-video.

Malcolm, J. (1990). *The Journalist and the Murderer*, New York: Knopf.

Needham, A. (2015). 'Robert Downey Jr calls British journalist "bottom-feeding muckraker"'. *The Guardian* online, 29 April 2015.

Perlich, M. (2003). *The Art of the Interview: A Step-by-Step Guide to Insightful Interviewing*, New York: Empty Press.

Sedorkin, G. & McGregor, J. (2002). *Interviewing: A Guide for Journalists and Writers*, Sydney: Allen & Unwin.

Online resources

Australian Story: www.abc.net.au/austory

Enough Rope: www.abc.net.au/tv/enoughrope

Ginger Baker interview: https://www.theguardian.com/music/video/2013/may/15/beware-mr-baker-qa-ginger-baker-video

Case study

Trent Dalton shows how he came to grips with interviewing one of the world's most important religious figures

Publication details:

'Orange crush', *The Courier-Mail*, *QWeekend* magazine, 9 July 2011.

The author:

Trent Dalton's journalism has appeared in *The Australian*, *The Daily Telegraph*, the *Herald Sun*, the *Adelaide Advertiser*, *The Sunday Times*, *The Walkley Magazine* and the *Griffith Review*. He is also a talented screenwriter, whose credits include a 2010 AFI nomination for the Best Short Fiction Screenplay Award for *Glenn Owen Dodds*, a film that won the prestigious International Prix Canal award at the world's largest short film festival (the Clermont-Ferrand in France). Dalton is an associate editor of *The Courier-Mail* in Brisbane.

The story:

The Dalai Lama's entourage approached *The Courier-Mail* a year before they visited Brisbane. Their question was simple: Would the paper be interested in a one-on-one interview with His Holiness? The paper's Editor-in-Chief, David Fagan, picked his main magazine feature writer, Trent Dalton, for the job. Dalton embarked on his research while also fielding questions from the Dalai Lama's public relations staff about the kind of questions he would ask. There was nothing signed or binding, but Dalton was made aware that 'hard questions' might not be desirable.

Dalton's research consisted of mining a range of YouTube interviews with his subject. Dalton was trying to work out a strategy for posing questions to a subject whose English is uneven, even if a translator is present. The end result was Dalton's decision to keep his questions really brief, even the more pointed and political questions that he wanted to ask.

There was plenty of other material about, including the Dalai Lama's new book, but Dalton's best source for his subject's personal history was a profile from an old *Life* magazine that he found on the internet. Dalton now had two of the three things he needed: a strategy for his questions and the background material to prepare himself for the interview. The third—and missing—element was to decide what his approach to the story would be. In the end, Dalton decided to keep that element simple.

'I was just going to do a fly-on-the-wall piece: 4000 words for our weekend magazine. And to tell it like I saw it,' Dalton explained.

The other consideration was timeliness. The Dalai Lama had already been to Melbourne and Sydney. Brisbane was the next stop, and Dalton's audience would have already seen and heard a fair bit about His Holiness by the time they got round to reading his story. That challenge was complicated by the arrival of a Channel 7 current affairs crew that was filming the Dalai Lama for the Sunday evening program.

As can often happen, the time a journalist spends preparing and researching a subject can actually increase anticipation and nerves when the interview finally occurs. Dalton, despite years of experience, was no different when his time came.

'I was incredibly nervous, but the Dalai Lama was the sweetest man, so generous,' Dalton said. 'There was something special about him.'

A scheduled 20-minute interview stretched to 30 minutes, and Dalton was able to ask some harder questions without his subject 'falling to pieces'.

Dalton describes himself as not being a religious person—and he had no particular view about the Dalai Lama before their interview—but he admits that there was something remarkable about the man. And that became part of the feature: the tension between His Holiness as an international spiritual figure and his very human qualities and habits.

It also raised some interesting questions about how Dalton should go about telling the story.

The first challenge was whether Dalton should tell the anecdote that opens the story, about the Dalai Lama using the toilet, the same lavatory that Dalton had used. The anecdote not only humanises His Holiness but also brings Dalton in to the story.

'I actually wrestle with being in the story. I want to give the reader every last thing. And I actually have a philosophy that "the reader wins",' Dalton said. 'But does the reader need to know this? Could I have told the toilet story without me [in it]? Yes, I could have but I told it not for ego reasons, but for what it reveals about character.'

The other reason is that the toilet anecdote is a telling detail. And Dalton loves details.

'I jot down every detail. That's all we feature writers have, all the non-verbal things, to see the little moments,' he said.

There were three other devices Dalton employed to good effect. One was the use of humour—not just with the toilet anecdote, but with references to the *Twilight* book and movie franchise, and the feature's final line. Dalton's reasoning for this was simple: it was to undercut the serious content.

'I really wrote the lighter things because I didn't want it be another earnest piece about the Dalai Lama,' he said.

He also focused on the mother and daughter who became caught up in the jostling for the Dalai Lama's attentions. 'I was looking around the crowd and I accidentally spotted her. [The mother's care for her daughter] was one of the most touching things I'd ever seen. There was only so much I could say about what the Dalai Lama was doing and saying—he was doing similar things—but this, her story, those stories, could actually mirror themselves,' Dalton said. He sought out the mother in order to get her details and then added her to the story.

The final element of the story was using Twitter to break up its length. Dalton is on Twitter and tweeted before the Dalai Lama interview what he was doing. That tweet generated the line from a woman who pointed out that His Holiness had a million followers (on Twitter), yet he followed no one. In addition to giving Dalton a good line, the use of Twitter to break up the story helps the reader 're-start' during the story when their attention might flag.

Writing sample

Orange crush

By Trent Dalton, *The Courier-Mail, QWeekend magazine,* **9 July 2011**

It's access all areas—behind the scenes and centre stage with His Holiness the Dalai Lama during last month's Queensland visit.

His Holiness the Dalai Lama—14th manifestation of the Bodhisattva of Compassion, Ocean of Wisdom, Sovereign of the High Land of Snows—has just ducked off to the men's room.

Long flight from Melbourne. A small group of red-and-gold robed Tibetan Buddhists wait patiently in the Brisbane airport office of Strategic Airlines. Whispers filter through the building, heads nod, flat-topped security men in black suits check wristwatches, relaying messages via earpieces as a matter of national security emerges— it's a possible No 2.

I was the last person to use that toilet and I'm praying, in my rush to meet the Dalai Lama on the tarmac, I left it in a condition pleasing to the holiest living spiritual figure in the world.

An impeccably dressed Strategic staffer waits nervously by the office's glass exit doors. 'You had a ciggy yet?' a male security officer asks her. 'No, I am not having a ciggy before meeting the Dalai Lama!' she says.

Justin Bieber has walked through those glass exit doors. Bono has walked through those glass exit doors. Kings of pop and rock. And here comes Jetsun Jamphel Ngawang Lobsang Yeshe Tenzin Gyatso: Holy Lord, Gentle Glory, Nobel laureate, exiled leader of the Tibetan Buddhists, 76-year-old lion-hearted and groundbreaking former political leader of the Tibetan government-in-exile, Yishin Norbu ('wish-fulfilling gem'), Kyabgon ('saviour'), Kundun ('presence'). A king of peace. There are 1,922,343 people following this man on Twitter. He's following nobody.

Some 50 waiting guests—airline staff, charity workers, high-ranking local Buddhists—form a path for His Holiness. He offers them his typical hands-raised, palms-together anjali greeting. He passes, smiling. I form a clumsy, unpractised greeting—part anjali, part yellow belt in karate—and he chortles. Empathetic.

Wise. Knows a try-hard when he sees one.

Outside the glass doors, he blesses Rachel James, wife of Strategic Airlines founder Michael James. He blesses the baby Rachel carries inside her. He leans down to a woman in a wheelchair: Shevaune Conry, the Brisbane woman with multiple sclerosis who inspired the creation of Youngcare, the Queensland organisation providing care for young people in aged and nursing homes. He cups her hands in his, leans in for a heartfelt blessing and tears fill Shevaune's eyes—all that pain, all those years her nerve cells betrayed her, writ large across her face. His Holiness nods.

And Shevaune nods gratefully. Something is exchanged and nobody knows exactly what, but four people are crying. 'Okay,' His Holiness nods. 'Okay.' He's not saying, 'It's okay'. But it feels like he is. Everything is going to be okay. That is his message to her. It's not heard. It's felt.

Today's Twitter feed, Wednesday, June 15:

'Taking care of our neighbours' interests is essentially taking care of our own future.'

His Holiness (from here to be known as HH) sits shotgun, his driver taking Kingsford Smith Drive to the city. The car behind him is filled with musclebound Tibetan agents in figurehugging suits with sharp eyes and big fingers clearly capable of gripping larynges and beating hearts. He gazes out his window to the Brisbane River. So far from home.

He was born a nobody to a penniless family in a northern Tibet village with no electricity and little food. But the boy could drink water from any stream. Modern China changed that.

Industry poisoned the waters of his home.

Now they're dirty, he says, as undrinkable as those of the Brisbane River.

At two, the boy was told by several wise and old men that he was a living god-king. At 16, this peasant farmer's son led a country under attack from Communist invaders. At 24, he was exiled to India as the world's most famous refugee.

HH pulls into the Stamford Plaza. In the hotel foyer, Brisbane-based Buddhists and Tibetan immigrants greet him with applause.

They wave Tibetan flags and bow gracefully.

Today he's the bringer of joy. The funny man. The embodiment of his key message of happiness above all else. The foyer crowd erupts with calls of thanks. Only the Pope really knows what this is like, to so frequently bring people to tears just by walking past them. The Pope and that guy from *Twilight*.

A TV reporter enters the hotel room designated for HH's two media interviews today in a top that hangs low on her cleavage.

'Is this appropriate for the Dalai Lama?' she asks. Even Keith Richards might find the top questionable. The reporter's producer rubs her chin: 'We were wondering about that.' The reporter corners HH's media adviser:

'Now, does he like being called His Holiness?' The Dalai Lama's private secretary, a fastmoving, well-built, grey-haired man named Chhime Rigzing Chhoekyapa, enters with three Buddhist monks trailing behind him. Chhime scans the room and turns his nose up at the many leads criss-crossing the floor, trip risks for HH.

'These will have to be cleared,' he commands.

He directs two assistants to lug an awkward square coffee table into the room's ensuite.

'There can be no objects in his way,' he says.

Thirty minutes later, the TV crew has gone.

HH rests himself before me on a maroon coloured two-seater couch that blends with his robe. The skin of his right arm is smooth and hairless. He spreads his legs and lifts the front flap of his robe so it sits between his thighs.

These are the legs that slogged 15 days across the Himalayas during his escape from the Tibetan capital, Lhasa, in 1959. He travelled through blinding sandstorms in the freezing cold of night to avoid Chinese guards.

He nods twice, smiles, adjusts his spectacles.

At 15, his tutor, Heinrich Harrer, suggested he wear glasses to aid his reading. The young Dalai Lama scoffed, considering them Western affectations. He sits opposite me now as one of the most widely read leaders in the world.

That smile. Straight from a black-and-white photograph I saw in an old *Life* magazine, May 4, 1959: A Famous Fugitive, A God King. That beautiful smile, all teeth and humility.

His translator, Ven. Ngawang Sonam, a warm-faced young man on his first trip to Australia, sits on the carpet beside my left leg.

'Okay,' HH says.

We talk about the people of Queensland who lost loved ones in the flood, the people still living in homes without doors in winter. He talks about hardship and how calamity and tragedy are already written. What isn't written is a human being's response to misfortune. That is determined by us. That is something we can control. He talks about visiting earthquake crippled Japan and being stunned by how little looting had been witnessed.

'Same thing I see here,' he says. 'Very little looting.' When he sees that, he feels great hope for the world. He praises the Queenslanders who united in catastrophe with 'the courage to face the tragedy'.

They say charismatic people draw you in, make you feel like you're the only person in the room worth talking to. The Dalai Lama leans forward so intimately, listens to questions so intently, that you feel like you're the only person in the universe worth talking to. He may speak like Yoda at times, in disjointed sentences that bounce randomly from subject to subject:

'From money, better education. More ambition.

More competition. More suspicion. More stress.

More frustration. More anger ...' But he's a masterful communicator. He's all presence. His restless eyebrows say as much about his message as his mouth does. '... but money,' he laughs, 'pay for my airfare.' I mention the 27th Australian soldier to die in Afghanistan. He reels at the figure, genuinely troubled. He speaks of karma. Happiness breeding happiness. Goodness breeding goodness. Then why, I ask, does a good and decent hard-working single mother of three kids in Bundamba, near Ipswich, have her home destroyed by flood; why do bad things happen to good people?

'God knows,' he says, shaking his head, smiling. He doesn't have that answer. He's not all-knowing. He's knowledgeable. People often ask him to perform miracles. He's often asked to heal the sick. If he could perform miracles, he says, he would fix a crook right knee that's been troubling him for years.

But he does know why I'm here. It's to write this story. And to be happy writing it. 'Why am I here?' I ask. I've been saving the question for God, but He rarely frequents the Stamford Plaza.

I'm being general. Why are any of us here? But HH gets all personal, addresses my own speck of dust-on-a-donkey's-backside role in the universe.

It's what he does with anyone he meets, tailors the big message so it suits the individual.

'You can bring joy,' he says. 'You can spread message around the world.' He raises his right forefinger to emphasise key words: 'Information! Knowledge! Happiness!' The message: If you do something, do it well. If you're a Christian, be a passionate Christian. If you're a carpenter, be a passionate carpenter. That will make you happy. And by being happy, your work here will be done. In the course of existence, the greatest thing we humans will ever manufacture is our own joy. 'Modernisation, more buildings, more cars will always grow,' he says. 'But still only human emotion stays the same. A thousand years from now, emotion still the same. So we change externally. Much change. But real human life, still always the same. We must focus on warm-heartedness. A spirit of forgiveness.

And that brings the spirit of dialogue. Whether you're a religious believer or non-believer, same human beings, part of the same humanity.' We discuss retirement. He leans back into the couch and reflects on his life's work.

'Satisfied,' he says. 'My life has become much more purposeful because of being a refugee.' Everything happens for a reason, maybe even two million Tibetans being murdered, starved or exiled by Chinese tyranny. 'If I still remain with all the formalities and ceremonies, I myself am not much useful,' he says.

He's most proud of his efforts to blend Tibetan Buddhism and modern science. 'And in the field of religious harmony I feel I have made some contribution.' He leans forward.

'You know, one Christian friend even described me as a good Christian.' He slaps his knees, giggling heartily.

Two hours later, at a packed South Bank Suncorp Piazza forum on the importance of never giving up, a ray of sunlight glares into HH's eyes on stage. He calls for his hat. His assistant digs in a bag for his favoured visor.

'No, my other hat,' he says. And he places a Maroons cap—it's State of Origin tonight, and earlier HH had also been gifted a team flag and maroon XXXX stubby cooler—on his head, bringing raucous applause, a near standing ovation, from the 4000 Queenslanders in attendance. He does it for the worthiest reason of all—for a laugh. And he has the crowd in the palm of his raised right hand.

'What matters is physical touch,' he says.

'We are all born from our mothers. We share common experience.' The crowd nods. Some weep. Others rock their heads back and forth in a trancelike state.

Everybody has their own reason for coming—for peace, to find comfort for cancer, for answers to the inexplicable. Some get their answers. Some don't. It doesn't matter. They have shared the presence of Kundun.

'Okay,' he says to the crowd as the sun begins to fall. 'I go home for sleep now. I'm hoping you also get some sleep. Goodnight.' He exits the piazza through a parted sea of followers. At the rear of the piazza he stops at a woman in a wheelchair, 32-year-old Naomi Curran. She has ovarian cancer. It's terminal. HH cups her hands and says something softly to her.

He says he will send her an Eastern medicine that has not yet been discovered by the Western world. Naomi weeps. HH moves on. An assistant scribbles Naomi's address in a notepad.

'What did that moment right there mean to you?' I ask Naomi.

She wipes away her tears. 'Hope,' she says.

Today's Twitter feed, Thursday, June 16:

'Non-violence is a sign of strength; violence is a sign of desperation and weakness.'

I'm staring at a young mother caring for a young girl in a wheelchair who has severe quadriplegic cerebral palsy, and is also deaf and epileptic, and the world, from this white plastic chair in the Sunshine Coast's Chenrezig Institute for Tibetan Buddhists, seems like a profoundly beautiful place. There are 3500 people around me gazing at the Dalai Lama, standing at a microphone on a stage at the bottom of a grassy slope bordered by tall hinterland trees blowing as gently as the prayer flags swaying above the stage.

These people have made pilgrimages from across the country to witness HH bless the institute's Garden of Enlightenment—a memorial ornamental garden set around eight ornate and vivid stupas (mounds) depicting the 'Eight Great Deeds of the Buddha's Life'—where guests can 'visit' their lost loved ones. The people at the front in Section A have paid $50 to be here.

Those at the back in Section B have paid $35.

HH is on stage talking about patience and compassion, about caring and commitment. And here is this mother, eight rows back, holding a hat over her disabled daughter's head to shield her from the sun. She's been holding it there for the past hour. Occasionally she places the hat on her daughter's head, but the girl shifts awkwardly in her wheelchair, lacking control of her movements, and the hat falls to the ground and the mother dusts it off and places it back.

This happens maybe 12 times during the Dalai Lama's two-hour speech. The girl is beautiful, maybe seven years old, with fair skin and strawberry blonde hair, perfectly plaited, tied with ribbons and ornate clips. She groans now and then to express things to her mum, who digs into her bulky carrybag and pulls out a plastic container filled with a yellow liquid homemade vegetable mix. She fixes a plastic tube to the container and unravels a pump mechanism that will feed the mixture gently to her daughter.

The mother turns to the stage to catch what the Dalai Lama is saying, tenderly strokes her daughter's shoulder with her left hand. Then the hat falls off again. The mother lifts the child from the wheelchair—unbuckling several straps and braces to do so—and carries her to a shaded area by the Garden of Enlightenment.

HH exits the stage. A woman comes to the microphone to make an announcement: HH's helicopter pilot is yet to present himself. 'Lindsay, if you're here, could you please make your way to the Garden of Enlightenment,' she says.

HH walks to the side of the stage and along a pebbled path to the Garden of Enlightenment. Several rows of the gathered crowd leave their seats to watch him pass and possibly, hopefully, make physical contact with him. But HH is heading straight toward the mother and daughter. The mother fixes her daughter's hair, straightens her own hair. But a group of camera-flashing onlookers moves in front of the mother just as HH passes, forcing her to humbly carry the girl out of the fray. She lays her down on a square of shaded grass, rolls her sleeves up and begins putting shin braces on the child's legs.

Her name is Nicole Thompson. Her daughter's name is India. Nicole is a midwife by trade and a full-time home carer by necessity.

Her days are spent visiting specialists, writing endless funding applications to governments, stirring liquid vegetable mixes. I tell her that I think she is the embodiment of everything the Dalai Lama just spent two hours talking about.

A helicopter's spinning rotor blade echoes across the grounds as 3500 believers look to the sky. The Dalai Lama's chopper makes a full, triumphant circle, then heads south toward Brisbane. 'I'm not particularly religious,' Nicole Thompson says. She's not here today for answers. She's not here for miracles. She's here today for India. 'We've come to one of these before,' she says. 'India finds it soothing to be around him.' Nicole nods her head. India lies with her back flat on the grass, staring dreamily into a sharp blue winter sky, perfectly serene.

Nicole smiles. 'I don't know what it is,' she says. 'She just likes being around him.'

Today's Twitter feed, Friday, June 17:

'HHDL's A Talk for World Peace' at the West Lawn of the US Capitol in Washington DC on July 9 at 9.30am, free admission.'

'Where you blokes off to?' the driver says.

'Botanic Gardens near QUT,' says photographer David Kelly.

'What's happening there?' the driver asks.

'We're seeing the Dalai Lama,' Kelly says.

'What's that?' the driver asks, straight-faced.

It's the last day of the Dalai Lama's southeast Queensland tour. Some 8000 people gather at Brisbane's Riverstage to hear him speak on 'Finding Happiness on Life's Journey and Overcoming Loss'. Irish singer and practising Buddhist Luka Bloom has been warming up audiences throughout the Dalai Lama's tour.

He takes the stage and looks out to the crowd gathered on a day so beautiful and clear it looks like the backdrop to a religious mural of heaven. Bloom sighs into the microphone: 'So this is winter in Queensland! When I visualise paradise I think this would be it,' he adds. He softly plucks an acoustic guitar and eases into a song called 'As I Waved Goodbye', which he wrote for the Dalai Lama in 2000: 'As I waved goodbye from the riverside, it was too much to take in / I could see the place, and imagine the face, of the young Tibetan God-King.' In a concrete room backstage, HH slowly makes his way around a circle of invited flood victims from Grantham, Toowoomba and Ipswich. There are 1000 more spread through the audience outside. A young girl hands HH a bouquet of roses. One mother weeps uncontrollably and HH cups her hands tenderly. Swimmer Dawn Fraser is in the circle. HH rests his forehead against hers gently. They share a quiet word about the pitfalls of ageing.

Bloom's lyrics echo backstage: 'It's a bad old wind, should no good begin, from a hurt that has been done / When the line was crossed and the land was lost, Oh, the holy exiled ones.' The crowd stands and applauds when HH takes the stage. 'Dear brothers and sisters, I am extremely happy to be with you,' the Dalai Lama says. He sits on a lounge setting that looks fresh from an Ikea box. ABC radio presenter, and today's MC, Richard Fidler sits respectfully beside him. Ipswich Mayor Paul Pisasale stands side-of-stage. 'See the badge on his robe?' he whispers. There's a gleaming metal badge near HH's right collarbone. 'Ipswich Pride Pin, mate!' There are four police officers guarding access to the left side of the stage. Two Tibetan agents guard the right side. Their heads turn swiftly as a man in a business suit walks uninvited onto the stage and sits down on the Ikea couch on the right side of HH. It's Mayor Pisasale. The flustered agents turn to Chhime for advice. Chhime's carrying a book under his arm called *Mirroring People: The New Science of How We Connect*. Chhime raises his eyebrows, part confusion, part despair. He gives the agents a calming gesture that suggests: 'Let it go, just another mystery of the West.' For an hour-and-a-half, HH fields questions from the audience.

'Your Holiness, my daughter has a disability and I'm worried about her life after I am gone ... ' 'Your Holiness, how do we learn to develop love for our perceived enemies?' 'Your Holiness, my son has joined the army. If he has to take the life of another, is there anything he can do to reverse the negative karma that killing causes?' They are deeply personal and extraordinarily complex questions. And they are answered with care and grace.

A woman stands up near the front of stage.

She says she has undergone nine brain surgeries in her life. She wants the Dalai Lama to help her deal with the deep sense of isolation that dwells within her. HH calls the woman on stage. She weeps at the invitation, makes her way reverently to the stage. HH places his palms gently on her cheeks. He embraces her. 'You are not alone,' he says.

'We human beings have the capacity to share each other's suffering. You are one of the six billion human beings.' He smiles. And the woman laughs through her tears. It's a beautiful sentiment, majestic from the mouth of a god-king.

The crowd is floored by the moment, drowned in an Ocean of Wisdom.

HH's interpreter sneaks a look at Chhime, who gestures to wrap things up. The interpreter gestures to HH and HH nods. 'Okay, finished?' he says, smiling to the 8000 in attendance. They stand and cheer. The triumphant roar follows HH as he waddles backstage, down a set of stairs, through a thin corridor and out the back door of a maintenance office to his awaiting vehicle. Tibetan aides check their BlackBerrys. Officials make head counts. Security guards pass messages through their earpieces, nod their heads in confirmation.

His Holiness has left the building.

5
Interpreting Your Data

'Once you know where a story is going and how you'll get there, it's a lot easier to pay attention to the scenery en route. In other words, by getting organised, you'll write not only faster, but better.'

David Fryxell, American magazine editor, in Garrison, 2004, p. 91

Objectives

In this chapter, you will learn how to choose the appropriate material for your feature and explore some techniques for making the best use of interview and statistical material accumulated during the research phase. You are asked to look at:

o   usefulness: what I have obtained and what it means

o   planning, organising and digesting

o   context, the key to success

o   what interview material to include

o   linking interviews with documentary evidence: in search of seamless writing

o   number crunching: data and statistics

o   a Case study: Leanne Edmistone reveals personal stories about a rare medical condition

o   a Writing sample: 'If there were a magic pill to suddenly be tall, would I take it? No', by Leanne Edmistone, *QWeekend* magazine, 2 April, 2016.

Gluing it all together

Having completed the research phase, you are probably surrounded by paper, transcripts of interviews, notebooks, thumb drives and computer printouts. It will look like organised chaos. But the article is there, just waiting to be drawn out. The end of the information-gathering process can be both liberating and daunting; the sense of freedom comes when you know you have completed your research, but the wave of intimidation is often not far behind.

Now comes the difficult part of building the feature, picking the pieces of information that you can then glue together into a seamless whole. Much of what needs to be done involves selecting the most relevant and important elements from the research. This can be time-consuming and taxing. It is really about organising your material. But writers should not be put off by this process. Those who find it too difficult—and opt for scantily researched features—will find that they not only struggle to write a compelling feature, but miss out on the rewarding experience of a deeper understanding of the information they have gleaned through their interviews and research.

It is often the review of the research that provides the vital insights and angles that can help transform a feature from something banal into an incisive piece of writing.

What have I obtained? What does it all mean?

The key test of all the information the writer has accumulated is its usefulness: How much of it is relevant to the article that is being written? The best way of assessing this is to test the material against the original idea or brief for the story. For example, a feature that is about the reasons for the resurgence of pub rock bands will be built upon the research and interviews directly related to that idea. There is no point including material about the state of clubbing, unless there is a causal link between the revival of pub rock and the decline of clubbing. However, a feature about online fashion shopping needs to include the state of retail or High Street fashion shopping, and some historical comparisons—how well did the bricks and mortar fashion outlets do before online shopping became so popular? Are people buying more fashion items now because they have so many digital and High Street options? Or has digital come at the cost of the High Street?

So, the writer's fundamental task when reviewing the information gathered is to test it against the original premise. Ask:

- Does this fact help?
- Is it relevant?
- What use is this quote?
- How does this piece of information help me?
- Does it advance the story or just repeat an earlier point?

An organised approach to sifting through your material is vital, because when the time comes to write the feature, you want to be able to sit down at your computer confident that you know exactly what information you need to use. One of the best ways to begin paring back the information gathered is to get rid of the irrelevant repetition of facts, observations and views, which only need to appear once (Blundell, 1988, p. 95). But there is no way around it: you will have to get your hands dirty and wrestle with the material. Be as rigorous with your research material as you are with your interview notes—as only some of it will be helpful in the eventual writing—but remember that ideally, most of the research you have done will be critical to your understanding of what you are writing.

One of the important elements that you are looking for is an anecdote or, ideally, several anecdotes. These small stories within the larger story will help introduce the feature and engage readers. They act like a mountaineer's food dumps; they are strategically placed points where readers can get extra nourishment to ensure they will complete their journey to the end of the feature. But anecdotes must have a purpose. Unless there is a real reason for them being used, anecdotes just clutter the feature (Sumner & Miller, 2005, p. 106).

The longer stories that demand significant research over several weeks often take longer to piece together. This is a reflection of the volume of material accumulated in the research phase, and also of the fact that it may take a writer some time to build up knowledge in a subject area they are not familiar with. They may need to spend the early days of research acquainting themselves with some basic information. When it comes time to write, probably only a very limited amount of the material collected early in the research phase will need to be included, simply because an article that is full of rudimentary data will turn off those who know a lot about the subject. Including such information would also eat up space in the feature that should be used for more important information.

Planning

There will be plenty of moments when the writer will stare down at their desk, covered in a mass of information, and decide that it is all too hard. In such a situation it is wise to take a deep breath and think calmly and logically about how to proceed.

This is where a plan is vital. Different writers will approach the specifics of a plan differently, but all of them will devise a plan or outline, because this will help organise their material (Garrison, 2004, p. 92). The most efficient way to plan is to identify the elements of your main theme or question, and then consider the beginning, the middle and the end of your piece—the big pockets into which you can pour information.

If you have chosen to write about the state of genetically modified crops in Australia, for example, you might have identified several key concerns—economic, social, community and political issues. Establishing those categories in the plan will make it easier to marshal your information and provide a structure for your feature (Hennessy, 1989, pp. 37–8).

One way of doing this is to start with a fresh piece of paper. Another is to use index cards. Whatever method you choose, you should find a way of drawing out the information and finding some coherence to help you form an early draft of the feature. Write the story brief at the top of the page. Then write down the main points of the story as you understand them. Next, go through the research, identifying sources, data, comments, quotes, observations and insights. Number these items of information down the left-hand side of the page. Put a number against the piece of research so you know where to locate the information when you are writing. This will provide an efficient way to sift your information.

If you were preparing the pub rock feature, for example, you could mark the data from the Australian Recording Industry Association about pub music as number one. You would then need to put the same number, and the source, on the relevant transcripts or notes so that when you return to the inventory you will be able to identify the information you need. You then continue, marking the second piece of information as number two on your notes and so on.

By the end of this process, you will have an organised view of what information is available. This will make it easier for you to digest the information and will help you identify whether there are any gaps in your knowledge. This system will also help you identify introductions and endings, and to highlight some other valuable ideas that will reinforce the main theme (Blundell, 1988, p. 96).

Your vision will follow the basic structure for the feature—introduction, middle and ending. In practice, you will need to choose many elements to incorporate within those broad areas to reflect the original story idea and the research you have compiled. For example, a feature on the decline of the Australian motor industry may be made up of an introduction (an anecdote from Holden, Ford or Mitsubishi) for two or three paragraphs, followed by the context or definition of the problem that the feature is addressing (the rapid decline and death of the local automotive industry). This could then be followed by a series of observations from experts—people in the industry—mixed with telling facts (sales figures, overseas imports, the decline in the number of Australians employed in the industry during the past 20 years) that illustrate the story idea. Finally, you might include another anecdote or even an observation that appears to encapsulate your argument or the consensus view of most of the experts.

Of course, another approach might suit you better. But whatever method a writer chooses, it must help them identify the material most relevant to the feature and therefore provide the basic information framework. Once that is in place, the stylistic elements of the writing—the nice lines, the sharp observations, the witty asides—can be added.

There is one potential problem that lurks at this stage of the process—the moment when you realise that you do not understand some of the information you have. The temptation is to abandon the material altogether. 'It's too confusing. I'll just cut it out,' you think. Instead, if you have time, call the person back, revisit the website or your original source, and try to clarify the point. Spend some time thinking and reflecting on the meaning. Otherwise, you may have problems writing about an important issue.

Context, context, context

If the writer is confused, how hard is it going to be for the reader? If you don't understand your context, it will show in your writing. Put simply, the writer has to wear their understanding of a subject lightly, while at the same time ensuring that everyone else understands as well. The vital rule for the writer is to write what they know and understand. Writers whose feature is built on the author's limited knowledge are easy to pick: the end results lack confidence and coherence. So good research and planning makes it easy for the writer to identify what they know and, therefore, what they can use with confidence. It is a difficult balancing act; in effect, you need to be a modest know-it-all.

The key to success is context. Context is the most valuable element of your feature at this stage because it will provide a framework for understanding, both for writer and reader. That framework can take a variety of forms. It may come from a piece of history (background to the development or issue), a personal insight (which helps provide a personal connection to a topic or piece of information that may otherwise be alien or beyond the understanding of many readers) or a social perspective (placing the topic or issue against the broader social trends or developments).

Context is present in every mainstream media feature. For example, in a feature about Adele, the context for the kind of 'normal' personality she purports to be is provided by contrasting her lifestyle with the wild ways of other singers, such as the late Amy Winehouse. Context in a feature about the premature death of a retired AFL footballer is provided by the documentation of the history of drug-related issues connected to his former football club. These factual elements are built into the features because new information cannot exist in a vacuum. Without context, a feature will leave the reader asking more questions that need answers.

Interview material

There is one question that is vital when choosing interview material for the feature. You must ask yourself: What are the best quotations? Interviews are about the personal insight or the telling summation of a situation. Readers love quotes. They want to hear what other people say and think, and not so much about what the writer says and thinks.

So when writers review their interview notes, they need to look for the quote that will give their feature some colour and insight. It might be the quote from the veterinarian about how they deal with putting to sleep the beloved family pet; it could be one from the guitarist about the boredom of long drives to country gigs; it could be from a celebrity talking about being ogled at nightclubs.

The elements that determine a good quotation are:

- a distinct turn of phrase, peculiar to the interviewee
- a fresh and engaging way of looking at the situation; that is, no one has said it quite like that before
- an accurate and concise summary of what everyone else you have interviewed has waffled on about.

Interview material that does not fit these criteria should probably not appear in the feature. Over time, writers become more expert at picking what will work best in the circumstances.

The golden rule is that if the interview yields good material that is not directly quotable, it should be paraphrased. Interview subjects have important things to say, but they might express them in an awkward way, or what they say might be too long to run as a direct quote. In these circumstances, try to find a way to place the material as a concise piece of paraphrasing. This will also help break up the quotes, or even provide a lead-in, or lead-out, to a quote.

All the remaining material needs to be assessed for relevance. Ask yourself:

- How much do I need this comment?
- Does it fit in with the overall direction of the feature?
- Does it advance the story at all, or does it just repeat an earlier point?

What the writer should be trying to do is pick the material that will advance the theme and objectives of the feature. For example, a feature on the security arrangements for the 2018 Gold Coast Commonwealth Games should look at the number of police on the streets in the build-up to the Games and during the competition; the increased surveillance at Australian airports and ports; and whether there are increased levels of electronic monitoring, such as CCTV cameras, in key areas of the Gold Coast and its Games venues. This data needs to be able to compare 'normal' levels of policing with the Games' staffing. In all likelihood, many other police officers from across the country will be brought in to the Gold Coast to help local police at the time. A feature needs to identify that and track how many police are descending on

Queensland and where they are coming from. Increasingly, technology and surveillance become a key part of any modern security strategy, so a feature should canvass those innovations. Heightened fears about terrorism, driven by all-too frequent international incidents, will drive reader interest and the feature needs to be measured and responsible so that facts, rather than emotion, are at the core of the feature, Inevitably, there will be some limitations to how much information will be officially divulged—secrecy is an appropriate part of security planning—but there should be a sufficient amount of information available to compile a credible insight into the precautions the city has taken for the Commonwealth Games. Too much background about international terrorism is wasted in such a feature. Readers are seeking reassurances that security measures are in place to enable them to experience the best of the Games. An acknowledgment of the security lessons learned from overseas terrorist attacks and a short summary of the perceived risk to athletes, administrators and officials during the Games would suffice before the writer worked through the main material of police numbers, security priorities and contingency plans in case of such an attack.

Linking interviews with documentary evidence

One of the difficulties of writing features is to make the writing appear 'seamless'. That means that there should be a smooth transition between one piece of information and another. This is particularly true of features that mix documentary evidence with first-hand accounts.

Most published features move between quotations and other material with ease. If only it were as easy as it looks! The best way to achieve seamlessness is to work at the linkages between the material. This can be made easier for the writer—and clearer for the reader, listener or viewer—by using the appropriate attribution. A constant use of 'she said' or 'Mr Stringbag said' at the end of a list of one-sentence quotes will do nothing for the flow of the feature, or for clarity. But a mixture of quotation and paraphrase, with the attribution made clear at the start of the particular section, will significantly help the flow.

For example, a feature on noted chef Luke Mangan contained the following paragraph:

> In some ways, Mangan argues, the restaurant industry has changed for the worse. He's not impressed when the parents of apprentices ring him to complain their offspring are being expected to work more than 40-odd hours a week. 'You can't learn what you need to learn in that time,' he says. 'I worked an 80 or 90-hour week and my father thought that was great. He understood that it was a discipline.'
>
> O'Neill, 2007, p. 85

This is a simple illustration of using paraphrase and a quote to reinforce the point, without overdoing the attribution. The other virtue of using this approach is that it makes the paragraph appear seamless because the placement of information follows Mangan's thoughts and line of argument. This is the key to linking paragraphs so that the story flows evenly. Unless the logic of the writer's thinking is made evident, then the material will not be coherent and the feature will be hard to read, as it jumps around in search of a central thought and without strong structure.

Consider this alternative example from a feature about an informant in the Melbourne gangland wars, which involved convicted murderer Carl Williams. The source material is a statement to police from the informant, Michael Thorneycroft. The feature attempts to move between the informant's statement and common knowledge about Williams' reputation.

> At this stage Williams was at the top of the gangland world, having organised the murder of enemies such as the Moran half-brothers, Mark and Jason, and other rival drug traffickers such as Nik Radev.
>
> Williams was known to refer to himself as 'The Premier'.
>
> 'Carl said he was the President or something like that, and that he wanted to run for Parliament,' Thorneycroft told police of his night in Williams' apartment.
>
> Anderson, 2008, p. 17

The first paragraph is supposed to be a launching pad, but the ride is bumpy because of the lack of smooth links between the paragraphs. As readers, we understand that the writer is trying to make a connection between Williams' self-appointed tag of 'Premier' and Thorneycroft's apparently mistaken rendition of this as the 'President', but it is a laboured link, which has not been made clear enough. As a result, the third paragraph loses its impact. A more direct and more explicit alternative to the second paragraph could have been:

> Williams came to believe his own publicity and referred to himself as 'The Premier', although this was lost on Thorneycroft, who was more intimidated than impressed when he met Williams.

That sets up the Thorneycroft quote and helps establish the informant's nervousness around the killer.

To be fair to the journalist, overzealous sub-editing can turn a carefully constructed feature into separate islands of information, which float throughout the story without connection to each other. But if this occurs, it may be because the writer has not written to length and the sub-editor has had to find ways to extract a large amount of copy to ensure the story fits the space available for it. Every writer needs to write to length. Otherwise, they run the risk of having their work presented in a way they might not wish.

Another important point to note is that marshalling material for a profile is far easier than for an issues-based story. The chronology of an individual's life provides the ideal framework to negotiate a feature—from birth, through schooling, career and relationships. Deciding on a framework can be harder when the writer has to cover a range of sources for a feature on drugs in sport, the obesity epidemic, or the pros and cons of a levy on plastic shopping bags. Such features will need a sure hand to find the right balance between documented information and personal reflection or opinion.

Here is an example of how linking interviews with documentary evidence can be done, from a feature about the ALP candidate Maxine McKew, who eventually unseated former Prime Minister John Howard from his electorate, Bennelong, in the 2007 federal election:

> Using the 2006 Census data, Bennelong is fifteenth on a scale of the ethnicity population, and it has the highest proportion of people born in non-English-speaking countries of any Coalition seat in the land.

But McKew is not relying on demographic shifts to deliver her Bennelong. 'I'm not going out of my way to target any particular group. The Chinese vote. The Koreans vote. I'm after Liberal votes. I have to persuade some of the people who have been voting, election after election, for John Howard that this time they should consider voting for me and for Kevin Rudd.'

Brett, 2007, p. 23

This works for several reasons. The first is that the writer, Judith Brett, has used the documentary evidence from the Census as what appears to be good news for the subject of her story. In theory, the change in the population profile of the seat might be expected to diminish its Liberal pedigree and enhance McKew's chance of winning it for Labor. Then we come to the small and subtle word 'but'. The use of 'but' gives the writer the chance to contrast the documentary fact with the interview material. The contrast helps shape our view about McKew because it tells us that she is not relying on changes in the electorate to win the seat. She is trying to avoid the appearance of complacency, but also fostering a sense of the difficulty of her task.

So the best way to put documentary facts together with quotes is to provide the linkages that work to the overall benefit of the feature. These linkages can be achieved by following the logic and thought processes of the interviewee; by inviting a source or individual to respond to or interpret the documentary data; or, finally, by using a simple word such as 'but' or 'and' to set up in the reader's mind a sense of contrast—or continuity—between the documentary material and the people in the story.

Number crunching

Sadly, writers are not always the most numerate members of the community. Well, you can't have it all! Writers know what they need to know, and they know about words. The downside is that features containing a lot of data can pose comprehension problems for some writers.

Issues of numeracy do not only apply to the more sober features on the state of the economy or concerning industrial relations. Numbers and calculations are involved in sports features (for example, a cricketer's batting or bowling average), IT features (for example, size and capacities of computer hardware and software) or even reviews of motor cars or boats (for example, engine size, top speed, acceleration rates etc.).

So every writer who embarks on a feature that contains such data should at least be armed with a calculator. However, a calculator can only solve part of the problem. The issue is often not only about doing the sums or working out the percentages, but about knowing what numbers or calculations to use in the first place. Deciding what numbers to use is similar to choosing what quotations to use for a particular feature: decide whether they are useful, distinctive and help advance the story. If so, use them. But don't use lots of numbers in the mistaken belief that you will dazzle the reader with maths. There are not many readers who are excited by a lot of numbers in feature articles and, if they are, they will be the first to tell the writer where they have made a mistake in their calculations. Nothing turns general readers off a feature quicker than numbers waving at them from the page. It is best, therefore, to select one or two sets of figures that are beyond dispute and are fundamental to the point of your story.

Before you insert the numbers, ask yourself three questions:

- Do I know what these numbers actually mean?
- How do these numbers help my feature?
- Have I checked that the numbers are correct? Errors can sneak into features if writers are not careful.

If you cannot give a resounding 'yes' to the first and last questions and a convincing explanation for the second, you will need to find another set of numbers, or use none at all. If there's someone you know who has superior mathematical and statistical skills, check with them. And then check again.

Unfortunately, it is also quite common for writers to take a set of numbers used in other features or news stories and build a paragraph or part of their feature around that data. But you need to be sure that you understand what those figures really mean. There is no point in lifting other writers' statistics unless you are sure that you are using them in the appropriate context. If you cannot be sure, don't use them.

There are, however, some times when it may be fundamental to your feature to use numbers that are disputed. For example, the debate over the so-called 'Stolen Generations' of Aboriginal and Torres Strait Islander children not only hinged on the concept of 'stolen', but also on the number of children involved. The numbers themselves became part of many features and columns written about the topic across the political divide. Needless to say, the rationale for using numbers became an integral part of the features themselves.

Summary

- o Organise your research material into the useful and the useless.
- o Make a plan about how to write your feature (identifying the structure and material you will need to use).
- o Make sure your feature has an introduction, a middle and an end.
- o Context is vital for understanding—for the writer and for the reader.
- o Look for anecdotes.
- o Use quotations that advance the story.
- o Beware of numbers. Are they essential? If so, check and double-check that they are right. If in doubt, seek advice.

Questions

1 How do you test which research to use and which research to leave out of your feature?
2 What is an anecdote?
3 A plan helps a writer to do what?

Activities

1   Go to your favourite magazine and pick a feature that interests you. Look at how the feature is structured. Identify the beginning, middle and end. Now look at the other parts of the feature. What information do those paragraphs contain? How many anecdotes are there in the feature? How many quotations?

2   Listen to a conversation between some of your friends. If you were writing a feature on them, how much of what they say would you quote directly? Think about the reasons for your choice.

3   Think about the funniest thing that has ever happened to you. Now write that episode as the introduction to a feature. Give yourself no more than four sentences to tell the story.

References and additional reading

Anderson, P. (2008). 'Living the high life', *Herald Sun,* 26 March, p. 17.

Blundell, W. (1988). *The Art and Craft of Feature Writing*, New York: Penguin.

Brett, J. (2007). 'It's Bennelong time: On the campaign trail with Maxine McKew', *The Monthly*, September.

Garrison, B. (2004). *Professional Feature Writing*, 4th edn, Mahwah, NJ: Lawrence Erlbaum.

Grobel, L. (2004). *The Art of the Interview*, New York: Three Rivers Press.

Hennessy, B. (1989). *Writing Feature Articles: A Practical Guide to Methods and Markets*, Oxford: Focal Press.

Malcolm, J. (1990). *The Journalist and the Murderer*, New York: Knopf.

O'Neill, H. (2007) 'Worth his salt', *Wish* magazine, October.

Perlich, M. (2003). *The Art of the Interview: A Step-by-Step Guide to Insightful Interviewing*, New York: Empty Press.

Sedorkin, G. & McGregor, J. (2002). *Interviewing: A Guide for Journalists and Writers*, Crows Nest, NSW: Allen & Unwin.

Sumner, D.E. & Miller, H.G. (2005). *Feature and Magazine Writing*, New York: Blackwell.

Online resources

RobertNiles.com: Statistics every writer should know: www.robertniles.com/stats

Case study

Leanne Edmistone investigates a rarely talked about medical condition

Publication details:

'If there were a magic pill to be suddenly tall, would I take it? No', *QWeekend* magazine (with *The Courier Mail*), 2 April 2016.

The author:

Leanne Edmistone has been a journalist for 20 years. She studied journalism at the University of Queensland and started her career at *The Queensland Times* in Ipswich. Leanne then worked for *The Sunshine Coast Daily* before she joined *The Courier Mail* in 2003. The story was a finalist in the Sporting Wheelies and Disabled Association 2016 Annual Awards, which recognise outstanding achievement in sport and healthy activity for Queenslanders with a disability.

The story:

Like many feature writers, Edmistone often finds her inspiration from the vast material to be accessed from overseas newspapers and magazines. A good idea in Washington or London is still a good idea in Australia. So it turned out for Edmistone when she came across a photographic essay on dwarfism in an English newspaper magazine 18 months before she actually wrote her feature on the subject. The idea stayed with her and although there were several Australians who appeared in the magazine photographs, Edmistone charted her own path and sought her own examples. She knew a couple of people who eventually appeared in the feature but her preliminary research was, Edmistone admits, a matter of getting to know the local landscape.

'I did the internet search to get the basic info, names and details of the support and advocacy groups and to familiarise myself with what was out there,' she says. Edmistone was also keen to find a new development that would give her feature some topicality. 'I contacted the [Lady Cilento] children's hospital to see if there was any [new] research into dwarfism—that was a bit of a fishing expedition, and I had a bit of a win with that one.' (Edmistone found physiotherapist Penny Ireland, who was about to lead world-first research projects into the development of fine motor skills among children with achondroplasia, the genetic condition that is the cause of the most common form of dwarfism.)

Edmistone's approach was to find a range of people with dwarfism, with different points of view and different experiences. But she found reticence among some support groups, who preferred to keep out of the media. Edmistone was, however, helped by an unrelated story she had done months before on a relative of one of the children—Quaden Bayles. His family trusted her after the earlier story and were supportive of Quaden taking part in the feature.

Edmistone's other main interviews—Kobie Donovan and Grant 'Scooter' Patterson—were both more at home in the media. 'Kobie is quite media savvy,' Edmistone says. 'She has her own agenda—she was warm, easy-going and, in some ways, had the best story to tell. She was more of an advocate. Grant is a good role model for his positive, give anything a go, don't care what people think, cheeky larrikin attitude, as much for the amazing things he's achieved against all odds and other people's scepticism.'

Once Edmistone found the right people to tell the story, there were additional and significant other challenges in writing it—the terminology, both medical and social, and the weight of the medical evidence that the story needed to describe the important differences between Kobie, Scooter and Quaden's conditions.

The words used to describe dwarfism are often pejorative—midget, for example, is not usually considered appropriate. So how did Edmistone deal with navigating her way through the right and wrong language?

'I just asked Kobie, "What's the right terminology?", and she said "short-statured, dwarf but not midget, although Scooter embraces 'midget'"', Edmistone explains. 'Most times, people in their situation are happy to educate you. There's no such thing as a stupid question. It's not about being pitied but being respectful of their challenges.'

When it came to the medical terminology, Edmistone read a lot of the original material and then tried to digest it into a reader-friendly format. 'I might repeat it back in simple language during an interview with the medical expert. That tends to make it easier.'

Edmistone felt she had a strong grasp of the medical terminology and felt confident with the subject matter too when the time came to write the story.

'This is a story about people, not the condition so I was careful not to have too many statistics. It's a fine balancing act and how much of the statistics you include is determined by what kind of story you're doing—if it's a story about the medical research, then it would have carried more data and medical stuff but it was the personal stories that shaped the content,' she says.

Writing sample

'If there were a magic pill to suddenly be tall, would I take it? No.'

By Leanne Edmistone, *QWeekend* magazine, 2 April, 2016

AS A student teacher last year Kobie Donovan received three invites to fifth birthday parties, was regularly beckoned to share lunch and games, and was often pointed out to startled parents in the school pick-up line. 'See Mum, I told you I had a little teacher!'

Donovan is 21 and 113cm tall—equivalent to the height of an average five-year-old child. She was born with spondyloepiphyseal dysplasia (SED), one of the rarer of more than 350 types of dwarfism and skeletal dysplasia, which affects about one in 95,000 births.

When Donovan graduates from the University of Queensland with her Bachelor of Health, Sport and Physical Education degree later this year, she believes she will be one of only three short-statured teachers in Australia and the only short-statured physical education teacher in the world.

'I did three years of uni not knowing if I could actually be a PE teacher, and then I got out there [on prac] and realised straightaway my height did not make a difference,' she says.

Donovan's most recent and longest prac stint was a semester at Emmanuel College, at Carrara on the Gold Coast, where she taught years 1, 8, 10, 11 and 12. In her first lesson with year ones, she allowed ten minutes' question time and good-naturedly permitted lots of 'I'm taller than you!' back-to-back height comparisons, while their regular class teacher buried her head in her hands, horrified.

'What did you do wrong to God? Were you born this big [holding finger and thumb 5cm apart]? How old are you? Where's your mum? Are you a mum?' were among the questions she was asked, Donovan recalls, barefoot and relaxed in shorts and singlet in the Gold Coast home she shares with her parents and two younger sisters.

Maintaining authority was an initial concern but her fears proved baseless, especially with older students. 'They already saw me as weaker so didn't need to test my authority. I played on it—those kids who muck up, I'd say, oh, can you please carry the bag of balls I can't carry? Sure, Miss,' Donovan laughs. 'The principal told me he'd never seen those kids help out in his life!'

Innovation is a skill people of short stature develop quickly. Donovan uses an iPad and PowerPoint because she's unable to write on the whiteboard, walks around the classroom rather than standing in front, and actively involves her students. 'I left that school thinking I just educated 1000 students and for half of them, I didn't have to mention dwarfism. Now when they see a short-statured person in public, they're not going to make a big deal. It's been normalised for them.'

Donovan felt physically ill the first time she met other people with dwarfism. She was 18 and on the same eye level as every other adult in the room. It was overwhelming.

Dwarfism is caused by spontaneous mutation of a protein needed for long bone growth and across the spectrum affects about one in 10,000 births. Achondroplasia, the most common form, affects approximately one in every 20,000 to 40,000 live births. By comparison, the most common birth defects in Queensland are facial clefts (1:700), spina bifida (1:1000) and Down syndrome (1:1100). Eighty per cent of people with dwarfism have average-height parents and siblings.

Achondroplasia is typified by a large head, short limbs and average torso, while the effect of spondyloepiphyseal dysplasia (SED) means Donovan's body is small but proportionate. Common complications across the spectrum involve the neck, spine, sleep apnoea, osteoarthritis and fatigue.

When newborn Kobie was handed to first-time parents Craig and Wendy in Proserpine Hospital, in the Whitsunday region, on March 21, 1994, after a normal pregnancy and natural birth, it was clear there was something different about her but no one could quite put a finger on it. Within 24 hours the family were transferred by ambulance to the larger Mackay hospital, as a precaution. A day later Kobie was diagnosed with achondroplasia. It took another 18 years and several other misdiagnoses, before genetic blood testing correctly identified her particular brand of dwarfism.

'My parents [said they] must have been the most relaxed, ignorant parents in the world,' Donovan says. 'Will she run, talk, hear, are her intellectual capabilities fine? The doctor's like, "yep; okay, so we'll just modify a few things to help her out".'

Craig, a logistics manager for a fuel company, and Wendy, a part-time school administration assistant, returned to their native Gold Coast to be closer to medical specialists. Here Kobie enjoyed an active suburban childhood, never realising her body was considered disabled. Sure, she was short but she could do, and did, everything sisters Courtney, now 19, and Brittany, 17, did.

Kindy, school, dancing, sport, sleepovers—all were navigated with the help of strategically placed stools, modified desks and tools such as makeshift levers on light switches. She learnt to jump (onto stools, chairs, toilets) with ease and always carries hand sanitiser because, even in the disabled toilets, she can't reach the sink. A neighbourhood seamstress alters her clothes, bought from both children's and women's retailers, as necessary. Shoes (size 13–1) are bought at Betts Kids.

Donovan passed her driver's licence on the first attempt and drives a modified Kia Rio. While friends routinely have their ID triple checked at nightclubs, she's never asked. Donovan wants a family, but is only interested in dating short-statured men. Yes, yes, she's limiting the number of fish in her sea but she wants to look into her beloved's eyes, not his crotch, on their walk through life together. Carrying a pregnancy to full term might be dangerous, if not physically impossible, but there's more than one way to have a child.

Donovan says payWave is a marvel when so many EFTPOS machines are affixed out of reach on store counters; she jangles car keys or pretends to use her mobile to look 'more adulty' when left waiting for service at the deli, and there's always someone happy to retrieve jars from top grocery shelves. Ironically, concerned attendants regularly upgrade her on domestic flights to a seat with extra leg room.

'It's funny the gestures people make for you. You order a coffee and although you're meant to wait at the counter, they're like, "we'll bring it to your table". I was fuelling up one day [at a servo] and the lady came running out thinking I couldn't do it. She's like, "no, no, stand aside", but I said, "no, I can fuel my own car".'

Sport is Donovan's lifelong passion, one doctors credit with staving off complications typically seen in others with SED at a similar age.

She played soccer, tennis and touch football until she could no longer physically keep up with teammates. At 14 she discovered athletics and the Paralympic Pathway. Her dream of becoming an elite athlete was achievable.

At 18, the talented sprinter and javelin thrower heard about the World Dwarf Games and Short Statured People of Australia (SSPA) Inc, a non-profit support organisation for people with dwarfism and their families. The 160-strong membership is centred in NSW and Victoria, but slowly growing in Queensland (15).

It was at an SSPA weekend training camp for the 2013 World Dwarf Games that Donovan first walked into a room full of physical peers, early preparation for mixing with almost 400 short-statured athletes in Michigan, US. Teammates still tease her for her initial, sickly reaction.

'[The Games event] was incredible. I'd run heaps of 100m races but I'd never run one with a full set of eight women, all the same height as me. There were no head starts, no modifications of time at the end. You just have to race and beat them over the line if you want to win, which blew my mind!'

Now a javelin world record holder and children's athletics coach, Donovan debuted for Australia at the 2015 International Paralympics Committee Athletics World Championships in Doha, Qatar, last year, and is hoping this month to be selected for September's Rio Paralympics. Next year she will lead a team of 40 into the 7th World Dwarf Games in Ontario, Canada.

An SSPA executive member and a motivational speaker, Donovan is determined to change the dominant conversation from the 'same old, same old short-statured medical story' or dwarfs being seen as an acceptable object of ridicule, particularly in the entertainment industry. She concurs with Peter Dinklage, star of *Game of Thrones* and arguably the world's most famous dwarf, whose 2012 comments are oft quoted: 'Dwarves are still the butt of jokes. It's one of the last bastions of acceptable prejudice.'

Donovan urges people of short stature to chase their dreams, flaunt their breadth of talent and 'show [everyone] who we really are'.

'Probably a generation ago, people with short-stature stuck to jobs behind a desk. My generation, we've got the mindset we can do anything. In the US, there are short-statured doctors, lawyers in the UK, here we've got people studying to be doctors, nurses, business managers. I've seen how much has changed in the past 10 years so I know it's just going to keep going forward. The next generation will be able to do absolutely anything.

'I tell kids, if there was a magic pill to suddenly be tall, would I take it? No. I love the way I am. I find it unique, not the plain old boring lifestyle you guys live. I get to see things from a different perspective. Yes, there are challenges, yes, there are bad days, but in the end I feel like I achieve a whole lot more.'

An Aussie larrikin with more cheek than a crowded beach and more one-liners than a comedy festival, it's hard to imagine a person in Cairns with a bigger personality than Grant 'Scooter' Patterson. Scooter is a straight-talking speed demon with a blond-tipped surfer's mane and an unquenchable thirst for adventure. He loves his many vehicles, spearfishing, running amok with his mates and carving up the dance floor, Bacardi and soda water in hand.

He's the champion Paralympic swimmer training every day with a determined eye on a medal in Rio, who has spent a lifetime showing people why it's dangerous to 'underestimate the midget'.

'I've got something called mongrel syndrome. When someone says, "oh, there's no way you can do that, how are you going to do that?" my silly brain goes: "F..k off, I can do that!" It just takes a little bit of work,' says Scooter, 26, so dubbed for his main mode of transport. Only parents Shelley and Steve, and little brother Mitchell, 22, call him Grant. 'My condition means it's pretty much impossible and impractical for me to do all that I've done. I'm not made like everyone else; I like to think I am but I'm not. I don't listen to the rules and that's why I get so far in life.'

Scooter was born with diastrophic dysplasia, a rare form of dwarfism which affects one in 110,000 births, typified by curvature of bones, a lack of cartilage in joints and a smaller oesophagus, which gives his voice a unique tenor. 'I always tell everyone that's my parents' chance of winning the lottery down the drain, gone. They have to put up with me instead,' he says. 'For Mitchell it was [a] one in four [chance], so he dodged a bullet. He avoided the washing machine incident when he was a baby—he didn't get shrunk.'

Climbing aboard a scooter aged seven to get around quicker and easier, Scooter went to Redlynch Primary and Smithfield High schools. He started swimming at 11, gave it up at 13, turned into 'a blob' and dove back into the pool with more serious intentions.

Scooter has since competed around the world, including the London Paralympics and three World Championships.

In July he completed the Cairns Half Ironman (1.9km swim, 90km cycle, 21.2km run) in seven hours, 48 minutes and 19 seconds—under the eight-hour able body time limit, in the process raising more than $9000 for an insulin pump for a local child with diabetes. His training consisted of eight pool and three bike sessions, averaging 150km on the road, a week.

'I didn't believe I could finish the bloody race! London was pretty good, but the ironman, the reception coming in at the end, was bigger,' he says. 'Everyone was whistling and yelling at the top of their lungs as I sprinted that last leg. It went nuts!'

Scooter credits his parents for not wrapping him in cotton wool and encouraging him to give anything a go for his active, healthy lifestyle. Attending a Little People conference in America at age 16 perfectly illustrated the alternative—'all the kids and older people had had an average of 40 operations; it looked like they'd been on the set of [movie] *Saw*, they'd been cut open that many times'.

He's had just one operation to straighten his ankles.

It's a hot, humid afternoon in Cairns. Scooter is on the phone, sitting outside Trinity Bay High School's pool ready for daily training with long-time coach, Andrew 'Herbie' Howard, after a big day at work. The natural chatterbox is usually banned from answering the phones at his family's business, Allied Bearings and Tools, where he's in charge of online sales, but with two staff absent he got a reprieve. 'You don't want to come to the shops with me ... everyone wants to have a yarn!' he laughs.

Scooter bought his first house in suburban Mt Sheridan, on the outskirts of Cairns, a few months ago. He lives alone and the only renovation he has planned is a new shed out the back for his beloved toys—Carly the 4WD, Darryl the jet ski, and Polly, his 850 Sportsman Polaris quad bike. Scoot, the, err, scooter, stays inside, doubling as a stool to reach the strawberry jam. He also has his 20-tonne slew crane, heavy rigid truck and skid steer (bobcat) licences.

'I'm saving my money for all the good stuff—the boat shed, the boat; all the other stuff I can make do, that's easy. In the kitchen I've got a hairdressing stool that I sit on ... and just bounce around the kitchen like a mad chef. One of my good dishes is a coconut and cashew creamy chicken. That goes down a treat with brown rice. You've got to make sure you've got plenty of extra cashews in there for more texture. It's all about the texture.'

Last year, with multimedia journalist Brett Frawley, Scooter co-wrote, co-produced and starred in *Scooter: The Movie*, making the top 50 of 650 entrants in Tropfest Australia, the largest short film festival in the world. When his swimming career winds down, he'd like to be an actor ... or race F1s ... or go-karts ... or maybe take up boxing.

Girls have, so far, come and gone. He'll date 'whoever is willing to give me the time of day; as long as they have a job and do something to keep reasonably fit, it doesn't matter what they look like'. As for kids—who have a 50 per cent chance of inheriting his condition—he'd love the chance to 'drag them around with all the awesome activities I do'. After all, as Scooter says, 'you only live once and nothing is impossible'.

In so many ways, Quaden Bayles is a typical five-year-old boy. He loves footy, Lego, Teenage Mutant Ninja Turtles, playing with his cars, filling his stomach and prefers his things to be blue or green, not pink or purple. Full of energy and mischief, he loves painting, learning Aboriginal dances and songs, and playing his clap sticks.

A proud Wakka Wakka, Birri Gubba boy, he is doted on by his poppy Tiga, single mum Yarraka and twin sisters Guyala and Yilan, 16.

So excited was Quaden about starting prep at the Aboriginal and Islander Independent Community School (better known as the Murri School), he was asking Yarraka to save dinner leftovers for his lunch for weeks, had his bag packed for days and—determined to make an impression—gave himself a 'dinosaur haircut'. (Mum did her best to tidy it into a modern Mohawk.)

Within minutes of walking into the Acacia Ridge school grounds, in Brisbane's south, the challenging reality of the big day—and the rest of his life—sunk in.

Why is your head so big? Why are you so small? Why does he look like that? He looks scary.

Quaden hates the words 'achondroplasia', 'special', 'different', 'baby' and 'little', and being handled by people he doesn't know.

He hates people talking about or staring at him and is not afraid to say it: mobile phone footage of him sitting in a shopping trolley, demanding 'Stop looking at me!' went viral. His Facebook photos and videos are routinely trolled.

Quaden is small even taking his achondroplasia into account; he's little more than half the size of most of his classmates. He is familiar with practically every corner of Lady Cilento Children's Hospital and has already had several major operations, with more spinal surgery on the cards. At school, he has a one-on-one support teacher daily but is still waiting for the special desk, chair, stools and wheelchair he needs. Fatigue from pain, severe sleep apnoea and trying to keep up with his classmates is constant.

Yarraka, 34, often finds herself suppressing tears as she fights to find ways to help her son accept and live with the challenges of his condition while having the confidence to chase his dreams. This is a boy *desperate* to pull on boots and play rugby league like his heroes. His knowledge of Indigenous players is encyclopaedic, his collection of signed balls extensive and players from both rugby codes including Johnathan Thurston, Beau Ryan, Nate Myles, Sonny Bill Williams, Willy Tonga and Quade Cooper have all sent him video messages of support. Hollywood heavyweight Russell Crowe introduced him to the boys at the South Sydney Rabbitohs. Ipswich team the Purga Wagtails have Quaden's handprint on their uniform. Crowds cheered as he led the Brisbane Broncos and the Queensland Murri team out on to match-day fields.

'But there are no dwarf rugby players,' sighs Yarraka, waiting in the school library while Quaden finishes his session with the school's occupational therapist. 'He just gets so angry and cries, because he doesn't accept it at all. He just says, "nah, I'm going to play footy, I'm going to get big and strong like Daddy"', she says.

'He just wants to be like everyone else.'

Three years ago Yarraka started the Facebook page Stand Tall 4 Dwarfism and is also an integral member of Dwarfism Awareness Australia Inc, a non-profit family support group established by Redbank Plains mum Stephanie Short after her son Xavier was born with dwarfism. About 20 group members with young children, from across south-east Queensland, meet regularly.

Yarraka uses the experiences of people such as American professional basketballer Jahmani Swanson, who plays in a New York pro-league team of dwarfs, American actor/producer Jason 'Wee Man' Acuna, of *Jackass* fame, and Melbourne motivational speaker Nick Vujicic, who was born without limbs, to show Quaden anything is possible.

'It's about focusing on the positives and making sure Quaden has those strengths, raising him to be confident,' Yarraka says. 'He's got the biggest personality, he makes a joke about everything ... I want people to see him for him. He's Quaden, there's so many different sides to him. Yes, he's different but we're all different, and we can learn to embrace that.'

One of Quaden's biggest advocates is fellow footy fanatic Taneya Shannen, 21, from Rockhampton, who also has achondroplasia. She has used her connections with various teams to buoy Quaden's spirits, particularly when he's been confined to a hospital bed. The third of four daughters born to Gayle and Rod, Taneya went to Rockhampton Grammar School and hopes to work in aged care. She recently completed her certificate of medical reception online, while caring for her grandmother Joan Shannen, 87.

'I'm really close to my Nan, she lives next door and I stay at her house every night, usually. We go shopping, eat out, whatever she wants to do,' says Taneya.

Fashion is a particular love of Taneya's and Joan is her chief seamstress, helping with any alterations necessary. A lower bench has been installed in her parents' kitchen to allow Taneya to prepare food easily, there are step-stools in every room, and she drives a modified Yaris.

A seasoned visitor to Canada and America, where she's also attended a number of Little People of America conferences and the 2013 World Dwarf Games, Taneya's dream is to explore Paris.

'Going out in public, there's still people that say stuff and try to take your photo, but I just ignore it. I go to schools to talk to kids and ask that before they speak, think: is it going to hurt someone?

'Everyone is the same, no matter what. Short, fat, poor, different colour, sizes, we're all the same people.'

WORLD FIRST MEDICAL RESEARCH

Brisbane physiotherapist Penny Ireland was asked to visit two families in a hospital labour ward. Each asked her 'very sensible' questions about their newborn babies diagnosed with achondroplasia. She couldn't answer. This experience drove her to focus her PhD—and the rest of her career—on the disease. Now, nearly 20 years after meeting those parents (with whom she's still in contact), Dr Ireland is an internationally renowned expert who will this year lead three world-first research projects looking at children with achondroplasia's development of fine motor skills, balance and mobility, and the condition's effects on their daily life.

'How terrible to have a sensible question that no-one can answer,' she says. 'I did this research to be able to have the conversation those families wanted to hear and couldn't.'

Ireland is collaborating with Melbourne geneticist Professor Ravi Savarirayan, of the Murdoch Children's Research Institute, who has had very promising results with his international drug trial promoting spine and bone growth in children with achondroplasia.

The ultimate aim is not a cure or standard height, but to decrease the risk of complications and the need for medical intervention.

'The first set of results, from the middle of last year, showed the group receiving the highest dose have grown 50 per cent [faster] than they were and there have been no serious adverse [side-effects],' says Savarirayan, who is hopeful the trial will be extended to Queensland families in the next 12 months.

The pair is also seeking funding to provide parents of every baby born with dwarfism with an eBook and DVD explaining the condition, the child's likely development, and ways to help the child manage daily life as he or she grows.

'My job as a physio is we *have* to work out the best way for these kids to be independent and we *have* to get the information out there, because it would make it easier for the school, it would make it easier for the health system, everything, if we can do that,' says Ireland, her passion palpable in the treatment room at Lady Cilento Children's Hospital where we meet.

'We've got to stop comparing apples with oranges. [These children] have got their own timeframe for doing things. That doesn't make it wrong. They're fine. We just have to know about it. If we can identify what's really tricky for them, then we've got a much better chance of going, okay, here's some strategies to help you deal with that.'

Ireland, a mother of two, also lectures at the University of Queensland and Griffith University, where she hopes to inspire young physiotherapists to specialise in achondroplasia and other rare conditions.

'It frustrates me that there isn't more research trying to find answers,' she says. 'It frustrates me that there must be families out there that wake up every day going, I don't know what's coming next.

'I really like being able to say, you know what, please enjoy your baby because you have a wonderful, brilliant little one; here's some thoughts and ideas of what's going to happen, here's some things that might be scary, here's a phone number to call.

'They're great families and they deserve as much input and as much care as [families] with other conditions where there might be thousands and thousands of kids affected. What makes these kids any less deserving of research and the time and the knowledge? Nothing. *Nothing*.'

6
Developing Writing Techniques

'All you need is the plan, the road map, and the courage to press on to your destination.'

Earl Nightingale (1921–89)

Objectives

In this chapter you will be shown how to take all your hard work and put it on the page. There is nothing more frightening than a blank piece of paper, so here you will be given structures to use, tips on how to start and finish your articles, and some advice on how to add flair to your writing. Armed with these techniques, you will find that blank page not nearly so daunting. This chapter covers:

o structuring your article

o different types of story

o writing leads: enticing your audience

o developing your language: creating mood

o a Case study: A structural analysis of Melissa Field's story for *Marie Claire* about overseas adoptions

o a Writing sample: 'If celebrities can adopt children from overseas ... why can't we?' by Melissa Field, *Marie Claire*, March 2008.

Creating structure

So, you have done your research and conducted your interviews—now what do you do? How do you take all that information and craft it into a feature article? This is where structure comes into play. Structure is the road map that helps you take your story from its origin as a great idea to its destination—the pages of the features section of a newspaper or magazine. There are a range of maps to choose from, depending on the style of story you are writing. In this chapter we will look at:

• the list story

• the Q&A

• the fact, quote and anecdote model

• chronological structure

• bookend structure

• the 'Sleepy P'

- the flashback
- tuning fork structure
- multilayer structure
- the breakout box.

The list story

One of the first articles you may be given to write, if you are lucky enough to garner a staff position at a magazine, is the list story. These fill the pages of glossy magazines and websites across all genres—appearing, for instance, in car enthusiast guides, girl mags and cooking publications. List stories usually take the form of a list of Top 10 (or whatever number) tips, tricks, DOs, DON'Ts, successes, failures or must-haves. Like most works of journalism, these stories are based on research and interviews, but unlike many works of journalism, they will rarely include quotes or refer to experts.

For these stories you will usually begin with a general introduction, which explains the topic and reveals why the reader should be interested in it. Then, in bullet-point form, you should provide a list. Each point on the list is given a heading (in which many publications will try to incorporate a witticism or pun) that is then explained in anything from one sentence to a few paragraphs. You need to order your list according to the needs of your readers—think about how to keep them interested in your story to the end (don't use up all your most interesting material in the first few points). You might order your points by price, 'newness', best to worst or vice versa, or try a chronological structure—it doesn't really matter how you do it as long as the order is logical and interesting.

The key here is to know your publication, to follow the way its established journalists write their list stories—how they use humour, how long their list points are etc. List stories are a great starting point in the world of features—they show your flair for writing without asking you to spend a long time formulating transitions between paragraphs, placing quotes or referencing expert opinion.

The Q&A

The Question and Answer story is a favourite style for an interview with a celebrity or prominent person. This structure is almost as simple as it sounds. Essentially, you conduct an interview and then transcribe it for your readers. Of course, there is a little more to do than that.

Most Q&As begin with a short introductory paragraph or two about the interviewee. This will usually reveal the relevance of the article (a new film released, a new political appointment, a new scandal etc.) and a small biographical note ('we've loved her since her first appearance on screen in 1990, but now this child actress comes of age in ...'). Then it's a matter of putting the most interesting parts of the interview on the page, dropping the boring stuff and making all this appear seamless to the reader.

The best Q&As will reveal a great deal about the interviewee through their responses to questions, which should become more probing as the story continues. These responses will be telling whether the celebrity is open and honest or tries to dodge the question or veers off-topic.

The fact, quote and anecdote model

Most feature articles will not work as list stories or Q&As because they require the journalist to explore the topic or personality in greater depth. There are a host of ways to structure a story; we will discuss a few in this chapter. The simplest structure was devised by Maurice Dunlevy and explained in his book *Feature Writing* (Dunlevy, 1988), where he argued that the typical feature article is made up of three ingredients: facts, quotes and anecdotes. By using these a writer can reveal another very important element—theme—which is discussed on pp. 102–3. First, we will consider the individual elements of Dunlevy's model.

Facts

Facts are an important part of every story; they provide the hard data—the dates, times, names and statistics—that backs up all the opinion and stories from your interviewees.

Quotes

Quotes are also an integral part of every story. They provide expert opinion, add another voice to your work, explain things better than you can, and reveal personalities and cultures. It is always better to have too many quotes than too few. But be careful: a quote is only one person's opinion and is tainted by their preconceptions, memory and what they want to believe and want others to believe. So, don't take what people say at face value—you will have to check the validity of their words by doing your own research.

There are three types of quotes you may use in a feature story. Which one you choose will depend on what sort of impact you are looking for and what kind of information you are trying to provide. The three types are:

1 direct quotes

    Example: 'I had no idea how bad things were going to get when I stepped into that warehouse,' Jack says.

2 indirect quotes

    Example: Jack explains he was unaware of the dangers inside the building.

3 dialogue

    Example: 'I had no idea how bad things were going to get when I stepped into that warehouse,' Jack says as he takes a sip from his beer.

    Ted smiles at his mate. 'You were a right idiot. Your first day on the job and you run head-first into a chemical fire.'

Anecdotes

Anecdotes are vital to any good feature. Anecdotes are those little stories we all tell about our lives: the day we lost our way home from school, the politician's first parliamentary blunder, the soldier's experience in enemy hands etc. Anecdotes are often what keep a reader interested—we love stories and we are fascinated with the lives of others. Think about one of your secondary school history classes. What did you find more interesting: a list of the dates when the kings and queens reigned, or the stories of their insanity, debauchery, triumphs and tribulations? Like a history lesson, feature articles need to be peppered with anecdotes to keep the reader awake.

With anecdotes, you either relay the little stories people tell about their lives, *or* you write what you saw and experienced:

- 'Jim had never seen a dead body before that day; he wonders what would have happened if he had just left that swinging gate alone ...'
- 'The hustle and bustle of life surrounds you as you step onto the platform, hundreds of busy commuters swarming between trains like ...'
- 'I stepped onto the red carpet, the bulbs flashed, the microphones pushed forward, the crowds gasped, "It's her!" I heard a woman squeal as teams of photographers whipped around in my direction, their lenses focusing on my stunned face. "Nope, it's nobody, false alarm," came the reply from one of the paparazzi. Like that, my moment in the spotlight was over.'

Theme

Theme is what keeps a feature hanging together—it is the glue that binds your facts, quotes and anecdotes. Theme is what your story is *really* about. Your topic may be Holocaust survivors but your theme may be 'love conquers all'. This theme would be revealed, perhaps, through the stories of the survivors. You might show that it was their love for each other, or their love for family who had escaped the camps, or their love for God, or a combination of all three that had enabled them to survive the horror of the war. You might write an article about an entrepreneur who began life in poverty but, despite the odds, built a multimillion-dollar company. A theme you might also choose is 'if you keep working for it, nothing is impossible'.

Your choice of theme will dictate which facts, quotes and anecdotes you choose. If you have done your job properly, you will have a mountain of information, or, to borrow from Ernest Hemingway (1966, p. 182), you will have an iceberg effect. Hemingway, a great journalist, not just a famous novelist, explained that an iceberg is always bigger than it appears—only one-tenth of it is above the waterline. This notion can also be applied to journalism—your article represents what we see over the waterline; underneath the water lies the real work, the research. For example, if you are writing a 2000-word article, you should have 20,000 words worth of interviews, facts and other research.

But how do you choose between all those words to make up your 2000-word article? You chop, select and organise all these facts, quotes and anecdotes according to whether or not they illustrate your theme. This method gives you:

- an easy way of wading through all that data
- an article with all its elements drawn together into a coherent whole
- a way to differentiate your story from all the others on that topic, whether it is about anorexia, Buenos Aires, primary education or a lagging sex life
- more than just a topic-based article—you have a story that can have universal meaning. All your readers may not want to start their own business, but with your theme of 'if you keep working for it, nothing is impossible', you have something that can resonate universally.

Dunlevy (1988, p. 5) took the elements of quote, fact, anecdote and theme and created a simple structure to follow:

- Begin with an anecdote (to buttonhole your reader).
- Follow this with a statement of your theme.
- Illustrate your theme with some facts and quotes.
- Brighten it with an anecdote or two.
- Illustrate with more facts and quotes.
- Brighten with another anecdote or two.
- Conclude.

This structure may not be the most creative in the world, but it works. If you are just beginning your journey as a feature writer, you'll find that this structure will be one of the handiest things in your tool box— it will provide a skeleton for you to flesh out with all your great writing and research.

Chronological structure

Another simple structure is that based on chronology. Essentially, you tell a story of an event or a person or group's life (or a slice of it) in chronological order. You start at the beginning (birth, or the start of the fire, or the founding of the society) and finish at the end (death, the fire is put out, the society's founder is assassinated and it disbands).

Chronological structure is particularly useful in the following scenarios:

- where time is integral—for example, a countdown to 11.45 pm, when the bank robbers arrive, or the terror attack begins, or you are born etc. (Cheney, 1991)
- when the story is complicated—involving politics, multiple characters, scientific discoveries etc. This structure is the most understandable for your readers. Why? Because our lives move chronologically, so we understand this structure instinctively.

Bookend structure

This structure is used mainly in conjunction with the 'fact, quote and anecdote' and 'chronological' methods, but it can be married with almost all the structures outlined in this chapter. When you 'bookend', you are mirroring the beginning of your story with the end of your story. You do this to provide your reader with a reinforcement of the theme and a satisfying conclusion to the article.

Remember that example of the entrepreneur who started with nothing but, despite all obstacles, fought his way to the top? You could begin the article with a description of this man as a small boy, playing in the field behind his home with some found objects he has turned into toys. This would reveal his background and point to the ingenuity that would make him a success. Then you could end the story with similar imagery, but this time you are describing the grown man, sitting on a bench in his opulent, manicured garden typing on his iPad, working towards his next goal. This reveals the theme 'if you keep working for it, nothing is impossible'. Your bookend introduction and conclusion have reinforced this theme and given the story, and your readers, a sense of closure.

The 'Sleepy P'

Once you have mastered the simple structures you can move on to the host of more advanced options. One of the classics is called '*in media res*', or what we call the 'Sleepy P'.

In media res means 'into the middle of things'—you start your story in the centre of the action, then you will usually come back to the chronological beginning of the story, work through to that exciting event, then move through it until the end.

For example, your story is about a World War II fighter pilot. You are telling the story from the day he enters flight school in peacetime until his celebration on VE Day. To start *in media res* you might begin with a description of the day he has to say goodbye to his wife before he departs for war (build emotion, set up some pressure, evidence of theme etc.), then go back to the beginning, work through to the first mission, then move on (Cheney, 1991).

Why do we call it the Sleepy P structure? Because that's what it looks like in diagrammatic form:

Figure 6.1   The Sleepy P structure

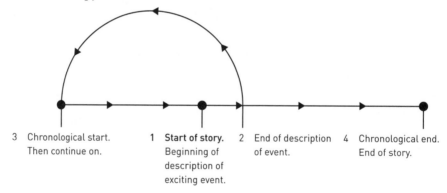

You can see how similar this is to the chronological structure—you just start in the most exciting, or most emotional, or most intriguing part of the story. You do this for an obvious reason—you need a stirring first few paragraphs to capture your readers' attention and ensure they will want to spend their time reading your story, and not skip ahead to read the next writer's hard work.

The flashback

This is a classic film structure (often used in B-grade movies, but occasionally in highly successful efforts such as James Cameron's *Titanic* (1997)) that allows you to move in and out of chronological time.

In this structure you usually begin with the end of the story—with someone looking back at a past event. Then you jump between 'today' and this moment in the past. The key is to ensure that the past event, as you describe it, moves forward in time:

- *Right*: John, in 2018 describes life in 1930s Melbourne: a day in June 1930, July 1930, January 1931, March 1932.
- *Wrong*: John, in 2018 describes life in 1930s Melbourne: a day in June 1930, March 1932, January 1931, July 1930.

If you jump around in time too much (such as in the 'wrong' example) you will confuse your readers.

With the flashback structure, you have the option of first using the interviewee in the 'today' time period to introduce the story and to conclude it, and dedicating the rest of the words to the past events.

Figure 6.2   The flashback: option 1

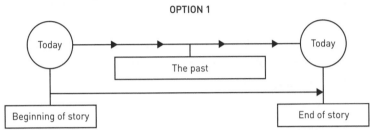

Alternatively, you can jump between 'today' and the past event so the interviewee can comment on their actions or on the event from today's perspective. Either method works, as long as you stick to the rule explained above—all events must move forward in time.

Figure 6.3   The flashback: option 2

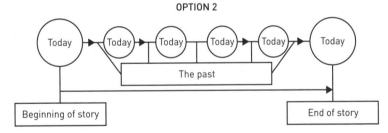

The flashback structure is particularly useful when you are telling the story of one person and their experience of an event. It can provide a sense of immediacy for your readers regarding the past and offers the interviewee's wisdom as they look back in time. This structure is also worth using because it enables you to show links between this past event and the world today.

Tuning fork structure

This structure, sometimes known as a parallel or convergent narratives structure, is also a derivative of the chronological structure (Cheney, 1991). The difference is that you share two stories with your reader instead of just one. With this method you tell stories that are seemingly unconnected (although you will have built the same theme into each story), then partway through the article you will show how these stories interconnect. Effectively, you create a structure that looks (in diagrammatic form) similar to a tuning fork. If used correctly, this structure should produce a harmonious article.

Figure 6.4   Tuning fork structure

This method is often used for love stories or reunion stories. A classic example would be the tale of two children who grow up with lives eerily similar, though they have never met. Then, in their thirties, through a chance encounter, they discover they are twins who were separated at birth and adopted by different families. If you are lucky enough to stumble onto such a story, the tuning fork structure is a great one to use. When done well, it builds suspense to a point that when the two characters finally meet, the readers are as excited as the people they are reading about.

Multilayer structure

This is a more complicated version of the tuning fork structure. Here, you take any number of people's stories that are seemingly unconnected and then pull them together (Cheney, 1991). Again, theme is an important element—it must be used to tie the stories together—you shouldn't just rely on the meeting point to do this.

With the multilayer structure, the stories usually connect at a major event. This could be something horrific like the 2017 Queensland floods, or something wonderful like a refugee becoming a citizen. You would write the story of each individual caught up in the drama, then at the end reveal how their stories are connected—that they all arrive at the town hall crisis centre, or that they step onto the stage at the citizenship ceremony. This is a difficult structure to pull off but when done well can illustrate the many faces and dimensions of an event (Cheney, 1991).

The breakout box

This is not so much a structure but an additional element to your chosen method. A breakout box is an important facet of many stories—it is the little sidebar or box that sits apart from the main story and adds extra information which, if included in the body of the article, might disrupt its flow.

For example, you have written a wonderful flashback story about your brother's experience of being deployed in the army to Afghanistan. You would like to include some of the key dates of the conflict, but to include them in the body of the story would destroy the reader's ability to get lost in the narrative. Here, the breakout box is one of your favourite tools. In the box you can list some key dates and statistics that readers can look to if they need information while reading the story, or they can choose to read them at the end.

Apart from providing additional facts or statistics, breakout boxes can be used to offer readers additional or contrary opinions (such as the male point of view in a story that focuses on women's experiences of adultery), quotes from experts, a list of celebrities who have experienced the same issue, tips on how to spot or deal with an illness or other problem, a vox pop or even contact information. Flip through your favourite magazine or the features section of your newspaper; every publication from *The Australian* to *Cleo* to *Vogue* to *FHM* uses breakout boxes, each in its own way. You'll see how these little fact blocks can add so much to an article in a very small word count.

Writing leads

Now that you have decided upon your structure, you need to start writing the story. Where else do you begin but with the introduction, also known as the lead. If you've written hard news, you know that when you sit down to pen one of these stories, creating the lead is an almost mathematical process. You've been taught to write down the *who, what, where, when, why* and, if possible, the *how* of the story, and once you decide what these things are, the lead tends to flow. With features it is not so simple. When writing hard news stories, you are trying to get across the most important information to the reader as efficiently as possible, but when writing features you have a different agenda. The hard news lead is all about *informing* the reader; the features lead is all about *entertaining* the reader.

While features (especially news or investigative stories) will often provide readers with detailed information, the introductory sentences are all about hooking the reader. The lead must be entertaining in some way or you will not convince your reader to come with you on a journey through hundreds or even thousands of words. If they just wanted the facts, they would go to an online news site. They are reading a feature for an in-depth explanation of an issue and for entertainment; they don't want to be bored along the way.

So, how do you come up with an enticing introduction? There are a number of methods available; it's just a matter of selecting them according to the publication you are writing for and the *theme* of your story. Theme is all-important, so don't forget it when you are writing your introduction; it should be a strong presence throughout the article.

Here we will discuss several types of introduction, or lead:

- the 'anecdotal lead'
- the 'mislead'
- the 'question lead'
- the 'quotation lead'
- the 'scene-setter lead'
- the 'get-the-reader-involved lead'.

The 'anecdotal lead'

This is the lead you will use if you follow the 'fact, quote and anecdote model'. You begin with a small story from one of your interviewees or from your own experience:

Third person—'Lee Miller: portraits of a life', *Marie Claire*

The beautiful blonde teenager was in a world of her own as she weaved her way through bustling downtown New York. Busy mulling over the day's plans, she stepped off the pavement, oblivious to the taxi speeding towards her. Horns blared and brakes squealed—but then, amid the press of bodies, a strong arm wrenched her back from danger. Her blue eyes wide with shock, 19-year-old Lee Miller turned to her rescuer and stammered her thanks. Little did she know that as well as saving her life, this valiant stranger was about to change it forever.

Burke, 2007, p. 246

First person—'Fabric conditioning', *GQ*

I have donned a wide array of run-of-the-mill, off-the-rack suits in my time: school uniforms, office wear, emergency funeral numbers, even a safari suit. My skin knows well the crass caress of cheap material, machine-cut symmetrically and factory-finished with all the care of someone stitching a tea towel.

And so it was that I one day found myself craving a suit made with me in mind. Something with a strong enough character to stay with me for years. Explaining all this one evening to a well-dressed relative, I was on the receiving end of some immortal words: 'My dear boy, you must visit Savile Row'.

Latham, 2007, p. 73

Of course, you don't have to use 'I' for it to be the first person. You can also use 'we':

First person—'The truth about Jebediah', *Rolling Stone*

It wasn't meant to be like this. Our interview was scheduled to take place hours ago in less risky confines, yet here we are in Jebediah's hotel room; well fed and on our collective ways to well drunk.

McMullen, 2011, p. 72

All of these anecdotal leads draw in readers by providing a sense of immediacy—taking them into the mind and experiences of the writer or transporting them to another world and into a key moment of someone else's life.

The 'mislead'

There is nothing worse than reading a story that promises something and never delivers. For example, you write in your lead about the difficulty of being single after 50, and then you spend the rest of the story describing a wonderful love affair between two people in their sixties. Or your lead explains how school years are the best years of your life, and then your story is about someone who has made it big their first year after graduating. What has the lead to do with the body of the story? Very little. You need to make sure that you give your readers what you have promised, that you don't *unintentionally* mislead them about your topic (Granato, 1996).

However, there is one exception to this rule and that is the *intentional* mislead. This is where you trick the reader into thinking one thing about your story and (this is the key) *quickly* reveal that the topic of the story is quite different.

'The power of positivity', *Marie Claire*

A group of teenagers and young children are on a weekend camp. They're yelling out over one another, trying to be heard. The younger ones are huddled together. A couple of the teenagers have their arms draped around each other. Everyone here has something in common that few people in Australia have—they are all HIV-positive.

Renkart, 2002

In the first four sentences, the journalist paints a portrait of normal kids hanging out together. Then the fifth sentence tells the readers what they are really experiencing—this is a day in the life of children with HIV. We can tell this lead is intentionally misleading because it reveals something to the readers. It encourages the reader to picture 'normal' children, and then tells them they happen to be sick. This juxtaposition is thematic—it says to the readers: yes they have HIV, but they're still 'normal', often happy, kids. Remember, as always, to be guided by theme when you are writing your lead, whether it is intentionally misleading or not.

The 'question lead'

The question lead is as simple as it sounds. You begin your story by asking a question of your readers. There is one catch though. You *must* answer the question. That seems obvious, but many new writers often forget this, or answer the question too far into the story. The rule is that you must answer the question within the next few sentences, as in the following examples:

'Billionaires' Ikea', *Forbes*

Want to own the chair on which Marie-Antoinette once sat? Knock on this Parisian door.

Numero 43, Rue de Monceau is an opulent town house in a quiet residential Paris neighborhood. There is nothing to tell you what goes on behind the massive wooden doors except a brass plaque with the name Kraemer.

Levine, 2007

'Celeb blog fantasies', *Cleo*

Ever had a creative girlfriend who would fuel your fantasies about Robbie/*NSYNC/The Backstreet Boys by inventing stories about them on the way to school? If the answer's no, hey— bad luck. But even if you had to rely on your own imaginations, it's likely you played the starring role. But now there's a growing Internet community of women writing pervy stories about their favourite bands and posting them online.

Valentish, 2007, p. 52

The 'quotation lead'

This lead sounds simple, but don't be fooled—you can't just start your story with any old quote. It must be a real attention grabber and something more interesting than you could have written yourself. This lead is often used when a celebrity has said something particularly outrageous or when a 'normal' person summarises a traumatic event in eloquent and heart-wrenching terms. Or, as you can see in the example below, when an interviewee says something your readers would only believe in between quotation marks.

'The mane attraction', *FHM*

'I have a whole series of shows planned in my head. I will pull an airplane with my teeth and I will pull an airplane with my hair. I will also be run over by an airplane. In between each of these acts, there will be lion battles.'

Smithurst, 2011, p. 45

The 'scene-setter lead'

This lead asks you to survey your surroundings and describe them to your readers so they can be transported to this place. Similar to the anecdotal lead, this is an account of somewhere you have experienced, though it does not have to be in the first person. What it must be is rich in detail; you should describe the textures, sounds and sights of the environment. This lead is particularly useful in travel stories and for articles on food, fashion, homewares and design.

'Liquid gold', *Gourmet Traveller*

It's mid morning in Cordoba and the air in the street is filled with the smell of a score of different kitchens as housewives prepare the daily meal: the sweet rich smell of onions slowly cooking down, the skin of a chicken being browned, and a mix of fresh seafood, probably squid, being sautéed with some punchy garlic. Despite the waves of different smells, there's one that unifies them all: that of olive oil. Spanish olive oil.

Cornish, 2011, p. 132

'Screen play', *Vogue*

On a low black lacquered coffee table in Gabrielle Chanel's apartment, among her ornaments and keepsakes, three cigarette boxes catch the light. The intricate little chests, each bearing the coat of arms of her beloved Duke of Westminster, are burnished in vermeil, a mixture of gold and silver, but once opened reveal an opulent lining of pure gold.

Spring, 2007, p. 132

The 'get-the-reader-involved lead'

This lead style is used a great deal in glossy magazines. It is designed to involve readers in the story, to assure them that you are speaking to them, that they have a stake in the topic at hand. This lead can be used in topics as diverse as fashion trends, dating techniques, sporting tricks or financial pitfalls, as the following examples reveal.

'Crush hour', *Vogue*

Picture this: it's Thailand. A quiet week away to steady city-jangled nerves in a jungle encircled meditation retreat. You spot his eyes across the room and all the *hatha* breathing in the world can't stop that wicked flame of awareness spring to life.

Lewis, 2011, p. 222

'Watch out ... there are millions of bedbugs about', *The Guardian*

You may want to be sitting down before you read this, but if you are on public transport/in bed/ensconced in that antique armchair, you might prefer to stand up. We are, apparently, in the grip of a bedbug epidemic. David Cain, who runs Bed-Bugs.co.uk, a dedicated bedbug obliteration service, says infestations have gone up by 500% in the last year.

Saner, 2007

Developing language

This chapter has armed you with an enormous array of ways to get your story on the page. But how do you write it? Of course you must write with your publication in mind (a topic discussed in depth in Chapter 10), but what else can you use to interest your reader?

Simile and metaphor

Two particularly useful literary devices are simile and metaphor. They add spice and life to your story and give your work that most elusive of qualities: style.

You create a *simile* by comparing one thing with another. This comparison adds to our understanding of the first thing in an interesting way. For example, you could compare the Los Angeles airport with the insanity of a store on sale day:

> I stepped into LAX and was confronted with men, women, children, crying, screaming, jostling for attention and escape. It was like the first day of the stocktaking sales.

This would be a perfect simile for a women's fashion publication. But what if you were writing for men? Perhaps you could compare the airport with the atmosphere of a bus after a grand final football match. Or, if you were writing for movie buffs, you could compare it with the out-of-this-world-hubbub of the *Star Wars* cantina scene. Just keep the comparison lively and relevant to your readers.

You create a *metaphor* not by comparing one thing with another, but by stating that one thing *is* another. This is a slightly trickier technique, and one that is more often used by fiction writers, but it can be useful in journalism.

Think about the power of the following statements:

1   He walked into the courtroom; he was like a jaguar, ready to pounce on the first man who disagreed with him.

2   He walked into the courtroom, a jaguar ready to pounce on the first man who disagreed with him.

The second example (which uses metaphor, unlike the first, which uses a simile) carries more weight, as it conjures up a stronger image in the reader's mind. You can see this barrister as if he were a predator waiting for the chance to take out his prey. Such metaphors can illustrate character traits beautifully and help point to the theme in your story.

Creating mood

You now have a fantastic structure for your story, rich with theme, facts, quotes and anecdotes. You are also entertaining and intriguing your reader with similes and metaphors, but there is one last thing you need to do. You need to think about your sentence length and word choice.

The length of your sentences and your choice of words will help to encourage mood in your work and give your readers more reasons to continue with your story. Take the following examples of the same event: a woman walking through the forest. Each description provides a different mood through the length of the sentences and the length of the words:

1   She walked through the woods, her hands lightly touching the leaves as she passed by, her fingertips caressing the outstretched green, the fine white veins pressing towards the surface, towards her.

2   She walked. Step, step, step. She was percussion in the forest. Her breath, in, out, in. Her fingers tap, tap, tapping on the leaves as she pushed through the trees.

In the first example, we are given a feeling of languor; an almost romantic mood is conveyed through the choice of a long sentence and long, soft words. The second version of the woman's walk uses a staccato rhythm—short, sharp sentences and words convey momentum. This sentence construction encourages the feeling of being chased. By creating mood in your story, you are transporting your readers into the anecdotes you have chosen, giving them a sense of what it is like to really be in that forest, or in Iraq, or at a celebrity party, or in the boardroom of a multinational corporation.

Writing is thinking. It involves evaluating the information you have gathered and choosing the best way of conveying it to your readers. As you have seen in this chapter, through structure, language and sentence construction you can pull you readers into another world and keep them interested in your story to the very end.

Summary

o   There are a range of structures you can use, depending on the topic and theme of your story.

o   Facts, quotes, anecdotes and theme are the building blocks for most feature articles.

o   There are myriad ways to start your feature; you need to use one that is relevant to your story and that will hook your readers.

o   It's not enough to have a great story idea and a great structure; you also need to develop your language skills to write great articles.

Questions

1 What are the key ingredients of a feature article, and how many ways can you structure one?
2 What methods can you use to keep the interest of your reader, from your lead to the conclusion?
3 What is the point of choosing a theme for your story?
4 Read the *Marie Claire* adoption story at the end of this chapter. What is the theme of this story? (Hint: look at the beginning and the end of the article.) How is this theme revealed and reinforced in the article?

Activities

1 Take a few of your favourite newspaper feature sections, magazines or online sites. Look at the way the journalists have structured the stories. Discuss why you think they decided on the structures and if these structures work.
2 Look at some of your past stories. Could they be improved by a structural change, or the application of theme, or better language techniques? Rework one of your stories with your new knowledge and try to have it published.
3 What makes a story interesting for you? Find some different articles on the same topic. Discuss which ones you find the most interesting and why.

References and additional readings

Burke, C. (2007). 'Lee Miller: portraits of a life', *Marie Claire*.

Cheney, T.A.R. (1991). *Writing Creative Nonfiction*, Berkley, CA: Ten Speed Press.

Cornish, R. (2011). 'Liquid gold', *Gourmet Traveller*, November.

Dunlevy, M. (1988). *Feature Writing*, Melbourne: Deakin University Press.

Field, M. (2008). 'If celebrities can adopt children from overseas ... why can't we?', *Marie Claire*, March.

Granato, L. (1996). 'Techniques of Feature Writing', RJet newswriting course.

Hemingway, E. (1966). *Death in the Afternoon*, Harmondsworth, Middlesex: Penguin.

Latham, E.W. (2007) 'Fabric conditioning', *GQ*, winter.

Levine, J. (2007). 'Billionaires' Ikea: Want to own the chair on which Marie-Antoinette once sat? Knock on this Parisian door', *Forbes*: www.forbes.com/free-forbes/2007/1008/328.htm.

Lewis, S. (2011). 'Crush hour', *Vogue*, September.

McMullen, A. (2011). 'The truth about Jebediah', *Rolling Stone*, May.

Nightingale, E. 'Earl Nightingale quotes', *ThinkExist.com*: http://thinkexist.com/quotation/all_you_need_is_the_plan-the_road_map-and_the/256121.html.

Renkart, E. (2002). 'The power of positivity', *Marie Claire*, October.

Saner, E. (2007). 'Watch out ... there are millions of bedbugs about', *The Guardian*, 2 October.

Smithurst, B. (2011). 'The mane attraction', *FMH*, September.

Spring, A. (2007). 'Screen play', *Vogue*, April.

Valentish, J. (2007). 'Celeb blog fantasies', *Cleo*, May.

Case study

A structural analysis of Melissa Field's story for *Marie Claire* about overseas adoptions

Publication details:

'If celebrities can adopt children from overseas … why can't we?', *Marie Claire*, March 2008.

The author:

Melissa Field

The story:

One of the best ways to understand structure is to read a story and break it down to its building blocks—its lead, conclusion, quotes, facts and anecdotes. This is a great exercise to do with your own work and your favourite features. To get you started we have broken down a 2008 *Marie Claire* article about overseas adoption that follows Dunlevy's fact, quote and anecdote model.

Writing sample

If celebrities can adopt children from overseas ... why can't we?

By Melissa Field, *Marie Claire*, March 2008

	Break-down
Marie Claire story	
AUSTRALIAN REPORT	Section
IF CELEBRITIES CAN ADOPT CHILDREN FROM OVERSEAS ... WHY CAN'T WE?	Headline

Sub-head

Angelina Jolie wants a 'rainbow family', while Madonna has added a Malawian baby to her brood. But if stars can make international adoption seem easy, the reality for Australians is very different. Melissa Field reports on our heartbreaking policies.

In an orphanage in Cali, Colombia, a couple sits nervously, clutching each other's hands as the director shuffles papers on his desk. The air is heavy with humidity and cicadas hum rhythmically outside the open window, a tattered curtain blowing listlessly in the breeze. On the other side of the closed office door, a 15-week-old, chubby-cheeked boy is being carefully dressed by his Spanish-speaking carer, her hands gentle as she eases him into a brand new Bonds jumpsuit. The clothing is a gift from the boy's new parents, the couple who are anxiously anticipating his arrival with repeated, surreptitious glances at the door.

Buttoning the last press-stud with a snap, the carer's young charge is now ready to leave the only home he has ever known to begin a new life on the other side of the world. He gurgles happily, unaware that his life is soon to undergo a profound transformation.

At last, there's a tap at the door and former high-school sweethearts Kylie and Peter Fitzgerald glance at each other, tears shining in their eyes. The small boy is carried into the room and gently placed in Kylie's outstretched arms, while an aide captures this life-changing moment on the couple's video camera. The date is 31 August 2004.

Anecdotal lead
These paragraphs introduce the story by describing someone's personal experience of the issue. In this case, it is the story of a new family brought together by overseas adoption.

Notice the small details used (the weather, the brand of the jumpsuit etc.) which increase the realism of the story.

'This is Julian,' smiles the orphanage director. 'Please, allow me to introduce you to your new son.'

For Sydneysiders Kylie, 34, and Peter, 35, this moment is the culmination of a two and a half year battle to adopt a child—a journey that has cost them thousands of dollars and hours of heartache. Contrast that with the experience of celebrities such as Angelina Jolie and Madonna, who seem to adopt children from overseas with ease. Jolie has even claimed she wants to adopt a 'rainbow family' of children from different countries and cultures.

The difference is that celebrities who adopt from overseas aren't working within the Australian system, points out Ricky Brisson, chief executive officer of Australian Families for Children, a non-profit organisation that supports couples seeking to adopt and helps facilitate overseas adoptions. In the USA, adopting a child from overseas might take just nine months; here, it can take as long as six years. In NSW, couples can expect to spend about $40,000 in the process.

While few would disagree that rigorous background checks are needed to protect children from predators, the adoption process seems mired in bureaucracy, believes psychologist Trudy Rosenwald, who specialises in adoption issues and is herself the mother of two adoptive children from overseas. 'Everyone accepts that safety measures have to be in place to ensure that children are placed in suitable families,' she says. 'The problem here is that the process is often so ambiguous it seems to many prospective parents as if the government agencies responsible are screening out families, rather than screening them in. In principle, it seems like you're deemed not suitable unless you can prove otherwise.'

Problems are compounded by the fact there is no national adoption system. 'Each state and territory in Australia has its own procedure to follow when approving applicants,' confirms Brisson. 'In NSW, the Department of Community Services [DoCS] is responsible for approving all adoption applicants, whether they're applying to adopt locally or internationally. Given DoCS's workload, I don't believe intercountry adoption is their top priority, which slows the process down.'

Quotes
This descriptive anecdote is completed with a quote.
Facts
Following Dunlevy's model, we have begun with an anecdote, then had a quote—and now we are presented with some facts and background information.

The facts continue—the writer explains the Australian situation. The first 'expert' is then introduced to add weight to the information provided.

A new expert is added for a different perspective on the issue.

Quote
It is time to have another voice in the story—that of one of the experts. Paraphrasing is rarely enough.

Another layer of expert testimony.

In late 2005, a report by the House of Representatives' standing committee inquiry into the problem, *Overseas Adoption in Australia*, stated, 'Australia's adoption rate is low and the weight of evidence of delays and hostility faced by the adoption community is too great to ignore.'

But its many recommendations—including the establishment of an intercountry adoption peak body regulated by the attorney-general's department—have been slow to come into effect. The Rudd government has announced plans to streamline the process, and advocates are lobbying hard to persuade politicians to put those plans into action.

Chief among those advocates is Deborra-Lee Furness, wife of Hugh Jackman, with whom she has adopted two children from overseas, Oscar and Ava, now 7 and 2. 'This is a humanitarian issue, and Australia has to step up to the plate and take its share of responsibility for the millions of orphans needing homes in the world,' insists Furness.

'Currently, our record is less than stellar on this. As it stands, Australia is the second lowest country in the world in terms of the numbers of intercountry adoptions we process each year. That fact alone infuriates me.'

In the meantime, abandoned and malnourished children around the world languish in dirty, overcrowded orphanages— or worse, are left to fend for themselves on the streets.

Given up by his young birth mother, who was unable to cope with the arrival of her third child and the breakdown of her relationship with his father, baby Julian's situation was no different from that of countless other adoptees. But he was one of the lucky ones.

'Peter and I feel incredibly blessed to have Julian in our lives and he was worth every hardship we went through to bring him home,' reveals Kylie. 'But we can't help but wonder, did it really have to take so long and be so difficult? I feel for anyone undertaking this process because it's incredibly stressful. You have to be mentally tough to get through it.'

Facts
Some more information—this time from a government source. The number and range of sources used in this story add to its credibility.

Quote
Another new voice—and this is one particularly interesting to the readers of *Marie Claire*. Furness is a famous actress, married to an even more famous actor. Celebrity opinion is always a great way to spark interest in your story and keep your audience reading.

Facts

Anecdote
The writer has encouraged us to read her story through her anecdotal lead, has revealed facts about the case through a range of different sources, and kept us interested through expert and celebrity testimony. Here she again persuades us to keep reading through returning to Kylie and Peter's emotional story.

After years of failing to conceive naturally, and reluctant to submit to the invasiveness and uncertainty of IVF, Kylie and Peter first explored the possibility of adopting in March 2002. Informed by DoCS that they could only apply for approval to adopt once they had attended an overseas adoption information seminar, the couple waited until the following August for a place to become available.

The next step was filling out the intensely personal application form, which thoroughly investigated every aspect of their lives, including finances, medical and career histories, and personal lives. Particular emphasis was placed on how they themselves were parented. Next, they underwent three in-depth interviews with a social worker within a six-week period, after which a detailed report on the couple, and their suitability as parents, was prepared.

The time between lodging an application and obtaining DoCS approval for adoption can be between six and 12 months. The Fitzgeralds lodged their application in August 2002, and were approved by DoCS the following July. Then, their application went to the orphanage of their choice (in their case, Chiquitines in Colombia) and the real waiting game began.

Months crept by. Peter and Kylie were on tenterhooks, continually checking their letterbox and jumping whenever the phone rang, waiting for that elusive call. Finally, on 30 July 2004, DoCS called Peter to say that he and Kylie had been allocated a child and that they should begin to expedite their travel plans to Colombia. One month later, the couple arrived in Cali, ready, at last, to meet their son.

Facts
Here we are given facts about their case which reveal the plight of many similar families.

Facts

Anecdote
Again, the writer ups the emotional tension of the story, explaining not just what Peter and Kylie did, but how they felt.

'The whole process was emotionally gruelling,' recalls Kylie. 'You're living in a heightened state of expectation for months and months, never knowing when or if you'll get the call. You're frightened you'll be rejected, your work suffers, your relationships become strained, and you can think and talk of little else apart from "the process". It's a nightmare to live through, made bearable only when you receive the call saying your child is waiting for you.'

Sitting in a Sydney café, Furness sighs with frustration when she hears stories such as these. After suffering miscarriages and enduring gruelling, yet unsuccessful, attempts at IVF, she and Jackman decided adoption was the best option for them, but it wasn't as straightforward as they had imagined.

'Having been through the pain of trying to conceive, I'd like to see adoption put forward as a choice much earlier in the picture,' she suggests. 'You might spend years on failed IVF attempts, beating up your body with fertility drugs and experiencing heartbreak if it doesn't work for you. Why not at least promote the alternative so that people know there are other options?'

Instead, when Furness and Jackman started their adoption journey 12 years ago, they quickly realised that Australia's system would be difficult to navigate. 'We went to an adoption information evening hosted by the Department of Child Services in Victoria, and the whole vibe was so intimidating, so negative and so disheartening that Hugh and I left before the tea and cookies—and I really like tea and cookies!' She's laughing, but it's clear Furness still feels angry. 'Before our eyes, Hugh and I just saw a whole roomful of people simply deflate, so I looked at my husband and said, "We're not doing this," and we left.'

That Furness possessed US residency meant the couple were able to pursue their adoption dream with an independent US agency. But she's all too aware that she and Jackman are often viewed negatively by the press, which slams celebrities for 'shopping for children' overseas—and it riles her.

Quotes
More than just an explanation of the adoption process; the following quotes from Kylie and Furness reveal their characters and the highs and lows of their experiences. This style of quotation encourages empathy between the reader and the speakers.

Anecdotal quote
Here we see into Furness's life— and through her own words. This further establishes the relationship between speaker and reader.

Facts

'We had another option available to us and we took it,' argues Furness. 'We know how lucky we were to have that choice. Having a baby is absolutely not a fashion statement. Who in their right mind would take on a child as a publicity stunt?

'It infuriates me that ignorant and mean-spirited people say Madonna and Angelina are just trying to create designer families for themselves, when what they're actually doing is giving needy children a chance in life. I'm thrilled they've brought attention to the issue. They could be out partying every night, but instead they're highlighting a problem that has simply been ignored for far too long.'

But it's the apparent ease with which celebrities are able to adopt that has many ordinary couples scratching their heads at the disparity between the adoptions they read about and their own tortuous progress. 'The expediency of "celebrity adoptions" is usually due to the fact that they're adopting through private agencies authorised to process the adoption,' says Brisson. 'They're at an economic advantage; they're able to pay for multiple agencies and legal teams to work on their behalf.'

As Furness recalls of her and Jackman's experience: 'The whole process in the US took us nine months. Here in Australia, to adopt a child from overseas you're sometimes looking at an average six-year wait. Six years! It's insane. If numerous other countries around the world can do their due-diligence checks and make this happen so much faster, why can't we? If intercountry adoption was a business here, we'd be saying, "Sack the CEO. It ain't working!"'

Furness was inspired to lend her voice to the campaign to overhaul our adoption system by one case in particular—that of adoptive mother Diana Liu and her daughter Zhen. When Liu's elderly parents found an abandoned baby in a village north of Beijing, Liu, a 39-year-old banking executive and Australian permanent resident, adopted the now three year old after her biological parents could not be traced.

Quote

Facts

Quotes
Here, expert testimony is used to reveal the experience of another interviewee.

Quotes
Back to Furness for more of her story. As you can see it is often much better to let interviewees speak for themselves—you gain great lines like 'Sack the CEO'—rather than to paraphrase their words.

Facts

Having been granted a Chinese adoption order, Liu has been unable to obtain a visa for her daughter to live permanently in Australia because she failed to go through the correct Australian adoption procedures.

Today, Zhen is living with Liu's parents, who are struggling to cope with a lively toddler. Immigration lawyers are acting on Liu's behalf in a bid to overturn the previous federal government's ruling that Zhen should be denied a visa. The case is still pending, and now rests solely on the ability of new Immigration Minister Senator Chris Evans to grant Zhen a visa on compassionate grounds.

An angry Furness says, 'I believe in the law, absolutely, but what I can't stand is injustice, and to me, Diana had no choice. What was she supposed to do? Leave Zhen on the streets or in an orphanage where she'll become institutionalised?'

Whatever the trials, inconveniences and heartaches involved in adopting a child from overseas, it's a struggle few families regret undertaking. In fact, Kylie and Peter are nearing the end of the process for a second time, hoping to welcome into their small family a Colombian sibling for Julian, who turns four in May. 'We've been approved to adopt for a second time. Now, we're just waiting for the phone call telling us our second child is waiting,' says Kylie, ruefully.

As for Julian, he is a happy toddler who chats continually, has exceptional manners and loves the family dog, Lucy, The Wiggles, *Thomas the Tank Engine* and, of course, Mummy and Daddy. Aware that he's from Colombia and that his birth mother still lives there, he is a well-adjusted child, secure in the knowledge that he is loved unconditionally.

'In some ways, the adoption process has been similar to how biological mothers describe childbirth,' muses Kylie. 'The pain is intense, but it's forgotten as soon as you meet your child. That has totally been our experience with Julian. Despite the agony we went through to become his parents, all he has to do is smile at us for Peter and I to be reminded that he was unquestionably worth the pain.'

For more information on intercountry adoption, visit the Australian Families for Children website at www.australiansadopt.org.

Anecdote
Here we have the introduction of another touching story. Not only does this tragic tale keep us reading, but it adds more weight to the argument that many people in Australia suffer due to adoption regulations.

Quote

Facts

Anecdote/bookend
Here we return to Julian, Kylie and Peter. This is a classic bookend structure. The article began with the couple adopting Julian and ends with him happily ensconced in his Australian life (and the family awaiting a new addition).
This ending not only offers a satisfying conclusion—emotionally and structurally—but offers a ray of hope. Adoption is worth all the pain and there is something you, the reader, can do to help.

BREAKOUT BOX 1

Adoption: the facts

Australia is second only to the UK in having the lowest rate of overseas adoptions among developed countries.

In 2005–06, 576 babies were adopted in Australia, 421 of those from overseas. In the same year, there were 155 adoptions of Australian children, with just 60 of those placed with families where there was no known relationship (i.e. a carer, step-parent or relative) between the parent and child.

In both local and intercountry adoptions, 91% of children were younger than five, with more than half of these aged younger than 12 months.

Adoptions overall have fallen drastically in Australia from a peak of almost 10,000 in 1971–72 to 764 in 1993–94, as fewer Australian mothers put their children up for adoption.

Every state and territory in Australia is party to the Hague Convention on Protection of Children and Co-operation in Respect of Intercountry Adoption. The convention was set up to establish international procedures and safeguarding measures to protect children. Australia ratified the convention in 1998, allowing us to facilitate adoptions from donor Hague Convention countries such as China, Colombia, Ethiopia and the Philippines.

Source: Adoptions Australia 2005–06, Australian Institute Of Health and Welfare.

Breakout boxes
Often a story will have at least one breakout box. A story of this length warrants a couple more.
The boxes have two functions.
The first and second boxes offer background information about adoption, while the third reveals what readers can do if they have felt moved by the story.

BREAKOUT BOX 2

Where do our adoptive children come from?

28% from China

Adoption is still considered a taboo subject in China. Its first overseas adoptions to the US occurred in 1988, with official legislation being put in place in 1992. Since then, China's one-child policy and its citizens' desire for sons has meant that increasing numbers of abandoned children have been put up for adoption. In 2005, about 8000 Chinese children were granted US immigration visas after being adopted by American families, while 140 children came to Australia.

24% from South Korea

South Korea has the world's oldest international adoption program, with more than 200,000 children adopted internationally since the mid-1950s. The program started after many children fathered by American soldiers during the Korean War were given up for adoption.

17% from Ethiopia

The HIV/AIDS crisis in Africa has led to an increase in the number of Ethiopian children being adopted overseas. Most go to the US, France, Ireland and Australia.

Source: Adoptions Australia 2005–06,
Australian Institute of Health and Welfare.

BREAKOUT BOX 3

How you can make a difference

Deborra-Lee Furness, Australian Families for Children and other agencies believe intercountry adoption needs to be streamlined and improved. They recommend the following:

- A federal peak body for intercountry adoption in line with recommendations made to parliament in 2005.
- The introduction of national, uniform procedures for intercountry adoption, so the process is the same for all Australian families.
- Tax relief for families who adopt children from overseas.

If you'd like to lobby the federal government to act on this issue, visit www.marieclaire.com.au, sign our petition and we'll forward your responses to the new Minister for Families, Jenny Macklin.

7
Getting into Character

You can tell a lot about a fellow's character by his way of eating jellybeans.

Ronald Reagan, 1981

Objectives

In this chapter you will learn how to take your feature stories to the next level—to improve your work with well-defined characters, telling quotes and dialogue, rich descriptions and your own point of view. The chapter covers:

o   character

o   quotes

o   dialogue

o   description

o   point of view

o   a Case study: How Rebecca Skloot finds stories and creates characters

o   a Writing sample: 'Fixing Nemo' by Rebecca Skloot, *The New York Times*, 2 May 2004.

Character—building the 'who' of the story

If you think about the stories that have meant something to you in the past, you will find they probably have one thing in common. Whether they were true stories told to you about friends or family, whether you read them on a website or in a magazine, or whether they were fictional stories in a novel or a film, you will find that it was the people in the stories that made them memorable. In screenwriting it is said that all stories should be character-driven. This is not a bad lesson to consider when you sit down to write a feature story. Humans are a narcissistic lot, and we love hearing about ourselves and about others whose experiences touch our lives. You can tap into this by developing characters in your feature stories.

This character development can be small; for example, you could add a few descriptions and pithy quotes to reveal a slice of someone's personality, or you could write profiles that are virtual character studies—written to reveal every aspect of the subject's personality (see the discussion in Chapter 12 on writing profiles).

But why bother revealing character in a feature story? There are two reasons. The first is that having a number of fleshed-out characters in a story makes it more interesting to read. Imagine reading a novel where you knew nothing about the people in the story, where only the events were explained. It wouldn't be much of a read, that's for sure. It is much the same for a feature story. If you want readers to accompany you over hundreds, even thousands, of words, you will need more than some great facts and a snazzy structure—you will need to populate your story with real people.

The second reason to make characters out of your sources is to affect your reader on an emotional level. This will encourage them to stick with your feature until the end, and may even help you to show them a new way of thinking or feeling about an issue or event.

When we use the word 'character' in the world of journalism, we are using it in a slightly different context from that of novelists or screenwriters. When you sit down to write a piece of fiction, you start with a blank slate. You have to build up your characters from scratch, inventing each facet of their personality, from their favourite ice cream flavour to the defining moments in their childhood. When you create characters for fiction, you may borrow pieces of real people you know—their mannerisms, part of their history, their aversion to broccoli etc.—but in the end these are fictional characters, creations of the imagination.

But in journalism nothing can be made up, fabricated, imagined or invented. The writer must stick to the facts. So in features your 'characters' are real people with real backgrounds and personality quirks. While in fiction you rely on your imagination for these things, in features you must discover them through interviewing, researching and observing. You will learn to understand the subjects of your features and then you will pass this knowledge on to your readers through quotes, dialogue and description. Journalists have one other important restriction—time and space: you won't always have a lot of time to study or observe your subject and you certainly won't have a lot of space to explain them to your readers. So you need to think about the best ways to communicate the character.

In Chapter 4 you learned about the interviewing skills you need to understand and reveal character in features. Interviewing is the main way to garner the information you need to present well-rounded characters. Remember Hemingway's iceberg effect from Chapter 6? You need thousands of words of background information for a story of only a few hundred words. You need to understand the subject of your story in great depth so you can present a smaller, but nevertheless accurate, portrait of the person for your readers. This involves two sets of interviews.

The first interviews are with the subjects of your feature. They need to be in-depth, so spend as much time as you can with your interviewees. If possible, take a leaf from the naturalist's book and observe the subject in their natural environment. If you are writing about a group of entrepreneurs, try to see them at work in their office; visit the doctor in the hospital, talk to the chef in the kitchen, or the golfer on the green. But for a great story, you should also try to see the subject away from their power-base—organise a second meeting at their home, or where they relax. The way their character shifts (or doesn't) in different settings will tell you a great deal about who they really are.

But don't only write down what your subject says in response to your questions; also note how your subject treats others. Mike Grenby, a syndicated columnist and feature writer (and the subject of the case study on pp. 204–7), once interviewed a businessman who purported to be a great humanitarian; but when he observed him ordering his secretary around like a slave, Grenby knew this man might not really reflect the image created in his media releases. He conducted some more interviews, did a little digging and had a much better story—thanks to his observation skills—than he would have had if he had stuck to what had been said in the PR blurb.

If your story is a character profile, or if your feature relies on a deep understanding or drawing of characters (such as a story on the effect of an event on an individual, community or group), you will need to do more than interview the subjects of your story. You'll need a second set of interviews. These will be with the people in your subjects' lives.

Imagine a profile piece on a young celebrity whose life had begun to spiral out of control. You would interview her, asking about the price of fame, the pressures of stardom, her hopes for the future etc. From this interview you would have a pretty good story that showed how this young woman had fallen from grace but wished to rise again. But imagine how much richer the story would be if you interviewed her friends—those who had known her before she was a star, others she'd come to know more recently. Then you could speak to other people in her life, such as her parents, fellow patients at her rehab centre, or her agents. Can you imagine how much better you would understand this celebrity now? You would know where she had come from and who she had been before she was propelled into the spotlight. You would know what the influential people in her life wanted the world to know about her, and what image of the girl observers of her less-than-glamorous moments had taken with them. This would make your feature more than the stock-standard superficial celebrity profile; this could now be a story with emotional depth, one that might touch on the truth of this young woman's life.

Whether you are writing a feature about a celebrity, a sports star or someone in your community, this depth of interviewing and observation will enrich your feature and take it to the next level. You may even produce a piece of creative non-fiction, a style of feature with characters so real that your work reads almost like a novel, though it still sticks to the facts.

Quotes—getting to know you

Chapter 6 outlined some of the many feature article structures. While a detailed character study might not be appropriate for a simple list story, or a 300-word bullet point 'how to', many other feature styles lend themselves to some level of character development.

In the last chapter we also looked at how quotes are necessary to provide expert opinion and different points of view for your story, as well as adding flavour to your features. In this chapter we take quotes to another level. Here you will learn how to use them to reveal character and even how to include dialogue in your stories.

When you write hard news, you have to give people information, quickly and efficiently. This often means taking quotes and paraphrasing them into news language. While paraphrasing is still a useful tool in features, you can greatly enhance your work by letting your interviewees talk for themselves.

Hugh Lunn, a Walkley Award-winning journalist and author of memoirs such as *Over the Top with Jim* (1999), said that paraphrased quotes are often the death of a feature story. 'A lot of people, when they write features, they have all the people they interview sound the same, so they're sort of short-handing them and writing their own version of what they said' (Lunn, in Blair, 2007).

As an example of how using what people say, rather than summarising their speech, can reveal a great deal about their character, Lunn used an incident involving colourful former Queensland Premier Sir Joh Bjelke-Petersen. 'You could say he said that: "The government is in a lot of trouble," or he could say, "They have one leg on each side of a barbed wire fence," which is what he would've said' (Lunn, in Blair, 2007).

What Lunn is revealing is that when you let people talk for themselves, you allow them to reveal parts of their personalities and, as an added bonus, you have much more interesting turns of phrase (such as the 'barbed wire fence' line) than you might have been able to come up with. Bjelke-Petersen had a reputation for mangling the language and referred to his press conferences as 'feeding the chooks', but his individual speaking style disguised a cunning political mind. It was that obvious tension between his political power and the cultivated ordinariness that helped illuminate how Bjelke-Petersen operated. And quotations such as the one above demonstrate that.

As we begin to know someone, we start to care about them a little, particularly if they are a sympathetic character. Their words help us to understand who they are and help us to sympathise with their predicament. As this sympathy is built into a feature story over a few lines, or a few paragraphs, we find an interviewee's words add more impact to the article.

This can be seen in an investigative piece published in *Marie Claire* magazine, which looked at the effect of DNA testing on securing the release of prisoners who were, in fact, innocent. The journalist, Claire Scobie, began her story by looking at two people touched by this technology: Jennifer Thompson, a rape victim, and Ronald Cotton, the man who was wrongfully convicted of the crime. It is through Thompson's quotes that we learn about the brutal attack and its effect on her.

Think about the difference in your understanding of the story from reading these two different accounts. The first uses paraphrasing, the second uses quotes.

1 Not long afterwards, Thompson was sitting, shaking and frightened, in a hospital cubicle when she heard a woman crying. A detective told her it was the other rape victim. Thompson says her heart broke; she empathised with the woman and knew she had to see her attacker brought to justice.

2 Not long afterwards, Thompson was sitting, shaking and frightened, in a hospital cubicle when she heard a woman crying. A detective told her it was the other rape victim. 'My heart broke,' she says. 'I knew how she was feeling and I was determined to nail whoever did it. I wanted him to burn in hell' (Scobie, 2004, p. 69).

As you can see, the second version is more revealing about Thompson's character and has more impact. It is also, obviously, the paragraph used in the *Marie Claire* article. From the quotes, we can sense the rage that boiled in Thompson in that hospital room, we can see the strength of her character, and we can understand the level of her compassion for the other victim. From the first version, we can feel sorry for her predicament and can be encouraged by her conviction to see her attacker behind bars, but not much more.

When it comes to your feature stories, remember to search in your interview transcripts for those all-revealing quotes. They will open your readers' eyes to the people you are writing about and give your story more impact than you could have produced with your words alone.

Dialogue—discussion for discovery

If you can see how one or two pithy quotes can spice up your feature and reveal character to your readers, imagine what you can do with dialogue. Dialogue is more than quotes strung together; it represents the way people really communicate with each other, such as their ticks, speech patterns and rhythm. Thus, a section of dialogue will take up a great deal more space than one or two quotes, so it works best in longer pieces of journalism.

There is another big difference between quotes and dialogue. Quotes are generally an interviewee's responses to a reporter's prepared questions. Dialogue, on the other hand, is most often the transcription of a spontaneous conversation between people. Through this spontaneity you will give readers a much more realistic view of the characters in your story (though you are still hampered by the fact that few people are completely relaxed in front of a journalist).

We see dialogue mostly in features that would be classified as creative non-fiction and in longer stories that would be published in literary journals or as books. There is a telling piece of dialogue in Margaret Simons' feature on the drug war in Manila, which appeared in *The Monthly* (2016). Filipino police Superintendent Redentor Ulsano is explaining to Simons the shooting death of a drug pusher.

> It was a buy-bust operation, he says. Undercover police went to purchase drugs, and then arrested the pusher…They were bringing him to the police station when he seized a policeman's gun and tried to shoot. The police killed him in self-defence.
>
> 'How many shots were there, sir?'
> 'One.'
> 'We heard five or six.'
> 'What? What did you say?'
> 'We heard six shots.'
> Ulsano stares and does not reply…
> 'Do your officers often make mistakes of this sort?'
> For the first time Ulsano looks angry.
> 'There is no mistake. It is not a mistake defending yourself, especially if you are in imminent danger of losing your life.'
>
> Simons, 2016

In this piece of dialogue Simons outlines her scepticism about what she has seen and heard. Like all good reporters, she is intent on testing the evidence before her. And in doing so, she reveals the police superintendent's defiant insistence on his version of events. At the heart of the dialogue is a cultural gap— that the Filipino police are determined to rid Manila of the drug scourge, even if it means operating outside the conventional standards of policing as we understand it. One of the most telling parts of the exchange is not what is said but rather what is not said—Ulsan's silence on the number of shots fired could be that he does know for sure or, as seems more likely, he is trying to communicate his version of what happened. And that's the beauty of dialogue—sometimes, the silences—or the physical actions of touching a nose, smoothing hair, averting eyes, staring out the window—can provide the feature writer with some extra telling detail that works in contrast to the dialogue.

To capture dialogue it is usually necessary to implement what is called 'immersion' reporting, or participant observation. This method comes from the work of the 'New Journalists', a group of unconventional writers in the 1960s and 1970s who were famous for returning to a literary style. Immersion involves spending time with the subjects of your stories, getting the feel of the locations, almost becoming part of people's lives—watching them in the mundane, as well as extraordinary, moments. This takes time, so it's not for everyone—especially not someone who has only a day or two before their story is due—but it adds more depth and power to your story than you can imagine. But don't forget, you can use other parts of your life— social, university studies, work—as fodder for your immersion reporting.

When Ted Conover—the author of a number of non-fiction books, including the lauded *Newjack* (2001)—was still at university, he decided to take time off to ride the trains with homeless people. A year later, he took his adventures and went back to university, where he turned them into his anthropology thesis. Another year later he published his first book, a creative non-fiction piece called *Rolling Nowhere* (1984). Through this experience Conover discovered that journalism and anthropology have a great deal to learn from each other:

> Participant observation, which is the anthropological method, is the way I prefer to pursue journalism. It means a reliance not on the interview so much as on the shared experience with somebody. The idea to me that journalism and anthropology go together, which sort of dawned on me while I was writing *Rolling Nowhere* (1984), was a great enabling idea for my life—the idea that I could learn about different people and different aspects of the world by placing myself in situations and thereby see more than you ever could by just doing an interview.
>
> Conover, in Sims, 1995, pp. 12–13

Sally Sara would agree. In her *Vogue* article on her journey discovering the lives of women in Africa, this Australian television and print journalist wrote about the lengths she was willing to go to for a great story:

> 'You can go in the shrine, but you must take off your top, Madam.' 'Sorry?' 'Madam, take off your top.'
>
> The village elders were staring at me. I threw a desperate look at my interpreter. He nodded. Bloody hell. I'd been shot at, chased and mobbed, but I'd never gone topless for a story.
>
> 'You must remove your shirt to enter the shrine. It's the rules.'
>
> The men were already getting undressed and wrapping brightly coloured cloths around their waists. I undid my shirt, one button at a time, slowly weighing up whether to pull out or not ...
>
> ... I had travelled hundreds of kilometres to reach this village in Ghana, and spent more than an hour trying to talk our way into the shrine. I was determined to see a priest who had held dozens of local women and girls in sexual slavery. I'd been interviewing one of his victims for the past week and I knew I couldn't write her story without seeing this man for myself.
>
> Sara, 2007, p. 44

In both Conover and Sara's cases, their immersion in their subjects' worlds enabled them to listen to the way people speak when they are not being interviewed. It also allowed them to have interactions as people (not just as journalists), and this makes for great dialogue.

There are risks, some very serious, when you immerse yourself in a situation while gathering the material you need, whether you do it by travelling with the homeless, visiting a new country, touring with a gothic band, witnessing a religious cult, or something else. Make sure you examine all the problems and dangers that can arise when you plant yourself in a world you may not have experienced before. Discuss these risks with someone who is knowledgeable in the area, and only set out on the adventure if you are fully prepared. Even then, be ready to walk out on the story if your safety is compromised.

There are two other dangers involved with dialogue. While they may not harm you physically, they may kill your story. The first writing pitfall to avoid is using dialogue as exposition. Exposition is a term often used in the world of film and is nicely satirised in the *Austin Powers* movies through the character Basil Exposition. This character does what you are never supposed to do: in his dialogue he simply *tells* the audience about other characters or situations, rather than doing what you are meant to do, which is to *show* your audience a character and their world through their own actions and dialogue.

For example, in the first *Austin Powers* film, Basil Exposition arrives and explains information that the characters, and the audience, already know. We enter the scene as the glove compartment in Austin's car revolves to reveal a picture phone—with the caller's name and position shown on the phone: 'Basil Exposition, Chief of British Intelligence'.

> BASIL EXPOSITION: Hello, Austin. This is Basil Exposition, Chief of British Intelligence. You're Austin Powers, International Man of Mystery, and you're with Agent Mrs Kensington. The year is 1967, and you're talking on a picture phone.
>
> AUSTIN: We know all that, Exposition.

Myers, 1997

Beware of such information dumping—now that it has been satirised on the big screen, your efforts on the page will only seem laughable to newspaper and magazine editors.

The second writing danger is to become too florid with your dialogue attribution—the short descriptions of who has spoken. There are few occasions when you should deviate from the old favourite: 'he said' or 'she said' (or 'says', depending on the tense you are using). A few variations on the theme are acceptable ('answered', 'explained', 'asked'), but other tag lines ('uttered', 'contended', 'espoused') can become intrusive in the sentence and break the flow of the story. If you feel you need to stray from 'said' in your story, do so sparingly and always with good reason.

Using the simple 'said' is great, but be careful you don't rely on adverbs (words that describe verbs and usually end in -ly) or adverbial phrases (two or more words that act as an adverb) to punch up the dialogue. The parts of conversation you have chosen to include in your story should stand alone, without needing what the horror writer Stephen King calls 'Swifties'. The term 'Swifties' comes from the name of the action-adventure hero of Victor Appleton II's books, Tom Swift. Appleton was known for adverb-laden attributions such as: '"Do your worst," Tom cried *bravely*.' King remembers a party game where the child with the wittiest 'Swifty' would be pronounced the winner. Memorable efforts included:

'You got a nice butt, lady,' he said *cheekily*.

'I'm the plumber,' he said *with a flush.*

King, 2000, p. 141.

Use dialogue in your stories to reveal character and bring the reality of the new world to your readers; just remember to avoid the pitfalls and you'll be another step closer to a great feature story.

Description—show, don't tell

'Show, don't tell' is one of the classic writing adages. But what does it mean and how does doing it reveal character? What this adage asks of you is to be creative and detailed, to be specific and expansive. Not only will you reveal the characters in your feature articles by doing this, but descriptions (when done well) are entertaining and will help keep your readers' attention on your words and away from the report on the latest tax hikes, or hem lengths, on page 24.

What if you are following in the footsteps of Hunter S. Thompson and writing about life in a bikie gang? You have begun to follow one of the gang members around and have recorded swathes of dialogue, but once you sit down at the computer, how will you describe him? You have two methods at your disposal: summary and description (Cheney, 1991).

With the summary method you will *tell* your readers what the bikie looked like and what he was interested in (Cheney, 1991). For example:

He was six foot four and liked loose women.

With the descriptive method you will *show* your readers the bikie and his character:

When he walked into the room, the men noticed him as much as the women. He towered over everyone, a walking totem pole clad in leather. His eyes flicked around the crowd, resting in the cleavage of a young, sequined dancer who had downed one martini too many.

Through both methods we find out that the man is tall. In the summary method we discover his height in inches, but we learn nothing about the way the man's height manifests itself. In the descriptive version we are given a much better idea of the 'who' of the story. It is revealed that the man towers over the crowd and the metaphor of the totem pole is used. Through these descriptions we realise that his height is a tool of power.

The summary method also *tells* us he is attracted to women of a particular type. But the descriptive method *shows* us his predatory nature by describing the way his eyes move and where they fall. That metaphor of the totem pole adds to this information. While in the first instance it informs us about the man's height, in the second it points to his personality, his animalism and, considering the size and shape of totem poles, his overt sexuality.

Think about the different ways you can describe something to keep your work interesting and to reveal character. For example, the woman in the sequin dress isn't 'sexy', or a 'temptress'; try writing something like:

She walked like molten gold, her hips swayed hypnotically under the shimmering fabric, her green eyes bore into me and I knew I was hers.

132 | Part A: Mastering the Techniques

Think about the difference in the ways your readers will view a character in your article, depending on the verbs you choose: 'she *strode* through the office' or 'she *slunk* through the office' or 'she *tottered* through the office'. Take the time to consider your choice of verbs, and remember the simplest is not always the best. If that woman was described as just '*walking* through the office', we would learn almost nothing about her.

Don't forget that it's not just what someone does or says that reveals their character. Descriptions of their surroundings and possessions can add a great deal. For example, you are interviewing a well-known, curmudgeonly writer in his home. You have described what the place looks like and described his outward appearance. You have noted his speech and the dialogue between him and his long-suffering wife. Then a cat leaps into his lap and he strokes it as he talks to you. You could, and should, mention the cat; it adds a warm dimension to his personality—but remember also to add the specific details. The man who loves his old and scarred ginger tomcat is very different from a man who obsesses about a diamante-bow-wearing Persian called Pookie.

The key to description is to note down every detail you see and hear, and to remember that the uninspired writer will *tell* the reader about a subject, place or personality, but the great writer will *show* that subject, place or personality in action.

Point of view—putting yourself in the picture

A great deal of time has been spent in this chapter discussing how to create characters from the people you witness and interview as part of your stories. But there is one other character you can't forget: yourself.

Often the journey you take while researching a story is so interesting that it begs to be included when you sit down to write. Or you might find that what you have discovered is so strange that your readers will appreciate having your voice to guide them through this new environment. The key is to know when it's time to speak up in your stories and when it's best to hide behind your byline and keep your opinions to yourself.

Most feature stories are written in the third person, with an impartial narrator who is a collator of information, or perhaps a witness to events. When the third person is used, people are mentioned as 'he' or 'she'; 'I' is never used—the journalist is endeavouring to be unbiased and not force their point of view in the story. For example:

> Jane walked into the blood bank and looked at the anxious men and women who were waiting
> for test results, and for the needle. She didn't want to be there either.

Writing in the second person is probably the least-used technique in feature stories. This is when the journalist writes the story through 'your' eyes, for example:

> You walk into the blood bank and look at the anxious men and women who wait for test results,
> and for the needle. You don't want to be here either.

It is often too distracting to keep this point of view throughout a story. However, this shouldn't be confused with the often-used technique of referring to the reader in a story. Most glossy women's magazines will speak directly to the reader, particularly in the headlines and subheadings. For example:

Headline: 'Our testing times'

Subheading: 'Thought you couldn't face getting tested? You can't afford not to.'

But the story itself will be written in the *third person*, with the occasional reference to the reader, *not* written through the eyes of the reader. For example:

> Jane walked into the blood bank and looked at the anxious men and women who were waiting for test results, and for the needle. Just like you, she didn't want to be there.

Then we have the first person—the 'I' story—where the writer takes the stage. For example:

> I walked into the blood bank and looked at the anxious men and women who were waiting for test results, and for the needle. I didn't want to be there either.

This technique is often used in works of creative non-fiction, whether they are memoirs, travel books, or one of the enormous number of harrowing stories from foreign correspondents that have hit the shelves in the past few years. The first person is also used in a range of magazines, including *Vogue*, *Vanity Fair*, *Esquire*, *Playboy*, *The Monthly*, and in most major newspapers.

Ted Conover, the writer who lived with the homeless for his thesis, realised the value of the first person when he turned his academic work into a piece of journalism:

> After I finished my anthropology thesis, an ethnography of railroad tramp life, I felt I had left out one of the most interesting things, which was what it was like for a person from a relatively sheltered middle-class background like me to live this way.

Conover, in Sims, 1995, p. 12

You too may find that you have a unique view on a situation, which might add more weight, power or interest to a story. In the book *War Reporting for Cowards* (2005), British journalist Chris Ayres takes the reader through his experiences of the horrors of 9/11, the anthrax attacks and the Iraq War. This is not just another report on modern conflicts; Ayres' work is fresh because of his unique voice. His tales are interesting because they relate these events through the eyes of someone who is afraid of everything around him. Who could say they wouldn't be even a little scared if bullets were zinging around their head, or if anthrax was mailed to their workplace? Not many, and Ayres taps into this potential for empathy between reader and writer.

In the following passage, Ayres is at a media initiation in Kuwait, preparing to be 'embedded' with the American troops in Iraq, and failing miserably at donning his gas mask:

> 'This guy,' [Lieutenant Tiffany Powers, army instructor] said, red-faced and pointing at me, 'is one very dead media representative. But well done the rest of you.'
>
> I made a second attempt to don the gas mask, with more success. My stubble, however, seemed to interfere with the seal. It was then I remembered reading somewhere that embeds had to remain clean-shaven. It made sense now. I was glad I had brought my Mach 3 razors and badger-hair shaving brush.
>
> By now I felt as though I'd lost 10lb in body weight through sweating alone. Inside my mask, I could feel beads of salt water drip on my nose. I instinctively lifted a gloved hand to scratch it.

The mask, of course, made it impossible. I felt dizzy. I needed a drink of water. Badly. I started to panic.

'Now we're going to learn how to rehydrate in a chemical environment,' said Powers. She lifted up an NBC-proof water canteen, pulled out a plastic drinking tube, and fitted it to a sealed attachment on her gas mask. It looked easy enough. In practice, however, I found it impossible to handle the canteen with my gloves, and I couldn't find the sealed attachment on my mask. I ended up pulling off the mask in frustration, unscrewing the canteen, and taking a swig.

I gave Powers a defiant look.

'Tut, tut,' she said, waving a thick finger. 'Dead again.'

Ayres, 2005, p. 174

Through Ayres' words we become sympathetic towards him, we learn what it must really feel like to step into a war zone, and we are interested in gaining a fresh perspective on what is normally viewed as the gung ho, bulletproof war correspondent.

In *Vogue*, we see another way to draw your point of view into the story. In Clare Press's article 'Stuff and nonsense', we find a discussion of the culture of acquisition—the desperation to have, despite having too much, in a world of excess. Her story begins:

Nutty the Cracker is an Alessi-made device featuring a very pleasing brown polyamide squirrel sitting atop an aluminium bowl. You slide a hazelnut under its cutesy metal teeth, push down and bob's your uncle: the nut's edible interior is released. This gadget is yours for $98 and, hey presto! you've got more stuff with which to fill your kitchen cupboards. You can, of course, buy the nuts ready shelled for $4.95. You can, but I didn't. I was seduced by the squirrel, you see.

Press, 2007, p. 106

Press introduces us to the topic not through facts and figures, or expert testimony, but through an anecdote from her own life. Here, she says, look at this: we're all susceptible to the gaggle of useless objects vying for our dollars. We, the readers, smile at her story and remember the many times we have been sucked in by some unnecessary trinket. Press has encouraged almost a friendship between writer and reader, formed a relationship with us so we will read her story to the end.

Ayres' and Press's pieces are, to take a phrase from the world of magazine writing, both DOs. Now let's look at the DON'Ts of the first-person point of view:

- Don't bring yourself into the story for just one or two comments—you must be a presence throughout the story.

- Don't bring yourself into the story in the middle or the end—your first 'I' should appear by the third paragraph, if not before. There are some good exceptions to this rule, but not too many, and all of them are written by very experienced feature writers.

- Don't put yourself into the story without a very good reason: a fresh perspective, to interpret a difficult-to-understand concept, to add humanity to an otherwise bleak or technical topic. You are a journalist, not a celebrity.

Summary

o To make your features more interesting, take your sources and flesh them out (only using real facts, not your imagination) so they become fully formed characters.

o Use telling quotes instead of paraphrasing—this technique helps to illustrate someone's character and keep your readers involved in your story.

o In longer feature stories and in book-length creative non-fiction, use dialogue to reveal the way your characters really speak and relate to others.

o Get out there and experience your stories; don't just sit at your desk researching with the internet and phone.

o Watch out for adverbs in your attributions, and for exposition in your dialogue.

o Show, don't tell, with your descriptions.

o Use detail to highlight a person's character.

o Utilise the first-person point of view to bring your unique understanding of a situation to a story.

Questions

1 What are the pros and cons of including dialogue in your feature story?
2 What are some of the ways you can use detail to reveal character?
3 When is it a good idea to use the first-person point of view in a feature story?

Activities

1 Pick up copies of *Vogue*, *The Monthly*, *Vanity Fair* and *Rolling Stone*. Find three feature stories that appeal to you. With different-coloured pens, highlight sections of character descriptions, telling quotes, dialogue and evidence of first-person point of view. How do the stories compare?
   a Which stories use more of the techniques than the others?
   b Which stories do you prefer, and why?
   c Do points a and b have anything to do with each other?

2 Practise writing descriptions. Describe someone in your family by using the summary method—*tell* the reader what they looked like and what they were doing at a given moment in time. Now describe this person using the descriptive method—*show* the reader what they looked like and what they were doing.

3 Find one of the feature stories you have written in the past and look at the point of view in the story. Now change the point of view: take one of the paragraphs and put it in the second person, the first person or the third. Ask yourself the following questions:
   a Has the story improved or is it worse for the change?
   b Has the market for the story changed?
   c Would readers better understand the story now?

References and additional reading

Ayres, C. (2005). *War Reporting for Cowards: Between Iraq and a Hard Place*, London: John Murray.

Blair, M. (2007). 'Putting the storytelling back into stories: Creative non-fiction in tertiary journalism education', PhD thesis, Bond University, Gold Coast, Qld: http://epublications.bond.edu.au/theses/blair.

Cheney, T.A.R. (1991). *Writing Creative Nonfiction*, Berkley, CA: Ten Speed Press.

Conover, T. (1984). *Rolling Nowhere: Riding the Rails with America's Hoboes*, New York: Vintage Books.

King, S. (2000). *On Writing*, London: Hodder & Stoughton.

Lunn, H. (1999). *Over the Top with Jim*, St Lucia, Qld: University of Queensland Press.

MacDonald, S. (2002). *Holy Cow! An Indian Adventure*, Sydney: Bantam Books.

Myers, M. (writer) (1997). *Austin Powers: International Man of Mystery* (D. Moore, M. Myers, J. Todd & S. Todd (producers)), USA: New Line Home Entertainment.

Press, C. (2007). 'Stuff and nonsense', *Vogue Australia*, April.

Reagan, R. (1981). in *The New York Times*, 15 January.

Sara, S. (2007). 'Out of Africa', *Vogue Australia*, August.

Scobie, C. (2004). 'I spent 19 years in jail for a crime I didn't commit', *Marie Claire*, March.

Simons, M. (2016). 'Duterte's Dirty War', *The Monthly*, December–January.

Sims, N. (1995). 'The art of literary journalism', in N. Sims & M. Kramer (eds), *Literary Journalism*, New York: Ballantine Books.

Case study

How Rebecca Skloot finds stories and creates characters

Publication details:

'Fixing Nemo', *The New York Times*, 2 May 2004.

The author:

Rebecca Skloot is a freelance science writer who has taught creative writing and science journalism at the University of Memphis, the University of Pittsburgh and New York University. She has written feature stories, essays and reviews for *The New York Times* and *New York Times Magazine, O: The Oprah Magazine, Columbia Journalism Review, New York Magazine, Glamour* and many others. She also wrote *The New York Times* bestseller *The Immortal Life of Henrietta Lacks* (2010), which has been made in to a film.

The story:

Rebecca Skloot enters the dramatic world of fish medicine—the vets, the owners and their love for creatures that were once flushed down the toilet if they looked a little green around the gills. She discovers a burgeoning industry, with fish owners lining up so their pets can receive enemas, have their broken bones fixed with plates and screws, have their scoliosis treated, or even be sent under the knife for plastic surgery.

For Skloot, finding a story is as easy as keeping an eye out for the unusual each day. 'I'm very big on finding stories in daily life, that's where my most interesting ideas come from,' she says. 'In this case, I was at the vet with my dog. A vet that I had never met before came into the waiting room and another staff member asked him, "How did it go?" He said, "Good, he's swimming around." The vet then went to leave the room and I said, "Wait. Did you say your patient's swimming? What kind of patient is this?" And then I began to interview him and learned about this world of fish medicine. I immediately knew there was a story there, I went online and discovered there was a great deal of work being done in the area, but no one had written about it. So I immediately emailed my editor and said "Hey, guess what ... ?"'

Skloot's next step, after preliminary research, was to track down interviewees. 'Finding the people is the first issue—I cast a really wide net—my stories are very character-driven, so I have to find the right characters to tell the story. The first thing I did was go online and I started looking for anyone who had said anything about fish surgery. There were chat rooms devoted to this on websites (there usually are for just about any topic). I posted on the chat sites saying that I was a reporter and I was looking for people who had taken their fish to the vet. I got a ton of responses back. I interviewed a lot of them over the phone—15 to 20 interviews of random people I found online who had some sort of intense relationship with their fish. I then decided who would be great to focus on as characters and did more in-depth interviews with them and people that they led me to.'

Skloot explains that it's not enough to have a phone interview and do some research to write a story with rich characters. For 'Fixing Nemo' she travelled around the United States, meeting with her interviewees. For her, interviewing is really 'hanging out' and involves observation as much as asking questions. Because Skloot spends days in their company, her interviewees eventually relax and she can begin to uncover their contradictions and quirks and paint accurate portraits of them in her stories.

'For daily newspaper journalism, when you have really short deadlines, phone interviews are fine,' says Skloot. 'But if you want to tell any kind of story, you can't do it unless you see it. So many of the sensory details you want to include in the story are only possible by being with the character. When it comes to the details of the fish surgery at the beginning of the story, it would have been very different if I had just called someone for the information. I would have had the facts without the story.' Essentially, if you want to capture the drama of a situation, you need to witness it—hearing the facts second-hand is always second best.

Capturing action and character details aren't the only reasons to get out from behind your desk and into the world of the interviewee. You'll find that the sources of your story are also invaluable when it comes to research. 'When I went to see Dr Greg Lewbart at his university, the first thing I asked was: "Can I have access to your library?" Most experts will have a great library of information at their fingertips. So when I visited North Carolina I spent a day in the library reading through journal articles and other information Dr Lewbart had pulled together. The historical information in the article is from that research.'

Some of the characters in 'Fixing Nemo' act differently from what many of us expect—spending $50,000 on fish surgery, for example—so Skloot realised she needed more than great characters in her story. She added her own voice to the article to help bridge the gap between the readers and the characters. 'I think that there are two or three times when writers should include themselves in the story. The first is if the story is about them or they've done something to change the course of the story—they've actually become involved in its development. The second reason is that the writer can serve as a bridge—which is what I was doing.'

Skloot chose to insert herself partway through the story, rather than at the very beginning, because she felt it was important to lay out the theme of the piece first. She wanted to drop readers into the action, into the surgery and the world of fish veterinarians, before she distracted them with her own voice. 'Right at the point that I thought people would be thinking, "this is crazy", I came in. It's a big stretch trying to convince someone that these characters are not insane, they just love their fish. So I am there to ask and answer the questions the readers would be asking.'

'Fixing Nemo' received rave reviews from readers, from the interviewees and from editors—the article has been reprinted numerous times, and Skloot was approached to do the story for television and radio. This story, about such an unusual practice, ended up having enormous appeal. This is because of Skloot's ability to capture character and to use detail and lively description to put the reader in the action, and because of her dedication when it comes to research.

Her final advice points to the reason for her successful career: 'Take time, because characters don't happen in half an hour.'

Writing sample

Fixing Nemo

By Rebecca Skloot, _The New York Times_, 2 May 2004

Dr Helen Roberts was about to make the first incision in what should have been a standard surgery—a quick in-and-out procedure—when she froze. 'Bonnie,' she said, turning to her anesthesiologist, 'is she breathing? I don't see her breathing.' Roberts' eyes darted around the room. 'Grab the Doppler,' she told her other assistant. 'I want to hear her heart. Bonnie, how's she doing?' Bonnie pushed up her purple glasses, leaned over the surgery table and lowered her face inches from the patient to watch for any signs of breath: nothing. 'She's too deep,' Roberts said, 'go ahead and give her 30 c.c.s of fresh water.' Bonnie picked up an old plastic jug filled with pond water and poured two glugs into the anesthesia machine. Seconds later, a whisper of a heart rate came through the Doppler. Bonnie wasn't happy: 'We have gill movement—but not much.' Then the Doppler went silent and she reached for the jug. 'Wait,' Roberts said. 'We have fin movement ... damn, she's waking up—30 c.c.s of anesthetic.' Roberts sighed. 'She was holding her breath,' she said, shaking her head. 'Fish are a lot smarter than people give them credit for.'

Yes, Roberts and Bonita (Bonnie) Wulf were doing surgery on a goldfish. Not the fancy kind that people buy for thousands of dollars and keep in decorative ponds (though they do surgery on those too), but on a county-fair goldfish named the Golden One, which Roberts adopted when its previous owners brought it into her clinic outside Buffalo, saying they didn't have time to take care of it. Which is to say, it's a regular fish that could belong to anybody. Just like Lucky, the one-and-a-half-pound koi with a two-and-a-half-pound tumor; Sunshine, who was impaled on a branch during rough sex; Betta, with a fluid-filled abdomen; and countless goldfish with so-called buoyancy disorders, like the perpetually upside-down Belly Bob, or Raven, who was stuck floating nose down and tail to the sky. All those fish went under the knife.

Ten years ago, the chances of finding a fish vet were slim. But true to its history, veterinary medicine is steadily evolving to meet the demands of pet owners. Through the early 1900s, vets treated livestock mostly. You didn't treat cats and dogs—you usually shot those. But by the mid-50s, the world was in love with Rin Tin Tin and Lassie, and people started thinking, I shouldn't have to shoot my dog. By the 70s, dogs and cats could get human-quality medical care—but treating birds? That was insane. Instead, bird advice came from pet stores (and birds died of a 'draft,' a diagnosis akin to the vapors). Yet by the 80s, avian medicine had its own academic programs, a professional society, at least one monthly magazine and a large clientele. Today we have surgery for parakeets, organ transplantation for dogs and cats, chemotherapy for gerbils. But people who want to take fish to the vet—those people are still crazy. At least for the time being.

'I have no doubt fish medicine will become mainstream much like bird medicine did in the 80s,' said Dr David Scarfe, assistant director of scientific activities at the American Veterinary Medical Association. 'It's actually happening far more rapidly than I'd imagined.' According to the AVMA, almost 2000 vets currently practice fish medicine. That number is steadily growing, and the market seems solid: 13.9 million households have fish and spend several billions of dollars annually on fish supplies alone—tanks, water conditioners, food—not including veterinary care or the fish themselves, which can cost as much as $100,000, sometimes more.

Fish diagnostics range from a basic exam ($40), blood work ($60) and X-rays ($55) to the advanced: ultrasound ($175), CAT scans ($250). Veterinarians tube-feed fish. They give fish enemas, fix broken bones with plates and screws, remove impacted eggs, treat scoliosis and even do fish plastic surgery—anything from glass-eye implantation to 'surgical pattern improvement,' with scale transplantation, scale tattooing or unsightly-scale removal.

But some of the most common and vexing fish ailments are buoyancy disorders. They involve the swim bladder, an organ in the digestive tract prone to infections, obstructions and defects that destroy a fish's ability to regulate air, leaving it 'improperly buoyant,' to the point of floating or sinking in odd positions—usually upside down. Surgically inserting a tiny stone in the fish's abdomen to weigh it down is the best option, but since that costs anywhere from $150 to $1500, depending on where and how it's done, many vets first recommend green-pea treatment: 'Feeding affected goldfish a single green pea (canned or cooked and lightly crushed) once daily might cure the problem,' Dr Greg Lewbart wrote in a paper titled 'Green Peas for Buoyancy Disorders'. Lewbart is a top fish veterinarian, but even he isn't sure how pea treatment works.

When I tell people I'm writing about fish medicine, their reaction is almost always the same: why not flush the sick fish and get a new one? Actually, for several reasons. First, there are the money fish. 'I've worked on several fish worth $30,000 to $50,000,' Lewbart once told me. These are the fancy koi that work fish shows for big prizes, then retire to a life of reproduction. 'I examined one in Japan an owner turned down $200,000 for,' Lewbart says. That's what he calls a big fish. 'People will spend thousands to fix them.' But not all koi are show koi; many are what Lewbart calls UPFs: ugly pond fish.

Which brings us to the human–fish bond, and people who gasp if you mention flushing because they swear their fish have personalities so big they win hearts. I heard stories of Zeus, who weighed two pounds but dominated the house cat by biting onto the cat's paw and yanking it headfirst into the tank when it swatted the water. There was Sushi, the 'gregariously affectionate' koi with recurring bacterial infections. And Zoomer, the 'koi with a vendetta,' who shot out of the water at her owner, David Smothers, and broke his nose—something his pet Ladyfish never would have done. She'd just cuddle with him in the pond and wiggle when he kissed her. David spent thousands trying to save Ladyfish when lightning struck near his pond, creating a shock wave that broke her back. He got X-rays, CAT scans, chiropractic adjustments and spinal surgery, then spent weeks in the pond, gently holding Ladyfish's tail during physical therapy. Nothing worked, and he still tears up when he talks about it.

The human–fish-bond people don't understand the money-fish people. 'They don't even name their fish,' Bonita Wulf says, sounding shocked. The organizers of the Singapore International Fish Show just announced a fish-adoption initiative, declaring that 'fish have their lives, and they have feelings, too,' so if fish don't win shows, it's 'more humane to bring the fish up for adoption,' rather than flushing them down the toilet. Others train fish to fetch and dunk basketballs. 'Some of fish personality might be a feeding response,' says Dr Julius Tepper of the Long Island Fish Hospital, 'but so is a lot of what we interpret as affection from cats.' Sushi's owner doesn't buy that. 'You have to meet Sushi to understand,' she told me. So I went with Dr Roberts to Marsha Chapman's house thinking, OK, Sushi, show me this personality of yours.

'Sushi's in here,' Marsha said, leading me to the 6-foot-long, 150-gallon tank in her family room. Marsha is a warm and motherly special-education teacher in her 50s who looks you in the eye and sounds as if she's talking to a room of second graders. 'Hi, baby,' she cooed. 'How's Mama's girl?' Sushi darted to the surface of the tank and started splashing frantically. 'That's right, show us how you wag your tail.' And Sushi did (though a wagging fish tail looks just like a swimming fish tail to me). 'She's just like a dog that way,' Marsha said. 'If I could hug her, I would.'

Aside from Sushi's size (two feet long), her looks are unimpressive. Mostly white, a few orange spots, short nonflowing fins, trademark carp whiskers. Lewbart would call her a UPF, though not around Marsha, who reached in the tank and patted Sushi's head. 'Look who's here, Sweetie,' she said, 'Say hi to Rebecca.'

Sushi ignored me. But she did the 'basketball dance' for Marsha, swimming in place, face against the glass, jerking back and forth and up and down. And Marsha did it right back. She put her red-lipstick-covered lips an inch from the tank opposite Sushi's. She clenched her fists, bent her elbows and knees, stuck out her butt and wiggled her body violently while making loud kissing noises. The more Marsha danced, the more Sushi danced. Then Roberts walked in the room saying, 'Isn't he cute?' and Sushi hid. 'Dr Roberts thinks she might be a boy, but Sushi is a girl's name.' Marsha tapped the tank. 'Don't be afraid, Dr Roberts makes you better.'

Roberts is a petite 'warm fuzzy fish vet' whose no-nonsense appearance—no makeup, a thick black plastic sports watch—almost clashes with the turquoise contacts that make her eyes beautifully inhuman. She surrounds herself with pewter fish and glass fish; papier-mache, metal, wood and stone fish; and of course, her pet fish: Splotch, Carrot, Harrison, Ford and about 32 others, including B.O. (Big Orange), her favorite. He's 'the dog of the pond' in the many fish pictures in her living room and office, or on her computer desktop. 'Come on, Sush,' Roberts said. 'I'm your friend.'

I stared into Sushi's tank for hours. Marsha put the *Twin Peaks* theme song on repeat, and I thought, Fun fish. She was active and sparkly, she swam back and forth, her muscles moving with the music in slow melodic waves. It was mesmerizing. But to me she was more like a Lava lamp than a pet. Then again, to her I was more like a piece of furniture than a human. I didn't feel Sushi's personality—I felt Dr Roberts' and Marsha's. When Sushi swam by, their eyes widened, they smiled, touched the glass, said hello. When she turned, they said things like 'Isn't she amazing?' and 'She's so funny.'

They know people might say they're crazy. 'I don't care what people think,' Marsha said. 'I use my relationship with Sushi as a springboard for teaching special-education students about affection for unconventional people, like themselves.' She stared into the tank, her voice suddenly serious. 'It enlarges the world when you see how much possibility there is for loving people and animals who aren't usually given a chance.'

The Golden One finally stopped holding her breath, which meant Dr Roberts could actually spay her. Well, at least that was the plan. 'I'm pretty sure she's a female,' Roberts said, 'but it's always hard to tell with fish. If she turns out to be a boy, it's no big deal. We'll just neuter her.' Roberts was born in England, raised in Italy and Georgia; her accent is soft, slightly rural and completely unidentifiable. 'Goldfish are the rabbits of the fish world,' she said when I asked why she was spaying her fish. 'I don't want to face the ethical decision of what to do with all those babies.'

Aside from the human-quality surgical instruments and monitors, the setup was 100% garden-supply store: one Rubbermaid tub full of pond water and anesthetic, clear plastic tubing attached to a submersible pump with duct tape. The Golden One lay on a plastic grate above the tub, yellow foam pad keeping her upright, tube in her mouth pumping anesthetic water from the tub, through her gills, then back again. Like a recirculating fountain.

It's the same setup used in the first account of pet fish surgery I could find, which was performed in 1993 and written about two years later by Dr Greg Lewbart at the College of Veterinary Medicine at North Carolina State University. Lewbart, a professor of aquatic medicine, has short brown hair, graying sideburns and a soft blanket of freckles—like someone misted him with tan paint. 'I don't tell my clients,' he told me, hesitantly, 'but I got into fish as a fisherman.' He couldn't help laughing when he said this. 'It's undeniably weird: I sometimes spend my weekends at the coast fishing.' Then he paused. 'I do mostly catch and release, but not always, and either way, it's unpleasant for the animal: I take the hook out, traumatize the fish, then throw it back in the water with a huge wound on its face or toss it into a cooler where it flops around for a few minutes. Then I go into work Monday, somebody brings in a goldfish, I console them, take their fish to surgery, then put it on postoperative pain medication.'

Lewbart loves fish medicine—he flies around the world teaching and practicing it; he publishes scholarly articles and books on it. But he's not all fish. 'My real love is marine invertebrates,' he told me, like snails, worms, horseshoe crabs. 'It's still a little down the road when people are going to start bringing those guys to the vet. But I think it'll happen in the same way fish medicine happened.'

Fish medicine actually dates to the 1800s, but it didn't start to catch on until the 1970s and 80s, when scientists started publishing research articles on everything from fish hormones and nutrition to pondside operating tables. But that had nothing to do with pets. Until Lewbart published his surgery paper, references to fish medicine came from fisheries, marine biology and wildlife.

In the late 70s, a few obscure papers mentioned the burgeoning field of pet fish; some even said vets should make the transition from aquaculture to pets. But that didn't happen for more than a decade, until koi exploded into a multimillion-dollar industry, the Internet appeared and owners started typing 'fish veterinarian' into search engines. When they found research papers by vets like Lewbart, owners started calling and e-mailing. 'I never thought of being a fish vet,' said Dr Tepper of the Long Island Fish Hospital. 'Then I got a call from a guy wondering if I treated fish or knew someone who did. I said, "No, actually, I don't." Then I was like, Why didn't I think of this earlier?'

Pet-fish medicine isn't exactly mainstream: many owners don't know fish vets exist; others look but can't find them. The AVMA and several vets are working on databases for referring clients, but they're not available yet. Until then, Lewbart will keep fielding 400 to 500 calls and e-mail messages a year from people with fish questions, and many owners will take matters into their own hands. Just like Bonita Wulf, who isn't an actual fish anesthesiologist; she's a fish hobbyist with a gravelly smoker's voice and a very large gun collection. (As Dr Roberts says, you don't joke about flushing fish with a woman like Bonnie.) Wulf talks to her fish and carries pictures of them in her purse. 'I've got grandkids too,' she says with a grin, 'but I only carry fish pictures.' She has taken more courses in fish health and medicine than most veterinarians, and she started by Googling the word 'koi.' Inevitably, that leads to KoiVet.com, an all-you-need-to-know-about-fish site, and Aquamaniacs. net. Between the two, thousands of fish hobbyists join message boards for moral support and immediate do-it-yourself help during fish crises. They're starting to refer one another to fish vets, though traditionally fish medicine is one of the few areas where pet owners, as a rule, know more than veterinarians. But things have changed: veterinary schools are starting to teach fish medicine.

I recently went to North Carolina to visit a seminar at one of the only aquatic-medicine departments in the world, which Lewbart oversees. He and his colleagues also run a one-week intensive fish-medicine course, as well as the world's only aquatic-medicine residency. Their courses are always full. On the first day of the seminar, eight vet students from around the country learned to catch, anesthetize and transport fish. They drew blood, took fin and scale samples, looked under microscopes for parasites. They saw an underwater frog with a fluid-retention problem, a turtle filled with rocks it wasn't supposed to eat. The seminar is about 25% aquatic reptiles and 75% fish, but the first day, there were no sick fish. And it was sunny out, so Lewbart took everyone to Ben & Jerry's for a fish-medicine lecture. As he sat in the sun wearing black plastic sunglasses—ice cream in one hand, fish book in the other—Lewbart talked about fish cancer and carp herpes. 'Are there any questions?' he asked eventually. A student from Pennsylvania raised his hand: 'Can a person make a living as a fish vet?'

The answer is yes and no: despite hourly rates up to $100 for 'tank calls,' business would be tight for a full-time pet-fish vet right now. Some successful pet-fish vets work in fisheries, public aquariums, zoos or the tropical-fish industry; others supplement their practices with teaching and research. But most pet-fish vets must treat other animals too. 'Dogs and cats are the meat and potatoes,' Roberts says. 'Fish are the spice.' That's likely to be true for a while. 'Fish medicine is still a hobby,' Tepper says. 'It costs me thousands of dollars a year.' He blames this in part on seasonality—koi are dormant in winter—so he and others are encouraging preventive fish medicine. That's what's unusual about the Golden One's surgery: she's perfectly healthy. Spaying means Roberts won't have to face the ethical baby-placement issue, but it's also a business move. 'If I can master this,' says Roberts, 'I can offer it to owners who say, "I really love this goldfish, I just don't want a thousand more."'

Fifteen minutes before the Golden One would be up and darting around her pond looking for food, Dr Roberts poked around in the fish's abdomen. She told Wulf about her new video game, then stopped suddenly. 'Look at that, Bonnie.' Roberts pulled a long yellow gelatinous strand from the Golden One's belly. 'That looks male, doesn't it?' Bonnie nodded. 'Yep, Helen, that's male.' Roberts laughed. 'How could you be male? You look so female!'

'Don't spay that one,' Bonnie said.

'OK,' Roberts shot back, chipper as always. 'We'll neuter him.' Then she turned to me and whispered: 'Fish medicine isn't an exact science yet. But we're working on it.'

8

Ethical Concerns

'The pen is mightier than the sword.'

Edward George Bulwer Lytton (1803–73)

Objectives

In the next two chapters we consider the consequences of actions journalists might take when researching and putting a story together. This chapter considers ethical concerns; the next chapter will look at legal issues. As we've discussed at other points in this book, journalism is all about making decisions. These can be straightforward or more complex. Straightforward questions are those relating to information-gathering and story-building strategies, such as: How am I going to tackle this story? Where will I find all the pieces to this jigsaw? Who do I interview? And what questions should I ask? Decisions become more complex when a journalist moves beyond questions of procedure to consider the consequences of actions they have taken or are contemplating. These actions might impact on the journalist, the organisation they work for, and the people about whom they are writing or who might be affected by publication of the story being researched. This chapter covers:

o   the need for journalism ethics

o   development of a moral compass—appropriateness of questions

o   guidelines for journalists—codes of conduct

o   the MEAA Code of Ethics

o   issues of concern for feature writers.

Understanding journalism ethics

One of the first lessons drummed into first-year journalism students is the need to behave ethically. Many lecturers will begin their discussion about journalism ethics by drawing their students' attention to the dictum by Lytton that heads this chapter: 'The pen is mightier than the sword.' While computers and digital recorders have largely replaced pens in the journalistic tool kit, Lytton's comment is just as apt today as it was in the nineteenth century, although it perhaps needs to be reworked to reflect the fact that in a digital age, the written word is just one form of journalism; today, much of what passes as journalism is provided in an oral (spoken) or visual (image) type form. The fact is that, in the wrong hands, words or images can be more damaging to an individual than a sword or any other weapon that has the ability to maim or even kill.

Words and images have the capacity to influence the way in which we regard people or events. This places a great deal of responsibility upon journalists to interpret events truthfully and fairly. On the surface, this may not appear to be such a daunting task. But words and images can convey subtle meanings, or even mean different things to different people. So we need to be careful. We need to think about the consequences of what we say or write, or even omit to say or write. Likewise, we need to think about the images, whether video or still, we employ to help convey a story. And if those words or images misrepresent a situation or suggest flaws in an individual's personality that may not exist, then we could cause serious damage to that individual's sense of self-worth, or to their reputation, whether we intend to or not.

Unfortunately, journalists are held in low regard by the communities they serve. We know this from the results of surveys conducted by the Roy Morgan Group and other companies that compare the ethical standing of different professions (for the 2016 results, see Roy Morgan Group, 2016). The reason why journalists fare so badly in these polls is difficult to ascertain. Perhaps it is because people do not like what they read and hear, an argument that has been reinforced by the *News of the World* scandal in the UK that broke in 2010. In an Australian context, the question of journalistic ethics has been explored by a number of inquiries beginning in 2011, inspired in part by the *News of the World* scandal. Journalistic standards have come under even closer scrutiny more recently following the election of Donald Trump as US President. As we discuss in the Introduction and Chapter 1, Trump's relationship with the media is a prickly one. He coined the term 'fake news' to describe any form of media reporting or commentary he doesn't agree with. His staff even came up with the term 'alternative facts' to differentiate between their interpretation of events, and that espoused in the media. Trump has also taken to using social media to tell constituents what he is doing, criticising the media in the process.

These attacks have damaged the media, and make it all the more difficult for journalists to do their job, particularly when it comes to performing a watchdog or 'Fourth Estate' function, that is to hold public figures to account. This is one important function. It comes out of a broader mandate: to tell society about itself. These important responsibilities are often difficult to fulfil, particularly when the media is under constant attack from people who have the power to criticise and to be heard.

Developing a moral compass

Fundamentally, most journalists are good people. They take their job seriously. They take pride in their work, in getting the story and in presenting it in a manner that helps people understand issues. Most journalists are also essentially ethical people. Like other members of the broader community, they have developed ethical or moral compasses that guide their behaviour (Tanner et al., 2005). These compasses enable them to distinguish between right and wrong, and to make decisions about whether their own conduct (or that of other people they are reporting on) is appropriate or not.

A journalist's moral compass will enable them to consider the appropriateness of questions they are proposing to ask a particular person. For example, should they adopt an accusatory tone or a conciliatory tone when seeking information from people who may have witnessed an event? What impact will the style of questioning have on the responses provided, or even on the well-being of the individual? These are issues we'll return to later in the chapter. At this point it is sufficient for us to point out that the type of questioning can have a significant impact on how a story progresses.

The individual journalist's moral compass develops over time. It is influenced by a range of factors, including the family environment in which they grow up, their life experiences, and the impact other people or groups have on them during their development. These may include friends, church, community, and sporting and political groups. Also significant are professional influences, including that of peers and the inevitable socialisation that takes place within a newsroom. The influence of a competitive newsroom can be especially strong and may even work as a counterweight to one's own moral compass, when individual journalists are seeking advancement, and the organisations they work for are vying to increase market share by publishing stories their competitors have missed.

Codes of conduct

Behaving ethically should not be a problem for journalists. There are a number of codes of conduct or guidelines they can draw on when seeking answers to an ethical conundrum. These include codes relevant to the industry in general, such as the Media Entertainment and Arts Alliance (MEAA) Code of Ethics, the Australian Press Council's (APC) Statement of Principles and Reporting Guidelines covering the print media, and the Australian Communications and Media Authority's (ACMA) codes of conduct for electronic media. There are also company-specific guidelines. For example, the ABC, SBS, Fairfax and News Ltd have all developed codes of conduct to help guide the behaviour of their journalists. The *Herald Sun* unveiled a new code of conduct in 2011 that is publicly accessible at <www.heraldsun.com.au>. Some of these codes are accessible online (see Box 8.1), although the direct links are often difficult to locate on the organisations' websites.

All these codes tend to be very general, although the advice is focused enough to provide guidance for a journalist under pressure.

Box 8.1   Codes of conduct

MEAA	www.alliance.org.au
APC	www.presscouncil.org.au
ABC	http://about.abc.net.au/wp-content/uploads/2016/05/ABCCodeOfPractice2016-1.pdf
SBS	http://media.sbs.com.au/home/upload_media/site_20_rand_2138311027_sbscodesofpractice2010.pdf
ACMA	www.acma.gov.au
IFJ	www.ifj.org/default.asp?Issue=ETHICS&Language=EN

In addition, there are a number of fact sheets designed to help journalists understand and report upon particular groups and issues within society. These include advice on reporting across cultures (Stockwell & Scott, 2000); on disability; on ageism; about suicide and mental health; and on ethnicity and religion. As with the codes of conduct, some of this advice can be accessed online (see Box 8.2).

Box 8.2 Issue-specific guidelines

Disability	http://www.inclusionwa.org.au/download/A%20way%20with%20words.pdf
	https://disabilitymediamatters.me/media-guidelines/
Ageism	http://www.humanrights.gov.au/our-work/age-discrimination/publications/age-discrimination-exposing-hidden-barrier-mature-age
Suicide and mental health	www.responseability.org
Ethnicity and religion	http://www.ifj.org/fileadmin/images/EFJ/EFJ_documents/Reports/Ethical_Journalism_Initiative_document.pdf
	https://www.article19.org/resources.php/resource/3093/en/getting-the-facts-right:-reporting-ethnicity-and-religion
	http://www.religionlink.com/pdf/primer2006.pdf
Terrorism	http://www.cjr.org/tow_center/guidelines_press_covering_terrorism.php?Daily
Cancer	https://www.cancerinstitute.org.au/about-us/Media/Writing-about-cancer-guidelines

---

Before embarking on stories about potentially sensitive issues, journalists inexperienced in these areas are advised to consult the relevant guidelines so they are aware of the pitfalls they might encounter.

The MEAA Code of Ethics

If you look at the codes identified in Box 8.1, you'll see that there is considerable overlap between them. Essentially, they cover the same topics and provide journalists with the same advice. In this chapter, therefore, we will focus on just one of the codes: the 12-point statement developed by the MEAA during the mid-1990s. This particular code is the latest iteration of a code for journalists that was first drafted in the 1940s and then expanded during the early 1980s.

On the surface, the Code is fairly straightforward. However, once you look more closely at some of the clauses, areas of potential difficulty become more apparent. Here, we briefly discuss each of the clauses to give you an insight into some of the issues you might face and the ways you might be able to deal with them.

Clause 1

Report and interpret honestly, striving for accuracy, fairness and disclosure of all essential facts. Do not suppress relevant available facts, or give distorting emphasis. Do your utmost to give a fair opportunity for reply.

There are a number of elements in this section that we need to think about. In the first part of the clause we are advised to '*report and interpret honestly, striving for accuracy, fairness and disclosure of all essential facts*'. We know that this means to report and interpret honestly. This is very easy if we have all the information laid out in front of us. But often we don't know whether we have all the pieces of the jigsaw puzzle in our grasp, particularly if we are researching a complex story such as an investigation that might have taken weeks or months to pull together. This is often made more difficult by the fact that we don't always want to flag that we are working on a particular story in case it undermines our investigation or tips people off.

For example, say you are working on a story about illegal immigrants being employed in the hospitality industry. You have spoken to some of the immigrants, to legally employed hospitality workers and to the union. They have provided some great background and even a list of people and restaurants 'they believe' to be behind the scam. But you are not convinced that everything you have been told is true. You suspect that this story might have been dreamed up as part of a political campaign to embarrass the government and to highlight working conditions in the hospitality sector. To make matters worse, you have not been able to raise the allegations of misconduct with any of the people purportedly behind the scam. You are also under pressure from your editor to publish the story before another outlet gets onto it. What do you do?

You need to be careful. It is tempting to cast stones, but there are legal and ethical considerations involved that all journalists need to consider. The key words are 'honestly' 'accuracy', 'fairness' and 'disclosure'. We can address the key concerns raised by the first part of Clause 1 by asking ourselves a number of questions: Are we being honest with the information? Are we being honest with ourselves, our readers, viewers and listeners? Are we presenting the information fairly and accurately? Are we disclosing everything that should be revealed in order for the full story to be told and for people to understand what we are trying to say?

This leads on to the second part of Clause 1: '*Do not suppress relevant available facts, or give distorting emphasis.*' As tempting as it may be to conveniently overlook some information, particularly if it does not fit in with our particular view of the world, we have to provide our readers, viewers and listeners with all the information they require to make a decision about a particular issue. We cannot make up their minds for them. We have to provide them with all the relevant information and allow them to make the decision or judgment for themselves. One key phrase in the clause is 'relevant available facts'. This can serve as an escape clause for journalists, who could be tempted to hide behind inadequate research or effort by saying, 'It was all the information I had'. However laziness is not an excuse, nor is suppressing information because it does not mirror your own world view. Journalists are obliged to seek out and present all relevant facts. This means making sure that we do not distort the story by providing more evidence in support of one side than the other. There are a number of ways in which we can achieve this. We can make sure we have all bases covered by seeking the views of a representative sample of people involved, or by highlighting differences of opinion (for example, between medical experts who disagree over different surgical strategies).

Media coverage concerning the Sydney neurosurgeon Dr Charlie Teo highlights this issue beautifully. Dr Teo has been profiled on a number of occasions (see, for example, Fairfax's *Good Weekend* magazine, 19 May 2007). In part, the media are interested in Dr Teo because of his success rate in highly risky operations. The journalists who wrote articles about Dr Teo could have focused solely on his successes and the adoration he inspires in his patients. However, by focusing on his personality and his relationship with his peers, some of whom questioned his approach to surgery, they added an important dimension to the story. If they had not done so, the journalists would only have been providing readers with a partial picture of Dr Teo.

It is the final part of the clause that can cause the most grief for journalists: '*Do your utmost to give a fair opportunity for reply.*' This is one of the tenets of contemporary journalism, so it should be second nature. But there are occasions when we write something about a person and either don't check it with them or don't allow them the opportunity to reply.

Take the hypothetical situation discussed earlier in this section. How would you deal with the 'illegal immigrants' story if your sources told you that the so-called prominent individuals behind it were members of a local bikie gang? Most people would probably support your decision not to approach this group for comment, particularly if doing so meant placing yourself at risk. But is that fair to the bikies, who may not have been involved and might welcome an opportunity to disavow any knowledge of the scam? Do you extend the right of reply to them before publishing the allegations, or do you wait and follow up in the next edition or bulletin, after they have come to you demanding satisfaction?

Occasionally, journalists—particularly those who see themselves as crusaders—ignore even that possibility. Remember, journalists have an obligation to be fair. We are not arguing that you have to be objective, as many American journalism ethics books preach. Objectivity is an unachievable goal. We all have inbuilt views of the world that help make us who we are, and thus we find it very difficult to shake them off, even for a while. However, we can be fair, even if it means acknowledging these inbuilt biases and prejudices, and we can produce feature articles that are balanced.

Before you decide to run with just one side of a story, you need to be pretty confident as to the authenticity of the evidence in your possession. You need to have a great deal of faith in your sources and preferably have hard evidence to support the allegations you are making. For example, if your story is about a heroin ring, ideally you would have seen the heroin and have photographs of the drug and the people you are accusing of trafficking it. Ideally, you should also advise your readers why you are producing just one side of the story and advise them that you plan to follow up with an alternative viewpoint.

In situations like the above, you should also question the motives of the people who are providing you with information, particularly if the story started as a result of a tip-off from someone you don't know particularly well. You should ask yourself why you, in particular, have been approached, rather than someone else. Is it because you have an interest in a particular issue? Or is it because the source considers you a soft touch—that is, someone who can be pushed in a particular direction or will accept information unquestioningly?

Clause 2

Do not place unnecessary emphasis on personal characteristics, including race, ethnicity, nationality, gender, age, sexual orientation, family relationships, religious belief, or physical or intellectual disability.

Again, this is one of those ethical rules that journalists look at and say, 'that's fair enough', but then breach it. In recent years there have been a large number of stories in which journalists have wrongly drawn attention to one or more of the characteristics identified by the clause. For example, race, ethnicity, nationality and religious belief have been widely discussed in the media in the aftermath of the attacks on the World Trade Center in New York on 11 September 2001 and a range of other terrorist attacks across the world since. Fair enough, because these attacks had their origins in issues of religion and ethnicity. But there is a difference between writing about race or religion in such circumstances and mentioning these issues when they are not central to a story. Many stories have been written since 9/11 that have served to incite ethnic and religious differences, rather than provide informed analysis of the issues that underpinned the terrorist strikes and subsequent events. For example, editorial decisions by newspapers, magazines and creative types led to attacks on Danish newspaper *Jyllands-Posten* (2005–10), French satirical magazine *Charlie Hebdo* (2011), and the murder of Dutch filmmaker Theo Van Gogh (2004) for criticisms of Islam and/or the Prophet Muhammad. Remember the old adage: 'a little knowledge can be dangerous'. It is one that journalists don't pay enough attention to, with the result that articles can be misinformed, or based on insufficient information.

Journalists frequently look for story hooks. Religion and ethnicity are just two of a number of possibilities. Gender, age, sexual orientation, family relationships and disability can also seem like strong hooks to hang a story from, but when writing about these topics, it is important to avoid perpetuating stereotypes. Too many stories about women, for example, focus on the deemed importance of child-rearing. For example, there were a number of stories about former Australian Prime Minister Julia Gillard's decision not to have children, on the style of clothes she wore, or the fact that her partner was a male hairdresser. The same could not be said of recent male prime ministers, although the media did find ways to have a dig at them (Tony Abbott's penchant for Lycra and Speedos; Kevin Rudd's wife's success as a businesswoman; and Malcolm Turnbull's wealth and his decision to live in his 'harbourside mansion').

Older people are also often stereotyped in the media, yet they shouldn't be, as they are all individuals, just like the people who write about them. Sexual orientation is less of an issue these days, although again, if mentioned, it should be relevant to the story. For example, during the gay marriage debates of 2011 there were a large number of stories that identified some federal MPs as gay or lesbian. In the context of the debates, this was probably reasonable, not only because the MPs concerned had previously announced their sexual orientation, but because it provided Australians with an insight into the personal lives of these MPs that may have explained their attitudes towards this issue. There was also considerable focus on the fact that then PM Tony Abbott's sister was gay. Again this could be considered reasonable, particularly given his opposition to gay marriage.

Family relationships always provide tempting fodder for the media, but again we should be careful about making linkages that are tenuous or that would place unfair attention on someone who is not directly related to the story. The media were justified, for example, in focusing on the relationship between then Prime Minister John Howard and his brother, Stan, the Chairman of National Textiles, when that company was reported to have received a $2 million federal government handout to pay employee entitlements when it closed down. This occurred at a time when other companies in a similar position did not receive government assistance. However, it is questionable whether the media were justified in highlighting the fact that the Prime Minister's son had been at a party where a young person died, allegedly of a drug overdose.

Finally, there are protocols that journalists should be aware of when conducting interviews with some groups of people, including Aborigines and Torres Strait Islanders, and people with disabilities. Indigenous Australian culture is complex and it requires expert knowledge to write authoritatively about related issues. For example, journalists will often talk about 'Aboriginal people', just as they refer to 'Muslim people'. Yet this is wrong in both cases, because there are different Aboriginal and Torres Strait Islander groups, each with their own customs and beliefs, just as there are differences of opinion among Muslims. You need to understand these differences. Sometimes they are very subtle, but if you get them wrong, you could offend many people. One example of a custom you should be aware of is that using the name of a dead Aborigine or Torres Strait Islander is frowned upon by many Indigenous people as it is considered disrespectful of the dead, hence the warning at the commencement of television programs warning people that the names of deceased ancestors may be mentioned.

Not only should you be careful about breaching customs, but you should also consider the manner in which you conduct particular interviews. How, for example, do you interview someone who is deaf? How do you interview someone who can't speak?

There are protocols that dictate how these interviews are conducted, and also the language you should use when describing someone who has a disability. For example, describing a person who uses a wheelchair as 'wheelchair-bound', or as being 'confined to a wheelchair', is viewed by many as inappropriate because the wheelchair provides that person with mobility and a degree of freedom to do things they would not be able to do otherwise. In addition, there are protocols that will help guide you about when or how to discuss sensitive subjects, such as sexual activity. These topics can be broached, but only with the right person and in the appropriate context. Again, the emphasis is on respect. Yes, you need to tell the story, but make sure the questions you ask relate to the story you have in mind. If you are planning to move down a sensitive path, flag that intention so the individual has an opportunity to prepare their answers.

Clause 3

Aim to attribute information to its source. Where a source seeks anonymity, do not agree without first considering the source's motives and any alternative attributable source. Where confidences are accepted, respect them in all circumstances.

Again, this is fairly straightforward. But there are issues that may impact on 1) your ability to source information and 2) the credibility of your story. Successful journalists build up a strong network of sources.

This can only be established over time, and is based on trust. The best stories have identifiable sources—people who are prepared to have their names attached to the comments they have made. This helps the journalist build up credibility with their readers, viewers or listeners.

Occasionally, journalists will receive hot information from a source who asks not to be named. This might be for any one of a number of reasons: the source didn't want to risk their job, or didn't want to go to jail (a possibility we discuss in Chapter 9). Finally, they might have felt that by being identified as the source of the information, they were placing themselves, friends or family at risk of physical harm. In these instances, the journalist has to ask: Will the story survive if I don't use this information? Am I justified in honouring the request for anonymity? Can I locate the information or similar information elsewhere?

There are a number of issues here. The first brings us back to an earlier discussion about the motives of the source. If you know the source, you can judge for yourself whether their motives are reasonable or not. If you decide they are reasonable and you need the information for your story, remember that you have to honour your commitment to maintain their anonymity. This could be problematic for you down the track, particularly if the story is the subject of legal action. You may find, as we discuss in Chapter 9, that a judge or magistrate could demand that you name your sources. There have been a number of high-profile cases involving journalists who resisted judicial attempts to make them reveal the names of their sources, and others where the journalists succumbed to legal pressure. So be warned: it is not an agreement you should enter into lightly. It is better that the source agrees to be named.

Clause 4

Do not allow personal interest, or any belief, commitment, payment, gift or benefit, to undermine your accuracy, fairness or independence.

In many respects, this is one of the foundation stones that underpin the MEAA Code. Belief and commitment are important traits of any journalist—if properly directed. But these need to be separate from the other elements identified in Clause 4, including personal interest, payment, gift or benefit. Outstanding journalists are often zealous and might be compared to a dog that refuses to give up a bone. But this zeal should be motivated by public interest and not personal interest. Journalists should not accept any form of reward, other than their salary and other benefits previously agreed to by their employer. For example, finance journalists should refuse discounted shares in companies they write about, or refuse to utilise any information they become privy to that is not public knowledge to buy or sell shares on the stock exchange; wine writers, restaurant reviewers, music reviewers, travel writers and other specialist journalists should be careful about receiving 'freebies', because these could compromise their independence. Journalists should be free to present stories as they see them. If they are receiving kickbacks from benefactors, then their judgment can be affected. Their reputation and their independence are at risk.

This is one area that has changed considerably in recent years. Some media organisations will not permit their journalists to accept freebies, or will limit the value of gifts. If a journalist travels as the guest of a particular company or organisation, a caption to that effect is included at the head or foot of the story. This is particularly relevant in the case of travel writers, a theme we return to in Chapter 17.

Clause 5

Disclose conflicts of interest that affect, or could be seen to affect, the accuracy, fairness or independence of your journalism. Do not improperly use a journalistic position for personal gain.

Again, Clause 5 is fairly self-evident, but worth considering nonetheless. There are a number of situations where a journalist may encounter a potential conflict during their professional lives. These can include, but are not restricted to:

- stories involving family, friends or colleagues (individuals, businesses etc.)
- stories involving an employer (or major advertisers the company is wooing or relies on—see also Clause 6)
- stories involving organisations the journalist might be involved with (sporting groups, political parties, churches, unions etc.).

We need to be careful when dealing with any of these situations, so rather than run the risk of being accused of favouritism, bias or the like, we could flag our interest from the outset, or hand the story over to a colleague. The last thing you want is for a story to be discredited because of a perceived conflict of interest that you refused to acknowledge.

It is also important to consider the second part of Clause 5: '*Do not improperly use a journalistic position for personal gain.*' There are a number of issues involved here. How do we define personal gain? Are we talking about monetary gain? Are we talking about those innocuous brown paper bags that pass between a corruptor and the person being corrupted? What about the boxes of wine delivered to the wine reviewer's home, the complimentary restaurant meals, the free use of a motor car while on holiday or for extended periods after a test drive?

The code is quite clear on this, as are the various media company policies, which tend to ban acceptance of any of these gifts or favours. They can all influence a journalist, and are designed to do just that. Such payments are apparently rare in Australia, but be careful; don't allow yourself to be swayed by the prospect of personal gain. Remember, there is no such thing as a free lunch—literally.

You also need to consider the danger of using information to benefit a group you are involved in (the local progress association, interest group etc.), and be careful not to be seen as a self-interested crusader. Crusading journalism can be a positive thing, particularly when you are using your position as a journalist to push for changes that will benefit the community as a whole. However, you can't use your position to crusade for a change that will benefit only a small number of people, such as a radical church or interest group. You have to think about those fundamental journalistic tenets of fairness and balance.

Clause 6

Do not allow advertising or other commercial considerations to undermine accuracy, fairness or independence.

This clause is really designed to protect journalists against unfair demands from their employers. All commercial media organisations are driven by the so-called financial imperative—the desire to make a profit. Media profits are linked directly to advertising revenue. Often, journalists—particularly young, inexperienced ones—are asked to write 'advertorials'. These are essentially product endorsements dressed up as editorials. There is nothing wrong with this, so long as the journalist is not forced to compromise their ethics by being asked to write a glowing story on a company they know to be shonky. Such stories should always include the banner or tag line 'advertising feature', or 'promotional feature' so that the reader or viewer knows that it is being written for a particular purpose and is not necessarily a personal endorsement—from the journalist, the publication, the program or even the holding company that owns the media outlet.

This clause is designed to protect the independence and integrity of journalists. However, a journalist is expected to be fair to the company concerned and perhaps even to its competitors. The clause would also cover the situation where a journalist might be asked to write about companies their employer or other members of the board of directors has an interest in. Should a journalist be cajoled into writing a story they believe is inaccurate or deceptive? The answer, according to this clause, is: 'No, the journalist should be able to write the story as they see it.' Reality, however, may produce a different outcome, as few journalists would want to jeopardise their position by antagonising their employers.

Clause 7

Do your utmost to ensure disclosure of any direct or indirect payment made for interviews, pictures, information or stories.

Clause 7 ties in with the earlier discussion of Clauses 4 and 5, which considered the issue of journalists accepting payment for what they write or don't write. In this case, we are considering the issue of journalists paying for information. This is a ticklish question (and, like much of what we've talked about above, involves questions of legality as well).

What is the big deal here? Surely there is nothing wrong with paying for information if it helps expose a wrongdoing? That depends. Remember the old saying, 'you get what you pay for'? That is not always the case. Sometimes you get more, or even less, than you pay for. You might be lucky and get what you need to pull your story together—that elusive piece that enables all the other pieces of the jigsaw puzzle to come together. Alternatively, you might get a lot less than you wanted.

There are countless examples of media organisations that have paid large sums of money for interviews that have, ultimately, provided poor television. Sometimes, the individuals involved have been poor performers. Sometimes, the information they claimed to have did not materialise. Occasionally, the person being paid to appear on television has felt duty-bound to 'dress up' their story so as to justify the money being paid to them. Under the television spotlights they have been exposed as charlatans, or as people seeking their 'fifteen minutes of fame' as Andy Warhol once proclaimed.

While newspapers tend to leave the big interviews to current affairs television and the magazines, there have been examples where newspapers have been caught out paying for forgeries. The German news magazine *Stern*, for example, paid for the rights to publish the so-called Hitler Diaries. These were subsequently proved to be fakes. There are instances in which expensive photographs have also been discredited. The message here is: if someone has an important story to tell, encourage them to provide the information gratis. Use the public interest argument.

Finally, you need to know whether the information or material being offered has been obtained legally or illegally. If it has been obtained illegally, then there are legal implications for you (you may be charged with receiving stolen goods). In this case, you are better off not accepting it, and certainly not paying for it. You also need to ask yourself whether, with a bit more leg-work on your part, you could find an alternative source for the information.

However, if you do decide to pay for information on the grounds that it is the only way you can pull your story together, then you probably need to advise your readers, listeners and viewers that you have paid for it (and even how much you have paid). It may be that they will judge the story differently than they might have done without this knowledge.

Ultimately, this is a question for the media organisation rather than individual journalists to make. Thankfully, fewer organisations appear inclined to engage in a bidding war such as that which followed the rescue of Tasmanian miners Todd Russell and Brant Webb in May 2006 after the collapse of the Beaconsfield gold mine. Australian media organisations appear to have mixed views on this question. This was highlighted in late 2011 in relation to the so-called 'Bali boy' story, involving the New South Wales teenager who was found guilty of drug possession in Indonesia. While the teenager was awaiting his hearing, Australian media organisations reported that one of the major television networks had negotiated a fee with the boy and his parents to tell their story upon their return to Australia. This was subsequently denied, although the claim was re-aired once the boy had been released by the Indonesian legal system and flown back to Australia.

Even more recently, the ethics of chequebook journalism were highlighted when *60 Minutes* reporter Tara Brown and her crew (producer Stephen Rice, cameraman Ben Williamson and sound recordist David Ballment) were jailed in Lebanon when a so-called 'child recovery operation' went horribly wrong. The *60 Minutes* crew were working with Sally Faulkner, the mother of two children taken back to Lebanon by their father, her estranged husband. Brown and her colleagues, along with Faulkner and a three-man extraction team, were arrested after snatching the children from Faulkner's mother-in-law. They were jailed, although the television crew and Faulkner were subsequently released and flew back to Australia after Channel Nine had negotiated a 'payment' with the children's father, which saw Faulkner give up her rights to see them. At the time of writing, the extraction team were still in a Lebanese prison awaiting trial. This story raises important questions, not just about the value of chequebook journalism, but also the risks associated with such stories: to the children, as well as to the reporters and other people involved. In this case, for example, the children's grandmother was knocked over when the children were snatched from her care.

Clause 8

Use fair, responsible and honest means to obtain material. Identify yourself and your employer before obtaining any interview for publication or broadcast. Never exploit a person's vulnerability or ignorance of media practice.

The three parts of this clause need to be dealt with separately, although the first and second are directly linked. The first has to do with avoiding deception, namely using *'fair, responsible and honest means to obtain material'*. Deception is a tough one from a journalistic perspective. Should you identify yourself as a journalist whenever you are researching a story? There are a number of elements to this. People will often say more to a person in what they consider to be a private conversation than if they believe their comments might be reported for all and sundry to read or hear. But sometimes that will result in you missing out on a story. If that is the case, can you justify it?

Some journalists use the 'sit in the corner and eavesdrop on every conversation that is going on around them' approach. This will provide good information, but is it ethical? Most people will say that overhearing information (particularly in a public place) is fine. It is what you do with it that creates the ethical dilemma. Should you publish it? This depends on whether you identify the speakers or not. If you don't identify them by name, you might be okay. But what if you identify them through association—that is, by saying where the conversation took place, on what day or at what time? Potentially, this might identify the speakers to other people who were at the venue, if not in the group.

Perhaps it is important—in a public interest sense—that the speakers are identified because of the content of the conversation. This is a tough decision, although it is definitely in breach of the Code because the methods being used are hardly 'fair and honest'. Whether the journalist is acting responsibly is also a moot point, one that depends on the outcome of the decision whether to publish or not.

The WikiLeaks debate in 2011–12 highlights some of the questions associated with this issue. The question of legality aside, this debate identifies some of the difficulties facing not only journalists, but also people working in positions that demand secrecy on the part of employees. WikiLeaks exposed a vast quantity of information which journalists—in fact, virtually anyone with a computer—could access. But most of this material had been provided to WikiLeaks in contravention of different countries' secrecy provisions. The fact that it had then been made accessible to journalists and others does not really change its status. What it does do is raise a question about whether 'fair, honest and responsible means' had been used to obtain the information. Certainly not on the part of the inside sources who provided the material to WikiLeaks. Can the journalists and media organisations rely on a public interest defence? Again this is a moot point, although the story was so big that media organisations would have ignored the tidbits provided to them at their peril.

Now let us look at the second part of this clause: *'Identify yourself and your employer before obtaining any interview for publication or broadcast.'* What about a deliberate deception, where you masquerade as something, or someone, you are not? There have been many instances where journalists have made a conscious decision not to reveal their identity, instead setting up elaborate disguises, posing in a range of occupations to gain their stories (as health-care workers, patients in psychiatric clinics, supermarket employees and proprietors of a city bar, for example). In all instances they were able to expose wrongdoing, although in some instances their conduct was said to be unlawful (another topic we will return to in Chapter 9).

In many respects, the decision whether to identify oneself as a journalist or not is part of an overall risk assessment. The journalist needs to ask: What are the consequences if I identify myself as a journalist?

Will it enhance or diminish my chances of getting the story? Am I placing myself at risk of physical harm? Would I be better to act as a fly on the wall or claim to be someone I'm not? The answers to these questions are linked to the possible outcomes. If there is a strong public interest argument, the journalist might be justified in making such a decision, but needs to consider the costs involved.

Finally, we need to consider the third part of this clause: '*Never exploit a person's vulnerability or ignorance of media practice.*' Too often this warning is ignored in the thrill of the chase. Journalists may overlook the fact that people do not understand how the media work or what the media are looking for. This is because journalists frequently work with media-savvy people—politicians, sports stars, people in the entertainment industry and business people—who rely on the media for their profile and often their success. Nowadays, such people are trained to deal with the media. They are told how to respond to questions and what answers to give. But many people in the wider community have not had media exposure or training, and often they are subjected to a media pack when they are dealing with a tragedy (covered further in Clause 11). Such people are often vulnerable and can be intimidated by journalists, especially those who are more interested in their story than in the welfare of the individual they are interviewing. It is important to consider the type of story you're researching and the people you're seeking to interview.

Clause 9

Present pictures and sound which are true and accurate. Any manipulation likely to mislead should be disclosed.

We will only touch on this one briefly as it really links back to previous discussions about truth, fairness and balance. It is often tempting to run footage or a picture just because it is technically good. But does it really present an accurate picture? Does it tell the full story or does it distort what you are trying to present? Should you crop people out of a photograph or leave them in? Is it appropriate to show old footage of the site or the individual that would give a different impression from the one people would receive if they were to visit the site or see the person today? The questions to ask here are: What are you trying to achieve? Is what you have produced justifiable in the circumstances?

Clause 10

Do not plagiarise.

Far too many journalists have been caught out in recent years claiming the work of others as their own. Plagiarism is a crime. It is intellectual theft and should be condemned as such. If you are going to use another person's words, work or even ideas, then give them credit for it. There is nothing wrong with drawing on the work of another person—we all draw inspiration from a range of sources. The sign of a good journalist is that they acknowledge doing so.

Clause 11

Respect private grief and personal privacy. Journalists have the right to resist compulsion to intrude.

Journalists and media organisations are often criticised for intruding in the private lives of individuals, particularly those who are grieving. Sometimes the criticism is justified, as journalists forget or deliberately ignore the protocols surrounding these issues. But there are also instances where the media are invited into private lives, for example by politicians, sports stars and personalities. The question for us is: When should journalists take that step? According to Hodges:

> It is just to violate the privacy of an individual only if information about that individual is of overriding public importance and the public need cannot be met by any other means. As a formal criterion, of course, this does not tell us what information to publish in specific cases, but it does provide a test for any particular decision on privacy.
>
> Hodges, 1994, p. 203

Arguing that the level of privacy a person is entitled to depends on their circumstances, Hodges lists seven categories. These are: public officials, public figures, celebrities, temporarily newsworthy heroes, criminals, innocent victims of crime and tragedy, and adult relatives of the prominent (Hodges, 1994, p. 203). To that should be added an eighth category: child relatives of the prominent (Tanner et al., 2005, p. 158).

A good example of a celebrity couple who allowed the media into their lives was Australian test cricketer Michael Clarke and his then fiancée Lara Bingle, who featured on the 'Where the bloody hell are you?' tourism advertisement. Given the access the couple had granted the media, it was inevitable when their relationship disintegrated that the media would continue to report on them, both at the time of the break-up and as they rebuilt their lives. It is interesting that Clarke—who went on to become Australian cricket captain and marry—became far more circumspect in his dealings with journalists, particularly as they related to his private life, while Bingle encouraged media coverage, perhaps a sign of their respective public personas.

Obviously, we need to be careful when dealing with anyone who is grieving, irrespective of whether they are a media-savvy public figure or a person who has been thrust into the spotlight by misfortune. People who are grieving can often act in unpredictable ways and, as journalists, we need to be ready for this. We need to be prepared for it when requesting an interview and we need to be ready for it when conducting the interview. We need to be aware that comments made in anger or grief should be carefully weighed up before they are published or broadcast. Remember, the prospect of a defamation action may not be far away.

Finally, this section of the Code does attempt to give journalists an 'out' if they do not want to cover such stories. But reality often demands otherwise. Journalists who regularly refuse to interview grieving parents, or relatives of a deceased person, will struggle to win promotion.

Clause 12

Do your utmost to achieve fair correction of errors.

At the start of this chapter we questioned why journalists and media organisations are not held in particularly high regard. Perhaps one of the reasons for this is the reluctance of media organisations to admit they 'got it wrong'. Considering our earlier discussion about the power of the word and its capacity to destroy reputations and lives, it seems a small 'ask' for journalists and their bosses to admit it when they make mistakes. Readers, viewers and listeners will respect you for it.

Summary

o Journalism ethics can be complex. It is easy to become bogged down in philosophical disputes about the merits of one particular course of action compared with another.

o Ultimately, such discussions should not be problematic. Journalists have a range of tools at their disposal, which should help them to act ethically.

o The first—and most important—tool is their own ethical compass, developed over a lifetime and reflecting the individual's outlook on life, including their beliefs and principles.

o Journalists can also draw on the various professional codes of conduct—the MEAA Code of Ethics and other codes or charters, both in-house and industry specific—when faced with an ethical dilemma.

o These tools should be sufficient to enable the individual journalist to act in an ethical manner.

o When in doubt, a journalist can always seek the advice of peers. If there are still doubts in their mind, they should think about the consequences of their actions and ask if they are justifiable or not.

Questions

1 What are the principal influences on individuals as they develop their moral compass?
2 To what extent does the MEAA Code meet the needs of journalists, or do you think it is outdated?
3 To what extent do you believe journalists are justified in not revealing their identity to people about whom they are writing or with whom they are discussing issues?
4 Should journalists be allowed to record conversations secretly, or to secretly take footage or photographs to support a story they are researching? What are the issues in support of and against this practice?

Activities

1 Using Factiva, or one of the other online databases, locate a story that involves a breach of ethics on the part of a journalist or media organisation. Write a summary of the allegations and then indicate why you believe the journalist's conduct breaches the MEAA Code of Ethics.

2 You are working as a motoring writer for a well-known car magazine. There are rumours circulating that a car which is about to be released on the local market does not satisfy Australian safety standards. A representative of the manufacturer approaches you and offers you a long-term loan of their luxury model, which is a proven performer. He says this is a 'no-strings-attached' offer. How do you respond to the offer? What are the issues involved?

3 Your magazine has a policy that no staff members are allowed to accept 'freebies' from clients. As a travel writer, you assiduously stick to this policy. What are the ethical conundrums that this policy seeks to overcome? Explain why you agree or disagree with the magazine's policy.

4 What are the lessons to come out of the *Charlie Hebdo* attacks for journalists and media organisations? Do you believe this attack (and other attacks, for example, the death of Theo Van Gogh, the condemnation of Danish newspaper *Jyllands-Posten* for publishing cartoons seen as critical of the Prophet Muhammad, or even the fatwa issued against Salman Rushdie) should serve to constrain the way in which journalists and other creatives write about or portray Islam? Explain your answer.

References and additional reading

Hodges, L. (1994). 'The journalist and privacy', *Journal of Mass Media Ethics*, 9(4), pp. 197–212.
Roy Morgan Group (2016). http://www.roymorgan.com/findings/
    6797-image-of-professions-2016-201605110031
Stockwell, S. & Scott, P. (2000). *All-media Guide to Fair and Cross-cultural Reporting*,
    Brisbane: Australian Key Centre for Cultural and Media Policy, Griffith University.
Tanner, S.J., Phillips, G., Smyth, C. & Tapsall, S. (2005). *Journalism Ethics at Work*, Sydney: Pearson
    Longman.

Online resources

ABC Code of Practice: http://about.abc.net.au/wp-content/uploads/2016/05/
    ABCCodeOfPractice2016-1.pdf
Australian Communications and Media Authority: www.acma.gov.au
Australian Human Rights Commission (2010). 'Age discrimination – exposing the hidden barriers for
    mature age workers.' http://www.humanrights.gov.au/our-work/age-discrimination/publications/
    age-discrimination-exposing-hidden-barrier-mature-age
Australian Press Council: www.presscouncil.org.au
International Federation of Journalists: www.ifj.org
Media Entertainment and Arts Alliance: www.alliance.org.au
Response Ability: www.responseability.org
SBS Codes of Practice: http://media.sbs.com.au/home/upload_media/site_20_rand_2138311027_
    sbscodesofpractice2010.pdf
Western Australian Government: http://www.inclusionwa.org.au/download/A%20way%20with%20
    words.pdf

9
Legal Pitfalls

'When men are pure, laws are useless; when men are corrupt, laws are broken.'

Benjamin Disraeli

'There can be no higher law in journalism than to tell the truth and to shame the devil'.

Walter Lippmann

Objectives

Journalists are not above the law, despite the importance we attach to our work. Like other members of society who break the law, journalists who do the wrong thing, whether deliberately or unintentionally, can find themselves the focus of legal attention. In this chapter we look at some of the areas journalists should be aware of when researching and writing feature stories, including:

o   contempt

o   defamation

o   trespass, deception and privacy

o   freedom of information

o   anti-terrorism

o   racial vilification

o   creators' rights.

Some words of warning

This chapter should not be read in isolation. It needs to be read in conjunction with the individual chapters that make up the second half of this book. For example, while we cover defamation in this chapter, we also return to it in Chapter 19, where we discuss restaurant reviews. Some of the other topics we discuss in this chapter are also revisited elsewhere, and specific examples are given.

This chapter also contains a caveat. The authors are journalists and academics, not lawyers. Media law is a complex area, particularly as it relates to defamation and contempt. While we draw attention to some of the consequences of, and even defences against, particular allegations, we recognise our own limitations and advise readers who feel they may have breached the law to seek professional advice. One of the reasons for this is that while there is some uniformity of laws as they apply to journalists, there are still jurisdictional differences in many areas, which can create traps for even well-meaning reporters.

The Australian legal system

The Australian legal system is complex and multi-tiered. We are not going to delve into the various responsibilities of the different courts here; you can explore this for yourself by accessing the websites listed at the end of this chapter. We suggest you do so, particularly if you are writing about the legal system, about people who work within it (lawyers, magistrates or judges), or about people who interact with it (because they have been charged with offences under Australian law, or are the victims of crime).

The Australian legal system is underpinned by a number of fundamental principles. These include:

- a presumption of innocence (until proven guilty)
- the right of the individual to a fair trial (there are a number of elements to this that we will return to later in the chapter)
- the principle of open justice (the belief that justice should not only be done, but also be seen to be done); however, there are some limitations to this, designed primarily to protect individuals (such as minors who are the subject of legal action, or victims of criminal conduct)
- the right to legal representation, in the case of criminal proceedings (this does not apply in civil cases, although the common law right to a fair hearing will ensure that parties to an action are not disadvantaged)
- the right to natural justice.

(For a more detailed discussion of the above concepts, see Pearson & Polden, 2014, 2011; Pearson, 2007; Beattie & Beal, 2007; and Cameron, 2007.)

The courts and the journalist

Feature writers can engage with the legal system at four levels. The first level is that of observer—that is, in situations where the legal system is the subject of the story the journalist is researching (for example, an article that compares sentencing standards for similar crimes across the different states), or where a person the journalist is interested in is the subject of legal proceedings. There have been a number of occasions when journalists have followed major stories through the courts, including cases in which former corporate high-fliers were charged after the collapse of their companies, and situations in which the court has been asked to reopen cases that allegedly led to a miscarriage of justice. For example, the HIH Insurance and OneTel cases in the early 2000s provided journalists with opportunities to focus both on the companies and on the lives of individual directors, including Ray Williams and Rodney Adler (HIH Insurance), and Jodee Rich, Larry Adler, James Packer and Lachlan Murdoch (OneTel). Turmoil on the share market may also play out in the courts, providing journalists with opportunities for stories that focus on the wiles of individual business people.

The second level of journalistic involvement in the legal system—that in which the journalist acts as a participant-observer—also has some strong Australian precedents. One of the best-known examples is that of West Australian journalist Estelle Blackburn, whose investigations into the jailing of John Button and Darryl Beamish led to their sentences for manslaughter (Button) and murder (Beamish) being overturned, albeit years after they had served their sentences and been released from jail. Both were jailed in the 1960s; Button was convicted of the manslaughter of his girlfriend, while Beamish, a deaf mute, was jailed for the murder of a wealthy heiress (see Blackburn, 2003; 2007). Another example involved Colleen Egan's role in the case of Andrew Mallard—a West Australian found guilty in 1994 of murdering Perth jewellery shop owner Pamela Lawrence, even though he had never met her. It took 12 years for his team, which included Egan, to mount the case that ultimately saw him released (see Egan, 2010).

While Blackburn's journalistic instinct told her there might have been a miscarriage of justice, she did not work her cases as a reporter. In fact, she acted as a primary investigator, alongside the legal teams established to plead the cases of Button and Beamish. Egan's involvement took a different course. She began as a journalist, before morphing into an advocate.

The third level of involvement, the journalist as participant, is the most unpalatable of the three, and concerns most of our discussion in this chapter. A journalist and/or the media organisation for which they work may become participants in the legal system if they are charged with breaching the law. We believe in taking a 'prevention is better than cure' approach. Our philosophy is that if you are able to recognise that the law proscribes certain behaviour, you will lessen your chances of becoming a statistic.

The fourth level at which a journalist may become involved with the law is as litigant. Generally, this involves the journalist seeking to protect their rights over the article, photograph, documentary or book they have created. This area is covered by copyright law, a topic we return to at the end of the chapter.

Responsibilities when covering court hearings

As previously indicated, journalists covering court hearings enjoy certain privileges. But with these privileges come obligations, some quite onerous. Journalists are expected to act responsibly when covering the courts (for guidelines on what you can and cannot do when covering a trial, have a look at the various online sites, legal texts or brochures produced by court-based public information officers; a number are listed in the References section at the end of this chapter).

There are a number of key points that journalists should bear in mind. For a start, they should make sure that any reports adhere to the law and ensure that the story does not jeopardise the right of the individual to a fair trial. Courts frown upon journalists (or other people) who seek to pre-empt a finding of the court (particularly if the trial is being conducted before a jury), by proclaiming a person innocent or guilty.

There are limitations not only on *what* journalists can write or say, but also on *when* they can publish or broadcast particular information. For example, journalists enjoy a virtual free rein in the period after a crime has been committed and before a warrant has been issued for the arrest of a suspect, or arrests have been made. However, once court proceedings are pending, the amount of material a journalist can publish is significantly limited. An individual's prior convictions cannot be published while the proceedings are active. Nor are photographs allowed in some situations, particularly if identity is likely to be an issue. This was highlighted in the case of *Who Weekly*, which in 1994 was fined $100,000 and forced to pulp an entire print run after publishing a front-page photograph of Ivan Milat, the accused in the so-called 'backpacker murders' case, before his trial had commenced. There are also strict limitations on the amount of material that can be published during children's court hearings, including information that might identify minors who have been charged, are victims of a crime, or are witnesses to a crime.

Breaches of these conditions can lead to an action against the journalist or their employer for contempt. Contempt can take several forms:

- **sub judice contempt:** this is information that is deemed to interfere with, or is capable of interfering with, the outcome of the case

- **scandalising the court:** this involves publishing information that is seen to undermine the administration of justice and the reputation of the courts

- **refusing to reveal the source of confidential information:** as mentioned in the previous chapter, this form of contempt was highlighted in the WikiLeaks case. No attempts have been made to prosecute anyone in Australia over the release of information to WikiLeaks, but there have been prosecutions in the United States, including the court martial of Bradley Manning (now known as Chelsea Manning), an intelligence specialist in the defence forces

- **revealing deliberations that have taken place among jurors:** unlike their counterparts in the United States, Australian journalists are not permitted to contact jurors during or after the trial. In Australia, any deliberations that take place within the jury room and between jurors remain confidential. Journalists— or jurors—who breach this covenant can be subject to legal proceedings

- **reporting what has taken place during closed court proceedings** (or when the jury is absent from the court): there are good legal reasons for the judge to ask the jury to leave the court, including discussions over points of law that might mislead jurors.

We will look briefly at the first three of these, as Australia has a long—and unfortunate—history of contempt involving journalists. In fairness, much of this is due to ignorance rather than any deliberate attempt to flaunt the law, but as lawyers will tell you, ignorance is no defence.

Sub judice contempt

Sub judice contempt is easy to avoid if you have an in-house lawyer you can turn to. Alternatively, follow the advice provided above and talk to the court's public information officer if the case is before the courts. If the case has not yet reached the courts, it is worth talking to police public relations officers, as they can keep you informed as to the status of the case—that is, whether warrants have been issued or arrests made (as different rules apply depending on what stage the case is at).

Michael Cameron (2007, p. 34) provides a good summary of what a journalist is allowed to do and when. He argues that before an arrest has been made, it is possible to publish the following:

- details of the crime; these can be quite extensive and include time, date, cause, possible motive etc.
- the police profile of any suspects, including identikit photos; it is also possible to write about the relationship between the suspects and the victim
- statements by witnesses and police
- an interview with the victim.

However, once a warrant has been issued or the individual has been charged, the amount of material that can be published is strictly limited. This is to protect the accused's right to a fair trial. Details about the offence must be broad; information about the accused is restricted to personal details (name, age, address, occupation). Witness or police statements should not be published, unless given in court. Nor should the journalist—or media organisation—provide any opinion on what the outcome is likely to be. Finally, photographs of the accused should not be published if identity is likely to be an issue during the trial. It is, however, possible to continue providing stories about the condition of the victim (Cameron, 2007, p. 34).

The risks journalists face in covering courts were highlighted in December 2016 when a young Yahoo7 reporter, Krystal Johnson, was found guilty of sub judice contempt. Johnson caused a Melbourne murder trial to be aborted after she published information that had not been presented to the jury. Johnson, who did not attend the murder trial on the day in question, based her report on factually correct information that had been presented at an earlier hearing, but had been withheld in this instance because of a risk that it may influence the jury. The information included a Facebook post from the deceased that she feared the accused may one day murder her. It was read more than 4000 times before being pulled off the Yahoo7 site. During the contempt hearing, the court was told that Johnson had not submitted her copy to sub-editors before posting it online. Johnson was placed on a good behaviour bond and Yahoo7 fined $300,000 (Crothers, 2017). The accused was subsequently found guilty of murder when the case was re-heard.

Scandalising the court

This form of contempt effectively involves bringing the court—or the presiding judge—into disrepute. In Australia this has been manifested in various ways, but predominantly by journalists criticising judgments or even delays in the handing down of judgments. There are some good stories to be told about the courts, about judicial office holders and the pressures under which they operate, as we saw in 2005 when News Ltd focused attention on the then Chief Justice of the Western Australian Supreme Court, the Hon. David Malcolm, AC. Chief Justice Malcolm was criticised by *The Australian* after supposedly giving incorrect directions to a jury in summing up a murder trial. However, the articles were not the subject of a contempt charge, despite the fact that they may, potentially, have been interpreted as a criticism of the judicial system.

There has also been a number of articles questioning sentences handed down by judges in various jurisdictions and states, and others querying comments made by judges when handing down their sentences (see, for example, *The Daily Telegraph*'s story on 22 February 2016, in which it said that eight sentences handed down by Judge Clive Jeffreys of the NSW District Court had been overturned on appeal because they were inadequate). It could be argued that these decisions have contributed to a community belief that the courts are soft on penalties, although this belief is not necessarily supported by the statistics (which in itself could be the basis of an interesting feature).

In 2011, in New South Wales, there was a series of stories discussing the future of two magistrates—Jennifer Betts and Brian Maloney—including whether they should be allowed to remain on the bench. In both cases the decision was referred to the Parliament after complaints to the Judicial Commission were upheld: Betts had been found guilty of bullying and intimidatory behaviour towards people who had appeared in her court; Maloney of inappropriate behaviour. Both magistrates argued that their actions had been influenced by mental illness—in the case of Betts it was depression, while Maloney had been diagnosed with bipolar disorder. In both cases, Parliament found in favour of the magistrates, who have been allowed to retain their positions. Interestingly, none of the articles was the subject of a contempt charge.

There is a fine line between producing constructive stories—those that could lead to positive outcomes—and writing those that bring the court into disrepute in the eyes of fair-minded Australians. Journalists should not be deterred from writing about the courts, or even about individual judicial officers; they just need to be aware that there are legal and ethical pitfalls if they should err (for example, see Merritt, 2011, which looks at the question of mental health and judicial officers).

Refusing to reveal sources

Finally, journalists can be held in contempt if they refuse to reveal a source of information that might be of interest to the court. This is a particularly problematic requirement for journalists because the MEAA Code of Ethics (discussed in Chapter 8) advises them to protect the identity of sources who have provided them with information on the basis that they will remain anonymous. Journalists are reluctant to break that trust on the grounds that it will jeopardise that relationship, as well as other relationships they rely on for valuable information, and because it could deter future whistleblowers from speaking out to other journalists—perhaps leading to corruption going unreported.

Three Australian journalists have been jailed for refusing to reveal the sources of information they published. Others have been charged with refusing to reveal their sources to the courts, including high-profile journalists Gerard McManus and Michael Harvey (2007); Richard Baker, Phillip Dorling and Nick McKenzie (2012), Adele Ferguson (2012) and Steve Pennells (2013).

McManus and Michael Harvey were found guilty of contempt in the Victorian County Court. They had received information detailing plans by the Howard government to reduce war veterans' entitlements by $500 million. The case led to a senior public servant turned whistleblower, Desmond Kelly, being charged. Kelly was found guilty in the Victorian County Court of leaking the information, a finding that was subsequently overturned on appeal to the Supreme Court (Ross, 2007). McManus and Harvey both refused to divulge to the courts the source of information used in their stories. However, this case took on a rather interesting dimension when the then federal Attorney-General, Philip Ruddock, said publicly that he did not believe the journalists should be jailed. They were, however, fined $7000 each and had their convictions recorded.

This issue arose again in 2012, when three Fairfax journalists—Richard Baker, Philip Dorling and Nick McKenzie—were ordered by the New South Wales Supreme Court to reveal the confidential sources they relied on for a series of stories about a relationship between Chinese-Australian businesswoman Helen Liu and former Defence Minister Joel Fitzgibbon. The articles alleged that Liu had provided Fitzgibbon with $150,000 'to cultivate him as an agent of political and business influence' (Hall, 2012, p. 2). Fitzgibbon denied receiving the money and sued for defamation. Tom Blackburn SC, counsel for Fairfax, argued that Fairfax and its reporters had two defences: 1) an implied right within the Australian Constitution to discuss matters of government and politics, and 2) the 'newspaper rule', which is designed to protect the identity of sources who provide information used in stories about politics or government. However, Justice Lucy McCallum described the newspaper rule as a guide, not a rule, and that providing absolute immunity to confidential sources—including sources of lies or misinformation—would impede democracy (Hall, 2012, p. 2). This is significant, given the denials by Liu, who questioned the integrity or authenticity of the documents relied upon by the journalists to justify their stories. *The Age* newspaper, which published the articles, subsequently sought leave to appeal the decision to the High Court. However this request was denied.

In 2014, Hancock Prospecting, the iron ore company controlled by Gina Rinehart, was ordered to pay the legal costs of Fairfax journalist Adele Ferguson who had written an unauthorised biography of the Rinehart family in 2012. Rinehart Prospecting had taken Ferguson to court, demanding that she reveal the sources of information published in the book. Ferguson refused. In another case, West Australian journalist Steve Pennells also had a win against Rinehart, who had taken legal action against him, seeking the identity of sources he had used for stories about the family. Pennells was able to rely on shield laws, which had recently been introduced in WA.

Today, most Australian jurisdictions have shield laws that are designed to protect journalists who refuse to reveal their sources either pre-trial or at trial. However, the effectiveness of these laws is yet to be truly tested (*Guardian*, 2013).

Defamation

While journalists need to be aware of the contempt laws, even greater traps are concealed in the defamation laws. These are a concern for a number of reasons. There is the obvious ethical dimension involved in the ability of journalists to destroy the reputations of individuals. Related to this is the fact that a successful defamation suit can financially ruin the journalist and the organisation that has published or broadcast the disputed words, pictures, footage or action. Even if the journalist and their organisation can handle the financial costs, their own reputation can be damaged as a result of a successful defamation action.

Simply stated, defamation is the release of material (in published form: printed, spoken or broadcast) that is capable of damaging the reputation of a person in the eyes of others. The range of material that can be defamatory is broad-ranging and can be conveyed via, for example, newspapers, magazines, newsletters, radio, television, public meetings, billboards, internet sites, emails, blogs, text messages, photographs, posters, cartoons, paintings and letters (Beattie & Beal, 2007, p. 43; Cameron, 2007, p. 11).

It is important to note that there is no real distinction between the written word (libel) and the spoken word (slander). In all defamation cases, libel and slander alike, the onus is on the complainant to establish that the defamation has occurred. There are three legs to such a case, requiring the complainant to prove that the material 1) has been communicated between individuals, 2) identifies the complainant and 3) defames the complainant (Cameron, 2007, p. 11; Beattie & Beal, 2007, p. 43; Pearson, 2007, Chapter 8).

The difficulty for journalists is that the very nature of our jobs requires us to be critical of people at times. But there is a difference—as defamation law recognises—between making comments that are justifiable and making comments that cannot be defended. According to Pearson and Polden (2011, p. 188), journalists should go through a two-step process when considering the potential outcomes of a proposed story or statement, asking:

- Is the material I'm about to publish defamatory?
- If so, is there a defence available to the publisher?

Ultimately, the court (which may be a judge sitting alone or a judge and jury) bases its decision on the imputation (that is, the meaning) of the words, images or actions in question. This can be a difficult decision, as there may be semantic subtleties that need to be considered. In some instances, the court may be asked to consider the explicit meaning of the words, images or actions in question. On other occasions— in cases where the defamatory statement may be based on innuendo, which by its very nature tends to be negative—the court may be required to read between the lines (Pearson & Polden, 2011, p. 192). Thus there could be a considerable gulf between the 'natural' or 'ordinary' meaning of a word and its implied meaning (Pearson, 2007, p. 185).

From a practical point of view, you should ideally have your stories 'legalled' (checked by lawyers) if you believe there is the risk of a defamation action. In addition, make sure you keep all the documents you use when researching your story. These could be called as evidence and might be needed to prove your defence.

(For further discussion of the legal issues identified here, see Pearson & Polden 2014, 2011; Pearson, 2007; and Beattie & Beal, 2007.)

Defending a defamation action

Journalists should not, however, avoid pursuing a subject or story because of the possibility of a defamation action. Remember, many powerful people will seek to intimidate journalists by threatening legal action. While some will follow through with the threat, many do not have the financial resources or the will to pursue a time-consuming court case, knowing that if they are unsuccessful they may have to pay not only their own court costs, but also those of the defendant. Journalists should assume that any defamatory comment will lead to court action, and they need to know that their action was defensible.

Defences to defamation are grouped under two headings: 1) truth and 2) public importance.

Truth as a defence

While this defence might seem relatively straightforward, the fact is that the onus of proof is on the defendant (the journalist or media organisation) rather than on the plaintiff. The court will start from the premise that the imputations are false (Pearson, 2007, p. 207), and the onus is on the journalist to prove that the statements were 'substantially true' (Beattie & Beal, 2007, p. 46). It is not sufficient for the journalist to *believe* the statements are true; they have to be able to *prove* the statements are true.

In practice, being able to prove the truth of something does not guarantee a risk-free publication, because proving the imputations that arise in a story can be a very different task from proving the facts upon which the imputations are based (Beattie & Beal, 2007, p. 46). For example, there is a difference between claiming outright that 'John Smith is corrupt' and making the claim by imputation. Often the latter is achieved through innuendo—for example, by the use of photographs that show the individual receiving a brown paper bag or envelope. Because we have been programmed by television dramas to associate brown paper bags and envelopes with corrupt conduct, we automatically jump to the conclusion that the recipient of the brown paper bag or envelope is corrupt, ignoring other possibilities, including the prospect that it might contain their lunch or an invitation to a party.

Public importance as a defence

There are a number of defences that fit under the 'public importance' category, including absolute privilege, fair report, qualified privilege, political qualified privilege, honest opinion and fair comment. There is also another category, where the defendant claims that the alleged defamation was unintentional or trivial. (For a discussion of these defences, see Beattie & Beal, 2007; Pearson & Polden, 2011, 2015; and Pearson, 2007). Significantly, the judge presiding in the case of the three Fairfax journalists, discussed earlier, indicated that the newspaper and its journalists could successfully rely on the qualified privilege argument in any defamation action 'if they could show their conduct in publishing was reasonable in the circumstances' (Hall, 2012, p. 2).

Trespass

Journalists chasing a big story are often tempted to go the extra distance to make sure they have every angle covered. Sometimes, however, this can mean that the line between staying within the law and breaking it is breached. For example, journalists can be charged with trespass if they enter property without permission.

Trespass charges are brought in a range of situations. The obvious situation is when a journalist or photographer enters a building or land when they are not invited (either implied or expressly) and then refuses to leave when requested to do so by the person who has legal possession of the property (an owner-occupier or tenant). Under the law, it is not trespass to enter a property to request an interview, although if the request is refused, the expectation is that the journalist will leave. If there are signs up saying that the media are not allowed, or the gates to the property are locked, then the implied right to enter the property to seek an interview no longer applies.

Drones, trespass and privacy

Trespass is also a factor journalists need to consider if they employ drones to research and/or supplement the story they are working on with vision or audio. While the law is yet to catch up with the growth in popularity of drone technology, the reality is that drones can be misused with the possibility that the operator may be charged with trespass, or breach of Australia's privacy, anti-stalking and surveillance devices legislation. Before using drones, or remotely piloted aircraft (RPAs) as they are known, it is important to investigate whether there are any federal or state-specific laws that need to be addressed. For example, there is no legislation designed to protect the privacy of individuals in Australia. Despite calls for a Tort of Privacy (supported by a parliamentary committee and the Law Reform Commission), the federal government has been reluctant to support this initiative. The *Privacy Act 1988* helps protect personal information, but it is not designed to stop the media pursuing an individual for a story. This has led to situations where celebrities have taken out apprehended violence orders (AVOs) against journalists and photographers. The best-known case in recent years involved Nicole Kidman, who believed paparazzi were stalking her and that a listening device had been attached to the fence of her property.

The ready availability of drones has added a new dimension to this, with the possibility that unscrupulous journalists (or anyone for that matter) could use a drone to surreptitiously take audio, photographs or video of individuals who believed they were acting in the privacy of their own homes or businesses. While any audio would probably be illegal under various state-based surveillance devices legislation (for example, see the Victorian Act), the situation regarding the use of video or photographs is less clear. While the Civil Aviation Safety Authority (CASA) has acted quickly to regulate the use of RPAs, its focus has been safety, rather than individual privacy. Nonetheless, some of the following requirements do have privacy implications. Under the new CASA rules, RPAs have been categorised by weight. The categories are micro (less than 100 g in weight); very small (100 g, but less than 2 kg); small (2 kg, but less than 25 kg); medium (25kg, but less than 150 kg); and large (more than 150 kg). The last three categories require the operator to have a remote pilot licence and operator's certificate. Micro drones do not require either a licence or an operator's certificate, whereas very small drones do, unless they are used for sport and recreation or are used 'within standard operating conditions'. Under the new CASA laws, standard operating conditions are defined in the following terms:

- The drone (RPA) must be operated within the pilot's visual line of sight;
- It must not be flown within 30 metres of a person not involved in the piloting of the RPA (or 15 metres if approval is given);
- It is operated at or below 400 feet above ground level by day (it cannot be flown at night, or into clouds);
- It cannot be flown over populous areas (beaches, parks, sporting events);
- It cannot be flown within 5.5 km of an aerodrome, or near or over prohibited or restricted areas (e.g. a military base).
- It cannot be flown over or in the vicinity of a public safety operation (bushfire, traffic accident, police operation etc.)

https://www.casa.gov.au/files/ac10110pdf

RPAs can be flown over private property, although a number of factors must be taken into consideration. The privacy of occupants must be respected. The RPA must be flown at a reasonable height over the property. It would not be appropriate to hover over individuals, take video of them, or hassle them in some way. We have already seen a number of instances where drones have crashed, potentially injuring innocent people, and CASA has issued fines to the operator and pilot.

From a media perspective, there is another factor that needs to be taken into account before an RPA is used. RPAs used for commercial purposes require CASA approval. In the case of RPAs weighing less than 2 kg, CASA requires at least five days' notice of the operation. This raises an interesting question in relation to drone footage that is provided to a media organisation by a non-journalist operator. If the footage and/ or audio is obtained illegally, is the media organisation also at fault?

Deception

As we discussed in the previous chapter, under the MEAA Code of Ethics journalists are not allowed to use deception to obtain information. The law frowns upon journalists who misrepresent themselves in order to obtain material for a story, including video footage. There are a number of layers to this, as in many states and territories the conduct of journalists is also governed by additional legislation.

Freedom of information

A high proportion of the stories that are produced by journalists—particularly feature writers—originate in government decisions (or the lack thereof). Often the material that prompts such stories is provided by sources within government departments and semi-government instrumentalities. But there are significant risks for government employees who provide journalists with unauthorised information, including jail under the *Crimes Act 1914*.

Australia does not have established whistleblower legislation to protect disaffected public servants who believe that government decision-making processes and decisions should be available for all to see. Nor do the shield laws provide the level of protection some advocates are seeking. Consequently, journalists either have to rely on the release of government-sanctioned information, which has often been sanitised to ensure that any criticism is limited, or they have to seek information through freedom of information (FOI) legislation. Journalists who understand the system, have good forensic skills and are persistent can use this to good effect.

In Australia, the Freedom of Information Act was introduced federally in 1982 and in all states and territories since. While there are some differences across jurisdictions, these are not significant from a journalistic perspective.

The main gripes journalists have relate to the costs and time delays involved in FOI applications. These applications can be very costly, particularly if they involve vast quantities of documents and considerable staff resources in allocating and copying those documents (or other data). While all legislation contains time limits—that is, it sets time frames in which public servants must respond to the request for information—often there is a capacity for these deadlines to be extended. Over time, governments have introduced a number of measures to prevent journalists from accessing information that might prove embarrassing. These can include 'conclusive certificates', commercial-in-confidence grounds and the fact that the documents had been prepared for Cabinet.

FOI legislation was introduced to make government more transparent and accountable. Individuals can use the legislation to ensure that personal information held about them by governments is correct (for example, hospital records etc.), but it was never intended that journalists use the legislation to obtain information about individuals—for example, about their criminal or educational records. FOI legislation has been used by media organisations to ensure that concerns about government mismanagement could be investigated and drawn to the public's attention. Examples include investigations into various state health systems, including waiting lists. As such, FOI, despite the criticisms, has been a valuable tool for journalists who are patient.

One of the mistakes journalists make in relation to FOI is in using it as a first port of call—almost like a government equivalent of a Google search. As the highly respected *Canberra Times* Editor-in-Chief Jack Waterford has commented, FOI should be a tool of last resort. Often, the information journalists seek can be located through publicly accessible sources, including government reports and online databases. The trick, according to Waterford, is to know who to talk to in the relevant government department, saying to them: 'I'm planning a story on X and wonder if you can head me in the right direction'. He says that often they will identify the material for you, without the time delays or costs associated with a formal FOI application.

If, however, you are required to make a formal application for information, Waterford's strategy can also help. He argues that an FOI claim should not be a fishing expedition. You should have a fairly clear idea of what documents you are looking for. Again, you can seek assistance through the designated departmental FOI officer. Ask them if you are on the right track, or if there are specific documents you should be asking for. If you don't, you may face a bill totalling thousands of dollars. You should also be wary if you are researching a story that might cause the government heartburn. Departmental staff look out for political time bombs. If they feel that a request may cause angst within the department or for the government, they are likely to contact the minister's office for advice. This could mean that the application will be held up or rejected.

Anti-terrorism, race hate and racial vilification

The area around activities to do with anti-terrorism, race hate and racial vilification is a legislative minefield and it requires considerable legal expertise to understand the implications of the relevant laws. Journalists working on stories involving national security should realise that the former Howard government gave Australia's intelligence organisations considerable powers to detain and interrogate people suspected of being involved in—or even contacting people suspected of involvement in—terrorist activities. For example:

- Under the *ASIO Legislation Amendment (Terrorism) Act 2003*, people suspected of such involvement may receive a five-year jail sentence; while the *Australian Security Intelligence Organisation Act 1979* allows one-year jail terms for various offences, which can include naming current or former spies.

- Journalists who make telephone contact with people suspected of having terrorist links may find that their phones are being tapped. Authorities have also been given powers to access SMS, email and other stored messages.

- Under the *National Security Information (Criminal Proceedings) Act 2004*, the courts have the capacity to limit the disclosure of information on national security grounds, even to the point of being able to hold proceedings *in camera* (that is, out of the public gaze).

In 2007, Australian broadcaster Alan Jones was found guilty by the Australian Communications and Media Authority (ACMA) of inciting violence on the basis of ethnicity and breaching the Commercial Radio Stations Code of Practice, in relation to his coverage of the 2005 Cronulla riots. This decision highlights the need for broadcasters and journalists to be careful about using their programs or columns to promote views that are considered undesirable or divisive. Equally, they need to be careful about allowing their programs or columns to be captured by interest groups that are seeking a respected or popular name to provide a platform for their views.

Journalists need to find a balance between promoting freedom of speech and being reasonable. The right to freedom of speech is implied, rather than expressly stated, in the Australian Constitution. It is also promoted by Article 19 of the Universal Declaration of Human Rights, to which Australia is a signatory. While the latter obliges signatories to protect 'free opinion and expression' (Beattie & Beal, 2007, p. 93), journalists need to be alert as to the potential consequences of allowing extreme views to be aired.

Australia has a range of laws (state and federal) that are designed to protect Australians against people who seek to vilify other members of society. At a federal level, the most important pieces of legislation are the *Racial Discrimination Act 1975* and the *Racial Hatred Act 1995*. The various states and territories also have legislation in these areas. Depending on the jurisdiction, people found guilty of breaching these laws can be fined or even jailed.

Some of the questions surrounding this topic were aired in 2011 when *Herald Sun* columnist Andrew Bolt was found guilty of breaching section 18C of the *Racial Discrimination Act*. The decision resulted from a class action brought by nine Indigenous Australians against Bolt and his employer, the Herald & Weekly Times. The applicants claimed Bolt had alleged that they used their Aboriginal heritage to claim professional advantage, including winning an arts prize and a scholarship. In his decision, Justice Mordecai Bromberg found that 'fair skinned Aboriginal people (or some of them) were reasonably likely, in all the circumstances, to have been offended, insulted, humiliated or intimidated by the imputations conveyed in the newspaper articles' written by Bolt and published in the *Herald Sun* (see Cohen, 2011). Significantly, Justice Bromberg ruled that Bolt and the newspaper could not use the fair comment or public interest defences to justify the articles.

This issue continued to simmer and in 2014, the Attorney-General George Brandis proposed changes to the Act. Brandis and other backbench MPs within the right wing of the Liberal Party argued that the Act restricted free speech. While Brandis's proposed changes were rejected, the issue was ultimately referred to a parliamentary committee which tabled its report in February 2017. Unfortunately the committee could not agree on an outcome, particularly in relation to S18C which makes it unlawful for someone to 'offend, insult or humiliate' a person on the basis of their skin colour or racial background (see: <http://www.aph.gov.au/Parliamentary_Business/Committees/Joint/Human_Rights_inquiries/FreedomspeechAustralia>).

Creators' rights

As with most of the topics covered in this chapter, this is a complex area. However, it is of particular interest to journalists as copyright owners of their own work. Be aware that the nature of your rights can be affected by any agreement you make, either with an employer (in the case of an employee) or with a publisher (in the case of a freelancer).

The creative rights of journalists are covered by the *Copyright Act 1968*, which provides that a right over a particular work is generated as soon as the work is created. This applies irrespective of whether the copyright symbol © is attached to the work or not. The *Copyright Act 1968* cannot apply to ideas or concepts, only to the expression of ideas or concepts in a material form (Beattie & Beal, 2007, p. 119). In the case of creative work, copyright generally extends for the life of the creator and for 70 years after their death, although in the case of photographs, the 70-year time frame begins from the date of publication. It is important to note that an individual work may have multiple copyright owners (for example, the photographer and the journalist).

Typically, journalists and other people producing copy for publication or broadcast have two rights: they have copyright and moral rights. Copyright owners have the exclusive rights to reproduce the work, publish it and communicate it (for example, via the internet, mobile phone, television or radio). However, while copyright is vested, initially, in the creator of the work, it can be transferred, usually for a cost (Beattie & Beal, 2007, p. 119). An issue emerges when someone breaches copyright without authorisation—for example, when someone publishes or reproduces work without permission.

Moral rights, on the other hand, refer to the right of the creator to be acknowledged as such. Whereas copyright can be transferred, moral rights are not exchangeable, even if the copyright changes hands (Beattie & Beal, 2007, p. 122). Generally speaking, authorship should be acknowledged whenever a work is published, printed, exhibited etc. Thus, if you assign copyright of an article to the publisher of a newspaper, they cannot claim the work to have been produced by one of their staff reporters. Morally, they are required to attribute the creative rights to you.

For more information on this topic, visit the Copyright Agency Limited (CAL) website: <www.copyright.com.au>.

Fair dealing

There are situations in which other people can use work that has been copyright-protected. For example, photographers and video operators are generally permitted to take photographs or footage of artistic exhibitions or works of art. Under the *Copyright Act 1968*, there is also a 'fair dealing' provision, which allows academics, students and others, including journalists, to use excerpts of a text or other document for research or study.

From a journalistic perspective, it is also permissible to reproduce an extract of a book, a film script or even an exhibit for purposes of criticism or review (see the discussion in Chapter 21). In addition, media organisations are allowed to use excerpts from other programs or publications in news bulletins (for example, a newsreader or announcer may read an extract from a newspaper or magazine piece, or a newspaper reporter may quote a story that was run on television).

However, if the use of published material is the subject of legal proceedings, the organisation being accused of breaching the *Copyright Act 1968* will be required to prove that the use was legitimate. This was tested in Australia in the case of *TCN Channel Nine v Network Ten*. Network Ten was sued after one of its programs, *The Panel*, was accused of rebroadcasting excerpts of items initially run on Channel Nine. Network Ten argued that the fair dealing defence applied, as the segments were being used for review and criticism. However, the court ruled against Network Ten, finding that the segments were used primarily for entertainment (Beattie & Beal, 2007, p. 125).

Obviously, it is possible for copyright to be re-assigned—that is, sold. Equally, the copyright holder can license another individual or company to produce items based on that product. While the assignment of rights is permanent, licensing can be temporary and even limited to particular purposes (for example, a one-off publication in a newspaper or a magazine).

This can be a complex area, and if you are negotiating the licensing of your work, you should have an agreement in writing that clearly defines the extent to which it can be used. For example, if you are a columnist, you might agree that your column can be published in a particular newspaper and then on-sold by the publisher of that publication to other newspapers in their chain. Under the agreement, you could, reasonably, ask for a percentage of the money obtained through republication. Equally, you could negotiate separate agreements for the hard-copy publication of your work and the soft-copy publication (that is, on the publication's website home page). You may decide to limit publication rights to a particular geographic area, so as to enable you to negotiate separate contracts with publishers in another geographic region. This is a popular strategy among novelists.

Freelancers seeking to negotiate contracts with prospective publishers should carefully consider any contracts they are asked to sign, so as to protect their rights from unscrupulous operators. In doing so, they can seek guidance from the MEAA, the Copyright Agency Limited (CAL) or a copyright lawyer. This is not necessarily required for a one-off article, but may be recommended for an ongoing column that might be syndicated.

Summary

o Australian journalists need to recognise that they are not above the law.

o Australian law is complex, particularly as it relates to areas like contempt and defamation. While there are defences to such charges, they are often difficult to prove, with possible consequences for the journalist including jail (in the case of contempt) or significant financial penalties (in the case of defamation).

o Because of this, journalists should ideally have their stories 'legalled' (checked by lawyers) if they believe there is the risk of a defamation action.

- Make sure you keep all the documents you use when researching your story. These could be called as evidence and might be needed to prove your defence.
- Journalists need also to be careful about trespass and deception. Both can lead to legal proceedings, as can a decision to secretly record conversations.
- While some legislation has been introduced that may assist journalists (for example, FOI), this legislation can also be used by shrewd public servants to block access to information.
- Journalists need to understand their rights when it comes to the sale and publication or broadcasting of their work. Guidance can be sought from CAL.

Questions

1 Name the different types of contempt.
2 What are the primary defences against a defamation action?
3 What rights does a journalist have over work they have created?

Activities

1 Using the Australasian Legal Information Institute (AustLII) website <www.austlii.edu.au>, select a recent case involving a journalist or media organisation. Write a brief summary of the facts, the arguments adopted by the plaintiff and the defence, and an overview of the decision. What is the significance of this decision from a journalistic perspective?
2 Identify a story involving the legal system (for example, comparing the case backlog of two states). How would you research this story? What legal bottlenecks might you encounter?
3 Having analysed the CAL website <www.copyright.com.au>, write a letter to a publisher you believe owes you money for publishing work for which you hold copyright. You will need to identify your rights over the content.
4 Briefly outline what you consider to be the main legal blocks standing in the way of journalists seeking to write about race and terrorism. To what extent does Australian law differ from that of other democracies?
5 Have a look at the ruling by Justice Mordecai Bromberg in the Andrew Bolt case: <www.austlii.edu.au/au/cases/cth/FCA/2011/1103.html>. What are the lessons to be learned from this for journalists?

References and additional reading

Beattie, S. & Beal, E. (2007). *Connect and Converge: Australian Media and Communications Law*, Melbourne: Oxford University Press.
Blackburn, E. (2003). *Broken Lives*, Melbourne: Hardie Grant Books.
Blackburn, E. (2007). *The End of Innocence: The Remarkable True Story of One Woman's Fight for Justice*, Melbourne: Hardie Grant Books.

Butler, D. & Rodrick, S. (1999). *Australian Media Law*, Sydney: LBC Information Services.

Cameron, M. (2007). *Australian Media Law: The Essential Guide for Journalists and Photographers*, Melbourne: News Custom Publishing.

Cohen, J. (2011). 'Andrew Bolt found guilty of breaching Australia hate speech law': www.internationalfreepresssociety.org/2011/09/andrew-bolt-found-guilty-of-breaching-australia-hate-speech-law.

Cranston, B. (2011). 'NSW magistrate appeals to keep her job', *Sydney Morning Herald*, 15 June: http://news.smh.com.au/breaking-news-national/nsw-magistrate-appeals-to-keep-her-job-20110615-1g3et.html.

Crothers, J. (2017). 'Yahoo7 fined, journalist Krystal Johnson given good behaviour bond over court report', ABC News, 17 February. Accessed from http://www.abc.net.au/news/2017-02-17/yahoo-7-fined-for-contempt-murder-trial/8279452

Egan, C. (2010). *Murderer No More*, Sydney: Allen & Unwin.

Eatock v Bolt (2011). FCA 1103: www.austlii.edu.au/au/cases/cth/FCA/2011/1103.html

Guardian (2013). 'Australia's shield laws, state by state', https://www.theguardian.com/world/2013/aug/07/australia-journalist-protection-shield-laws

Hall, L. (2012). 'Journalists told to reveal sources', *Sydney Morning Herald*, 2 February, p. 2.

Merritt, C. (2011). 'Legal academics call to track fitness of judicial officers', *The Australian*, 24 June: www.theaustralian.com.au/business/legal-affairs/lega-academics-call-to-track-fitness-of-judicial-officers/story-e6frg97x-1226080858909

Moses, S. (2007). 'Victory for online buyer in court dogfight', *Sydney Morning Herald*, 4–5 August, p. 2.

Pearson, M. (2007). *The Journalist's Guide to Media Law*, 3rd edn, Sydney: Allen & Unwin.

Pearson, M. & Polden, M. (2011). *The Journalist's Guide to Media Law*, 4th edn, Sydney: Allen & Unwin.

Pearson, M. & Polden, M. (2014). *The Journalist's Guide to Media Law*, 5th edn, Sydney: Allen & Unwin.

Ross, N. (2007). 'Saga's true winners', *Herald Sun*, 26 June, p. 2.

Online resources

Amnesty International, December 5, 2016. 'The Racial Discrimination Act: The two minute version': https://www.amnesty.org.au/racial-discrimination-act-the-two-minute-version/

Australian Legal Information Institute (AustLII) provides a database of legal resources, including Acts of Parliament and judgments from all Australian jurisdictions. It also has an excellent database of international judgments and legislation: www.austlii.edu.au

CASA 2017: https://www.casa.gov.au/files/ac10110pdf

Copyright Agency Limited: www.copyright.com.au

Justinian, an Australian legal magazine produced by journalist Richard Ackland, provides an interesting insight into the profession and judgments: www.justinian.com.au

Media guidelines

Federal Circuit Court: Information for the Media: http://www.federalcircuitcourt.gov.au/wps/wcm/
connect/fccweb/about/media/

NSW: Land and Environment Court (NSW): Media Contact Information: www.lawlink.nsw.gov.au/
lawlink/lec/ll_lec.nsf/pages/LEC_mediaguide

NSW: Law Reform Commission of New South Wales: Contempt by Publication: The Media and
the Courts: http://www.lawreform.justice.nsw.gov.au/Pages/lrc/lrc_completed_projects/lrc_
completedprojects2000_2009/lrc_contemptbypublication.aspx

NSW: Supreme Court of New South Wales: Media: www.lawlink.nsw.gov.au/lawlink/supreme_court/ll_
sc.nsf/pages/SCO_media

NSW: Supreme Court of New South Wales: Supreme Court Policies: www.lawlink.nsw.gov.au/lawlink/
supreme_court/ll_sc.nsf/pages/SCO_scpolicies

NT: Media Guide: Northern Territory Courts: www.nt.gov.au/justice/ntmc/media/documents/Media_
Guide.pdf

Queensland Civil and Administrative Tribunal: Media Policy: www.qcat.qld.gov.au/about-qcat/
media-policy

SA: A Handbook for Media Reporting in South Australian Courts: http://www.courts.sa.gov.au/
ForMedia/Pages/default.aspx

Tas: Covering the courts: A basic guide for journalists: http://www.supremecourt.tas.gov.au/__data/
assets/pdf_file/0010/297622/Covering_the_Courts_-_A_Basic_Guide_for_Journalists_Tasmania.
pdf

WA: Guidelines for the Media Reporting in Western Australian Courts: http://supremecourt.wa.gov.au/
M/media.aspx?uid=5248-6373-3309-4990

Court contacts

High Court of Australia: www.hcourt.gov.au

Supreme Court of the Australian Capital Territory: www.courts.act.gov.au/supreme

Supreme Court of New South Wales: http://www.supremecourt.justice.nsw.gov.au/Pages/sco2_
newscarousel/media_resources.html,c=y.aspx

Supreme Court of the Northern Territory: www.nt.gov.au/ntsc

Supreme Court of Queensland: www.courts.qld.gov.au/courts/supreme-court

Supreme Court of South Australia: http://www.courts.sa.gov.au/ForMedia/Pages/default.aspx

Supreme Court of Tasmania: www.supremecourt.tas.gov.au

Supreme Court of Victoria: www.supremecourt.vic.gov.au

Supreme Court of Western Australia: www.supremecourt.wa.gov.au

10
Editing and Polishing Your Work

'It isn't so important for a writer to use one particular method rather than another (although some are inherently superior). What is crucial … is that every writer have a method of some kind: routines to cling to when everything goes wrong, rules to follow when you're blocked or frustrated. After all, there are an infinite number of ways to organise one's writing life.'

Robert S. Boynton, American author, 2005, p. xxxiii

Objectives

It is now time to consider whether your work meets all the objectives you've set for yourself, as well as the requirements of the commissioning editor. This chapter will help you to answer the following questions:

o   does your story satisfy its objectives?

o   have you covered your key themes in detail?

o   is the language appropriate to your target market?

o   have you eliminated the jargon and clichés?

o   do your transitions work?

o   have you illustrated your article (with charts, diagrams, pictures, video footage or audio)?

Take pride in your work

While many journalists think that their responsibility is to produce a draft article that will invariably be corrected by a sub-editor and turned into a polished piece of writing, we strongly believe that all journalists should work at producing good copy; that is, you should take pride in your work, perhaps even consider it a work of art in the making. This goes beyond identifying the story, asking the right questions and tacking together a draft that you know will be reworked by someone else. As a writer, you should be your own harshest critic.

Taking pride in your work means revising your story until you are proud to have your byline attached to it. Some journalists have tremendous research skills. They have an innate ability to locate information and to ask the right questions of their subjects. But the best journalists have an additional skill: word-craft. This means having a command of grammar, syntax and word use. Journalists who have mastered these skills have the capacity to bring their stories to life through the language they employ. They are wordsmiths, as opposed to 'word-mongers'.

Wordsmithing involves thinking about what you want to say or write and considering how it can be conveyed in a way that says to your readers, listeners or viewers: 'Not only do I know what I am talking about, but I can also speak and write in a way that conveys my mastery of the language.' Word-mongering, on the other hand, is a somewhat derogatory term. Someone who engages in this practice is, according to the *Shorter Oxford Dictionary*, a person who 'deals in words, but especially strange or pedantic words, or in empty words without sense'.

Does your piece cover its objectives?

On the surface, this question appears to be straightforward. In fact, if you have been thorough in your research and writing you should be able to deal with it very quickly. Let us assume that you were able to locate the information you needed for your story, you have interviewed all the people identified as being able to contribute to your piece, and you have produced a draft. Now you need to ask yourself:

- does my story answer all the questions?
- are there any gaps in the information provided?
- if so, how can I fill these gaps (by asking additional questions, conducting more research or expanding my interviews to other people)?
- are there any gaps in the logic of the story?
- is the story fair (or at least justifiable)?
- are there legal considerations I should be aware of (or need to address)?

Essentially, the first four questions deal with content. They point to a critical question, namely: Have you covered your key themes in detail? If you can answer yes to this question, then you can move on to the final two questions. These are directed more at the consequences of the material than the content and are covered more fully in chapters 8 and 9.

Remember also that superficial stories will always come across as such, irrespective of how beautifully they are written. As William Blundell (1988) points out: 'A well shaped idea, convincing illustration and interpretation of it, and sound story structure count for more than artful and impeccable use of the language.'

Be aware that sometimes writers reach the point where they sit down to write, only to find that their story has moved in a completely different direction from that which they—or their editor—had originally intended. This need not be a bad thing, unless the editor is expecting a particular piece and won't shift from that. But generally speaking, editors are quite flexible and if the story develops into something much bigger or more important than they had anticipated, so much the better.

Readability

It is important that your story is 'readable'. George Klare (1963) describes readability as 'the ease of understanding or comprehension due to the style of writing'. As William DuBay (2004) points out, 'this definition focuses on writing style as separate from issues such as content, coherence and organization'. It can be equated with clarity, which is defined by Gretchen Hargis and colleagues. (1998) as the 'ease of reading words and sentences' and was one of the three key ingredients of journalism identified by Murray Masterton (1991).

Essentially, readability involves presenting your material in a way people can understand 'without stumbling over complicated words' (Letham, n.d.). Obviously, there will be instances where some readers will struggle with the meaning of individual words. But if you understand the audience you're writing for, the majority of your readers should readily understand what you are saying without having to reread the sentence (Letham, n.d.). Over the years, a number of tests have been developed to measure readability. Among the best known are the Flesch, Flesch-Kincaid, Gunning Fog, Cloze, Lexical density and Coleman-Laui Index. Some of these link readability with educational grades—that is, the level of education required to understand a particular text.

Understanding your audience

When it comes to readability, publishers and broadcasters cannot afford to 'get it wrong'. If a text is too dense for readers, or the speech adopted by a broadcaster is over the heads of their listeners or viewers, these audiences will quickly abandon the publication or program. For this reason, media organisations regularly conduct market research designed to enable them to stay in touch with their target audience.

The research—which may take the form of telephone interviews, online surveys, self-administered questionnaires and focus groups—is designed to tell the media organisation what their readers, viewers or listeners like and dislike. The people surveyed are asked about different sections of newspapers or magazines, and about different segments of radio or television programs. As a result of audience feedback, the organisation then makes decisions about how its product—the publication, program or website—can be improved. This information is fed directly back to the editorial staff, who respond by adding new sections to their site, publication or program and, in worst-case scenarios, by removing those sections that are not popular with the audience.

This is an important—and ongoing—process, one that begins even before a new program, site or publication is launched. Early research seeks to give the media organisation an idea of whether the proposed site, publication or program will find a niche in an often crowded marketplace. To survive, new publications, programs and websites need to distinguish themselves from those that already exist. To do this, they need to either offer something different or appeal to a different demographic. In journalistic terms, the term 'demographic' is used to define the audience. Audience demographics can be measured in a number of ways, including, but not limited to, gender, age, income, occupation, interests and suburb of residence.

Media organisations will seek to appeal to people who possess a combination of these demographic characteristics, depending on the publication or program they are proposing. For example, car magazines are traditionally aimed at men. Within the car magazine market there are generalist and specialist publications, each appealing to a different demographic, the former to people on average incomes, the latter to people who have niche interests (for example, luxury cars or racing cars). While the luxury car publication is clearly aimed at the higher income segment, the racing car magazines are directed at a much broader demographic, including women, where income is not necessarily a factor.

There are also a significant number of publications that are produced in smaller print runs and cover more specialised subjects. These can include self-help, specialised craft and collecting publications. There is also a category of publication that is pitched at an even more targeted market, namely people working in a particular industry sector or who have a particular research interest. (For a list of Australian magazines and their circulation, see the internet links at the end of the chapter.) If you are seeking to pitch an article to a particular magazine, program or website, it is worth having a look at that outlet's own website. This can provide you with important information about its circulation/reach and readership/audience.

Accessibility

Assuming that you have considered the above factors and have a clear picture of your target audience, you now have to think about ensuring that your article or program is accessible to the majority of people you are seeking to reach. This is where the earlier discussion about readability becomes important. According to Cheryl Stephens (n.d.), the English language contains more than 490,000 words, with an additional 300,000 technical terms. But, says Stephens, 'It is unlikely that an individual will use more than 60,000 and the average person probably encounters between 5000 and 10,000 words in a lifetime.'

This sounds like a lot of words, but bear in mind that literacy is a problem in Australia, both among young people and adults. The Australian Bureau of Statistics 2006 Census found that approximately 54 per cent of Australians aged 15–74 years had prose literacy skills (that is, the ability to read a newspaper), with 53 per cent having document reading skills (the ability to read bus and train timetables) (ABS, 2007). This was reinforced in a 2011–12 study conducted by the ABS in conjunction with the Organisation for Economic Co-operation and Development (OECD). According to the Programme for the International Assessment of Adult Competencies (PIAAC), Australia ranked fourth in terms of literacy skills among adults aged 15–74. However, the results of the test did point to significant problems, with nearly 44 per cent of Australians having literacy skills at or below Level 2. (The scale is accessible at <http://www.abs.gov.au/ausstats/abs@.nsf/Lookup/4228.0Appendix202011-12>.)

This—as well as ongoing debate in the media about declining literacy standards among school-aged children—must be a concern to newspaper and magazine publishers who are battling declining circulation figures across their traditional publications. Of particular concern is their inability to encourage young readers to develop the reading habits of their parents and grandparents. There are clearly a number of reasons for this failure to appeal to young readers, but journalists themselves can help address the problem.

No matter whether you are writing for a mass audience or a specialised market, you must ensure that the language you use can be understood by those you are seeking to reach. This requires particular skill, particularly for freelancers, who will write for a range of different publications, programs or even websites on a weekly basis. As a freelancer, you might write an article on a murder trial for a tabloid newspaper one day, and a longer piece about the discovery of a genetic explanation for autism for a specialist medical publication the next.

While the writing required for each article must be accessible, the chances are that the reading abilities of the two target markets will vary significantly. While the members of the scientific community are likely to understand the story written for the tabloid newspaper, it is highly unlikely that the majority of newspaper readers would understand the medical terms discussed in the medical journal. Or it might be that you are asked to write the autism article for both of these publications. While you would be expected to boil it down to the nuts and bolts for the tabloid market—focusing on the *who, what, when, where, why* and *how*—the readers of the medical journal would expect a far more detailed piece that not only employed the language they use in their work, but provided considerably more detail about the discovery, focusing especially on how the breakthrough occurred.

As the readability tests suggest, individual publications are pitched at people with different educational levels. We're not aware of any directly relevant Australian research on this topic, but we can provide some first-hand knowledge. The authors began their journalistic careers at the Launceston *Examiner*. Early on they were told to write using language that would be understood by 13-year-olds. This was for news stories; for features there was a little more scope, but not much. The fact was that we were writing for a generalist audience, most of whom had high school rather than university educations.

You can draw comparisons between the language adopted by regional newspapers and that preferred by the larger state-based dailies. It is also worth drawing comparisons between tabloids and their broadsheet rivals. The former use shorter sentences and less complex language than the latter. While two of Australia's best known newspapers, the *Sydney Morning Herald* and *The Age* have recently succumbed to pressure and changed from a broadsheet to tabloid format, they nonetheless maintain the seriousness of broadsheets as reflected in their language. This is also reflected in a comparison of *The Australian Financial Review*, a tabloid-sized specialist business newspaper, and *The Australian*, a broadsheet. Both adopt similar language and sentence structures, thereby reflecting the similar demographics—including educational levels—of their target audiences. Yet, if subjected to a Flesch or Gunning Fog test (see the internet links at the end of the chapter), both would possibly achieve a higher readability score than *The New Yorker*, which is a quality magazine.

Challenges of an idiosyncratic language

The English language is complex; of that there is no doubt. It is a mishmash of languages. It started borrowing characters and words from Roman, Irish and German tribes more than 1500 years ago (Cook, 2004, p. vi). Gradually, words were borrowed from many other languages, including Latin, French, Turkish, Arabic, Italian and Japanese (Cook, 2004, p. vi). As English has become an international language, it has incorporated a huge number of words, with many more—often idiosyncratic words—being added each year. This has added a new layer of challenge for journalists (and their audiences). In particular, journalists need to be aware of the dangers of using jargon, clichés, euphemisms and slang.

Jargon

Jargon ('buzzwords') is essentially technical language; it contains words that are relevant to a specialist audience—say, doctors, engineers or astronauts—but not ordinary readers. If you are writing for a specialist audience, then invariably you will be required to use jargon, but don't overdo it. And if you do use such words or phrases, make sure you understand what they mean. Also, it is important not to fall into the trap that many professions or occupations fall into—namely, developing a style of writing that is basically unintelligible, even to insiders.

This problem has been highlighted by a number of writers. For example, Don Watson, a speechwriter to former Prime Minister Paul Keating, was a critic of what he termed 'weasel words'. Watson wrote a book titled, appropriately, *Death Sentence: The Decay of Public Language* (2003). In it, he criticises journalists for adopting the language of the people they write about when, with a little thought, they could write in a more accessible and understandable manner. For example, he talks about the willingness of journalists during the first Gulf War to adopt the nonsensical language that flowed from the Pentagon or the media centre in Doha.

One of the words such journalists adopted was 'degraded'. Most people have a fair idea of what 'degraded' means, but what about in this context: 'The military said they had degraded by 70 per cent a body of Iraqi soldiers'? Used here, it means that 70 per cent of Iraqi soldiers had been killed. Why not just say 'killed'? Other language used during coverage of this war included reference to being 'on message' or 'embedded'. The latter phrase quickly developed a pejorative sense, meaning 'in bed with'. But the military also used terms such as 'attrited' and 'deconflicted'. With a little semantic gymnastics you can work out what they mean, but why do journalists need to use such words when it would be much easier and less frustrating for the readers if they used words they understood?

Clichés

Clichés are phrases, or expressions, that have been overused to the point of becoming redundant, so you should avoid them like the plague (to illustrate a point by falling into such a trap). Journalists who regularly use clichés are saying to their audience: 'I'm sorry, I'm not a particularly imaginative person and my grasp of the language is limited.' Sadly, this is often the case with sports writing, an area of journalistic endeavour that has the capacity to produce beautiful writing or commentary, but often fails dismally. A good example of a phrase that is threatening to become a cliché is 'back to the future'. This phrase regularly appears in journalistic writing, but rarely with the gusto that accompanied its use during the 2017 Australian Tennis Open when Rafael Nadal and Roger Federer and the Williams sisters—Venus and Serena—fought their way through to the finals. While these two showdowns were unexpected, given that all four were aged in their 30s and three of them had significant layoffs due to injury, it was the use of this phrase to hark back to their glory years, particularly in the case of Venus Williams, that grated because every journalist and commentator seemed to 'jump on the bandwagon' rather than search for a different combination of words to describe what was happening.

Alternatively, they may be taking a condescending approach, saying: 'I'm using this language because I think it is all you'll understand.' Don't patronise your audience, but do show them that you have a strong grasp of the language and can present your work in an original form.

Another thing to remember if you are still tempted to use clichés is that while some sections of your audience might understand what you are saying, others—particularly those for whom English is not their first language—may find the phrase or expression confusing. For example, the saying 'think outside the box' is a popular cliché. Most Australians understand that it means to try and think creatively, or to come up with an original idea or solution. But what about someone who has only recently starting speaking English? For them it would appear nonsensical. The same with three other popular clichés: 'The grass is always greener on the other side', 'The apple doesn't fall far from the tree', and 'You can't judge a book by its cover.'

Euphemisms

Euphemisms are less problematic, but can nonetheless be frustrating. Remember the incident mentioned in Chapter 4, when one of the authors—who had been asked to write an Anzac Day feature including comments from surviving veterans—was told about the veteran he was seeking to contact: 'He's no longer with us.' The soldier's widow was using a euphemism, rather than saying straight out that he had died, but because the journalist had not understood this, he persevered, asking: 'Can you tell me when he'll be back?' This unfortunate incident highlights how euphemisms can cause problems not just for journalists, but also for audiences. Euphemisms are a polite or indirect way of saying something that may be construed as being harsh, vague, or even unpleasant to hear. Another popular euphemism for 'he has died' is 'he has passed'. It used to be 'he has passed away', but today, 'away' is frequently eliminated from the phrase. Another example of a euphemism is 'a few extra pounds' meaning the person being referred to has put on weight.

Slang

As with jargon, slang can have a place in writing, particularly in features and longer-form writing. But again, it should not be overused. Like jargon, slang tends to be used to exclude some people. A good example is the language being adopted by teenagers when talking to their friends via SMS. Their friends will understand what they are saying, but the chances are that their parents will not.

Slang is known as the language of the streets. It is a colloquial language, which may be known to people within a particular geographical area, but not necessarily to people outside that region. For this reason, slang can both support and undermine your writing. If it is essential to the story—particularly if it is adopted by your interviewees, or helps your audience gain a deeper understanding of them or the issue you are writing about—then use it by all means. But don't overuse it, particularly if it is likely to confuse or offend. For example, 'kick the bucket', 'sick' and 'photo bomb' are all examples of slang. Kick the bucket (to die) is an oldie. But what about 'sick' and 'photo bomb'? For older people 'sick' means to be ill, but for younger people it can mean 'awesome' or 'cool'. To 'photo bomb' means to impose yourself, intentionally or not, in a photograph.

Other checks

There are a number of other checks you should also make. First, avoid using too many words. Ask yourself: Can I say this more fluently? Remember the KISS (Keep It Simple, Stupid!) principle. This works just as effectively with feature writing as it does with news writing. Eliminate redundant words from your sentences (that is, words that don't add to the meaning of your statement, or are tautologies, meaning words that say the same thing). A popular example of a redundant word is 'eliminate altogether', when 'eliminate' would suffice. Another is 'revert back'. There are many others. See if you can locate some.

Finally:

- Check to ensure that, where possible, you are using active rather than passive voice; if you do decide to use passive voice, make sure it is immediately followed by active voice.
- Ensure the tone of your writing is consistent throughout.
- Don't write negatively.
- Check for poor punctuation and spelling.

Do your transitions work?

One of the skills of a great writer is producing copy that flows. It draws in the reader, listener or viewer; and once drawn in, they will want to keep reading, listening or watching. In part, such a skill depends on the language employed, as we discussed above. But it also links back to the content. The content must flow. Every sentence and paragraph must lead seamlessly to the next. You don't want your audience to say: 'Why did they say that?' or 'What is the relevance of that comment?' Transitional sentences connect the themes. Some journalists will use a quotation as a transitional device, others may use a description. It doesn't matter what you use, so long as you continue to engage your audience.

Some writers seek to engage the audience by adopting a light-hearted approach. The approach adopted will obviously be influenced by the nature of the story. A light-hearted approach, for example, won't work with a hard-hitting investigative piece, but can work for a celebrity interview.

Tone and voice

As a journalist, you will gradually develop a writing or speaking style that is distinctly yours. It will become your signature and part of your identity. Broadcasters such as Alan Jones and Phillip Adams, and commentators such as Janet Albrechtsen, Andrew Bolt and Robert Manne all have their own distinctive styles. Some—particularly broadcasters like Andrew Denton and Sir Michael Parkinson—have adopted a conversational style. This does not mean that we should always write as we speak—most of us are in fact better writers than speakers. With writing we have the chance to reflect, to rework the sentence, to tone down what we were thinking to make it more palatable. With oral conversation we often don't have the power of reflection. However, we should seek to write in an engaging style that makes use of both tone and voice. Clearly, tone and voice will change according to the nature of the story we're working on. And our ability to express these clearly links directly to our command of the language.

Polishing your writing

Polishing your writing can be the most challenging and most rewarding activity for a writer. There are several important elements to be considered when reviewing your work. As we have said on several occasions already, clarity is vital. A clear exposition of the feature idea is the greatest gift a writer can give the reader. But how does a writer achieve that?

Word-craft is the cornerstone. However, this is of little value unless the writer is prepared to be ruthless about paring back their work and making absolutely clear what they mean. The key to this is not to over-write. The quickest way to lose a reader is to build sentences that are full of layers, sub-clauses and qualifications. Some sentences need to be heavy with detail—and they can often work well if they are surrounded by short sentences—but mostly the formula is one idea for each sentence. Keep it simple. If need be, you can build around the simplicity. That means using adjectives and adverbs sparingly.

It pays to remember what you were told in primary school: that adjectives are 'colour words'. As such, when they are overused they can produce lurid prose. Avoid adjectives. Resist their siren-song. Many budding writers confuse good writing with writing that contains an excessive number of adjectives. Good writing contains a few well-chosen adjectives used at the right times for maximum impact. Think of them as a currency, and remember that you are on a tight budget. Imagine a friend approaching you for a loan. Yes, you want to help, but no, you cannot afford it. Well, perhaps a small donation—not much, mind you, just a little. So, use one adjective when you can, and when you really need to use it. And be careful about the adjective you use—is 'tiny' the word you want, when 'microscopic' is more accurate? Is 'old' too banal and clichéd? If you think so, choose another word, even a simple word, such as 'aged'.

If there is a rule for writers regarding adjectives, it is that less is more. Apply this rule rigorously and you'll be amazed at what a difference it makes to your prose. Suddenly, the other words have to work harder, the sentence is leaner and, as a result, the meaning is clearer. Consider this:

> The tall detective walked into the extended office, which was bathed in a harsh yellow light from an angled, large window, cut into the wall.

Compare it with this example, in which the adjectives have been taken out:

> The detective walked into the office, which was bathed in light from a window cut into the wall.

Excessive use of adjectives rarely amounts to good writing.

Writers also need to be aware of the use of adverbs. These are the words that modify verbs and often end in -ly—such as 'sharply', 'aggressively' and 'remarkably'. Adverbs can trap writers, who may find themselves using them unnecessarily. Here is an example from a contributor to a weekend newspaper review section. The writer is talking about a photograph of his father in his cricket outfit:

> He gazes at me from the sideboard, my dad. He stands self-consciously in front of a rustic score-board. The tops of his grey canvas pads sag limply over their bulging knee-rolls ... His club cap perches awkwardly on his head, shadowing one eye ...

Thompson, 2008

The writing is affectionate and poignant, but it does not need the adverbs. Look at two adverbs in the quoted sentences—'limply' and 'awkwardly'. 'Limply' follows the word 'sag'. Does 'limply' add anything to 'sag'? No. Why? Because 'sag' implies 'limply'. It works well enough on its own. 'Limply' is unnecessary. We already have the visual idea of what is occurring in the photograph. The writer makes the same mistake with 'awkwardly'. The hat is already 'perched'—isn't that awkward enough? The adverbs just clutter the sentence, slowing the pace without adding anything to the meaning. So see if you need to get rid of adverbs when you review your work.

The final consideration in word-craft is knowing which word to use. This is a problem for many writers who get caught up in the vernacular. While it is important to write as we speak and think, we do not need to choose words that are imprecise and inaccurate. This can be a challenge for writers because language needs to be dynamic, but many words are used inappropriately once and the mistake is then perpetuated. One such word is 'decimate', which is taken these days to mean kill or destroy a large number. In fact, the word's original meaning was to destroy one in every ten (Moore, 2004).

Illustrating your work

Remember the adage 'A picture is worth a thousand words'? Today, with the development of online media sites, that saying has taken on a new meaning, with journalists increasingly being expected to produce stories suitable for a range of platforms. In fact, some stories will not even be considered for publication or broadcast without photographs, other visuals or even audio. Today, many experienced journalists are being retrained so they are multiskilled. Fairfax and News Ltd, for example, are training their newspaper journalists to use video cameras so they can take footage and conduct interviews that can be quickly uploaded to the internet. The footage can be converted to stills for the traditional newspaper and the content turned into a written feature.

As a journalist—particularly if you're working as a freelancer and have to sell your story idea before getting a commission—you need to ask yourself:

- How can I best illustrate this story? Should I be looking at both still photographs and video footage?
- Do I need action shots (ideal for a sporting feature) or interior and exterior shots (in the case of a home renovation or profile)?
- Do I have the capacity to take these shots myself or should I team up with a professional photographer or cameraperson who has skills in this particular area? Remember, photographs for magazines such as *House and Garden* or *Vogue Living* require specialist skills. The lighting can be complex, and often amateur photographs are too cluttered for these magazines. It would be a pity to lose a commission because your photographs are not of a sufficiently high standard. This is easy to avoid, however. Check with the publication or website to see if they have particular requirements for photographers.

Try to take photographs of people you interview (remember, you'll need to ask their permission). If you are writing about someone who is dead, approach the family for a photograph. If the person was well known and you do not have family contacts, you can contact the local historical society, archive or library. An organisation the person belonged to could have a photograph it would be prepared to lend. Obviously, if you are writing your piece for a local newspaper, then the paper is likely to have file photographs that can be used. Make sure the photographs reflect the story you have produced.

If you are writing about a historical event or figure, it can be worth trying to include photocopies, photographs or transcripts of relevant documents. These could include maps, letters of appointment, other letters, extracts from diaries, even a photograph of their headstone or a monument erected in their honour. All of these can add an important dimension to your story.

So too can charts, tables, artists' impressions or even plans. Remember, people respond to visual cues and may have a greater understanding of a concept you are talking about if there is an illustration that helps to contextualise your explanation. Obviously this does not apply to all people. Whereas most people can understand artists' impressions of how a building will look, their eyes will often glaze over if you provide them with a detailed plan. The key is to think about who you are writing for. Is it a specialist audience or a generalist one? The specialist audience will undoubtedly appreciate the inclusion of a detailed plan, whereas the general reader would be happy with the artists' impression.

Given that journalists are often required to work across different media, it is also important to think about how you can take advantage of the new media to present your story. For example, radio lends itself to the use of background music and other sounds. This also applies to television and online sites. It may be that you have some archival material (music, an interview, a speech or even dialogue from a play) that may enhance your written piece. While it may lose its impact when transcribed for a written piece, a strategically placed link in an online article may provide the reader with an opportunity to appreciate the atmosphere or other element you are seeking to convey when you refer to the extract or excerpt in your writing.

The red pen treatment

One of the best ways to find your own mistakes is to cast a critical eye over the work of professionals (or that of your peers or classmates). Go through a range of stories (your favourites and those that have bored or irritated you), get out your 'red pen' and assess the strengths and weaknesses you find.

Go through this process a few times, then return to your own work. You'll find it much easier to find the holes in your stories and come up with solutions to enhance and enrich your work.

Below is a 'red pen worksheet' to help you assess your stories. It covers many important points discussed in this and other chapters. You will need to evaluate if the story is written with the audience in mind, if it is written well from beginning to end, if it utilises research and interviews appropriately and if it illustrates the story when necessary.

Read through the story you have chosen, then give it a grade next to each of the criteria listed. Then come up with a couple of suggestions for improvements at the end.

Red pen *worksheet*

Story topic is appropriate for the publication:

Opening: ☐

Use of quotes/dialogue: ☐

Use of research: ☐

Choice and use of structure: ☐

Use of language: ☐

Use of theme: ☐

Conclusion: ☐

Use of additional material (examples: photographs, graphs, transcripts): ☐

Grammar and spelling: ☐

Overall grade for story: ☐

Suggestions for improvement:_____

_____

_____

Summary

o   As a writer, you should be your own harshest critic.

o   As a critic, you should get rid of those unnecessary words and also consider the structure and content of your story.

o   Ask yourself the following questions:

   a   Have I put in too much description (or not enough)?

   b   Does my story flow?

   c   Does it get bogged down in detail?

Questions

1   List the key elements a writer should look for when editing their own work.

2   What are the rules regarding the use of adjectives and adverbs?

3   How do magazines and newspapers seek to keep in touch with their readers?

4   How is readability measured?

Activities

1 Go online and read explanations of the Flesch and Gunning Fog readability tests (URLs are given on p. 193) or one of the others. How do these tests work? See if you can apply these tests to your favourite newspaper and magazine.

2 Select a piece of your own writing. Based on the discussion in this chapter, what are its main weaknesses? See if you can edit it to improve its readability, structure and use of language.

3 Select a piece of writing from a scientific or business magazine. See if you can rewrite the piece so that the material is understandable to an audience of your peers.

4 Try to develop a demographic profile of a magazine or newspaper you read regularly.

5 Go online and put together a list of clichés, euphemisms and buzzwords you find in published articles. Provide a separate list of alternative words and phrases that would be more appropriate or would improve the readability of the articles.

References and additional reading

ABS, *see* Australian Bureau of Statistics.

Alley, M. (2000). *The Craft of Editing: A Guide for Managers, Scientists and Engineers*, Blacksburg, VA: Springer.

Australian Bureau of Statistics (2007). *Adult Literacy and Life Skills Survey, Summary Results, Australia, 2006*, cat. no. 4228.0, Canberra: ABS: www.abs.gov.au/ausstats/abs@.nsf/mf/4228.0

Blundell, W.E. (1988). *The Art and Craft of Feature Writing: Based on the Wall Street Journal Style*, New York: Penguin.

Boynton, R.S. (2005). *The New New Journalism: Conversations with America's Best Nonfiction Writers on Their Craft*, New York: Vintage Books.

Cook, V. (2004). *Accomodating Brocolli in the Cemetary: Or Why Can't Anybody Spell?* London: Profile Books.

DuBay, W. (2004). 'The principles of readability': www.impact-information.com/impactinfo/readability02.pdf

Garrison, B. (2004). *Professional Feature Writing*, 4th edn, Mahwah, NJ: Lawrence Erlbaum.

Hargis, G., Hernandez, K., Hughes, P., Ramaker, J., Rouiller, S. & Wilde, E. (1998). *Developing Quality Technical Information: A Handbook for Writers and Educators*, Upper Saddle River, NJ: Prentice Hall.

Klare, G.R. (1963). *The Measurement of Readability*, Ames, IA: Iowa State University Press.

Letham, S. (n.d.). 'Cut the fog! The readability factor': www.write101.com/letham2.htm

Lockwood, K. (ed.) (2005). *Style: The Essential Guide for Journalists and Professional Writers*, 3rd edn, Melbourne: News Custom Publishing.

Masterton, M. (1991). 'A new approach to what makes news', *Australian Journalism Review*, 14(1), pp. 21–6.

Moore, B. (ed.) (2004). *The Australian Oxford Dictionary*, 2nd edn, Melbourne: Oxford University Press.

Stephens, C. (n.d.). 'Cheryl Stephens on plain language': www.plainlanguagenetwork.org/stephens

Strunk, W. Jr & White, E.B. (2000). *The Elements of Style*, 4th edn, New York: Longman.

Thompson, G. (2008). 'This (cricket-loving) life', *The Weekend Australian Review*, 19 January.

Watson, D. (2003). *Death Sentence: The Decay of Public Language*, Sydney: Random House.

Online resources

Audit Bureaux of Australia: www.auditbureau.org.au

Australian Bureau of Statistics, 1996 Census Data: www.abs.gov.au/AUSSTATS/abs@.nsf/
96cdbygeogtype?openview&restricttocategory=Main%20Areas&Expand=1&

Flesch Readability Index: http://www.readabilityformulas.com/
flesch-reading-ease-readability-formula.php

Gunning Fog Readability Index: http://gunning-fog-index.com/

Information Access Group, Literacy in Australia: http://www.informationaccessgroup.com/docs/
PIAAC_A4booklet_web.pdf

Juicy Studio: Readability Tests: http://juicystudio.com/services/readability.php

Magazine Publishers of Australia: http://www.magazines.org.au/about/

National Inquiry into the Teaching of Literacy, 2005: http://research.acer.edu.au/acer_history/26/

11
Selling Your Story

'Failure is the condiment that gives success its flavour.'

Truman Capote

Objectives

Throughout this book, you have been practising techniques and strategies to write great stories. In this chapter we will show you how to take all that hard work and turn it into dollars. Here you will learn how to publish your stories and become a freelance writer. This chapter covers:

o   what you need to sell a story

o   how to identify a possible publisher

o   wooing the publisher

o   negotiating payment

o   a Case study: Freelancer Mike Grenby talks about life as a journalist and how he sold his foray into food writing

o   a Writing sample: 'Dainty plates eatery all the rage in London' by Mike Grenby, *Calgary Herald*, 30 June 2010.

What you need to sell a story

You've done your research, conducted your interviews, considered your structure, worked on your theme and written your story. What next? This is when you enter the world of publishing. It can be cut-throat, insensitive and disheartening, but it can also be very rewarding—emotionally and financially. But before you grab the phone or type out your email pitch, you need to look at your story one last time.

Your story needs to be original, creative and polished in order to be published. And as you start to formulate your pitch, consider what the editors of the US National Public Radio say works for them: 'Good pitches include basic narrative elements: a specific focus, a central question, stakes, a conflict and/or a central character. Ideally something *happens* in the story' (MacAdam, 2017). You might not have all those elements, but getting most of them will certainly make for an eye-catching pitch.

To ensure you're ready to make your pitch, check your story against these questions:

1   Does your story present ideas in an interesting way? Will the reader be engaged by the characters, the story, the themes and the structure?

2   Has your story been proofread? Are the facts, grammar and spelling correct? Is it well written?

3   Is your story on Paris, scoliosis, space exploration etc. different from the rest?

4   Does something actually happen?

If you can answer all these questions positively, you have a good chance of having your story published. While all the points on the checklist are important, you may not have considered the second last one. Sadly, there is no such thing as a completely original story, but you can always come up with a new angle on a topic.

Remember that when starting out, you may complete your story before approaching editors; however, more established writers will pitch and sell an *idea* before doing the actual writing.

When editors review story ideas sent in by freelancers, they often ask themselves this question: Is this just something one of my staff writers could cover? This means you have to be original—what can you do that staff writers can't? Freelancers were for some time an expense that cash-strapped newsrooms found they could not use as frequently as they would have liked. But with newsrooms shrinking, there are more opportunities for freelancers, especially those with specialist interests and the technical skills to drive a multimedia package that the mainstream media outlets will be keen to use.

In fact there are several advantages freelancers may have over staff writers. The first is time. Staff writers are working to strict deadlines—they don't always have weeks or months to research and write a story; sometimes they only have hours to knock something together. As a freelancer you do have time (in between classes, or your job, or your family commitments) to undertake long-term research and/or experience a story as it develops over time. You may even have the time to make yourself part of the story.

This brings us to the second important advantage that freelancers have—themselves. You are a unique person, with a unique point of view, unique experiences and unique style. You can use your own voice and past to increase your 'publishability'. Take a travel story on Bangkok, for example. This city has been written about numerous times, so how can you sell a story about somewhere everyone knows about? Start by thinking about what might have been different about your trip. Perhaps you volunteered at an orphanage while you were there, learned about the best places to buy impossible-to-pick copy handbags, stayed in one of the gay and lesbian resorts, did a culinary tour of all the weirdest food imaginable. Getting off the beaten track and trying something new, or something very 'you', could give your story the originality you need.

Some magazines have sections dedicated to stories about the lives of 'real' people. These magazines, like *Cleo*, *Cosmopolitan* and *Take 5*, ask readers to send in their stories of pain, horror and surprise. Often these story ideas are then turned into 'as-told-to' stories. They are then developed and rewritten by a staffer (often with the benefit of an interview), but in the first person, as if written by the woman or man the story is about. As you can see from the examples below, the story begins with a catchy quote headline, is followed by a general summary subheading, and the main body of the story is presented within quotation marks.

Cosmopolitan:

'I went to the toilet and a baby fell out'

Michelle Kitchener was every bit the fun-loving party girl about to turn 21. But after one quite memorable toilet trip, her life changed forever.

'I've never suspected that I was pregnant. I'd only been with my boyfriend for three months and I was on the Pill the whole time. When we broke up, I continued getting my period regularly, though it was lighter than usual. I thought you didn't get your period when you were pregnant. I thought I was safe ...'

Tarca, 2005, p. 92

Mother & Baby:

'I delivered our baby by YouTube'

Meet Marc Stephens, 28, Internet savvy super dad.

'Whenever I hear a story about a silly video on YouTube, I have to smile. Most people log on to look at footage of dogs on skateboards. Luckily, there are plenty of informative videos posted there as well. It was one of those that helped me bring my baby boy into the world—and might just have saved his life.'

Walton et al., 2010, p. 36

But, if you are already a journalist, you can pitch your own true story to these magazines and explain that you can write it yourself. So, if you have a story about how you were brought up by a Wiccan coven, or survived a strange life-threatening disease, or were stalked by your old English professor (or something equally as interesting or harrowing), you might have a good chance of being published.

The other advantage you may be able to offer is simply your expertise. Specialist knowledge is increasingly valuable when newsrooms are staffed by journalists with broad general knowledge. If you have, for example, a blog about a local football league, a particular area of science, or have developed a website that is a resource for dog trainers, there may be opportunities to leverage that specialist knowledge into standalone features for mainstream publications.

Identifying a possible publisher

To enter the world of freelancing you first need to come up with a great and original story idea. Your next job is to find an appropriate publisher. But rest assured, a great idea that makes an editor want to know more is the best possible step towards publication. When the time comes to go to market with your idea and story, you will need to become familiar with the plethora of publications in Australia (a nation with some of the highest magazine sales per capita in the world) and what stories they include. To help you in this endeavour, books such as *The Writer's Guide* by Irina Dunn and websites like the one created by the Magazine Publishers of Australia, or the others listed at the end of this chapter, are very useful.

Once you understand the myriad options available, you'll need to select the newspaper, magazine or website to pitch to, depending on your topic and the style you intend to write in.

Topic

There is nothing worse than pitching a completely inappropriate story to a publisher. Not only will your story be rejected, but the editor will realise you have no real interest in their publication. They will also wonder why *anyone* would employ someone to write a story if they don't even know how to research the outlet they want to write for. Don't get yourself blacklisted—think before you decide on a publication. Don't pitch a profile to a magazine that doesn't publish profiles; don't pitch a literary piece to a news magazine; don't offer a political insight piece to a teen magazine.

The key is research. Spend time developing a long list of bookmarked websites, a library of magazines and newspaper sections—particularly ones you'd like to write for.

Work out what sort of features these publications specialise in, and (just as importantly) what style of article they would never include. If you find you are cash-strapped and can't afford a slew of publications, spend time in newsagents or bookshops that carry magazines and papers and simply write down the article names and topics in a notebook. You can also check out your local library—many include a range of newspapers and magazines on their shelves.

You also need to make sure you know what stories your chosen publication has published in the last 12 months. It is very embarrassing if you offer a story to an editor who published a similar story in a recent edition. You can do this through your library, via searches of the publication's website and through online databases such as Factiva and Nexis, which store information about newspaper and magazine articles. The databases are only for subscribers, so you can pay for the service or, if you are studying, you may find you have free access through your university. Some state and local libraries also provide free access to these databases for residents.

Style

Now that you have your story idea and your target publication, you will need to write according to the website, magazine or newspaper's style. This means you have to think about audience and detail.

Audience

Who are the readers of this publication? How old are they? What sex are they? What are their incomes? These are questions you need to be able to answer if you are going to write a story that sells.

Each demographic has a style of its own. This is clear if you look at the tone in *Women's Health* and compare that with *New Idea*, then with Jetstar's in-flight magazine, then with *Home Beautiful*. You'll notice the language differs: some publications will use a large number of colloquialisms; others will use technical terminology, and some may even change spelling to keep up with the habits of their audience (such as using text spelling: 'we luv him', 'its gr8', 'they're 4eva' etc.).

You'll also observe that some publications will feature high-end options, such as yachting holidays and reviews of tailors, while others will focus on ways to cut down on family spending, or how to caravan with a pet. This is because publications are demographic-specific, and editors understand their readership intimately. You need to know what your readers expect if you want an editor to buy your article.

You can find demographic information on the internet (publications often have pages for advertisers that list a range of details about their readers). One of the easiest sites to navigate is for Bauer magazines: <http://www.bauer-media.com.au>. There you can find all the data you need for a host of magazines from *Australian Geographic* to *Woman's Day*. These days, audience profiles are far more sophisticated than they used to be: good editors know the data and what their readers want. You have to be mindful of the audience at every step of the process, from the idea, to the research, the writing and finally the pitch.

If you can't find the details for your chosen publication on the web, you can call the publication's advertising manager or examine a few copies from cover to cover. Don't just look at the feature stories to understand the readership; also look at the advertising and pictorial spreads; this will tell you about what the readers want to have and how much they are willing and able to pay.

Detail

As they say, the devil is in the detail. You may know your audience and have chosen a perfect topic for your publication, but you also need to make sure that all the little details of the story are correct. These details are usually contained in a publication's style guide (which is sometimes published to the general public). But if you can't get hold of the official style guide, you can create your own. Again, this involves reading a number of copies of your chosen publication. You'll need to create a database of style points for the magazine or newspaper you'll be pitching to.

These points are:

- What is their rule with numbers? (Not all use the standard rule of one to nine in words and 10 and above in numerals.)

- What attributions do they use (only 'said'/'says' or can you also use 'explained', 'assured', 'demanded' etc.)?

- What tense do they use for their stories and for their attributions?

- What point of view do they use (first, second or third person, or a combination, depending on the story)?

- How do they treat names? (Do they use first names or last names? Are there exceptions for celebrities or children?)

- What is the minimum and maximum length of the paragraphs in the publication?

- Do they use breakout boxes?

- What is the average word count for each style of feature they publish?

Wooing the publisher

In your journalist's toolbox you need more than just great writing, research and interviewing skills; you also need to be able to sell yourself (not always the easiest thing for writers, who are renowned for being shy, introverted types). When you start your career, you won't usually have to sell yourself to an editor face to face, or even over the phone (which cuts down on how scary the process can be). Instead you will approach publications via email; it's simple, inexpensive and what the majority of publications expect.

To find the email addresses of your chosen publication's features editor, you can look inside the front cover of a magazine, in the front of the features section of a newspaper or in the 'contact' section of a website's drop-down menu. If all else fails, call the publication (their number should be on the website or in the White Pages) and ask for the features editor's name and email address. Or you may know someone who works there—a former student colleague of yours perhaps—who can not only give you an email address or direct phone number for the features editor, but can maybe even mention to the editor you will getting in touch.

Once you have the editor's name and email address, you need to woo them with a great pitch. The following is a workable template that has led many new writers to publish their first feature stories. Similar structures are also used by established writers like Rebecca Skloot to sell stories to the most respected (and lucrative) publications in the world:

1. Address the email to the specific features editor of that publication—do not send out any generic emails.

2. Start by introducing yourself (you don't need to mention your name till the end) and explaining what publications you have written for previously (even if this is only a university newspaper or magazine) and what makes you perfect for this story or publication (for example, you're pitching to a youth surfing magazine and you won the Gold Coast Grommet Championships two years ago).

3. If you know the editor, mention this. You could know them via a third party or you might have seen them at a conference or an event (which are vital networking opportunities—go to every party, awards night or industry get-together you can).

4. Show you know the publication by stating something like: 'Your readers enjoy ..., so this story would appeal to them because ...'

5. Write your pitch the way you will write your story. You have already done your preliminary research and perhaps an interview; you should now explain the story to the editor with a lead, headings and an overall structure—perhaps with a bookend (explained in Chapter 6). This shows the editor you know how to write and you know how to structure. Don't forget to use the language of the publication—write your pitch in the style of the real story; that means using whatever lingo and details are particular to the publication. But don't get too wordy. Shorter is always better. If you cannot express the core idea in a sentence or two, then the editor will have moved on long before you get to the punchline.

6. Add in a couple of other story ideas. You may find that the editor doesn't like your main pitch, but may be interested in one of your other suggestions.

7   If you have published previously, offer to email the editor copies of your stories or direct them to a website you have set up to showcase your feature writing (you can do this cheaply through sites such as Wordpress—but make sure these sites are for your freelance work only and are not mixed in with personal content, as this can make you look unprofessional). If you are unpublished, you might offer to write the story 'on spec'. This means you will write the story and then send it to the editor, who, after reading it, will decide whether or not to publish and pay for your work. This is a particularly good option if you have written, or are writing, stories for a course you are doing—you have to write the story anyway, so you may as well offer it to a publication. But whatever you do, *do not* send anything with the initial pitch; you have to offer this option to the editor and then let them take you up on this opportunity. Editors will never open emails that contain attachments—they look like spam mail.

8   Say goodbye, thank the editor for their time reading your pitch, and tell them you'll be looking forward to hearing from them.

Here is an example of a short email pitch to a travel publication:

Pitch	Comments
Dear Ms _____,	The email is addressed to the editor of the publication.
I am a freelance writer and former newspaper journo and photographer and I'd love to contribute to your magazine. As a former international flight attendant I am always interested in travel stories, and I love _____'s mix of information and entertainment.	The writer begins with an introduction, their credits and what makes them special.
While I might live in your 7th worst holiday destination, here in Port Laurie, when we're not putting up garish high rises, we produce great feature articles (at least that's what we think). So, I have a few story ideas for you.	This is a reference to a story from an edition of the publication—it shows that the writer reads the magazine. It also employs the humorous tone of the magazine.
After reading some of the reviews in your magazine, I thought you might be interested in a look at Adelaide after the sun sets (I'll be visiting the city in August). 'Adelaide night life: a bar crawl of biblical proportions' explains that while Adelaide may be synonymous with stone cathedrals and Victorian morality, at night the tiny city shrugs off its choirboy robes and puts on its boogie shoes.	An explanation of the story begins, utilising the publication's language and style, and again shows how the writer understands the publication.

Pitch	Comments
This city has a bustling nightlife worthy of any die-hard clubber, cocktail connoisseur or wine bar aficionado. This story will take your readers on a journey of the best places in Adelaide to while away the wee small hours and mention some places to avoid.	The writer explains what will be covered in the story.
Or why not take advantage of my experience as an air hostess? I could write a survival guide for travelling the skies in comfort.	The writer now offers alternative story ideas.
Please let me know if you are interested in these ideas or if you'd like me to cover any events or destinations in south-east or rural Queensland. I look forward to hearing from you, and if you would like to see copies of my previously published work, please don't hesitate to ask. Regards, Jane Writer	The writer signs off and offers to send the editor copies of published stories.

When you send out your pitches, remember that freelancing is tough. You should expect to be rejected a number of times; it happens to the best of writers, especially early in their careers. You need a thick skin for the freelance business and you need to have confidence in your own abilities. Just because one or two editors don't like your work, it doesn't mean you're a terrible writer; you might just be pitching to the wrong publication or one that doesn't take submissions from people who don't have a long list of credits (there are many of those).

You can start by pitching at the top of the list of your favourite publications, but don't be discouraged before you work your way down. You may find you aren't successful in selling your travel piece to *Vogue Entertaining + Travel*, but you may make it into a street-press publication or a travel e-zine. The money isn't as good, or you may be working for free, but you are constantly building your credits and this is the way to start a great career.

Negotiating payment

You would never be a writer for the money. You rarely hear of a journalist buying a personal jet or a private island, but you can make a living in this business. There are few things more satisfying than paying the rent by doing something that you love, and freelancing can be lucrative, depending on who you sell your stories to and how many stories you can write.

The Media Entertainment and Arts Alliance (MEAA) is the representative body for journalists (among others) and publishes rates for freelance writers on its website: <www.alliance.org.au/media-summaries>. In 2016 their freelance minimum rates were:

- $986.00 per day
- $657.00 per half day $\left(\frac{2}{3} \text{ day rate}\right)$
- $246.00 per hour
- $1001.00 per 1000 words or less, then 93c per word.

Do not get your hopes up with these figures. While many publications use these 'per word' rates, or provide even better rates (the more glamorous and prestigious the publication, the more money you should make), they are not used across the board. Many of the smaller publications offer lower per word rates no matter how many, or few, words they require. Some of the free press and internet publications do not offer any remuneration, but may instead offer free subscriptions or just the excitement of seeing your work in the public domain. Many reputable publications only offer 25–50c a word. It is rare to find an Australian mainstream publication that pays a dollar a word.

The decision is yours. Bear in mind that there are some unscrupulous characters who will try to take advantage of you, and you shouldn't let them do so. If you are dealing with a major publication, then you should be paid, but if you are dealing with a smaller outfit, you may choose to waive the dollars for the excitement of seeing your name in print.

Summary

o Make sure your story is original, polished and engages an audience with a story where something happens.

o Think outside the box when it comes to your story ideas.

o Try writing from a personal angle to increase your 'publishability'.

o Find an appropriate publisher for your story.

o Make sure your topic and style fit the publication you target.

o Pitch your story the way you'll write your story.

o Try to get paid when you publish a story—and don't let anyone take advantage of you.

o Never give up! All the great writers have had a door shut in their face at least once. Don't let this discourage you; keep writing and keep pitching your work.

Questions

1 How can you find the demographic details for your selected publication?
2 What are the important steps to follow when you write an email pitch?
3 What should you expect to be paid for a freelance story? Would you ever accept less? Why?

Activities

1   Examine your top three favourite publications and create a database of their style points.
2   Take one of the stories you have written, edit it so it fits a publication and then pitch it!
3   What are some intriguing things about you that would make an interesting story? List them and come up with publications that would be interested in stories based on these ideas.

References and additional reading

Dunn, I. (2002). *The Writer's Guide: A Companion to Writing for Pleasure or Publication*, Sydney: Allen & Unwin.

Grenby, M. (2010). 'Dainty plates eatery all the rage in London', *Calgary Herald*, 30 June.

MacAdam, A. (2017). 'What makes a good pitch? NPR Editors weigh in', www.training.npr.org/audio/what-makes-a-good-pitch, January 24.

Tarca, S. (2005). 'I went to the toilet and a baby fell out', *Cosmopolitan*, February.

Walton, J., Dickinson, B., Moore, A. & McMillam, G. (2010). 'I delivered our baby by YouTube', *Mother & Baby*, June/July.

Online resources

Factiva: www.factiva.com

Nexis: www.nexis.com

Magazine sales sites:

-   Bauer magazines: http://www.bauer-media.com.au
-   iSUBSCRiBE: www.isubscribe.com.au
-   Magazine Publishers of Australia: www.magazines.org.au
-   MEAA Rates for Freelance Writers: www.alliance.org.au/media-summaries

Case study

Freelancer Mike Grenby talks about life as a journalist and how he sold his foray into food writing

Publication details:

'Dainty plates eatery all the rage in London', *Calgary Herald*, 30 June 2010.

The author:

Mike Grenby has earned much of his living for the past 35 years by selling freelance writing to newspapers, magazines and other publications. He pioneered the idea of a money column in the late 1960s, while at *The Vancouver Sun* newspaper, and his column continues to appear in Canadian newspapers every week. He also contributes articles on travel and other topics to various Australian and Canadian newspapers and magazines. His books (which have sold more than 100,000 copies) include *Suddenly ... It's You! A Guide for Lottery Winners*. Grenby graduated with high honours from the Graduate School of Journalism, Columbia University, New York, and is an assistant professor at Bond University, where he teaches journalism and public speaking.

The story:

Mike Grenby is an accomplished freelancer and teaches courses in freelancing and travel writing. He knows how to find the angle that will draw in the reader and (importantly if you are a freelancer) the editor. 'It is vital to come up with ideas that are both exciting and topical,' he says. 'You need to be aware of what's happening in the areas you are visiting and what will be interesting to your readers back home.' In this case he had found a restaurant that was on the cusp of becoming the latest 'in' place in London, and knew he could use it as the focus for a travel piece.

One of the keys to a successful career as a freelancer is to use your life as fodder for your work. Grenby always wears his journalist hat, even when choosing somewhere to eat while on holiday. He loves a good meal (and a big one), so the idea of sitting down to 18 courses of food wizardry was appealing to him and he knew it would be to others. 'I was right when I said that Viajante was London's hottest new restaurant,' he said. 'I was lucky I took the opportunity to eat there at the beginning of my trip. I went to book again on a return visit and I was told the restaurant was fully booked until the following week, and by that time I was due to be in Paris.'

With Viajante's star on the rise, Grenby realised that an article on the restaurant was a perfect idea for a freelance story. The world is being taken over by television shows based around food, and his angle would tap into a current interest in the marketplace. Grenby also managed to find a food-obsessed travel editor whom he knew would be interested in an up-and-coming restaurant in England.

When Grenby returned to Australia, armed with photos, facts, anecdotes and memories of delicious flavours, he approached the *Calgary Herald* with his idea. Once he had a commitment from the editor, he put pen to paper, making sure he followed the publication's style and tone. 'With this story I chose to send my ideas to a specific editor as I knew she was a real foodie at heart,' he said. 'Normally I wouldn't be so narrow with my pitch, I usually send feelers out to a number of newspapers and see who is interested in commissioning my work.'

As he is an established journalist, Grenby always waits for the editor to agree to publish his work before he starts writing, but he says even this is no guarantee that the process will be smooth. 'The best experience is a commitment followed by publication and payment; the worst is commitment (approval of story idea) by an editor ... and 18 months (and several changes of travel editor) later I'm still trying to either have the article published or be paid a kill fee.'

As payment for his story, Grenby was happy, like many others, to take the newspaper's standard pay rate. But he reminds us that you can get more than one cheque with a great story idea. 'I often ask if a publication would mind if I approached a competitor with a rewritten version of the story,' he said. 'Also, what can often happen is that a newspaper can offer the article to other papers in the chain—usually with some payment going to me.'

Grenby says that although pay day is wonderful, it is often worth writing for free or giving up your rights to an article to get started in your freelancing career. That is unless 'the article is so big/important that the writer could do better on her/his own'.

According to Grenby, the key to a great career in freelancing is simple: work hard and often, and use your imagination to generate great new ideas. 'Always be pumping something into the end of the pipeline—and be prepared for several things to pop out at the other end at the same time, often necessitating a few all-nighters to write, revise, etc.' He also suggests that you never give up. It's always hard at the beginning of your career, but one day, like Grenby, you could be indulging in a sumptuous feast—and getting paid for it.

Writing sample

Dainty plates eatery all the rage in London

By Mike Grenby, *Calgary Herald*, 30 June 2010

LONDON—When Nuno Mendes dishes out lunch and dinner, he often uses tweezers to put the food on the plate.

That's because some of the ingredients are so small he couldn't handle them with anything else. And he needs to make sure many of the food items—like tiny flowers—are the right way up.

Mendes is the chef-owner of Viajante, one of London's hottest new restaurants. Opened in April, the 40-seat restaurant offers only three choices for dinner: a tasting menu comprising six, nine or 12 courses.

You are introduced to each course as it appears on the table. (If you insist, you can get a copy of the menu after the meal.)

At Viajante, which means 'traveller' in both Portuguese and Spanish, the diner is meant to take a journey with every mouthful.

'I want my food to surprise and delight my guests,' said Mendes, who grew up on his family's dairy farm in Portugal.

'It's not about being shocking, but it is about being playful. Each ingredient should taste as perfect as it possibly can, its flavour never lost or masked but rather developed and combined in exciting ways that make you fall in love with it all over again.'

The 12 courses I sampled, which according to the number of photos I took actually came to 18 courses by the time you add the complimentary appetizers and desserts and special bread, included dishes like:

- Squid tartare and pickled radishes, samphire (a green plant that grows in tidal marshes) and squid ink jus (frozen like a slushie).
- Olive soup with Greek yogurt, ginger and pistachio crumbs.
- Pig's neck and prawn, savoy cabbage, fried capers and grated egg.
- Aged sirloin of beef and chunky miso, ramson onions and burnt fennel.
- Carrot mousse, sweet and pickled, buttermilk and granité (again, a frozen slush).

Mendes left Europe in the 1990s and trained at the prestigious California Culinary Academy in San Francisco before going on to work with some of the world's leading chefs.

He said he has also been inspired by travelling through Japan where he tasted freshly made umeboshi (a tart, tangy, salt pickled plum), and learning the bold flavours of south-west US cuisine in New Mexico.

He avoids too much fat, salt and sugar in his dishes, favouring various herbs and spices instead to give the food interesting and appealing flavours. I'm sure that's the main reason, along with the small portion sizes, my four-hour dinner left me feeling comfortably rather than uncomfortably full.

'I am passionate about the food I cook,' he said, 'from the ingredients we source to ensuring that every meal is indulgent but healthy.

'It's hard work, experimenting to combine different flavours and textures, dealing with the failures as well as the sudden inspirations that lie behind the final success.'

In the short time Viajante has been in business, its food (the menu items change regularly) and chef have attracted rave reviews in the newspapers here:

'Flawlessly presented, exactingly executed and wildly innovative'—*Metro*. 'One of the hottest young chefs around'—*The Guardian*. 'A meal here's a fun ride that's worth the price, if you are prepared to pay the price'—*Time Out London*.

'I hate to think what a meal like that costs, but no more than staying in a nice hotel no doubt, and far more memorable,' said Marny Peirson, a traveller from Vancouver when she heard about the tasting menu at Viajante.

That's a good way to put it into perspective. The six-course tasting menu costs $95, the nine-course $125 and the 12-course $140. These days, you wouldn't find much of a hotel room in London (or many other cities) for $95–$140. There's also a three-course lunch for $40.

Add a wine pairing—a different wine for almost every course (I counted 12 wines for my dinner)—and you are looking at an additional $50, $75 and $100, respectively.

Mendes said about 10 per cent of his dinner customers choose the six-course menu, 60 per cent go for the nine courses and 30 per cent for the 12 courses.

Diners sitting in the front section of the restaurant have a great view of all the food being prepared in the open kitchen. The staff use a book to keep track of which courses have been served to which tables.

Most of Mendes' employees are under 30. 'I believe in giving something back by helping train young people who are interested in the business,' he said.

His partner, Clarise Faria, runs The Loft Project. Originally set up as a temporary supper club and personal test kitchen, the Loft has now become a platform for the next generation of talented chefs to take up residency and showcase their food. Chefs are invited from top kitchens around the world to host dinners for guests around one communal table in Mendes' own home.

Former Herald *money columnist and now travel writer Mike Grenby is assistant professor at Bond University on Australia's Gold Coast.*

Part B
Different Styles

12
Profiles

Question to actor Keanu Reeves: How do you feel about being a sex symbol?

Answer: I think it's cool.

Q: What did you like about the script when you first read it?

A: I opened up the page and it said, Speed, and I went, 'Cool, I like that'. The situations were very cool.

Q: There's a lot of emphasis on your looks, though?

A: I think that's part of the genre, it's cool.

Rachelle Unreich, 2004, p. 16

Objectives

This chapter sets out to identify the techniques used for writing profiles. It should be read in conjunction with Chapter 4, because the craft of interviewing is integral to good profile writing. A range of profile categories, all of which pose some challenges to the interviewer and writer, are considered here. Each profile involves its own pressures and expectations, so this chapter presents some general approaches to the profile, irrespective of the subject. It covers:

o   what a profile is

o   politicians

o   business people

o   celebrities

o   ordinary people

o   obituaries

o   a Case study: What do you stand for? Joshua Robertson on the challenges of profiling an unconventional politician

o   a Writing sample: 'George Christensen on poverty, priesthood and a flirtation with One Nation' by Joshua Robertson, *The Guardian* (online) 26 September 2016.

Introduction

One of the most coveted jobs in any feature-writing department is that of the profile writer. Profile writers get to meet celebrities, ask them cheeky questions and write a piece that is almost guaranteed to have an audience. Why? Because people from all walks of life love reading about what makes people famous, successful or desirable. And the profile writer knows that better than anyone. This privileged position does not, however, mean only one writer can do profiles. While writing a profile does take some art, perception, interviewing skills and usually a great deal of research and hard work, it is a task that most writers can achieve. But there are some caveats to consider.

What is a profile?

Profiles are potted biographies, or snapshots of lives still being lived (Ricketson, 2004, p. 1). Profiles remain popular with readers because people are fascinated by others.

There are two kinds of profile. The most common is the profile undertaken with the subject's consent. It can involve just the subject or it may extend to the subject's circle of friends and enemies. The second type of profile—sometimes called the *Esquire* profile, after the American magazine that championed it—is assembled without the consent or cooperation of the subject, from observation of the subject and anecdotes, views and opinions supplied by friends and enemies.

One of the famous examples of this is Gay Talese's profile of Frank Sinatra, entitled 'Frank Sinatra has a cold', published in *Esquire* in April 1966. It is a masterful piece of writing that Talese composed after tracking Sinatra for several weeks without once getting a chance to interview him. The story showed it was possible to write a penetrating portrait without direct access to the subject (Granger, 2003). As an example of New Journalism, it has few peers. It starts: 'Frank Sinatra, holding a glass of bourbon in one hand and a cigarette in the other, stood in a dark corner of the bar between two attractive but fading blondes who sat waiting for him to say something' (Talese, 1966). This sets the scene perfectly and echoes the writer's own struggle to hear something from Sinatra.

Not every writer agrees with this approach to the profile, or indeed sees value in it. English profile writer Fiametta Rocco believes such an approach gives the profile a 'hollowness' at its heart. 'People are complicated, and the best profiles need help, not for what he or she will tell you in words but for the subtler, deeper, more irrational things that get conveyed in other ways' (Rocco, 2000, p. 49). The reality is that writers do not always have a choice; their editor might demand a particular profile subject, and if that subject is not interested in being part of the exercise, the writer will probably still embark on the profile.

It is worth remembering that such profiles can be published in the modern era of celebrity-driven and entertainment-related journalism. Celebrities, sports people and business people who have no need to build their identity or add to their fame may not cooperate with a writer who believes there is a good—and fresh—story to be told. Yet a subject's refusal should not be seen as a provocation to do a 'hatchet job' on them. There may well be a range of good reasons for the subject to cry off on a profile; writers should not take this refusal personally.

But such refusals should act as a reminder that the majority of profiles are written about artists, musicians, sports people, business people, writers and politicians when they have something to promote—and that is, at its most basic, themselves. So how do you manage to get the best out of the exchange under those circumstances?

Politicians and business people

There are two things that unite politicians and business people as profile subjects. The first is their tendency to express themselves in jargon (relevant to each of their areas). The second is that there is not much general public interest in what either of them do or how they do it. For politicians, this is partly a reflection of a widespread apathy about politics in Australia, and also the fact that politics, at state and federal levels, is dominated by certain key portfolios that are headed by prominent individuals such as prime ministers, premiers and treasurers. Political profiles tend, therefore, to focus on those incumbents.

Politicians

The good political profile is a rare event in mainstream publishing. Why? Largely because politicians from the major parties have similar backgrounds and often hold similar views. Modern politics is not known for its capacity to provide a succession of diverse and interesting candidates for public life. Party unity tends to shave off individual distinctions and ideas, while political or bureaucratic jargon represents the final impediment to a compelling political profile.

But there are always exceptions, and the exceptions prove the rule. Check out the George Christensen profile at the end of this chapter. He is interesting because he doesn't sound—or look—like most politicians. The impact of former Queensland independent MP Pauline Hanson is another illustration of this. Hanson lost endorsement by the Liberal Party in 1996 for airing some contentious views, but she won the federal seat of Oxley as an independent and then started to gain national attention. After a range of implosions and controversies that saw her lose her seat and disappear from the national debate, she returned in a blaze of publicity in the 2016 federal election to secure a Senate spot. Hanson was interesting because she was unfashionable, unpredictable and uncomfortable in the public gaze. She was loathed and loved in various degrees, but she was compelling because she was not a conventional politician, and therefore was an ideal subject for a profile. Fairfax's *Good Weekend* magazine sent its best profile writer, David Leser, to do the job.

Hanson invited Leser back to her house to do the interview. Writing later about the role observation plays in completing the profile and rounding out an individual, Leser explained:

> I stood in the kitchen drinking Bundies and dry and watching the chops fry. I looked at the CD collection when no-one was watching. I saw a house devoid of furniture or mother love. Again, the art of observation, but not necessarily of interviewing.
>
> Leser, 2001, p. 8

Leser's reliance on observation shows how details can help inform the larger picture of the individual. They were vital to an understanding of Hanson—who is fundamentally a person with simple views that are shared by many Australians.

The hurdle for writers attempting a political profile is that most senior politicians have been interviewed so often they have little that is new to say, and even if they are willing to talk, they often do so in an uninteresting way. The onus falls on the profile writer to find ways to change the dynamics of the interview. This could involve doing the interview with the politician at home with their family, or perhaps conducting it in the presence of their closest colleague. Try to resist all efforts for an office-based interview. One union official (later to become a federal Labor MP) used to take the initiative with journalists who wanted to profile him: he insisted they join him while he drove around Melbourne visiting union sites. It was a perfect way for the writer to see the unionist in his natural environment, and—to the unionist's benefit—among friends and supporters.

But once again, the keys to a good political profile are extensive research, and perseverance during the interview in order to diplomatically explore personal motivations. The reason a person has sought a career in public life is interesting, as is the reason for certain decisions made in government.

Aberrations are interesting too. One of the infamous moments in former Prime Minister Malcolm Fraser's otherwise distinguished career was the mysterious loss of his trousers during a visit to Memphis in the United States. Some years later, writer Paul Toohey embarked on an inspired journey to retrace Fraser's steps. This humorous reconstruction of the episode revealed a lot about Fraser. It was not a conventional profile, but it provided fresh insight into a man whose public image had been one of certainty and rectitude (Toohey, 1996, pp. 7–26). Thinking conventionally about a profile can be the first step towards producing a stilted or predictable outcome. Fresh thinking tends to produce interesting results, as Toohey proved.

Business people

Business profiles are common enough in specialist business media. Business subjects feel more comfortable talking to an audience that understands what they do. The way many successful business subjects express themselves is how they identify with the people who move in their circles. So, unless writers are prepared to deconstruct the jargon for more general consumption, business profiles are unlikely to find a wider audience.

Business profiles in mainstream Australian publications tend to focus on the very wealthy and the very famous: the Packers, the Murdochs, the Lowys, the Holmes à Courts and, more recently, the Rineharts (dynasties carry an inherent reader interest; we are all part of a family). These profiles often follow the *Esquire* method, because the very rich and famous tend to avoid regular engagement with writers—they just don't need it.

This tendency among celebrities to avoid such coverage is amplified among successful business people. Many business people believe what they do is a private activity, even if they head a public company. There is something old-fashioned about this and it can be frustrating for writers who believe that what is happening in business deserves wider exposure. The proliferation of so-called mum and dad shareholders demands a series of meaningful features on the chief executive officers running many of the companies in which they hold shares. That such features are not being written reflects the unwillingness of the subjects to cooperate with the interviewer, either out of anxiety about giving up something of themselves for scrutiny or out of concern about revealing too much about their business practices in a competitive marketplace.

However, there is another way of achieving a satisfactory result. It is a compromise driven by the subject, but it has appeal for the writer too. It is the 'sanctioned' *Esquire* profile, which offers the subject a rare degree of control over the outcome without appearing to dictate the content of the feature. One of Australia's wealthiest men, the late Richard Pratt, used this technique. When one of the authors approached Pratt's office, he was told politely that Pratt would not grant an interview, but that the office would provide a list of contacts—friends and associates—who would be happy to talk to the writer about Pratt. The office was also pleased to offer assistance by providing some recent speeches and anecdotes that would help the story.

This represents a tantalising offer for any writer. Here was access to several big businessmen in Pratt's home town of Melbourne, and the chance to talk to them about Pratt. One of the problems with this kind of profile, however, is that business colleagues are unlikely to be completely objective about the person who nominated them as a mouthpiece. But the writer agrees to this approach knowing that pitfall. Each party knows where they stand.

Celebrities

Some years ago, before Arnold Schwarzenegger entered politics and was still in the movie business, one journalist admitted to Arnold's publicist that he needed more than half an hour with the actor to do his intended profile justice: 'if I'm going to do the profile properly, I'd want to hang around over a few days,' the writer protested. 'Oh God,' the publicist replied, 'this wouldn't be one of those profiles where you try to *figure him out*, would it?' (Farndale, 2002, p. 10). Every celebrity interviewer wants to be able to 'figure out' their subject—especially because they feel that there is something to 'figure out', despite all that has been written about the celebrity.

This may be partly explained by the following observation from British profile writer Lynn Barber: 'I like and need the competitive edge of going where many journalists have gone before and trying to do better' (Barber, 1991, p. viii). But the writer (of this chapter) also believes that celebrities are just waiting for a chance to talk candidly about themselves, and it is this optimism that helps drive the massive commitment to celebrity profiles.

The celebrity profile is the most common kind of profile undertaken in newspapers, magazines and online. It is an industry in itself. Profiles for some magazines are often assembled from other interviews, snippets of information from overseas sources and internet gossip to shape a story that has, at best, a slender association with the truth. Some publications conceive story ideas built around pictures and headlines ('Alicia's baby dream', 'Jude's home alone' or 'Rove's new love')—an inversion of the usual and ethical practice—which become the basis for rebuilding a new profile of another celebrity. The one unadorned truth about these profiles is that very few of them are actually profiles; they contain scant personal detail, have no insights, include little personal history and contain little original content. But when you come across a real celebrity profile, you know it.

One of the major difficulties confronting the celebrity profile writer is the 'junket' interview, where the journalist joins other writers in a hotel room with the celebrity to discuss the latest film or online extravaganza. Time is short and often the expectation from the magazine or newspaper is high: a lot of words are required from a shared 20-minute interview. This can tax the writer's resources, as Rachelle Unreich found when she interviewed actor Keanu Reeves for a 3000-word magazine profile. Unreich, an Australian writer then based in the United States, was confronted by an interview subject who didn't have much to say. She opened her profile with some paragraphs about Reeves' hairstyle. 'But can you blame me? One of Keanu's juicier quotes in that interview was: "I wasn't very happy with the script"' (Unreich, 2004, p. 16).

So writers who desire to find something fresh to say about a celebrity face many challenges. Apart from the time constraints, they are often faced with uninterested or uninteresting subjects who have nothing much to say. However, as Lynn Barber (1991, p. viii) identifies, the upside is that the writer does not have to waste time in the piece explaining who the subject is.

Given these limitations and opportunities, there are several ways to go about a celebrity profile:

- Do it straight: conduct a formal interview and observe the techniques outlined in Chapter 4.

- Do it straight, but add a twist: talk to the celebrity in a conventional sense and then add yourself into the picture to include your reactions and asides to what the celebrity says and does during the interview.

- Do it only with the twist: this is really a profile with an attitude. The tone of such a profile is the critical factor—it can be simpering or flattering, but more often it will be sarcastic with a tendency to lampoon the subject. This may be great sport for the writer, but it assumes the reader feels the same way the writer does about the celebrity. This approach is best left to those writers who are assured of their style and observations, or it can look precocious and nasty.

The final approach will be determined by the writer's experience (both as interviewer and writer) and the publication that is running the profile. For example, *Rolling Stone* will run a different profile of former US Vice President-turned-environmentalist Al Gore from that which would appear in *The New Yorker* because their audiences are different. *New Idea*'s profile of Nicole Kidman will be radically different from *Good Weekend* magazine's story on the same actor. *Good Weekend* prides itself on rigorous, multi-sourced profiles. For instance, David Leser's profile of broadcaster Alan Jones for the magazine involved interviews with a hundred people before Leser actually interviewed Jones (Leser, 2001, p. 8). By contrast, *New Idea* will rely on one interview with the actor as the basis of a profile. But *Good Weekend*—and magazines of that ilk—tries to avoid spending too much time on celebrities. The publishers of such titles believe their readers want a range of profiles. That is not necessarily the case with other mainstream magazines, which are particularly aware of the commercial impact of having certain identities (such as Kate Middleton's sister Pippa) placed on the front cover. Such frequent coverage of certain 'star' celebrities means that what does appear is not necessarily a profile that documents their life. Instead, these profiles show an incremental development in the saga of the celebrity's life, which has been documented in previous magazines. Many mainstream weekly glossy magazines build celebrity profiles over a period of weeks or months, while other, more diverse publications do a profile once and leave it at that. There are also plenty of news-based websites that 'scrape' the magazines for fodder and turn it around for an international audience. It's not journalism— it's just cutting and pasting from somewhere else.

Ordinary people

It is rare for so-called ordinary people to be the sole subject of a profile. It may be that ordinary people are part of a series of small features about a particular habit, skill or lifestyle that is one of the add-on elements in many magazines and supplements. But generally, ordinary people are not thought to be sufficiently different from the intended readership to be considered legitimate profile subjects. Rightly or wrongly, this approach has persisted over time, with only a few exceptions.

The first exception is the profile of a range of ordinary people who are in some way linked by either an event or other circumstances. For example, a series of profiles on former asbestos workers could be linked by the fact that all of them have developed mesothelioma. Each of their stories might be unremarkable, save for the shared circumstances of their work, which led them to develop the same fatal disease.

The second exception is rarer, but arguably better known. It is the profile of the ordinary person who has been transformed into an extraordinary one. The most obvious example of recent years is that of the two miners in Beaconsfield—Brant Webb and Todd Russell—who became heroes after their remarkable survival despite being trapped underground for two weeks in May 2006. Profiles of the pair appeared and even a book was published about their friendship, their work and how they came to survive. The rarity of their survival and their basic 'ordinariness' were the prerequisites for the profiles. The fact that ordinary people have done the impossible makes them fascinating and inspiring subjects—if they can do it, why can't we?

Yet the reality is that most ordinary people are uncomfortable about being the subject of a profile, and in some cases they are unhappy with the end result. It is worth remembering that people who are used to being interviewed—whether they are celebrities, sportsmen or businesswomen—have a basic understanding of the dynamics of the interview and the profile form. They have been through the process before. This is rarely the case for ordinary people, who are often flattered at being approached for a profile but are unfamiliar with the process or the end result.

As a consequence, the writer should tread carefully and be honest and clear about what they want from the interview and what they are going to do with it. For the subject, this may be their only chance to be profiled, so the writer should aim to make it a valuable experience for both themselves and the subject.

Ordinary people will usually be free of the jargon and agendas that often characterise other more worldly profile subjects. They can be candid and wise, so their quotes are often fresh and insightful. There is much rich material in the profiles of ordinary people.

Being able to draw out that kind of information is increasingly valuable to readers because of the range of community awards and celebrations for volunteers for good causes. These include the Australia Day and Queen's Birthday Honours lists, which provide an opportunity to reward thousands of Australians for making a contribution to the nation. Each of these ordinary people has a story, and each local newspaper will attempt a short profile of the most recently decorated member of the community. These are perfect (happy) circumstances for the interviewer to elicit information from the award recipient about their life and achievement. However, moments of disappointment, grief and loss are more challenging. In such circumstances, the writer needs to connect with the person they are interviewing for the profile at a level of humanity that enables the interview to be held in a genuinely inquisitive and non-threatening or intrusive way.

Obituaries

Obituaries are short biographies of the recently deceased, which demand many of the same skills necessary to write a profile of a living person. It would be wrong for the writer to assume that obituaries need to be dull or colourless. As the Obituaries Editor of *The Times*, Ian Brunskill, noted: 'Obituaries are about lives, not death' (Brunskill, 2005, p. xiii). Indeed, a good obituary will bring a person to life, and many have contained the kind of detail that helps celebrate the person's individuality. The former Obituaries Editor of *The Daily Telegraph* in London, Hugh Massingberd, explained his approach: 'All my life I had seen history and biography as a marvellous excuse to tell funny stories, strange anecdotes, about people' (Massingberd, 2001, p. xi). And this is the key to writing a good obituary—it is vital to capture the essence of the individual.

The challenge for the writer is to balance the research to reflect both the public and private aspect of the person. A well-known public figure, such as a politician or television personality, will have an extensive series of clippings that cover their public life. But what about the rumours about their private life—that the politician had a mistress and the television personality had a drug habit? How much of this can a writer use in an obituary?

The reality is that there is no law about defaming the dead, and consequently there is a risk that some of the more lurid and untested rumours may find themselves in the public arena through an obituary. This is when the writer has to exercise restraint and stick to the basic premise of the feature: if it cannot be verified, it must not be printed. The death of an individual does not absolve the writer from exercising basic decency and professional ethics, of being accurate and truthful.

A practice favoured by many publications is to prepare the obituary well in advance of the person's death. That gives the writer the opportunity to talk to the subject and their friends to ensure they get the basic details of the subject's birth, birthplace, family and career correct. It sounds almost ghoulish, providing for the subject a moment to confront their own mortality, but it is the best way of ensuring the central facts of the person's life are correct. The nation's major newspapers always have extensive obituaries of international and national identities—such as Queen Elizabeth II and Nelson Mandela—written and edited, sometimes years in advance, ready for publication when they die.

These days, obituaries are often written from reminiscences and tributes submitted to publications from family and friends, and edited by the resident obituarist, who is usually an older staff member on the major publications, with extensive experience and contacts. Often they know the subject of the obituary and know how to convey an accurate sense of the individual without offending family and friends or misrepresenting the subject. This is where the writing skill reaches its peak. The best feature writing is distinguished by nuance, but underpinned by an explicit understanding of the subject.

Obituaries appear when reader interest is greatest, but when grief is still prevalent and the immediate family audience is at its most vulnerable. The obituarist must be aware of the family sensitivities as well as the reader interest. Consider this example, from London's *The Daily Telegraph*, for a minor member of the British aristocracy:

> Denisa, Lady Newborough, who has died, aged 73, was many things: wire walker, night club girl, nude dancer, air pilot. She only refused to be two things—a whore and a spy—'and there were attempts to make me both,' she once wrote.
>
> in Massingberd, 2001, pp. 6–7

There is plenty for the passing reader in such an obituary, but the more vivid elements are actually supported by the subject of the obituary in her own words, the perfect outcome for the obituarist.

Now consider the death of Australian actor Heath Ledger, who was only 28 when he died in his New York apartment in 2008. Ledger's acting ability and early death revived memories of other Hollywood stars whose careers were over too soon, such as James Dean and Marilyn Monroe. Premature ends to famous lives usually catch the obituarist unprepared. In Ledger's case, the obituaries were also overlaid with constant speculative reports about the circumstances of his death and the state of his personal and financial affairs. There were 24,267 stories on Ledger published around the world in the three weeks after his death, but only a fraction of those could be considered obituaries (Norris, 2008). This rampant speculation reflects the nature of modern celebrity, but the obituarist cannot become too involved in wondering what happened to their subject and why. In this case, the difficult task was to marry the basics of reporting the key moments of Ledger's life with fast-emerging sentiment surrounding the young actor's death. Hence, the obituary in *The Times* in London said:

> Ledger was a big, muscular, blond Australian and was initially dismissed as just another pretty pin-up boy. He seemed determined to prove detractors wrong, doing much to obscure his handsome looks and plumb the despair of a series of complex characters. Inevitably there will be comparisons with James Dean and River Phoenix, who also played conflicted, alienated characters and died in their twenties, leaving behind a sense of loss and waste.
>
> Savage, 2008, p. 27

Such instances are rare. Most obituarists will have to content themselves with following the basic requirements of the task—the subject's full name, birth date, place of birth, family, occupation, marriage and surviving family. These constitute the platform on which the obituary must be built. The banal obituary will closely follow the person's life progress, from school, to university, to career, to marriage, to family, to retirement. But obituaries need the telling anecdote, the insightful quote or the distinctive detail to lift the life beyond such chronology.

This can be difficult if the writer is not familiar with the subject. One of the authors recalls working with a young journalist who was reporting the death of Australian novelist Patrick White. The journalist found himself talking to a famous Australian poet about White. Once he had finished the telephone interview, the journalist hung up the phone and said: 'Got some quotes from a bloke called A.D. Hope.' It is a safe bet that had the journalist known more about Hope's esteemed place in Australia's literary life, he might well have gleaned more from the interview and put more into his story.

There is an increasing tendency in some publications to have obituaries supplied by a member of the community who best knew the subject. Sometimes they can come from an immediate family member or a close friend. The result is smaller obituaries that often lack insight and detail but are a strong testament to the individual's decency and contribution to society. This kind of writing is largely uncritical and celebratory. But the goal of every obituary should be to give a rounded picture of the subject, and the writer who seeks to do so will benefit from the opportunity to test their writing skills by assembling facts of an individual life in a compelling and respectful manner.

Major newspapers' websites have provided increased opportunities for obituary writers. *The New York Times*, for example, regularly supplements its written obituaries with photographic slideshows, video footage of significant events in the individual's life, or even interviews. This is exemplified in the case of famed boxing personality Angelo Dundee, who worked as trainer, manager and cornerman for a number of famous boxers, including Muhammad Ali (Cassius Clay) and Sugar Ray Leonard. *The New York Times* obituary of Dundee included a written report and a slideshow (Goldstein, 2012). It is an excellent example of how well-written obituaries can bring individuals to life, even after their death.

Summary

o   Most readers love stories about people (famous or ordinary).
o   Most people love talking about themselves.
o   Try to avoid repeating jargon in profile interviews.
o   Don't take it personally if a profile subject turns down your request for an interview.
o   Try to find something new to say about someone who has been frequently profiled.
o   Obituaries are about lives, not deaths.

Questions

1   What are three ways you can approach a celebrity profile?
2   Who is likely to provide the best information for a profile about a business person?
3   Who do you need to talk to for an obituary?

Activities

1   Think about a person you believe you know well: it could be your partner, sister, brother, father, mother or grandparent. Then think about what you don't know about them and write it down in the form of questions. Next time you see the person, ask them the questions. Watch and listen to their answers and reactions.

2   Go to a magazine or newspaper that contains a celebrity profile. Read the profile and then do an internet search for articles about the celebrity that were published around the same time. What are the similarities? What are the differences? How would you have done it differently?

3   Write a list of five people from all walks of life whom you think deserve to be profiled. They could be the local social worker, a budding sports champion or an international figure. Write one reason next to each of your choices for why you think they should be profiled ('being famous' is not a reason). Now start researching each of them. Which one interests you most? Why? Would they interest others?

References and additional reading

Barber, L. (1991). *Mostly Men*, London: Viking.

Brunskill, I. (ed.) (2005). *Great Lives: A Century in Obituaries*, London: HarperCollins.

Farndale, N. (2002). *Flirtation, Seduction, Betrayal*, London: Constable.

Goldstein, R. (2012). 'Angelo Dundee, trainer of Ali and Leonard, dies at 90', *The New York Times*, 1 February: <www.nytimes.com/2012/02/02/sports/angelo-dundee-trainer-of-boxing-champions-dies-at-90.html?pagewanted=1&_r=2>

Granger, D. (2003). 'Foreword', in A. Miller (ed.), *Esquire's Big Book of Great Writing*, New York: Hearst, p. x.

Leser, D. (2001). 'The interview: art or a confidence trick?', *The Walkley Magazine*, issue 13, pp. 8–9.

Linnell, G. (1999). 'Making the hard yards', *The Walkley Magazine*, issue 6, pp. 8–9.

McGregor, C. (1990). *Headliners*, St Lucia: University of Queensland Press.

Massingberd, H. (ed.) (2001). *The Very Best of the Daily Telegraph Books of Obituaries*, London: Pan Macmillan.

Norris, C. (2008). 'There were 24,267 stories about Heath Ledger in the three weeks after his death. Some of them may have been true', *The Weekend Australian Magazine*, 8–9 March.

Remnick, D. (ed.) (2000). *Life Stories: Profiles from The New Yorker*, London: Pavilion House.

Ricketson, M. (ed.) (2004). *The Best Australian Profiles*, Melbourne: Black Inc.

Rocco, F. (1999). 'Stockholm syndrome: journalists taken hostage', in S. Glover (ed.), *The Penguin Book of Journalism*, London: Penguin, pp. 48–59.

Rocco, F. (2000). 'Stockholm syndrome: journalists taken hostage', in S. Glover (ed.), *The Penguin Book of Journalism* (paperback edn), London: Penguin.

Savage, M. (2008). 'Heath Ledger: The *Times* obituary', *The Times*, 23 January.

Stark, N. (2006). *Life After Death: The Art of the Obituary*, Melbourne: Melbourne University Press.

Talese, G. (1966). 'Frank Sinatra has a cold', *Esquire*, April.

Toohey, P. (1996). *God's Little Acre: Journeys into Australia*, Sydney: Duffy & Snellgrove.

Unreich, R. (2004). 'Talking fluent celeb', *The Walkley Magazine*, issue 27, pp. 16–17.

Case study

What do you stand for?: Joshua Robertson on the challenges of profiling an unconventional politician

Publication details:

'George Christensen on poverty, priesthood and a flirtation with One Nation' by Joshua Robertson, published in *The Guardian* (online) September 26, 2016, https://www.theguardian.com/australia-news/2016/sep/26/george-christensen-on-poverty-priesthood-and-a-flirtation-with-one-nation

The author:

Joshua Robertson has been a journalist for 12 years. He started his cadetship in far north Queensland with the *Tully Times* and became an investigative reporter at *The Courier Mail* in Brisbane. He became Brisbane correspondent for *The Guardian* in 2014.

The story:

One of the challenges of writing a profile of a well-known figure is finding something new and fresh to say. When Josh Robertson embarked on researching a profile of federal Queensland MP George Christensen, he knew there had been a lot of words already written about the views of the notoriously provocative politician. But then again, how much did people *really* know about him?

'The instruction from HQ [*The Guardian*'s office in Sydney] was: where does George Christensen come from? We knew some of his background and his passion for *Doctor Who*, but really, so little was known,' Robertson explains.

'He's an arch-conservative from Queensland, who stokes all these stereotypes about Queenslanders. And I wasn't sure I'd be able to say anything fresh.'

So Robertson armed himself with extensive research, searching for something that hadn't been written or observed about Christensen. He went back to the MP's maiden speech, which helped him with some family angles. Robertson had spoken to Christensen months before the profile, to quiz him about his attendance at a Reclaim Australia rally and propose a week with the MP on the looming federal election campaign trail. Follow-up calls to explore that opportunity went unreturned and Robertson was concerned that by the time he was researching the profile, Christensen had frozen him out. At that stage, the profile was shaping as a piece that would be collated from other people's views of George, rather than containing the voice of the man himself. Then Robertson got lucky.

'I came across George's father's mobile number on an old electoral slide used in an earlier campaign. So I rang his dad and he said: "He won't talk to you if it's going to be a hatchet job" and I reassured him it was going to be fair,' Robertson recalls. About 90 minutes later, Christensen rang Robertson. The interview lasted well over an hour and Robertson was able to glean fresh material—including his time in the seminary and something of his disarming sense of humour.

The feature itself, however, was a fundamental contrast between the progressive world view of *The Guardian* and Christensen's conservatism. Robertson was 'acutely aware of striking the balance'. There were key questions and issues—including Christensen's views on climate science; his provocative statements on Islam, immigration and conservationists—that Robertson knew he had to address. 'I would have been eviscerated in the Comments [section] if I didn't address those issues, but George was happy to go there,' Robertson says.

Robertson approached the interview with some broad areas, and basic talking points enumerated in his notebook. 'I'm not slavish to a structure for these kinds of interviews—you have to go where the interview takes you,' he says.

And it led to some insights—about Christensen voting for One Nation in the 1998 Queensland election, which Robertson was delighted to learn because 'it speaks to the link between One Nation and the traditional Liberal–National Party supporters [in Queensland].'

But perhaps more importantly, it also gave Robertson a stronger sense of where Christensen comes from and who he represents. 'People like George don't occur in a vacuum. As he says in the story, there are people he meets who don't think he goes far enough.' Others think he goes way too far. 'He's routinely vilified on social media. One hopes that people perceive George as a person who has his own humanity and comes from a particular community. His prejudice is no different to some other prejudices,' Robertson says.

And although Robertson doesn't necessarily identify with Christensen, he is familiar with the views the MP holds and the way he expresses them. 'I did my cadetship in deep North Queensland and I've still got family up around there. I think that helps.'

But it also helps if the reporter doesn't become too engaged in the interview, on one side or the other. 'Empathy is more important than sympathy with an interview subject,' Robertson says. 'I've reported a lot on organised crime and bikies—you don't have to like someone to be a fair reporter.'

Perhaps the final test was the reaction to the profile. Christensen didn't respond but several conservatives thought that 'for *The Guardian*, this was pretty good.'

Writing sample

George Christensen on poverty, priesthood and a flirtation with One Nation

By Joshua Robertson, *The Guardian* online, 26 September 2016

A few weeks shy of George Christensen's 20th birthday, having let his National party membership lapse and getting 'itchy feet thinking about One Nation', he voted for Pauline Hanson's party in the 1998 Queensland election.

The next year, having seen how One Nation's 11 state MPs—three of them in electorates straddled by Christensen's now federal seat of Dawson—were 'all over the shop' in parliament, he resumed paid-up membership of the Nationals.

While Hanson had poached National members en masse by espousing similar views about 'race-based welfare, the flag and a whole heap of other things', Christensen came to 'figure at that stage it was better trying to sort these issues out within the National party rather than a new vehicle'.

That flirtation with One Nation was not the only alternative path Christensen explored on his way to Canberra, where the self-described 'humble backbencher' arguably now rates as the most influential figure to emerge from Queensland National ranks since Barnaby Joyce.

Twice, like his political ally Tony Abbott before him, Christensen seriously contemplated becoming a priest.

At 21, he was accepted into a seminary in Melbourne but withdrew after a couple of weeks.

'It's probably going to be controversial [but] one thing I can say is that there were some blokes you immediately identified as gay and I think there is that element that do go there but then there are other people in there who you were quite sure they weren't gay,' he observes.

Asked about his feelings on celibacy, Christensen recalls an exchange between a seminary tutor and 'one of the blokes who immediately took a shine to me and was showing me around'.

'The tutor's come in and said to them, look, no real work this week because you're doing this instead, so do a 200-word essay on celibacy and what it means to the priesthood.

'The tutor walked away and the guy looked at me and said, "200? I'll just give him two".' Christensen roars with laughter at the memory.

About five years later, he again thought strongly about joining the priesthood, holding 'some serious discussion with the local bishop but it didn't go anywhere else'.

'Anyway I ended up nominating for the LNP instead,' he says, again with a laugh.

An arch conservative provocateur and lightning rod for furious disagreement from the progressive left, Christensen grew up poor in the sugar belt city of Mackay.

His parents met by chance in a Brisbane rehabilitation hospital, where his father Ian, the scion of a Mackay cane farming family, was recovering from losing a leg to cancer aged 19.

His mother Margaret, a migrant with her family from the UK, had cerebral palsy and severe epilepsy.

Ian says: 'Both of us are disabled and George was our first-born son and we struggled mightily for a number of years.'

Their son was a bookish and 'placid' boy, Ian observes.

Christensen recalls developing 'a bit of a thick skin' from teasing at school for showing up without shoes, which 'I couldn't afford basically'.

'There were only two types of kids that went to school barefoot: all the Aboriginal kids and me,' he says.

'They'd call me the barefoot bandit, which was kind of funny. There were other instances like that where you couldn't go on excursions because your family was too poor. You got used to it.

'So I became academic, probably because people took the trouble to read to me as a kid and I got interested in books.'

Among his father's interests to rub off on the young bookworm was the TV series *Doctor Who*.

In 2013, Christensen, wearing a *Doctor Who* scarf, put up a motion in parliament calling for funding to lure BBC producers to film their 2015 series in Australia.

Ian recalls his son as a toddler bursting into tears at hearing he planned to order a miniature Dalek from the UK 'because he thought it was going to come to life in the night and zap him'.

There were other apparent villains on TV introduced to Christensen via his father.

Ian says: 'I've probably got to blame myself for George being the political animal because coming from an agricultural family, of course we had ties to the National party, and of course we'd sit down for the evening meal and watch the news and here's Bob Hawke and Paul Keating on there and I'd be passing somewhat less-than-glorious comment about these gentlemen.'

As influential was his parents' resistance to the option of life on a disability pension. Ian took a job in a taxi call centre, moving on to driving and owning his own taxi, before eventually establishing a motor parts manufacturing business with Margaret.

It's a story of individual agency that profoundly affected Christensen as he began pondering 'life and the social strata' as a teenager.

'You can get trapped very easily in the idea of being in a family where welfare is the driver of your family economy,' he says.

'The more I read about it, there was two ways of looking at life. You can say, woe is me, my life is terrible, I go to school barefoot every day—by high school I wasn't—why is it so unfair these other kids have got Nikes on?

'Or you can get on with it and do what you need to do to ensure one day you're going to purchase at least Dunlops. So you're not the barefoot bandit any more.'

Christensen won a place to study constitutional law at Griffith University but had to turn it down because moving to Brisbane was unaffordable.

Instead he studied at Central Queensland University, settling on majors in journalism and public relations.

As the teenage editor of a student newsletter, Christensen sowed the seeds of his first national controversy by publishing, in apparent satire, slurs on Jews, gay people and women.

'My thoughts: the truth is women are stupid and that is that,' he wrote in one piece, raising in another concerns about a new Bible edition that 'removed accusations that the Jews killed Christ'.

Christensen was hired after graduation by then Dawson MP De-Anne Kelly, working alongside a close friend from school in her electorate office for more than two years.

He won a seat on the local Mackay council in 2004, augmenting what was then a part-time wage by starting up two local newspapers with a girlfriend.

His political training ground was a city in the 'full swing' of an overnight mining boom.

'It was fantasy land: people would drop out at grade 10, do half a year work earning $97,000 and then you're bumped up to $120,000. Where on earth can that happen?

'It really was a crazy time and people thought it was going to go on forever, that's why [the downturn] is such a shock to the system in Mackay.'

Christensen recalls learning the bread and butter of constituency work that enabled him to ultimately 'walk into the job of a federal politician knowing half of the job'.

He made some local notoriety for himself aged 25 railing against the council wasting money on 'frilly bits as opposed to the basics'.

In terms of courting controversy, Christensen was just getting started.

Preselected to run for the now-merged Liberal–National party in Dawson in 2010, the unearthing of those student newsletters put the 32-year-old candidate on the national radar.

Ian remembers being shown the newsletters at the time and telling his son: 'If you've got any ideas of a political future, maybe you shouldn't have said that.'

Still, he found 'Kerry O'Brien interrogating Tony Abbott on the 7.30 Report' on the issue 13 years on to be 'completely over the top'.

Christensen apologised 'without reservation for those dumb comments made as a teenager over a decade ago'.

The list of outrages attributed to Christensen since is long: his statements on immigration and Islam and his endorsement of Geert Wilders and the Reclaim Australia movement; his attacks on the 'gutless green grubs' and 'terrorists' of the anti-mining conservation movement, and likening the Safe Schools anti-bullying program to 'grooming' by paedophiles; his call for the reintroduction of the death penalty and public canings of drug dealers.

Christensen says there's a 'standing joke that [the prime minister's office] don't even bother phoning George any more' to suggest he pull his head in.

'That has been the way for a while, I've got to say,' he says, adding his biggest regrets in federal politics are when he didn't speak up to oppose things such as tobacco taxes.

Having called for a royal commission into the science of climate change in his maiden speech as an MP, Christensen still believes that 'in 50 years' time we'll probably all look back on it and go, "what was all that about?"'

These kinds of pronouncements, particularly on social media, paint Christensen as the consummate right wing troll. Not the first to observe that the left wing platform of choice seems to be Twitter, and Facebook for the right, Christensen is active on both.

In return, Christensen has earned the distinction of being the most heavily abused federal politician online. He sometimes shows his father the feedback.

'I think, boy, if that was me I'd be a bit miffed. He just laughs and smiles about it,' Ian says. 'He does have a well-honed sense of humour.'

One response that did unsettle Christensen came because of something he said—and now regrets—in the wake of his encounter with abject poverty in south-east Asia, including the infamous 'Smoky Mountain' community based around a rubbish dump in the Philippines.

He invited critics of the 'infamous 2014 federal budget' to 'do a tour of Asia and live like these locals'.

'A bloke wrote to me and told me that I had become a "mark" and he included a photo of a guy whose head was blown off and told me that some Australians still had guns,' he says. 'And that shook me a little bit.'

Amid the needling and vitriol online, Christensen has shown a willingness on occasion to admit fault or see the joke when he's made the butt of it (such as when a bikie tattooist made him into a nude caricature).

When his brother Antony was jailed in 2014 for a home invasion and assault on the lover of his former de facto partner, Christensen did not try to distance himself, supplying the court with a character reference.

Ian says of the episode: 'Yes, well, the truth is always the way to go.'

On whether there's a side to his son that enjoys baiting ideological opponents, Ian says: 'Don't in any way, shape or form be confused about George or where he's coming from: he's a true blue conservative.'

'These people that attack him for the things he says, he's just reflecting what the community's thinking and how it is on the ground.'

Once in a while, a 'salt of the earth' LNP supporter in Mackay called Shane Maloney would lay out a spread of scones, tea or beer on his verandah where locals bend Christensen's ear.

That's where, amid complaints about foreign ownership of Australian properties and tree-clearing restrictions, Christensen cops it for not going far enough.

'It's interesting, it's a ferociousness from people who are of the same ilk as me in my own electorate, who are upping me as the representative of the LNP or the National Party for not doing enough on these issues,' Christensen says.

'I have to say to them … "can I just tell you I would love it if the entirety of the nation was like all you people sitting on the verandah here". But we've got people that are diametrically opposed to what you're saying and what you think. That's unfortunately the art of politics, doing what's possible, not doing what you'd like to do all the time.'

A single week this month, in which three big political stories revolved around Christensen, showcased his rising influence in government.

After Christensen addressed a packed media conference to praise the government for scrapping superannuation changes over which he'd threatened to cross the floor, Fairfax Media observed that a Martian visitor would 'be forgiven for thinking he was running the show'.

Christensen's speech calling for immigration bans on countries with jihadi extremists gained no purchase within government but got just as much attention.

Then a story highlighting a pre-election comment that he'd quit the government if it didn't scrap the backpacker tax prompted speculation he'd join One Nation. Joyce spoke of the need to keep a rising 'leader' in the Nationals tent lest he become a Bob Katter-style independent.

'That's the problem sometimes, three big things in one week you start to look like a bit of a show pony and the third was not intended,' Christensen says. 'There's a danger in overegging it and last week unfortunately because of that story it got overegged.'

Christensen says his 'poor choice of words' about quitting simply reflected his confidence the government would fix the backpacker tax.

'Immediately Paul Bongiorno is putting stories on Channel 10 that I'm going to go to One Nation and a source saying, is this the next Bob Katter?

'I think to myself, "bloody hell. I want to stay in the government, I don't want to leave".'

Asked whether he's well-placed to help the government deal with the resurgence of the party he once voted for, One Nation, Christensen notes the splits that tend to emerge in minor parties elected on the strength of a 'cult of personality' of a single leader.

'We saw that with the Palmer United Party most recently,' he says. 'I don't wish that on One Nation now. I hope that Pauline has that all under control and to a degree it looks like she does. I think Pauline's a lot different to Clive.'

13
Issues-based Features

'She combines a cold eye with a warm heart.'

James Cameron on Martha Gellhorn, in Kerrane & Yagoda (eds), 1997, p. 422

Objectives

In this chapter we turn our attention to what we call 'issues-based features' and look at some of the more popular areas that generate such features. They include:

o   politics

o   business

o   the arts

o   'real-life' and 'as-told-to' stories

o   A Case study: Alexandra Fisher on her Walkley Award-winning documentary that investigated sex trafficking and prostitution in Mexico.

The how and the why

Issues-based features are really the bread and butter of feature writing and quite often are written to accompany a developing news story. As we discussed in the early chapters, news stories can deal with the *who*, *what*, *where* and *when*, but they don't always explain the *how* or the *why*. Finding the answers to these questions is generally the responsibility of the features desk. Frequently, the responsibility for producing such pieces will be allocated to a specialist. This might be someone who is on staff, or equally, it may be a commissioned piece produced by a freelancer or even a non-journalist who has a particular interest in the topic being explored. In an age of multimedia, such pieces may be produced by a team of people, including writers, and specialists in audio and video, or by an individual who can work across all of these platforms. Later in this chapter we reveal how Alexandra Fisher, a brave young freelance journalist, produced one such story. Acting on little more than a hunch, Fisher produced a powerful story on sex trafficking in Mexico City, despite not knowing the language (Spanish), and arriving in the country without any contacts through which to develop the story. The resultant piece was subsequently commissioned by the ABC and won Fisher a Walkley Award for Best Young Television Journalist/Video Journalist of the Year in 2013.

Politics

Political writing has long been a staple of journalism. Not a day passes without media outlets devoting considerable space to covering new or ongoing political stories. This is part and parcel of living in a democracy, where people expect to know what is going on, what governments have done and why, and even what they are contemplating. In liberal democracies the government is expected to be open and politicians to be accountable for their actions. The media have a watchdog role: they are entrusted with the responsibility of keeping society abreast of what governments—and other sections of society, including business and sport—are doing. However this can be a difficult ask, particularly if politicians can avoid the mainstream media and talk directly to their constituencies via social media as we're seeing in the US following the election of Donald Trump as president. This task is being made doubly difficult by the fact that in an era of so-called 'fake news', younger people are less likely to access mainstream media (print, electronic or online) than their parents, and are increasingly vulnerable to information that supports their world view, rather than being willing to at least contemplate alternative views or opinions.

In mainstream Australian media, issues-based political features tend to be produced by two groups of people. The first comprises political journalists, the majority of whom operate out of either the Canberra Press Gallery or one of the press galleries that are attached to the various state and territory parliaments. The second group does not include journalists, although some may have worked in the media previously. Rather, they are specialists in a particular area. They may be academics, former politicians or advisers, or representatives of interest groups—for example, the Wilderness Society, Greenpeace, the Australian Bankers' Association, the National Roads and Motorists Association or the National Farmers' Federation. There are an enormous number of such bodies, and collectively they represent the interests of a large number of people. As such, they are often given an opportunity by the media to 'express their views', either as a source cited in a detailed feature or in a stand-alone opinion piece.

A good example is the media's coverage of the complex 12-nation Trans Pacific Partnership (TPP). When the landmark deal was signed in late 2015 the reaction to the treaty was mixed, as reflected in a series of articles the *Sydney Morning Herald* published on this issue on 7 October 2015. The pro argument was presented by Donald Robertson, a partner with law firm Herbert Smith Freehills, while the counter argument was written by Leon Berkelmans, director of the Lowy Institute (<http://www.smh.com.au/business/the-economy/tpp-will-the-transpacific-partnership-really-benefit-australia-20151006-gk24so.html>). Even these articles, however, only provided a summary of the arguments for and against the proposal. To do this issue justice, the media needed to talk to spokespeople from all the industry sectors likely to be affected. And they needed to seek multiple opinions from within these sectors, as attitudes were mixed, with considerable disagreement within and across various sectors as to the benefits or demerits of the deal. For example, in the primary industry sector, Fonterra, a large multinational dairy producer, was critical of the TPP, whereas the National Farmers Federation, which represents farmers across a range of sectors, supported it, believing that it would help to eliminate tariffs and gain broader access to international markets. A further level of complexity was added to the story during the US presidential election campaign when Republican front-runner, now US President, Donald Trump said he would tear up the TPP if he won office. Trump won, and he did tear up the agreement as one of his first decisions as president, leaving the other partners, Australia included, scrambling to resurrect it minus the US.

Sometimes the stories are staring us in the face, as Fisher's story on sex trafficking in Mexico City reveals. It is a political issue that appeared to have been virtually ignored at a local level. But sometimes it takes an outsider—or a person with a particular agenda—to draw attention to such problems. Sometimes it simply involves asking the right questions of the right people, as Alexandra Fisher was able to do. Sometimes it takes a group of affected people to bravely draw attention to an issue which has been kept under wraps by the authorities (as we're currently witnessing with the inquiries into child abuse in the churches). Sometimes it takes a high-profile person to draw attention to the problem, as has been the case in Australia with Fortescue Metals Group founder Andrew Forrest (discussed later), who has used his wealth to draw community attention to the plight of Indigenous Australians, as well as to the problem of human trafficking worldwide. Journalists who pick up on these stories, whether through their own initiative, or because they have had an issue brought to their attention by others, can play an important role in helping to right significant social wrongs.

When discussing the role of feature articles, it is important to distinguish between those produced by journalists as part of their daily reportorial responsibilities and those produced by the weekly columnists or commentators. The latter are commissioned to produce articles that have a particular ideological bent. For example, Piers Akerman, the former Melbourne *Herald Sun* editor, Janet Albrechtsen, a columnist for *The Australian*, and Gerard Henderson, the *Sydney Morning Herald* columnist, are all considered to be right-wing commentators. Phillip Adams, the ABC Radio National host and columnist for *The Australian*, is unashamedly left-wing, while Robert Manne is a contrarian.

People who seek out and follow these commentators do so with the knowledge that the argument presented will be inspired by a particular ideological viewpoint. Compare these with features written by well-known past and present gallery journalists, such as the late Matt Price, Michelle Grattan, Laurie Oakes and Alan Ramsey. While these writers have been critical in their writing, they can always be expected to be balanced.

Journalists producing issues-based political stories need to know who to turn to for information about a particular topic or issue. The best journalists maintain a contact book that contains information about a range of sources (including their areas of expertise, positions, qualifications, email addresses and, most importantly, telephone numbers, both work and after-hours). The information should be regularly updated, with new contacts being added all the time, even if they may not be considered particularly relevant at the time.

Types of stories

Because politics is so diverse, journalists are regularly presented with opportunities to produce issues-based features. These can be built around the following:

- policy initiatives
- legislation

- reports (departmental, parliamentary committees, industry groups, political interest groups)
- social issues
- changes of government and elections
- leadership challenges, ministerial reshuffles, portfolio changes
- inter-governmental relations (international, federal–state, state–state, state–local)
- personal wrongdoing (moral scandal, corruption, breach of the law).

Most people who have an interest in politics could quickly point to examples of stories that fit under each of the above headings. Obviously, some of them may overlap. Policy initiatives, for example, frequently lead to legislative change (or the introduction of new legislation). Often the precursor to policy is the preparation of reports by the relevant government department or departments. Such reports may even follow discussions with non-government bodies (industry groups and interest groups, for example). Sometimes they don't, however, as the highly contentious announcement in July 2016 by the then Baird Government in NSW that greyhound racing would be banned reveals. This decision was announced without forewarning, including discussions with the greyhound racing industry. The government clearly didn't anticipate the negative reaction to this decision, one it overturned just three months later after losing a critical by-election.

These changes are often foreshadowed in news reports. However, news reports, particularly those on radio and television, rarely have the capacity to cover such stories in detail, particularly if they involve complex legislation or reports. Often there are subtleties (or nuances) in the legislation, the report, or announcement that require space to be examined properly. Not only that, but the journalist may need to cast wider for expert opinion to help explain the technical details and/or consequences of the proposed legislation or policy.

This is highlighted each year when the federal and state governments release their Budgets. While the Budget speech is generally produced in plain English, the supporting documents (which usually amount to thousands of pages) can be complex, and to interpret them can take days and a degree in economics, accounting or business. While Budget coverage and other major government announcements are usually left to the senior journalists, there comes a time when younger journalists are provided with an opportunity to step up and cover these major events. At first glance they can appear daunting, but they need not be.

To produce an issues-based feature drawn from a Budget, policy launch or release of a government discussion paper is a relatively straightforward task, so long as the deadlines are realistic. Much of the basic information will have been covered in the news stories that accompany the launch or announcement. These stories may even have been written by another journalist. Your task, as the feature writer, is to pull apart the Budget, announcement or report in order to add an additional dimension to that of the news coverage.

Issues-based features provide the writer with the opportunity to dig deeper and to find answers to the questions that invariably go unanswered in press conferences or government PR blurbs, because they are too difficult, embarrassing to the government or just unpalatable. The federal Budget provides a huge mine of information for journalists, with stories invariably crossing a range of issues, including federal–state relations (funding for schools, roads, health) and international issues (defence expenditure, international aid etc.).

But these issues are not limited to the Budget, as we have found in recent years. Since the attacks on the US World Trade Center on 11 September 2001, the world has been on terrorist alert. Journalists have produced millions of words addressing a range of questions their audiences are asking:

- Who is behind these attacks?

- What prompted them?

- Are they likely to cease?

- Should countries like Australia continue to maintain troops in Iraq, Afghanistan and other international hotspots?

- What role should we play in helping to eliminate ISIS?

There are of course other spin-off questions, including the extent to which Australia's involvement in the so-called 'war against terror' has impacted on its relationship with other countries, particularly the United States and Britain. Journalists play an important role in giving expression to these questions, both in their news stories and features. Clearly, war and terrorism are highly emotive issues, and journalists need to be careful when covering them. As we found during the conflicts in Iraq and Afghanistan, journalists who questioned the government's line could be accused of disloyalty.

Obviously elections provide another important source of issues-based feature material. This was highlighted in the 2016 Australian federal election, which spawned a range of feature articles covering topics as diverse as profiles on political hopefuls, detailed comparisons of the electoral prospects of individuals and parties, and discussions about the policy performance of the incumbent government and the plans of the Labor challenger. While some of these clearly do not fit under the heading of issues-based features (for example, individual profiles, which we discussed in more detail in Chapter 12), the majority clearly do. In politics, the term 'issues' is broadly interpreted.

For example, in recent years, Australian federal politics has been characterised, some people might say plagued, by a series of leadership challenges. While it is not unusual for these to occur within the opposition, in recent times the target has been the prime minister. This started during the Hawke years, when there were regular rumblings about a transition from Hawke to Keating, a change that ultimately occurred when the latter challenged. It continued during the Howard years, although in this instance the challenger, Peter Costello, did not move on his boss. Howard's successor, Kevin Rudd, was subsequently rolled by his deputy Julia Gillard, whom he then successfully rechallenged for the top political job in Australia. Rudd was defeated at election by Tony Abbott, who in turn was challenged and defeated by one of his colleagues, former merchant banker and lawyer Malcolm Turnbull, just 12 months into his term. Even as this book was going to press, Abbott and his backers within the right wing of the Liberal Party continued to cause grief for Turnbull, thereby providing journalists with considerable material for ongoing stories, including speculation about yet another challenge.

Another issue that captured the attention of political journalists in 2016 and continued into 2017 was the ongoing political and economic turmoil in Europe and the United States. This included Brexit and the US presidential election. Both have had considerable impact on Australia, particularly the rush by new US President Donald Trump to try and undo as much of his predecessor Barack Obama's legacy as he could in as short a time as possible. This has had significant implications for Australia at both a political and trade level, including Trump's decision to withdraw from the Trans Pacific Partnership (TPP), and to impose a freeze on immigrants with a Muslim background. Trump's unpredictability on policy issues, his inexperience as a politician, and his decision to sideline the mainstream media, sections of which he accuses of engaging in fake news, has created many opportunities for journalists, particularly those political commentators who are trying to understand the new president.

Finally, we need to turn briefly to the subject of political wrongdoing. Again, this can be a staple of issues-based political features, as Australian journalists found during the late 1980s and through the 1990s, when federal and state governments were accused of wrongdoing at different levels. During the late 1980s there were corruption inquiries in Queensland, New South Wales, Western Australia and Tasmania. Several ministers, a former premier and a deputy premier were jailed. In Queensland a police commissioner was dismissed and jailed, and in Tasmania a prominent media magnate was jailed—all after being found guilty of corruption. These events provided journalists with opportunities to question the political standards of some politicians, and to consider the temptations that were placed in front of them and whether there were adequate accountability measures to stop such wrongdoing.

While the number of corruption charges against former and standing politicians appears to have declined in recent years, a number of public figures have been subjected to public scrutiny over claims of self-interest (including defrauding the Commonwealth of funds—the so-called Travel Rorts inquiries (most recently involving then Federal Health Minister Sussan Ley; see the writing sample in chapter 14 for an explanation of how this story was pulled together)); of making decisions, while serving as a minister or parliamentary secretary, which could have benefited companies or interests with which they were associated (for example former NSW Labor ministers Eddie Obeid and Ian MacDonald); of holding a seat in parliament while ineligible (Senators Bob Day and Rod Culleton); of continuing to manage business interests while a Member of Parliament (Clive Palmer); and of misusing union funds before entering parliament (Craig Thomson). All of these stories provoked a barrage of feature articles that asked important questions about the conduct of elected MPs and the temptations or pressures they encountered.

Summary: politics

- Politics provides a ready source of stories for issues-based features. In many respects the difficulty for journalists lies not so much in locating topics of interest they can write about, but in separating the really important stories from those that are interesting but of less significance.

- Information for issues-based stories can be found in a wide range of material, including details of personal contacts, policy announcements or statements, legislation, reports, statements made during parliamentary Question Time and via media releases.

- Political journalists should always be looking for information that helps to explain the questions that an announcement provokes. Issues-based political journalism enables writers to go beyond the *who*, *what* and *when*, to answer the *why* and *how* questions that lead to a greater understanding of the rationale behind a particular decision or policy and its potential consequences.

Business

The Australian share market boom that occurred in the first years of the twenty-first century was to a large extent sustained by the resources sector. The impact of this boom was to generate keen interest in the share market by the so-called 'mum and dad' investors, who watched their superannuation funds grow by double-digit amounts year after year.

The growth of online share trading also meant that many of these investors were actively buying and selling stocks, thereby adding significantly to their retirement nest eggs. One of the spin-offs of this was a growth in the number of magazines (such as *Personal Investor* and *Your Money*) and websites or blogs directed at these investors, and an expansion of the coverage of the share market in the business pages of daily newspapers.

With this has come increased investor knowledge and thus higher expectations of publications, programs and individual journalists. Consumers are demanding more—and better quality—information. For example, during the sub-prime mortgage crisis that hit the United States in the late 2000s and caused a significant sell-off of Australian shares, particularly those companies exposed to the US market, investors were seeking answers to a range of questions, such as:

- What caused the collapse of the US sub-prime mortgage market?
- Why did that collapse cause a fall in other share markets, even though they had little direct exposure to the US market?
- What are the likely consequences of the sell-down?
- Will it lead to a recession, or simply to a correction in the share price of locally listed companies?

On the surface, the first two questions were relatively straightforward and were addressed by journalists talking to a range of experts, including share market analysts, bankers and economists, who willingly proffered opinions as to what had caused the sub-prime collapse and what had been its impact on other share markets, including Australia's. However, the third and fourth questions—which everyone wanted answers to, particularly those with money invested—were far more difficult to answer. The experts were more guarded in their responses, many declining to commit to a definitive answer, in part because they did not want to trigger a sell-off on the market, particularly given the impact that emotion can have on investment decisions, especially during times of uncertainty.

All of this has provided opportunities for journalists to produce features that deal with a range of issues, including:

- the vulnerability of the Australian share market to international factors
- how to recession-proof your portfolio
- companies that are considered less vulnerable during a bear market or even a recession
- taxation strategies.

Business stories can flow from a range of sources, including contacts the journalist has developed over time, media releases, company reports, filings with the regulators—the Australian Securities Exchange (ASX) or the Australian Securities and Investments Commission (ASIC)—and investigations.

When writing about a specialist topic such as the share market or the economy, journalists are rarely the experts. In most instances journalists will be collating and presenting the views of recognised experts—authoritative people who work in the sector they are writing about and whose statements and opinions underpin the main points the writer is seeking to make. This is the key to producing an authoritative piece: knowing who to talk to and asking the questions your audience is seeking answers to.

Invariably you will find that views differ, particularly when it comes to complicated issues, such as the likelihood of interest rate rises, or a share-market correction following the election of President Trump in the US. If this is the case, you need to consider the standing of the sources you are quoting:

- How senior are they?

- How highly regarded are they among their peers?

- What qualifications do they have?

- How long have they been working in the sector?

- What other experiences underpin their comments (or ability to speak on this topic)?

- In the case of share market downturns, have they experienced such a situation before (in a professional sense, rather than simply during their lifetime)?

If you are writing about the possibility of a recession, it is important that you obtain as many viewpoints as possible from highly regarded experts. In this situation, one or two opinions are not sufficient. Also, you should seek to canvass the views of people across different sectors (and don't forget to include comments, where relevant, from the government, and from statutory authorities such as the Reserve Bank, particularly in the case of features that look at the reasoning behind increases in interest rates and their impact on home affordability). It is always a good idea to provide a historical dimension: when did the previous crashes or recessions occur? What triggered them? How long did they last?

Remember, short-term share market changes are often driven by emotion, rather than by the fundamentals (financial health and performance) of the listed companies. This places considerable responsibility on journalists not to overplay the prospect of a crash or other negative events, as doing so might trigger such falls and thereby cause small investors to lose their life savings.

One of the consequences of a vibrant share market is an increase in the number of companies that list on it and invite investors to invest through IPOs (initial public offerings). In some instances these companies take advantage of investors' confidence in the market and their belief that the share price can only increase. This is confirmed in boom years when a large number of speculative mining companies list on the ASX. Many of these companies are explorers, which begin with no real asset bases or guaranteed resource deposits. As such, many are too small—and considered too risky—to be covered by the large investment houses. But a small number have fired the imagination of investors and journalists nonetheless.

When writing about companies, there are a few points you should bear in mind. Despite the fact that many people are interested in the share market, they are not necessarily financially literate. The readers of a daily newspaper, for example, may struggle to understand terms like 'price/earnings ratio', 'earnings per share (EPS)', 'hedging' and 'cash flow'. They may not even understand the difference between a profit and loss statement and a balance sheet. Readers of specialist newspapers (*The Financial Review*, for example) and magazines such as *Business Review Weekly* and *Personal Investor* will understand the jargon. So the trick is to write for your audience: don't seek to bedazzle them with your command of the language; write in a way they will understand.

Make sure you explain relationships between companies and individuals. For example, in the case of a takeover, check to see if some or all of the directors have multiple directorships. Are there any potential conflicts of interest? Do they have previous histories that might impact on their ability to manage the company?

While journalists have an obligation to their audiences when reporting on business affairs, they also have responsibilities. They have a duty to be fair to the subjects they write about, be they companies or individuals. Just as journalists can destroy political careers, so too can they destroy corporate careers and potentially bring companies undone, although sometimes their dire predictions are proved wrong.

For example, one of Australia's corporate success stories has been Fortescue Metals Group (FMG), a company built up by West Australian mining magnate Andrew Forrest. When listed in 1987, the company was worth a few cents per share. Forrest, the chief executive and major shareholder, later boasted that it would become the 'third force in iron ore', rivalling international heavyweights BHP Billiton and Rio Tinto. Many journalists scoffed at Forrest's claims and intimated that the company was likely to fail, pointing to his record as chief executive of the ill-fated explorer Anaconda Nickel. However, under Forrest the FMG share price rose, reaching $83 before the company opted for a 10:1 share split. It was not until FMG shipped its first load of iron ore to Chinese mills in May 2008 that journalists reluctantly began to accept the Forrest story. All along, they were waiting for Forrest to trip up and for the venture to fail. Even today, there are some business journalists who consider the Fortescue story too good to be true, and who impose a questioning tone on anything they write about Fortescue or Forrest (who in 2011 stepped down as chief executive, to move into the chairman's position). Despite this, Fortescue has continued to weather the vagaries that saw the price of iron ore fall dramatically (from $150 USD per tonne in mid to late 2012, down to less than $40 USD per tonne at the start of 2015, to rebound to $80 USD per tonne in February 2017). Along the way, Fortescue focused on cutting costs and reducing debt.

Another great story has been the emergence of Gina Rinehart from virtual obscurity to become one of Australia's richest people. Rinehart has an interesting pedigree. The daughter of pioneering West Australian prospector Lang Hancock, she has endured a number of battles, including one with her stepmother, Rose, to build and diversify the company that her father started. Along the way, the very private Rinehart has managed to shield herself from too much media scrutiny, although that proved more difficult in the period 2011–16 when a number of events conspired against her. First, the tumbling iron ore price saw her fall from her position as the wealthiest person in Australia (estimated net worth of $20 billion). Second, two of her four children used the courts to successfully wrest control from her of a family trust that held 24 per cent of the family's wealth. Finally, she guaranteed media interest in herself when she purchased significant stakes in Fairfax Media and Network 10.

The business world is a good source of stories. Since the late 1980s there have been a number of prominent corporate collapses, which have provided considerable fodder for journalists (for example, HIH, OneTel, Harris Scarfe). Not only did the demise of these companies cause a number of prominent individuals to fall from grace, several even ending up in jail, but it promoted a greater scrutiny of the business and finance sectors. Some very strong articles have been written on the duties of directors and senior executives, on the salaries these people were being paid; and on the severance packages they were receiving even after they had run companies into the ground. Despite the tendency of the media and regulators—such as the ASIC, ASX, Australian Competition and Consumer Commission (ACCC) and Australian Prudential Regulatory Authority (APRA)—to turn their spotlights on these companies, it is likely that there will continue to be situations involving wrongdoing or incompetence to write about in the future.

Clearly, however, business stories are not limited to the share market, individual businesses or even the behaviour of individual business leaders. The business sector has an impact on all sections of society, including government. A healthy resources sector means that governments benefit from the royalties mining companies pay to extract resources from the ground. A healthy housing sector benefits state governments through stamp duty revenue. A healthy share market means that government coffers benefit from increases in the tax being paid, such as capital gains tax, company tax, payroll tax etc. A healthy business sector means that there is an increase in expenditure on infrastructure, equipment, research and development. This could also lead to increases in wages and employment levels. Increases in the share market, wages and employment mean that people are likely to spend some of their increased wealth or income. This has direct benefits for other sectors (discretionary consumables etc.). The downside is that such spending can force inflation up, thereby putting pressure on the Reserve Bank to increase interest rates (and thus force families to cut back on their discretionary expenditure).

All of these events provide story opportunities for journalists.

Summary: business

- A vibrant share market and economy have provided business journalists with considerable opportunities to write longer-length explanatory features and opinion pieces. These articles have covered a range of issues, including the reasons for the rises and falls in the share market and their subsequent impact on the economy.

- The key to writing successful stories on business, economics and finance is to understand your limitations. Remember, this is a highly specialised area. If you don't have a university degree in one of these areas, try to develop a number of contacts who can help to explain the technicalities of company reports, geological reports and other documents that you might have to interpret in the course of writing a particular feature.

The arts

In many respects this topic is covered in chapters 21–24 (when we look at reviews) and in Chapter 12 (on profiles). It is also covered by our previous discussions in this chapter of politics and business. The reasons for this are clear: much of the funding for the arts comes either from government or from charities and private benefactors, such as the late Richard Pratt (the billionaire businessman). However, there are many people who have a lower profile than Pratt and yet give tirelessly to the arts in Australia. These include philanthropists like Peter Weiss, Betty Amsden, Tim Fairfax, Simon and Catriona Mordant, Harold Mitchell and David Walsh (see ArtsHub under Online resources later in this chapter).

Many issues-based feature articles about the arts seem to focus on the question of funding. A lot of these organisations lead a hand-to-mouth existence; that is, they rarely receive sufficient money from the government (state or federal) to enable them to plan too far into the future. They invariably have to go to the relevant minister or funding bodies for top-ups to guarantee their survival for another 12 months. Or they need the support of people like those we mention above.

Like the journalists we discussed earlier in the chapter, arts writers need to maintain a strong list of contacts. These can include artists and managers, curators and people in senior management positions (bureaucrats who control the purse strings, gallery directors and the heads of various arts bodies). However, even the writers with the best credentials also need to know who the benefactors are. More importantly, they need to be able to access them and to have a relationship with them that allows them to be able to ring and ask potentially difficult or even embarrassing questions.

Richard Pratt and his wife Jeanne were long-time supporters of the Melbourne arts scene, providing millions of dollars over the years. However, in March 2000 the Pratts were the subject of intense media scrutiny when it was revealed that Richard Pratt had had a child by his young lover, Shari-Lea Hitchcock. There were a large number of stories about Pratt, his family and Hitchcock over a period of months. Not surprisingly, there were questions raised about whether the coverage would result in the Pratts withdrawing from public life and from their support of Victorian arts and charities. Fortunately for the arts community, they did not.

The coverage of this story was handled by general reporters, rather than by arts specialists or even business specialists, with whom Pratt would have developed a relationship throughout his career. However, a later scandal, involving Pratt and price-fixing allegations, was covered by business writers. In many respects the reluctance of arts writers to touch the earlier story was understandable, even though there was clearly a connection between this story and continued support for the arts. The latter story, however, was rightly left to business writers because of the complexities involved. The question that remains unanswered in relation to the first story is whether the arts writers could have used their relationship with the Pratts to turn this particular issue into a major feature on philanthropy and the extent to which turbulent times can test the commitment of a philanthropist to their chosen cause.

There is an interesting footnote to this story. Even in death, some people cannot avoid media attention. In 2010, nearly a year after Pratt's death, Hitchcock and her daughter with Pratt, Paula, announced plans to contest the terms of Pratt's will. The will had made significant provisions for Paula. She was to receive nearly $30 million in shares, as well as almost $6 million in shares held in trust for her and her mother out of Pratt's then $5 billion estate. By May 2016 when the BRW 200 Rich list was published, the family's wealth (now managed by son Anthony) had nearly doubled to $10.35 billion (*Australian Financial Review*, 2016). This case was finally resolved in 2015, with the outcome kept secret, although it is believed that Paula did receive a larger slice of the estate (*The Australian*, 2016).

However, another claim against Pratt's estate has been resolved. In 2011, Madison Ashton, Pratt's former mistress, had claimed in the New South Wales Supreme Court that Pratt had reneged on a promise to set up a $2.5 million trust fund for each of her two children, as well as pay her $500,000 a year. On top of that, she alleged that Pratt had agreed to cover her annual rent bill of $36,000 and business expenses of $30,000 a year. However Justice Paul Brereton dismissed the claim, arguing that the claim was not enforceable because Ashton had accepted $100,000 in February 2005 'in full and final satisfaction' (Carson, 2012).

As we discuss in more detail in chapters 22–23, arts writing tends to be highly specialised. Journalists are likely to cover one of the arts (music, drama, visual arts, literature) and then specialise even more (for example, in classical music, jazz or contemporary rock; or in theatre, film or television; or in painting, sculpture or photography; or in fiction, non-fiction or poetry). This is not to say, however, that a general feature writer could not produce a competent issues-based piece on arts funding or on trends within a particular discipline.

Summary: the arts

- Arts writing can overlap with politics and business, although it can also stand alone.
- Arts writers are often specialists, but can also have the capacity to write across different areas on generic topics.
- As with the other areas discussed in this chapter, arts writing is about developing contacts and trust. If you have a broad range of contacts who trust you, even if you are tough on them or their work, they will continue to speak to you, and thereby provide you with the information you need to sustain your career.

The 'real-life' story

If you want to break into the world of feature writing, one way to do so is through freelancing, and one of the simplest stories to have published is the real-life story. Editors love using freelancers for this sort of story, because they can often uncover stories staff writers could never access. This type of story is published in a multitude of women's magazines including *Cleo*, *Cosmopolitan*, *New Idea* and *Take 5*. Some men's publications, such as *FHM*, also include this style of feature.

Real-life stories often come under the title 'It was my worst nightmare' and catalogue the sort of tales that you would never believe if you hadn't seen them in print, or heard them on radio or television. These are the articles about people who are not celebrated in the arenas of politics, business or sport, but who nevertheless have a great story to tell. You'll find real-life stories about women who give birth, never having realised they were pregnant; about a couple that can't be married because they have just discovered they are twins separated at birth; about the horse whisperer who lives alone in a slab timber hut; or the hunter who discovered Australia's biggest gold nugget when out shooting kangaroos.

The hardest thing about these stories is finding them. Yet even this is not as hard as you think. If you are a staff writer, you will be sent letters and emails from people who want to tell their story. If you are a freelancer, you won't be receiving this sort of mail. Instead, you need to start talking—to your friends, family and co-workers. If you are studying at university, talk to other students, your teachers and to people in the cafeteria.

Often the question 'What's the weirdest thing that's ever happened to you?' will open the floodgates and reveal a great tale. If that doesn't succeed, ask the person about their friends and family. If you find something useful, get that person's contact details and hear the story from their own lips. You'll be surprised how quickly you'll unearth a juicy tale.

The 'as-told-to' story

While many of these real-life stories are written in a standard feature style, many more are written in the format of the 'as-told-to' story. What this means is that you conduct the interview with the person who has the great story, but rather than writing about them in the third person, you write in the first person. The story will appear as if it was written by the interviewee, but the reader will usually find the words 'as told to [name of writer]' at the bottom of the page.

Because this story reads as one long quote, you will not include opinions from other people involved in the incident, quotes from experts or the sort of background information that is usually found in a feature article.

The formula

- Find a juicy story.

- Write the headline, which for most publications is written in a quote, such as 'My ex-boyfriend kidnapped me!'

- Write a general third-person introduction that introduces the person being interviewed and usually involves the readers. For example:

   Ever worried how your boyfriend would react if you told him it was over? Jane Smith never suspected that telling her man she wanted to break up would lead to her being locked in a car boot and taken interstate. Jane tells her story …

- Write the story using quotes from the interview. You will often have to restructure the quotes, and occasionally writers change what was said to make things clearer for the readers. If you do this, make sure you call your interviewee and double-check that they approve of the changes you have made.

- Most publications will want you to provide a breakout box that includes information not contained in the body of the story. This could be:

   - tips/explanation/warning signs from an expert

   - a range of quotes to show how other people dealt with the same situation (vox pop)

   - which celebrities battled this condition/dealt with this issue etc.

- what it's like on the other side of the fence; for example, if the story is about someone who has conquered anorexia, you could have one breakout box from an expert about the disease and another featuring four friends or relatives speaking about having someone with anorexia in their circle.

Summary: 'real-life' stories

- Real-life stories are a simple way to start your freelancing career.
- Finding a story is as easy as talking to your friends and family.
- Follow a simple formula for an 'as-told-to' story: headline, general introduction, first-person story, breakout box.

Summary

o Issues-based feature writing is an essential part of journalism. While we've focused on four areas—politics, business, the arts and 'real life'—the fact is that this type of writing lends itself to virtually any subject matter.

o To be a solid writer, you need an excellent—and eclectic—list of contacts. These should be nurtured across a broad range of disciplines because you never know when you may need that killer quote to launch or wrap up a story.

o The key to all issues-based writing is research (see the discussion in Chapter 3). You need to do the legwork before you commit yourself to conducting interviews (a topic we discussed in detail in Chapter 4).

o Finally, you need to have a clear idea of where you think the story might head before you begin the interviews. This is where the research phase is so important. However, you should always be flexible enough to permit the story to move in another direction.

Questions

1 What are the similarities between politics writing and business writing when it comes to issues-based features?
2 What are the key issues confronting the arts from an issues-based perspective?
3 What sets 'real-life' and 'as-told-to' stories apart from the other types of issues-based features covered in this chapter?

Activities

1 Go online to the federal government's website, or one of the state government sites, and locate a copy of a recent Budget speech. Read the speech and identify an initiative you believe would make an interesting issues-based feature. Turn to the supporting Budget documentation (Budget papers and media releases)

and see if you can pull out enough information to constitute the bones of a story. List at least six questions you believe still need to be answered.

2   Access the federal government's website and locate a media release that deals with federal–state relations. Follow up by scanning the Factiva online database of newspaper articles for the following two weeks to see how the story was covered in newspapers and magazines. See if you can find at least two feature articles that explore the deeper questions behind the issue. Describe the deficiencies in the articles and suggest how they could be improved.

3   Visit the Australian Bureau of Statistics website <www.abs.gov.au> and go to the latest Census data. Write a feature article that looks at historical changes in Australia's demographic profile over at least 30 years.

4   Inflation is one of the key challenges for the Australian economy. Research and write an article that looks at changes in Australia's inflation rate over the last decade and what the Reserve Bank has done in response to these changes.

5   The mining sector is said to have driven the most recent boom in the Australian economy. Write a piece looking at how the mining sector has contributed to that growth.

6   Provide a plan, including a list of who you would interview, for a feature about the arts in Australia.

7   See if you can come up with your own 'as-told-to' feature by talking to family and friends. Write this up in a style suitable for a magazine that publishes this sort of story.

References and additional reading

Australian Financial Review (2016). 'BRW Rich 200 List 2016': http://www.afr.com/leadership/brw-lists/brw-rich-200-list-2016-20160526-gp4ejn

Australian, The (2016). 'It's a battle of wills when estates are contested': <http://www.theaustralian.com.au/news/inquirer/its-a-battle-of-wills-when-estates-are-contested/news-story/87ccb8b42cb74f683b5376ebf0fbb61c>.

Carson, V. (2012). 'Richard Pratt's former mistress loses court battle for his millions,' *Daily Telegraph*, 16 January: www.news.com.au/business/the-late-richard-pratts-former-mistress-madison-ashton-loses-her-court-battle-for-his-millions/story-e6frfm1i-1226245217231

Kerrane, K. & Yagoda, B. (eds) (1997). *The Art of Fact: A Historical Anthology of Literary Journalism*, New York: Touchstone.

Roth, M. (2000). *Analysing Company Accounts*, 3rd edn, Melbourne: Wright Books.

Online resources

ArtsHub: http://www.artshub.com.au/au/news.aspx?contentTypeCatId=114&CategoryId=740&ListingId=186651&HubId=0&CategoryGroupId=${mapfile_categorygroups:}

Australian Bureau of Statistics: www.abs.gov.au

Factiva: www.factiva.com

Case study

Alexandra Fisher ventured to Mexico as a young video-journalist to pursue a story she believed was worth the challenge and the risk

Publication details:

'Thousands of Mexican women trafficked for prostitution', *Lateline*, 13 February 2013, http://www.abc.net.au/lateline/content/2013/s3695795.htm.

The author:

Alexandra Fisher started her career with the Australian Broadcasting Corporation after graduating from the University of Wollongong with a Bachelor of Journalism. She reported for ABC online, radio and TV over five years. She won the Walkley Young Australian TV Journalist/Video Journalist of the Year award in 2013 for her story on sex trafficking in Mexico. In 2016, she moved to East Africa to work as a freelance journalist.

The story:

As Alexandra Fisher's flight into Mexico City descended, the then 23-year-old's anxiety rose. She was out of her depth.

The fledgling video-journalist had ventured alone to the foreign land, where she couldn't speak the language (Spanish), had little money, no connections and under two weeks to delve into a story powerful criminals wanted to keep hidden.

Fisher learned about sex trafficking in Mexico while visiting the United States a few weeks earlier. Traffickers were kidnapping and forcing thousands of Mexican women into prostitution in Mexico, the US and around the world. The story of their tortured lives was largely unknown in Australia. Many of the victims were Fisher's age and much younger; that tore at her.

After arriving in the capital, Fisher used Twitter to connect with Rosi Orozco, then a Mexican congresswoman behind an anti-trafficking law in the country. They met for coffee and Orozco invited Fisher to spend the next day with her. The congresswoman proved invaluable. Fisher joined her in attending back-to-back meetings and a sitting of parliament. The journalist was able to secure interviews with high-profile people she wouldn't have otherwise gained access to: from the businessman who owned more than half the country's nightclubs to the head of prosecutions in Mexico City.

Earning people's trust was key to transforming the story into a reality. And for one reason or another, people not only gave the 23-year-old their trust, but their time.

Among these people, most remarkably, was veteran police commander Carolina Hernandez. The woman was a family friend of a young Mexican man Fisher met at the hostel where she was staying. Without hesitation, the commander risked her personal safety to show the journalist the illegal sex trade first-hand: a place in Mexico City controlled by traffickers, dangerous even for police. Hernandez changed into plain clothes and drove the journalist undercover into the area. Women lined the roads like mannequins, displayed under city lights as their masters watched from the shadows.

The hell those girls were living was revealed to Fisher by trafficking survivor Elizabeth, called 'Isabel' in the story for her safety. The journalist met her through a local refuge only two weeks after her rescue. Elizabeth, aged 23, was a mother of twins to her pimp. He raped her repeatedly over her four years of capture.

To this day Elizabeth reminds Fisher of the unique privilege journalists have in delving into the dark chambers of a stranger's life. Elizabeth's hopes had been engulfed by pain. That pain burned from her deep brown eyes and into Fisher's memory.

Elizabeth's testimony drove the story that was later commissioned by ABC's *Lateline* program and earned Fisher a Young Walkley Award. More importantly, it moved Australians to donate to efforts to rescue the thousands of girls still trapped in the trade.

14
Investigative Journalism

'At the core of investigative journalism is exactly the same thing that drives a page-turning thriller: telling a great story.'

Hank Phillippi Ryan

Objectives

This chapter provides an introduction to the world of investigative journalism. Long considered one of the benchmarks of longer form journalism, it generally involves a doggedness and determination to uncover a story or information that someone doesn't want told. While investigative journalism can take weeks, months, even years, to produce, the skills required are also beneficial for other forms of journalism. This chapter covers:

o   The history of investigative journalism

o   The research process

o   The interpretation of your results

o   A Case study about Annika Smethurst.

Introduction

Much has been said and written in recent years about the pending death of traditional journalism. One form of journalism that was slated for extinction is investigative journalism, often considered the preserve of the best and brightest, the most dogged and morally driven of our journalists. And while we've seen some contraction in the amount of investigative journalism produced, there certainly has been no reduction in the quality. Australian journalists—like their counterparts elsewhere— continue to produce outstanding work that shines a spotlight on the deeds—and misdeeds—of people in public office, as well as those working in the private sector. The reality is that there continues to be—and hopefully always will be—a demand for investigative journalism, or as it is sometimes called, watchdog journalism, even crusading journalism.

History

Investigative journalism in its various forms has a strong and proud history, both in Australia and elsewhere around the world. Investigative journalists, and other journalists using investigative techniques, have played an important role in keeping governments, businesses and individuals accountable for their actions. For example, most journalism students have heard about two of the great investigations: the Thalidomide investigation headed by London's *Times on Sunday*, and the Watergate investigation that led to the impeachment of US President Richard Nixon led by the *Washington Post*. These two investigations—along with others—helped to spawn a generation of journalists who wanted to uncover the truth, no matter where it was hidden. That was certainly the case in Australia, although it should be noted that *Four Corners* on ABC Television was established in 1961, well before these investigations. The success of investigative journalism is highlighted by the number of Walkley Awards individual journalists and teams of reporters have received over the years for turning the spotlight on stories that needed to be told. Significantly, however, while journalists from different organisations often worked on the same story, they did so independently, as was the case with the separate award-winning investigations into corruption in Queensland during the 1980s by Chris Masters (ABC/*Four Corners*) and Phil Dickie (*Courier Mail*).

But it is not just the big ticket stories that investigative journalists pursue. They also pursue the smaller fish, those that have the capacity to impact on our daily lives—the dodgy cab driver or whitegoods repairer, the hypocritical council CEO, vulnerable people who are taken advantage of by faceless bureaucrats. In some instances, there will be someone to blame. In others, it will just be a mistake or an oversight that a journalist doing their job can rectify.

In more recent times, the changes taking place within journalism have led to a reduction in the number of media organisations that support dedicated investigative teams. Instead, we've seen a sharing of intelligence between different media organisations, as well as the teaming up of journalists across different platforms to conduct investigations. For example, journalists working for the Melbourne *Age* and the ABC have teamed up to produce cross-platform reports on a range of topics, including 'The Money Makers', an investigation into Reserve Bank of Australia subsidiaries Note Printing Australia and Securency in 2009, and the two-part joint investigation by Fairfax Media and the ABC on the 'The Mafia in Australia' (29 June and 6 July 2015).

We have also been witness to the emergence of organisations such as WikiLeaks that acts as a storing-house or a repository for sensitive information leaked from governments and corporations and then shared with media organisations that produce stories based on the information received. Finally, we've witnessed international collaboration between media organisations and journalists who are members of the International Consortium of Investigative Journalists (<https://www.icij.org/>). Recent ICIJ investigations include the Panama Papers (<https://panamapapers.icij.org/>) and Skin and Bone (<https://www.icij.org/tissue/video-skin-and-bone>).

These, and a host of other investigations around the world (for example *The Boston Globe's* investigation into sex abuse in the Catholic Church that led to the movie *Spotlight*), suggest that investigative reporting is not only alive and well, but that it plays a critical role in helping to expose dishonest people, and holding governments to account for their actions. It is because of this that we have included a chapter on investigative journalism techniques in this revised edition of the book. However, given the complexity of investigative journalism, we can only hope to provide an overview of the techniques employed by investigative journalists. If, after reading this chapter, you want to investigate further, we suggest you have a look at our companion book *Journalism Research and Investigation in a Digital World* (Tanner & Richardson, 2013).

What does it take to be an investigative journalist?

Despite its hallowed status within the profession, the reality is that the skills required to be an investigative journalist are no different to those required for other forms of journalism. To be a successful journalist at any level, you need to be inquisitive, have an interest in the world around you, and be prepared to keep asking questions until you get what you consider is the correct answer. That is, don't allow yourself to be fobbed off by someone who may feel threatened by your investigations or even the questions you are asking. Having said this, however, often the people you are investigating are playing for much higher stakes than those people you may cover in a different beat. For example, have a listen to Caro Meldrum-Hanna's (2016) investigation into cheating and corruption within the greyhound racing industry, 'Making a Killing'.

This highlights some of the challenges—perhaps even risks—investigative journalists face, whether investigating illegal practices in sport, murder, or corporate or political corruption. While not all investigations are risky, there is no doubt that some unscrupulous characters will do everything they can to dissuade the reporter from digging too deep, including physically threaten journalists and their families. This is highlighted by the number of journalists killed while on the job (See, for example, the various statistics compiled by the Committee to Protect Journalists (<https://www.cpj.org/killed/2016/>). These statistics do not cover just investigative journalism—in fact in recent years, most journalistic deaths tend to have occurred in war zones. However, this is not to lessen the risks associated with investigative journalism in some regions, including Asia, Africa and South America.

What are the skills associated with investigative journalism? The first of these we touched on above. It involves being inquisitive. All journalism involves building networks of people who can provide you with information. In some instances it might be the tip that starts off an investigation. In other cases it could be a piece of the puzzle that connects other bits of information you currently have, but can't necessarily see the link between. However, while most people are generally willing to talk to journalists 'on the record', in the case of investigative journalism, much of the information you receive is provided secretly, or in the case of sources you know, on the understanding that they are granted anonymity.

This can pose some interesting challenges for the journalist. One of the first questions you need to ask if someone you don't know, or only vaguely know, cold calls or offers you information in an unsolicited manner is: 'why me?' The why me question is important. Many media organisations encourage the unsolicited provision of information, often via their websites, where anonymity is promised. But this tends not to be targeted at individual journalists. Sometimes individual journalists do receive information because the individual providing the material believes they have a reputation for good work. But sometimes, especially if you are a young reporter just starting out and have little background in investigative journalism, it is worth asking 'Why me?' Is it because the people providing the information believe you might be a little more gullible or less questioning of information that is not as strong as a cursory glance would suggest? This is not to suggest that you reject the information out of hand. Rather, it means that you should seek to establish the veracity of the claims being made.

Often this is a straightforward process. If you have a well-established contact book you will have alternative sources you can approach to determine whether a claim or allegation is justifiable. If you don't, then you need to ask yourself some follow-up questions, including: 'What are they hoping to achieve by undermining the individual or people involved?' For example, in the case of claims against a political foe, are the allegations simply part of a targeted power play between factional rivals? Or, in the case of allegations about underworld figures, is the claim part of a broader turf war?

The second skill is linked to the first and involves knowing what questions to ask and, ideally, who to ask these questions of. There is a third element to this, namely knowing when to ask the questions. As we've discussed elsewhere, there are different interviewing strategies available to the journalist (see Chapter 4). Which of these you choose to adopt depends in part on the person you are interviewing and the types of information you are seeking from them. Again, you need to ask yourself some questions before tackling your interviewee. How well do you know them? Do they respect and/or trust you, or do they see you as 'the enemy'? Are they the focus of your investigation, or simply someone who can help you fit the pieces of the jigsaw together? Are you seeking information from them that only they are likely to know and, if so, are you placing them at risk?

The research process

Before you conduct your interview (or interviews), you need to conduct some research. This is not to say that you don't ask some preliminary questions. In all likelihood you'll need to, especially if you're following up on a tip or an information dump from an unexpected source. But generally the definitive interviews, particularly those involving the accused, will come much later in the investigation. Before that, you'll need to do some background work. Clearly the research you undertake will be influenced by the type of story you are investigating, the amount of information you already have, where that information came from, and what form it takes.

Prior to the development of the Internet, journalists wishing to undertake investigations generally relied upon hard copy files. This meant that their task was a difficult one, as the documents were often difficult to trace, and might have been stored in dusty archives, government departments, or even old boxes or suitcases in attics or cellars. Often the custodians of those documents had little knowledge of what they possessed, so a request for information was hit and miss. Even when people did know where particular documents were, they may have been reluctant to share them with journalists because of a concern about their own reputation, or the reputation of the person the documents referred to.

Today, however, journalists have access to vast quantities of information, some of it placed on the Web by unsuspecting individuals, companies and governments, others mined by unscrupulous individuals and organisations who have hacked into government databases and released the resultant data for all to see (think Wikileaks; Bradley (Chelsea) Manning, Edward Snowden, or even the Ashley Madison relationship site). Much of this information can be located through a simple key word search. For example, it is relatively easy to trace individuals online, through one of the various social media sites, and/or their professional associations. But a word of warning: just because information is available online, doesn't mean that it is correct. For example, autobiographical or biographical information is often not subject to second- or third-party editing and individuals will often claim credit for qualifications or achievements to which they are not entitled. Likewise, some sites are user-generated and editable. Take the Wikipedia site, for example. There have been a number of occasions in which information has been maliciously changed by individuals because it did not agree with their world view.

The lesson from this: always verify or corroborate information you are provided with, irrespective of whether it is provided verbally, via hard copy documents or online. There is a good lesson for journalists in the experiences of Ralph Willis, the Treasurer in the Keating Government. In the last days of the 1996 federal election, which Labor lost, Willis received a forged document that claimed dissension between federal opposition leader John Howard, and Victorian Liberal Premier Jeff Kennett. Willis did not realise the document had been clumsily forged (the text was photocopied onto an old Premier's Office letterhead). He and the government were severely embarrassed when that fact was drawn to his attention during a press conference.

The sheer quantity of information available on the internet means that journalists need to be constantly on their guard. If you are accessing such information, have a look at the source providing it. Start by looking at the website address. Does it have a .gov, .com, or .org suffix? Generally such sites are reputable, but not always, particularly if they have been hacked. It is always worth doing a background check on the political party, government department, company or organisation involved, so that you can gain some sense of the possible motives at play.

This is particularly the case if you venture into the so-called Deep Web and Dark Web. The Deep Web, also called the Invisible Web, is said to represent more than 90 per cent of all information stored on the Web, including email and chat messages, and private content that is generated by social media sites as well as information generated by banks and health providers (bank statements, electronic health statements etc.). This information will not be uncovered via traditional search engines, such as Google, Yahoo or Bing, unless it has previously been located and made accessible via the visible web. To access it, you need either access privileges (usually password protected, or a Virtual Private Network (VPN)). For more on this, see http:// whatis.techtarget.com/definition/deep-Web.

The Dark Web is a key part of the Deep Web and a veritable goldmine for investigative journalists. The Dark Web is the repository of mainly illegal information, such as drug-selling sites Silk Road, Agora and Evolution, or sites specialising in child pornography, the sale of illegal weapons and counterfeit documents. As with the Deep Web, it is impossible to access these sites via conventional search engines because they conceal their URLs. Journalists wishing to access the Dark Web need specialised anonymity software such as Tor or I2P to gain access. Often such software can be downloaded free of charge. Wikileaks used Tor and the Dark Web to create a site where anonymous sources could deposit leaked material. This has since been developed into SecureDrop, software that works with Tor to enable media organisations to receive anonymous submissions (<https://www.wired.com/2014/11/hacker-lexicon-whats-dark-web/>). From a journalistic perspective, it enables the user to surf the web anonymously (that is without leaving a trail that can be easily followed, perhaps by the people or organisations you are investigating).

What are you looking for (and where should you look)?

In most cases, journalists don't need to trawl the Dark Web or even the Deep Web in search of information. Much of what you will be searching for is available through more conventional sources. The critical question to ask is: 'who (or what) is likely to possess the information I need?' If you're looking for information about an individual, there are plenty of sources you can tap into, depending on whether they are still living or deceased. If they are a high profile individual (a politician, businessperson or sportsperson), chances are there has been plenty written or said about them in the local media. Thus a simple online word search is likely to produce at least some information that might help you. If they are deceased, an archives search could be a useful starting point, particularly in the case of early settlers or convicts. All Australian states have archives that hold enormous amounts of information, much of it now available online (see links at the end of the chapter). Even genealogical websites such as Ancestry.com can prove helpful. Of course, social media sites such as Facebook and Twitter, or professional sites such as LinkedIn can provide background information, or links to networks of people who may know the individual you're asking about. In recent years many good stories have been initiated, or enhanced, by journalists going online and asking for information via Twitter or Facebook.

If you are investigating a company, there are a number of places to begin your search. Most companies have their own website that provides a range of information (names and profiles of senior staff and board members, company history, financial statements and annual reports, media releases, speeches etc.). The media is another worthwhile starting point, particularly in the case of public companies (those that are listed on the local share market), but also privately controlled companies. It is often easier to find information on publicly listed companies because they are required under corporations law to provide regular updates to the market on matters that impact their share price (changes in key staff, profit warnings, takeovers etc.). In Australia a great deal of this information, and more, is held by the regulators, including the Australian Securities and Investment Commission (<www.asic.gov.au>) and the Australian Competition and Consumer Commission (<www.accc.gov.au>).

When investigating the financial health or corporate behaviour of a company, there are a number of independent sites that can provide good information, including the Australian Stock Exchange (ASX), the Australian Shareholders Association (ASA) and in the case of companies that have failed or been delisted from the ASX, Delisted (<www.delisted.com.au>). The Internet also plays host to a number of chat rooms in which investors discuss companies and issues. Sometimes it is worth just lurking in the background to hear what people are talking about. If they touch on something you're interested in, you can join in the conversation.

Privately controlled companies are far more difficult to investigate, as the reporting requirements are not as onerous and there is no requirement that such information be made publicly available. Again, the media is an obvious starting point, particularly in the case of high-profile companies (those that launch with a fanfare or great promises, or are involved in major projects that receive media coverage). But if you really want to find out what is happening (as in the case of a major builder who has been declared bankrupt and left his suppliers and sub-contractors tens of thousands of dollars or more out of pocket, you need to look further afield, particularly if it is alleged that the people behind the company have done this previously. In such cases, it is important to tap into people who may be close to the company you are investigating, for example, suppliers, sub-contractors, customers, members of the local chamber of commerce or industry body.

If it's politics you're investigating, then there are a number of resources you can access, depending on the type of story. If you are researching a story on branch-stacking within one of the major political parties, you need to talk to a range of people, including those who have been accused of such behaviour. But before you do that, you need to talk to those who are making the allegations, and those who have been affected (the unsuccessful candidate who was a victim of such a practice, and the grassroots supporters who have been effectively disenfranchised). Obviously you would also talk to senior elected members of the party itself, opposition MPs, and academics who might be able to provide you with some historical background to this issue. And, as is the case with all such investigations, see if you can get hard copy evidence of such wrong-doing, to help back up your claims (letters, memos, recordings of conversations etc.).

However, if your research is policy-focused, then your starting point would be quite different. For example, say you have received a tip off that the government has received a major donation from an overseas company that had recently purchased considerable parcels of prime agricultural land. The purchase had allegedly followed a discussion between senior executives from the company and a government official, during which the company was told that the government would fast-track legislation to allow the company to dam the Murrumbidgee River and create flood plains. The company planned to breed a new genetically engineered species of frog that initially would be sold to the restaurant trade in Europe and Asia, ultimately replacing aquaculture as one of Australia's key resources.

There are a number of ways to research this story. The obvious starting point is to ask the relevant minister whether the claims are true or not. At the same time, if you know the name of the company, you could approach it directly. But, if both are reluctant to talk, then you will need to adopt other strategies. One approach would be to talk to contacts you might have within the government, including relevant ministerial advisers or departmental people. Obviously any such conversations, if they occur, would be off the record. But if the issue is seen to be politically delicate, you may have to formally request the relevant documents via Freedom of Information channels. Australia has had Freedom of Information legislation since 1982 federally and at a state level since the mid to late 1980s. This enables Australians to request, check and amend personal information government holds about them. Significantly, FOI also enables journalists to request documents that cover policy decisions. While there are some caveats on what journalists can obtain, including so-called commercial-in-confidence clauses, there can be considerable delays while you wait for the claims to be processed. FOI can, therefore, be an important tool for journalists who face stone-walling from government.

If you do place an FOI request, you need to be strategic. It is pointless embarking on a fishing expedition and asking 'for everything to do with discussions between the government and company x regarding y'. Some of the material may already be excluded by the exemptions covering Cabinet documents. If the agreement has been the subject of Cabinet discussions, or even a briefing paper prepared on behalf of Cabinet, then it won't be publicly released for anywhere between 25 and 30 years depending on the government involved (for more on this, see Kirkpatrick, 2002; 2013). As Waterford points out (2002), you need to be very specific when it comes to FOI requests, so that you get what you're actually seeking.

Given the inevitable emotion attached to such a story, there are a number of other potential sources who may help you, including the Greens, local environmental groups, downstream water users whose entitlements may be affected by any proposal to dam the river, ecologists and, of course, local businesses that stand to be affected. Another obvious source of information is the landowners who sold their properties to the company, although they may be prevented by non-disclosure clauses from talking about the sale. Invariably, however, you will find that many people are prepared to talk, and that ultimately the noise generated will force the government to respond.

Sometimes the piece you are researching is fairly mundane and may involve a rumour about an MP, or one of their staffers. Such stories can develop very quickly as we saw in late 2016/early 2017 when the question of MP entitlements arose following the revelation that then federal Health Minister Sussan Ley had bought an investment property on the Gold Coast while allegedly on official business. Ley is not the first MP—federal or state—to fall foul of the court of popular opinion over this issue. However, since the introduction of Registers of Pecuniary Interests (see Parliament of Australia in the References later in this chapter), MPs have been expected to become far more transparent about their dealings in and outside of their official duties. As Ms Ley found out, it is very easy for journalists to trace property purchases that appear on the register, irrespective of how vague the declaration may have been. It is also relatively easy to link purchases with so-called official trips and begin to ask questions about the appropriateness thereof.

Interpreting the information

As the above discussion reveals, investigative journalism is akin to puzzle solving. Once you know where to locate the information, the pieces will ultimately fit together. However, sometimes we receive so much information that we can feel overwhelmed. In such cases, it is often worth using a software package to help either analyse the data or even establish relationships between different documents or people you are investigating. When it comes to establishing relationships, there are a number of proprietary products that are designed to help conduct qualitative analysis. Popular programs include software such as NVivo, QDA Miner, Saturate, Raven's Eye, Atlas.ti, HyperResearch, MAXQDA, f4analyse, Annotations, Focuss On, Qiqqa, XSight, Quirkos, Dedoose, webQDA (for an analysis of these programs, see <http://www.predictiveanalyticstoday.com/top-qualitative-data-analysis-software/>). Predictive Analytics Today has also identified a number of free software programs, including QDA Miner Lite, Coding Analysis Toolkit, (CAT), Computer Aided Textual Markup and Analysis (CATMA), Cassandra, LibreQDA, RQDA, TAMS Analyzer, Elan FreeQDA, QCAmap, Connect Text, FsQCA, Transana, Visao, Tosmana, GATE and Kirq. These programs will not only help identify relationships, but also assist in transcription, content and discourse analysis.

Sometimes we're given material that is presented in spreadsheets. This can be intimidating, but need not be. A basic understanding of Microsoft Excel, particularly its mathematical formulas, will enable you to interpret all but the most complex of data. This is particularly the case with financial data. Let's face it, most of us are not forensic accountants. We might have some understanding of how a company report or balance sheet is laid out, but lack the capacity to tell if someone is 'cooking the books' so to speak. If that is the case, it is a good idea to ask for help. Team up with a specialist who can help you to understand the material you're dealing with. It might be an accountant, a lawyer, a doctor, even a geomorphologist. It is much better to seek assistance—and share the glory—than it is to wallow around and not fully understand the issue you are trying to come to grips with.

While much of the aura surrounding investigative journalism attaches to the quest for information and the interpretation of the material you locate, the reality is that at the end of the day this can mean little if you are unable to present your findings factually and in a way that non-expert audiences will understand. While you are writing up your findings, you need to think about the ethical and legal implications of what you have done, or what you are saying. This is discussed in more detail in chapters 8 and 9. However, a number of issues stand out, particularly from a legal context. First, the investigative journalist's greatest risk is defamation. People will do everything they can to stop journalists or media organisations from publishing or broadcasting information that is detrimental to them. There are a number of legal avenues they might pursue to prevent this from happening. They may seek an injunction (a court order that prevents the journalist or media organisation from publishing all or some information, pending a court hearing). Some will threaten journalists with a defamation action. These can be very costly and time-consuming, therefore journalists and media organisations need to be confident that what they have found, and what they are saying, can be justified if a court action proceeds. There are also issues around trespass and being provided with information that was illegally or secretly obtained (again see Chapter 9). Finally, in the current environment, in which terrorism is on everyone's lips, there are provisions within Australia's anti-terrorism legislation that have implications for journalists.

From an ethical perspective, the critical questions revolve around principles of fairness. Have you done everything you can to ensure that your story is fair and factual before going to print? Are all sides of the story represented in a balanced way? Have you given the appropriate people an opportunity to respond to allegations and, if not, is your decision to exclude them from the story reasonable?

You also need to think about how best to present the material. Is it a piece that could benefit from the use of data visualisation? There are some outstanding examples online of how media organisations have presented material in an interactive way (see, for example, the BBC's map which details every fatal accident in the UK between 1999–2010, Bloomberg's 'Deadliest jobs in America, or ProPublica's 'A disappearing planet'). Perhaps the piece doesn't lend itself to data visualisation. But that shouldn't rule out other forms of enhancement, including video footage, audio, still photography, or images of relevant documents.

Summary

o Investigative journalism can be challenging, even time-consuming and risky. But it can be enormously satisfying to pull together a story that proves that someone has been engaged in illegal or shonky behaviour.

o Many of the skills investigative reporters employ can be applied more broadly to journalism, including the art of interviewing, locating and interpreting information, and then presenting information in a way non-experts can understand.

Questions

1 To what extent do you believe there is a future for investigative journalism?
2 What can daily journalism learn from investigative journalism?
3 What are the major ethical and legal issues investigative journalists should consider?

Activities

1 Go online and see what you can find out about either the Thalidomide story or the Watergate scandal. In what ways do you believe that they helped promote a sense of investigate zeal by journalists?
2 Have a listen to the Caro Meldrum-Hanna story mentioned earlier in the chapter (the link is in the References). See if you can identify the various stages Meldrum-Hanna worked through in pulling this story together.
3 Go online and find some examples of data visualisation. What is it about these stories that appeals to you?

References and additional reading

Meldrum-Hanna, C. (2015). 'Making a killing': http://www.abc.net.au/4corners/stories/2015/02/16/4178920.htm

Kirkpatrick, R. (2002). 'The glory of the revelator: historical documents as a resource.' Chapter 7 in S.J. Tanner (ed.), *Journalism: Investigation and Research*, Longman: Frenchs Forest, NSW.

Kirkpatrick, R. (2013). 'Research strategies.' Chapter 6 in S.J Tanner & N. Richardson (eds), *Journalism Research and Investigation in a Digital World*, Oxford University Press: South Melbourne.

Parliament of Australia. Register of Pecuniary Interests: http://www.aph.gov.au/Senators_and_Members/Members/Register/Previous_Parliaments/44P_Members_Interest_Statements

Ryan, H.P. http://www.azquotes.com/quote/1136216?ref=investigative-journalism

Tanner, S.J & Richardson, N. (eds) (2013). *Journalism Research and Investigation in a Digital World*, Oxford University Press: South Melbourne.

Waterford, J. (2002). 'The Editor's position.' Chapter 3 in S.J. Tanner (ed.), *Journalism: Investigation and Research*, Longman: Frenchs Forest, NSW.

Online resources

Australian Securities and Investment Commission: www.asic.gov.au

Australian Competition and Consumer Commission: www.accc.gov.au

BBC: http://www.bbc.com/

Bloomberg, 2015, 'The deadliest jobs in America': https://www.bloomberg.com/graphics/
2015-dangerous-jobs/

Boston Globe: http://www.bostonglobe.com/news/special-reports/2002/01/06/church-allowed-abuse-
priest-for-years/cSHfGkTIrAT25qKGvBuDNM/story.html

Delisted: www.delisted.com.au

International Consortium of Investigative Journalists: https://www.icij.org/

Panama Papers: https://panamapapers.icij.org/

Predictive Analytics Today: http://www.predictiveanalyticstoday.com/
top-qualitative-data-analysis-software/

ProPublica, 'A disappearing planet': http://projects.propublica.org/extinctions/

Skin and Bone: https://www.icij.org/tissue/video-skin-and-bone

TechTarget: http://whatis.techtarget.com/definition/deep-Web

Wired: https://www.wired.com/2014/11/hacker-lexicon-whats-dark-web/

Case study

Annika Smethurst discusses political scandals

The author:

Annika Smethurst studied journalism and international studies at Monash University, graduating with honours. She worked with the *Bendigo Weekly*, dabbled in radio with the ABC and worked for a state government politician before landing a traineeship with News Corp, based at the *Herald Sun*. She was promoted to the State Government round within six months and was part of the Victorian state politics team that was nominated for a Walkley Award for its work on the Baillieu government's secret tapes bombshell. She joined the *Herald Sun* team in Canberra in 2015. She won the 2016 Walkley Award for her 'Choppergate' story and two Melbourne Press Club awards. In 2017, Annika became News Corp's national political reporter for its Sunday mastheads.

1 Where did the idea for the politicians' expenses story come from?

The expenses of all federal MPs are released every six months on a website. The documents include everything from office supplies to overseas travel. There are pages of documents that not only cover current MPs but also former prime ministers and even their spouses, who are still entitled to bill taxpayers for a few items. The documents are usually released late in the day at the end of a sitting period making it difficult to get a cracking yarn for the next day's paper—unless you know what you are looking for. In most cases the stories that make the paper the following day are often accumulated travel bills for the Prime Minister or Foreign Minister because the figures look big but mean little without any context or analysis.

In both the case of Sussan Ley and Bronwyn Bishop, the stories didn't emerge until weeks later. Political staffers, journos and MPs spend weeks looking through the expense reports, particularly over the summer and winter recess when MPs return to their electorates and news can be hard to find.

Charter flights are listed separately within the documents and I had heard that there were a few questionable flights listed from the last six months of 2014— during the period of the Victorian election. Charter flights normally have to be approved prior to travel by the Special Minister of State, unless you are a Presiding officer—a Speaker or the President.

Bronwyn Bishop had listed a charter flight in November 2014 from Melbourne to Geelong. As a Victorian I knew this was a short route to charter a flight. Looking through the pages of expenses it was clear to see that MPs in remote areas primarily used chartered aircraft because it was easier than travelling by car to their nearest capital city and taking a commercial flight. I had worked at *The Geelong Advertiser* as a cadet and driven the Geelong Road many times. The drive takes just under an hour; it seemed strange to take an aircraft for such a short distance given the need for a chauffeured ComCar [Commonwealth Car] at each end. It was worth asking the question.

In the case of Sussan Ley, sources had told me the Health Minister had purchased a property on the Gold Coast on what was believed to be a taxpayer-funded business trip. It then became a matter of lining up the documents.

Alongside expense reports, MPs and senators are also required to list any financial interests they have such as shares or properties. Sussan Ley had added a new Queensland property to her Register of Members' Interests. Recent sales data is also readily available and includes the purchase date, property address, vendor and the name of the person who made the purchase. Once the dates lined up it again became a matter of asking the question.

In both these cases the original story was never enough for the minister or Speaker to resign; in fact neither story ran on the front page. It was stories from my newspaper and other media outlets in the days that followed that really put pressure on the government. In busy news cycles stories often die as quickly as they are born. It's about continuing to dig.

2   At what point did you realise you had a story? And how much more work did you have to do to 'land' the story? What was the hardest part of doing the story— finding it? writing it? getting reaction?

With Bronwyn Bishop the hardest part was getting an answer from her office, which probably should've been a sign that I was onto a story. Naively, I believed that if the Speaker had taken an aircraft from Melbourne to Geelong it must have been due to a tight schedule or because she had made a separate visit to a school or hospital. After a few days of silence I eventually rang the media office of then-Prime Minister Tony Abbott asking for a response. Initially it was not clear what event Ms Bishop had attended. She maintained all travel was 'in accordance with the guidelines and within entitlements'—but did it pass the pub test? The day after the original story about her charter flight was published, sources came forward and told me it was a Liberal Party fundraiser. After three days of stories, Ms Bishop agreed to repay the money and held a now-famous press conference where she continued to insist she had done nothing wrong. The following day, I looked into another charter flight and found she had again travelled to a Liberal fundraiser—this time in rural NSW—using a taxpayer-funded aircraft. For 18 days the *Herald Sun* ran stories about Bishop's expenses over her decades in Parliament. Eventually she was forced to resign.

With Sussan Ley, her media team also gave the same defence—all travel was within the rules. The pub test is often more important than the rules. Voters often have their own gauge of what is right and what is wrong. Flying to the Gold Coast to purchase a property using taxpayer funds was not passing the pub test. Prior to changes announced by Prime Minister Malcolm Turnbull in January 2017, expenses were something of a grey area, and many questionable trips may have been ticked off because the behaviour appeared within the rules. But with a government cutting welfare and funding for schools and hospitals, the bar for what the public would accept had been lowered.

The reaction to both these stories was intense and hit me quite hard. I remember standing by my stove doing some late-night baking when the Bronwyn Bishop story went up online and the reaction was huge. While Twitter isn't always the best tool to measure the impact of a yarn, I knew this was not going to go away. Similarly when the story about Sussan Ley buying a property on a taxpayer-funded trip hit the website, the reaction was swift and all one way. Readers weren't happy and any doubt I had disappeared.

3 How careful were you to keep it to yourself? Canberra's a very gossipy place. A Press Gallery veteran told me once: 'You rarely break a story here—often, you just get increments on stories'. Is that your belief? In the digital era, is it harder/easier to find these kinds of stories?

After stories break it becomes quite competitive to break more updates and new exclusives. Often the original story is easy to keep to yourself. Unfortunately in the 24-hour news cycle it's harder and harder to drag yourself away from the hourly updates and break your own yarns. Staying ahead of a story is the most difficult task. The internet is a great way to update the stories and stay ahead of the curve. With Bronwyn Bishop we were the first news website to publish photos of Bronwyn Bishop's helicopter flight. We also used the website to update details of the police investigation. But the hard copy of the newspaper still has a huge impact in setting the agenda for the day ahead. Publishing exclusives in the daily paper was still one of the most important parts of keeping the yarn alive.

4 Would you call it 'investigative journalism' or something more like 'just following your nose'? Why/why not?

In both these stories the saying 'where there's smoke there's fire' proved correct. Once the original breach was identified, it became easy to see a pattern. Bronwyn Bishop's helicopter trip triggered a full review of her expenses over her entire career—not just by the government but by members of the Press Gallery. Similarly with Sussan Ley, a pattern emerged; it became obvious that she was taking a lot more trips to the Gold Coast than many of her colleagues.

Elements of both these expenses stories were based on investigative journalism, but trawling through documents is not the only way to break yarns. In both these cases, political sources played a huge role in breaking further exclusives. Hitting the phones is important to get a sense of how the stories are playing out internally, but looking outside the Press Gallery bubble and engaging with the general public is really important. Readers contacted me with both the Bronwyn Bishop and Sussan Ley stories to contribute information. Often a lot of incorrect information filters through but it's important to follow leads when your nose tells you to.

http://www.heraldsun.com.au/news/victoria/brownyn-bishop-splashes-5000-for-charter-flight-from-melbourne-to-geelong/news-story/889fcecab07e491dcd389b43d05412f6

And here's the Ley story.

http://www.heraldsun.com.au/news/national/federal-health-minister-susan-ley-buys-gold-coast-flat-on-taxpayerfunded-trip/news-story/bb78f8800f38aaac2b2ffe64573fd8f7

15
Sports Features

'You know, we've got 700 print journalists covering [AFL] nationally, which averages out at one per player. So if you think about the newspapers, you think about online media, and the speed of this media now, you think about television ratings, it's an explosion of coverage.'

Andrew Demetriou, former Chief Executive Officer, AFL, 2010

Objectives

In this chapter you will learn about what makes a good sports feature, but just as importantly what pitfalls await the enthusiastic sportswriter. Sport is perceived as a glamorous activity and it is very easy to fall for its charms. So to help you navigate some of those potentially fraught moments and emerge with a strong sports feature, this chapter will cover:

o   why sport matters to readers

o   the tradition of sports writing

o   what happens if you prefer computer games to any other type of game

o   the traps (and some of the solutions)

o   the components of a good sports feature

o   a Case study: Michael Gleeson on the strange collision between a footballer and a tram

o   a Writing sample: 'Who gets hit by a tram?' by Michael Gleeson, *The Age*, 22 November 2008.

Why sport matters to readers

The sheer number of sportswriters in Australia tells us one thing: there is a lot of sport covered in the nation's media. The fact—yes, fact—that the number of people covering one sport—AFL—outnumbers those covering national politics in the Federal Parliamentary Press Gallery by about 3:1 tells us something else: that media organisations believe sport is more important to Australians than federal politics. And while politics can be glimpsed in a range of human activity—in the office, in the kitchen and even in the playground—sport, as award-winning British sportswriter Simon Barnes notes, is 65 million years old, dating back to the basic competition within nature (Barnes, 2006, p. 360). This means that the appeal of sports writing lies in our instinctive understanding of what sport is often about: the survival of the fittest, to deploy an (appropriate) cliché.

Yet amid this age-old charm, there is a more modern view about those who actually write about sport: that they, in some ways, are less serious, less engaged and less intellectual than those who cover politics, the arts or business. Not for nothing was the sports section of newspapers called the Toy Department. Part of this misplaced snobbery was a durable preconception among many readers (and some other journalists) that covering sport is one of those jobs that is a) easy, largely because b) it's usually done by sports fans, for whom it is a dream job. The second preconception has some truth, although being a sports fan and covering sport can lead to some horrible predicaments and lamentable outcomes amid the pleasure, the front-row seats and the travel. And that is why the preconception about sports reporting being easy is totally wrong. To be a good sportswriter takes more than just being a fan. It takes intelligence, curiosity, passion, a sense of humour, patience and perseverance. In fact, the best sports reporters will tell you their experience as general reporters was the critical element in them becoming good sports reporters. Specialise too soon in your dream job and you run the risk of losing perspective on sport. Give yourself a solid grounding in the craft of news reporting and you will be able to apply the basic tenets of journalism to the sporting arena. More importantly, such experiences will equip you with the skills to push beyond the conventions of sports reporting and become one of the rare breed of sports feature writers, winning the coveted place in the sports pages, or in the rapidly growing number of sports websites, where there is space to display your writing.

The tradition of sports writing

In the range of feature writing practised across journalism's history, it has been sports writing that has occupied a particularly revered place. The reasons are simple: there have been some wonderful examples of the craft over the years, especially in the United States and the UK, where writing about sport goes beyond the mere outcome of a contest. American writers such as Red Smith, Gay Talese, W.C. Heinz, A.J. Leibling, David Halbetstram (a former distinguished war correspondent), Gary Smith, George Plimpton, Hunter S. Thompson and Tom Wolfe wrote about sport with conviction and perception, especially for magazines such as *Sports Illustrated*. In the UK, a different range of writers, such as Neville Cardus, Brough Scott, Hugh McIlvanney, Ian Wooldridge, Nick Hornby, Frank Keating, Matthew Engel and Lynne Truss, have occupied newspaper pages with whimsical, compelling and revealing pieces on sport.

The Australian tradition is different. Our early newspapers were strong on sport, indicating the importance of sport to the colonies, especially in Melbourne, where the reporting of the fledgling Australian football, cricket, cycling and other amusements was distinguished by a robust engagement with the issues around the game. Ex-players taking up the writing—such as the former Australian test cricketer Tom Horan, who wrote under the name Felix in *The Australasian*—helped set a benchmark for lucid renditions of cricket matches. Indeed, it is possible to argue that sports writing in Australia up to the 1950s was full of longer-format reporting that took the reader behind the scenes of a match or an individual performance. But then for about 30 years, until the 1980s, a lot of Australian sports writing was trapped in the blow-by-blow accounts of who won, who did well and who was injured. It is hard to fathom exactly why this was the case, and although there are traces of it in contemporary Australian sports writing, there is now significant nuance to the sports pages afforded by commentators and feature writers such as Greg Baum, Malcolm Knox, Peter Lalor, Chloe Saltau, Emma Quayle, Samantha Lane, Gideon Haigh, Linda Pearce, Nicole Jeffrey, Caroline Wilson, Mark Robinson and Ron Reed (note the number of women in the list, a trend that has appropriately got stronger during the past decade). And there is also a strong list of book-length sports writing from Graem Sims, Ben Collins and Glenn McFarlane, although these are predominantly biographies of historical sporting figures.

Taken together, these approaches represent different opportunities for readers to get more insight into the issues, results and personalities that dominate sport. But the fundamental approach, no matter what era and whoever the writer, remains the same: the reader needs to find out something that they didn't know. It sounds straightforward, but the extra layer of challenge to this quest for sportswriters is simply because so many of their readers are so well informed about the sport already. They are often lifelong fans who have an opinion on team selection, a player's capability, a club's fortunes, an administration's inertia or just what they saw at the ground earlier in the day.

Veteran Melbourne football writer Mike Sheahan put it this way:

> And we're under probably more scrutiny than any journos in the business. People don't care about how BHP runs day to day but they care about how a footy club runs because they barrack for someone. So that scrutiny, whatever the story is, people out there have a working knowledge of the subject. And a view.
>
> in Bodey, 2011, p. 27

There is also a deeper discussion occurring. As former England test cricketer Ed Smith observed: 'Sports fans argue about anything and everything ... Unravel the ideas behind the arguments ... and you will find questions about evolution, destiny, psychology, the free market, history and many other disciplines' (Smith, 2008, p. xiii). As Smith goes on to suggest, that might sound daunting, but the charm of sport is that it can be enjoyed at a number of levels. And it is bringing those levels alive—and providing the basis for readers to find something that snags their attention—that is the job of the sports feature writer. It is vital to remember that social media is a powerful adjunct to the circulation of sports stories and key to promoting the important debate and engagement that is at the heart of being a sports fan. Sports journalists for every mainstream media outlet try to develop a profile that will help bolster their social media traffic with an eye to increasing interest in and exposure of their stories.

Most of the principles of feature writing we have explained in this book apply to writing longer stories about sport. Good research, balance, a number of voices, strong interviews, telling anecdotes and a solid structure are vital elements in sports stories too. And like other features, sports features fall into the broad categories of profiles, issues, context and comment.

But there are several distinguishing elements that we need to explore to ensure that sports features have the necessary freshness and flavour to be good reads. The first of those is working out if you are sufficiently interested in sport to commit to researching, interviewing and writing a feature on a game, a sporting issue or a sportsman or woman.

What if I prefer computer games to any other type of game?

For all the enthusiasm many sportswriters have, it is also true that some of the best writers about sport, or any other topic, are often those who have no long-term interest in it. In fact, their ignorance can be a virtue that enables the writer to see things that the more devoted follower of that particular area might take for granted. Fresh eyes can bring alive a contest or a personality. The jaundiced view, the conventions of the contest, the glib resorting to clichés are often absent from the writer who is tackling a subject for the first time. Here is former literary editor and novelist turned sportswriter Lynne Truss talking about why she wrote about sport for *The Times* in London:

> Sporting knowledge was not what I'd been hired for by *The Times* sports desk; just a cheerful nature, an open mind, a clean driving licence and an idiot willingness to deliver 900 words on deadline from any live sporting event, including those I didn't remotely understand.
>
> Truss, 2010, p. 2

Truss's ignorance was her point of difference from all the other sportswriters who were covering such events, and that difference was used by *The Times* to help engage readers who, like Truss, did not necessarily understand or regularly follow certain sports. It was a smart way for the publication to try to find a new audience by using a fresh approach to an established part of the paper.

It is equally true that if you understand the nature of competition, whether it's a game of dominos or *Call of Duty*, then you will probably also understand the forces that drive sportsmen and women: the urge to compete and the lure of victory. These are simple impulses that many of us share. It helps to remember that the basic premise of sport—competing against either yourself or someone else—is a fundamental aspect of human nature. It is what that challenge reveals about us as individuals that should form the bedrock of a successful sports feature. Indeed, such human elements are the basic fodder of all good writing, whether it is covering the events on the oval, in the boardroom or in cyberspace. Or as Barnes puts it: 'Sport is the most intensely physical thing that humans do, or do in public, anyway. And yet the tales we tell are not of bodies, but of hearts and minds and souls' (Barnes, 2006, p. 12).

However, it is true that many sportswriters are passionate about sport, usually one sport in particular, and are determined to cover that sport. The passionate devotee brings many good things to their work: understanding, years of knowledge, commitment to the job, and an enthusiasm that is almost tangible for some readers. Over time, these writers build not only a wealth of knowledge, but also a reputation that sustains a personal following. Readers will turn to their stories because they are a trusted source. It takes years of writing well, being right in what you write and displaying a breadth of understanding to get to that point. And an indefatigable commitment to covering that sport.

The traps (and some of the solutions)

Before we look at the components of a good sports feature, it is appropriate to start with the traps that sportswriters should avoid, because they need some discussion. These are also the criticisms most often levelled at sportswriters by readers, sports administrators and players. They are legitimate traps that the best practitioners of sports feature writing avoid or find ways of overcoming.

I'm a fan. What's wrong with that?

As we have seen, being a fan of all sport, most sport or one sport can be a terrific advantage. It can also be a liability if the feature writer doesn't manage their passionate interest appropriately. As in all journalism, the principle of objectivity should be observed. Readers are fans too, but they still want information they can rely on, and that means information that is not filtered through the writer's prism of partiality. The double-whammy for sportswriters is that they can be passionate not only about a sport, but about a particular team or individual. Sportswriters, especially early in their careers, need to maintain balance. That amounts to covering every team and every individual with the same level of critical observation.

Being a passionate follower of a particular team or game is useful when the feature in question is a first-person account of a lifelong devotion to the cause. This type of feature is often a nostalgic recollection published when a club is entering the finals or is on the verge of major changes. However, the more often a sportswriter indicates who they support, the harder it is for them to deal with other clubs. Those clubs' communications teams know who the sportswriter barracks for: can they rely on the writer to treat their club fairly when the writer is so partial? It is a legitimate question for journalists and one that really only occurs in one other area of journalism—politics, where again there is a contest, this time for power and ideas, between the major political parties. Partiality in political writing is a dangerous path to take because it polarises readers, let alone the impact it has on alienating some political contacts. The same is true for sports journalists who fail to keep their allegiances to themselves.

The corollary of being a fan is that it can also get in the way of the journalist doing their job. If you get the chance to interview your 'heroes'—maybe swimmer Mack Horton, surfer Stephanie Gilmore or footballer Moana Hope—it is human nature that you will probably find yourself awestruck, even intimidated by their success and fame. If that happens, the interview and resulting story will resemble nothing more than a fan's happy encounter with their idol. No one really wants to read that. The greatest service a journalist can do their reader is to tell them something new. If you are a fan, you are ideally placed to ask your hero something interesting because you know all about them. That is an opportunity every journalist who is given the chance should take. The alternative is what is called a 'puff piece', which tells the reader nothing they didn't already know about that particular athlete, other than that the author of the story is an unashamed fan who couldn't get over their own devotion to the athlete in the story.

They've got nothing to say. Why did we bother talking to them at all?

This is a legitimate beef from many sports journalists when the time comes to interview sportsmen and women. There are several obvious reasons for this. One is that in the era of professional sport, most successful athletes have really only experienced life in the bubble of training and competing. Many of them have started young and been part of a cosseted and privileged world that is alien to most people. The end result is an individual who frequently does not have much to say about anything other than their sport and their approach to the latest contest. Many athletes have skipped tertiary study or are doing it on an extended part-time plan to accommodate their sport. It is easy for sports journalists to be snobs about this. As cricket writer David Frith noted in a press conference with 'articulate' West Australian cricketer Michael Hussey:

> When he stated that he and all Western Australians were a 'parochial' mob, it was the longest
> word I had heard used by an Australian cricketer at a press conference since [spin bowler] Tim
> May trotted out 'tautologous' at Edgbaston [Oval] in 1993.
>
> Frith, 2007, p. 143

There is some truth in this, but it is not the role of the sports journalist to point out the understandable deficiencies in someone's education or life experience. These athletes are good at what they do. That is why stories are done on them. They should be treated with respect. This is especially true when dealing with teenage talent, which can be excruciatingly difficult for the interviewer and interviewee. The teenage years are hard enough without the burden of competition and comparisons with other athletes, let alone the expectations that go with excellence. This burden is particularly oppressive in Australia, where new talent is often lauded quickly in the media and then casually disowned when the talent does not mature in line with those high expectations. A compassionate and understanding approach to dealing with such formative talent is the best way to ensure a more relaxed response from the teenager, and this may also provide a good memory for the athlete and become the basis for an ongoing working relationship between the sportswriter and the athlete.

Why say something new when a good cliché will do?

Australian sports writing is often replete with clichés and hackneyed phrases that don't actually tell the reader anything much at all. Clichés are the literary equivalent of fast food: they are quick, convenient and, after a little while, you're still hungry. Many occupants of sports departments in the major publications think that clichés are the best option, especially when they are so busy filing for online publication, creating video, feeding Twitter and filing for the next day's paper. The challenge really is to create the word pictures that enable the reader to see what the journalist sees. This has to be a priority for sports feature writers, who have the scope to explore a subject or individual in more depth than their colleagues, who are constantly filing results and updates. It behoves every sports feature writer, whether they are writing a colour piece for page one or a profile piece for a weekly magazine, to avoid the clichés that are an antidote to clear thinking and fresh insights.

There is one significant caveat to this discussion of clichés. Clichés are often supplied not by the writer, but by the interview talent. This occurs with such frequency these days that it is regularly lampooned: 'We're taking it a week at a time', 'I thought the boys really stood up tonight', etc. These pieces of waffle, like most clichés, might have been meaningful once but now they obscure meaning. So why do coaches, captains and athletes use them? Because they actually meet the requirement of saying something without saying anything. And increasingly, sportsmen and women are given media training by their clubs and managers to ensure that when they appear on camera and in print, they don't say anything remotely controversial. Most sportswriters rail against these ridiculous phrases—but some of them trot out their own clichés, even when describing their annoyance with the same habit on the other side of the fence.

The momentum for this range of tosh, especially from coaches and sports administrators, comes from the requirement to respond to the media in mandatory media conferences. That demand for 'talent' at the end of the match, before the match or at the end of the day provides the athlete with the opportunity to reflect on their performance. There is often precious little insight to be gleaned from these routine events. For many athletes, the media conference is a ritual they would happily skip. But some sports, such as tennis, levy a hefty fine on players who do not attend the post-match conference, a burden for many players having to confront the disappointment of losing in a Grand Slam event.

The end result is a tightly controlled environment where the athlete is often a reluctant participant who mouths predictable grabs while the assembled media become quickly bored with the repetition of content. It also means, however, that the sportswriter trying to find a fresh angle on an athlete will struggle to get past the athlete's agent or PR assistant because they a) want to protect their client from too much media exposure (for any number of reasons) and b) can justify not cooperating with the writer's request because there are official media conferences for the writer to ask a question. All this amounts to a particular challenge for the sportswriter trying to find a new angle, a fresh voice or a unique insight into a game, or a match, or its players.

I know all about this, so let me tell you what I think

A frequent problem that emerges for sportswriters is simply the prevalence of opinion in the most basic of sports writing.

Writers who are passionate will appropriately have opinions. Should there be more teams in the AFL women's competition? Was Black Caviar better than Phar Lap? What impact will the Big Bash have on the fortunes of the Australian Test cricket team? These tend to be imponderables, but sportswriters are often experts in their field and believe they are qualified to address the issues. But as we've seen throughout this book, having an opinion is fine as long as it is presented as such, in a column or an article clearly labelled 'opinion'. There is no place for opinion in general sports reporting. Sports feature writers might proffer an opinion, but the good writers test the opinion with their sources, against their experiences and often with the subjects of their articles. That way the writer's opinion can be tested against those directly involved and become a legitimate part of the writing.

There's a problem here. What are the administrators doing about it?

There is a tendency among sportswriters to identify issues within games as responsibilities of a sport's administrators, the law of the land or indeed a sporting club and its culture. When sport is so important to a readership, it is vitally important that sports coverage canvasses the bigger picture, around issues that range from drugs in sport, sportspeople's use of social media (for good or bad), funding for facilities, the advent of new clubs and their impact on the competition, or the influx of overseas talent in the Melbourne Cup. These are legitimate points of discussion and will often find their way into columns. However, any sports feature that looks at such issues needs to examine the layers within the issue, and that necessitates talking to a range of sources. It is not good enough for a sports feature to identify a problem and then call on the sport's administrators to fix it. For example, cricket fans know match fixing has occurred. The International Cricket Council (ICC) has acted. The question for any feature on this topic is not what the ICC has done, but why it needs to do more and what are the impediments or incentives for doing so.

Consider an alternative example: the arrival of the AFL women's competition in 2017. This became such a rich area for reporting that it led to an unprecedented coverage of women in Australian sport. There were features about the clubs, the players, the draft of players, their salaries, and once the competition was underway, the massive interest from spectators at the ground and on television. In many ways, the triumph of the blanket coverage of the women's competition was how similar it was to the coverage of the men's game—this was partly driven by several of the established clubs putting teams in the competition (Collingwood, Carlton, Melbourne, Western Bulldogs) but also helped by the game not being too different to the men's rules, so that every fan knew where they stood with the new League. The upshot was that it relegated some of the intense—and often excessive—media exposure of the men's game, to a second-order issue. And that too was a stunning achievement.

Nothing's more important than sport

Get a grip. Get some perspective. There is a durable corps of sportswriters who believe that the people they are writing about are heroes, gods, superhuman, and that what they do in sport will transform the nation, the world and everyone else's lives. Well, yes, that is a piece of hyperbole but it appears to be the subtext of some sports features. The reality is that sport at the highest level is still fundamentally an entertainment. Professional sportsmen and women earn high salaries from doing what they are good at. Certainly, they often capture readers' imaginations and tap in to a range of emotions that include patriotism, nostalgia and sentimentality. On occasions, they will also provide us with the opportunity to stake out the high moral ground and make a judgment about human behaviour. But if you are writing about sport, you need to remember that it is a diversion for most people and employment for only a very small number of people. The key question for the sportswriter is: Who is your audience: the athlete or the spectator? The answer is a simple one.

The components of a good sports feature

While sports features are designed to be read in their entirety, from beginning to end, the writer stands a better chance of that happening if they start with a compelling introduction.

The common denominator among readable sports features is an introduction that provides an instant entrée into the world of that particular sport or individual. So it is worth taking time to craft an introduction that gives you the opportunity to say something fresh or insightful, to perhaps set a scene or outline a puzzle, all of which can be played out and resolved in the feature.

The introduction needs to be sharp and avoid spending too much time building to the point of the story. In most sports features, there is little space to spend 10 to 12 paragraphs slowly tightening the focus on your subject. You need to assemble the angle and lead with it from the start, in crisp and concise language. This will set you up to draw on the ingredients of a good sports feature that will shape the final outcome. Here's an example from one of the best sportswriters of his generation, Ian Wooldridge, on England snatching victory from Australia to win the 2003 Rugby World Cup:

> 'Had a fiction writer submitted it for publication it would have bounced back with a sarcastic rejection slip. Handsome, modest hero wins World Cup with last kick and extra time on zero? Too fanciful by far, old boy. Just a little more plausibility please. And yet that's precisely how it was...'

Wooldridge, 2008, p. 361

Key ingredients

A satisfying sports feature is usually distinguished by several key elements. These are set out below, and an example is included with each. All of them—or at least some of them—are usually present. And these ingredients remain true for someone writing about an amateur soccer match for a suburban newspaper, or covering the Olympics for an international website.

A sense of place

This can be a venue, such as a sports ground, or a particular location, such as the host city for the Olympics, a cricket ground in India, a river used by rowers, or a golf course. The sense of place helps provide a physical context for the story and is the equivalent of a theatre stage for the telling of the (sporting) drama. This is often an indicator of the sportswriter actually having seen the event or the moment they are writing about. It can be a vital part of the feature because it conveys a sense of authenticity: the writer knows the area or the ground and can sketch an accurate picture of the surroundings. It is an aspect that works across sporting profiles, sporting issues or comment. Example:

> The FerOz Shah Kotla stadium, with its weed-strewn terraces and grotesque concrete grand-stand, its wreath of smog and its shroud of dust, looked to the Australians a likely place for a calamity. The pitch was pocked and powdered as the façade of the stand. Its condition was not due to artless workmanship. Rather, it was the careful cultivation of a surface on which Indian spinners could have their wicked way while an injured Shane Warne was not about to retaliate in kind.

Baum, 1996, p. 26

A sense of competition

This is really an understanding of rivalry and the parameters of the contest (how hard or easy it was). It includes the factors that impact on the competition, such as the strength of the rival, the strength and weakness of the individual sportsman or woman or team involved, the history behind the contest and the preparation involved—or the sheer effort involved in conquering an injury, which is just another form of contest, albeit an internal battle for the injured athlete. Example:

> After breakfast and the playing of a short film on American football, [North Melbourne coach Ron] Barassi rose to speak. Sensing the mood of his players, he opted for a low-keyed address at this early meeting. Speaking with uncommon gentleness he reminded them that: 'Last week you had the premiership in your mitts, and you let it slide out. *That's* the reason you must win today. There're a million other reasons, but that alone should be enough—because you're the guys who let it slip.'
>
> Powers, 1978, p. 139

An epiphany, perhaps

This is where that team or that athlete discovers something about themselves, collectively or individually, and builds a change in fortunes around it, for better or worse. This is about identifying a significant change in thinking, preparation or personnel, and charting the effect it has on the individual or team. Example:

> One day [Tracey Menzies] was a 29-year-old suburban high school art teacher, coaching swimming part-time, doing wedding photography on weekends and planning nuptials of her own. The telephone rang—the world's best swimmer, fresh from winning six gold medals at the Commonwealth Games in Manchester, called to say he was leaving his coach. Menzies didn't understand at first that [Ian] Thorpe was offering her the job ... Then he called back and dropped the other shoe. 'I'd like you to be my coach,' he said.
>
> Jeffrey, 2004, p. 1

A sense of excellence (or ordinariness)

Sport is about success most of the time, so outstanding performances are recorded. Losing is valuable if it is part of the development of a new talent or rehabilitation of an older athlete. Excellence is often measured in sports features by talking to an athlete's peers or previous players to provide a perspective on those achievements and motivations. But often, portraying an average performer, or an ordinary athlete with something to say, illuminates the bigger issues in sport and is an antidote to the excessive glamour and hyperbole surrounding elite sport. Example:

> His full name is Charles Valentine Holten. Most people call him Val. But in sub-district cricket circles he is invariably referred to as 'the great Val Holten'...
>
> He learnt to bat by watching his father, who played in the Subbies for Brighton. A few years later, his coach at Melbourne Grammar, Bert Davie, gave him some advice: 'Play the good balls and hit the loose ones.' The words stayed with him like a song. Holten went to district club Melbourne as a 16-year-old and three years later was in the First XI.

But the Demons were a powerful club and after he was dropped, Holten sniffed better opportunities at Prahran. It was a wonderful move for him. He established himself as one of the competition's leading batsmen and in 1952 was selected to play for Victoria, against Queensland.

He was a bag of nerves but twice got to 20. But the fact that he was bowled on both occasions brought home to him the gulf between club and first-class cricket.

Amy, 2008, p. 35

A sense of action

This is vitally important. When you write about sport, you are writing about a physical, intellectual and emotional activity, whether it's chess or whitewater rafting. There is action in every moment of the competition if you look carefully enough. The athlete at the centre of this activity is, at that moment, defined by what they are doing. The sportswriter needs to capture that action because it will help readers understand how the athlete competes, and often, as a by-product, why they compete. Example:

> [Alisa] Camplin believes it's imperative to 'practise as you mean to compete', so she lines up for another shot at perfection. She focuses her thoughts and tips forward down the in-run, gathering speed. She flies into the air, twisting and flipping her body, in the three-and-a-half-seconds she has before landing. Her timing is fractionally out, and she flips past her feet straight on to her back, smashing her in to the snow. The impact, from 13 metres in the air is three times her body-weight. The lights go out.

Yallop, 2004, p. 12

A sense of history

Sporting success is a comparative exercise, and understanding the history of sporting performance provides an indicator of the importance of a new record, whether it is a high jump mark or consecutive Melbourne Cup wins. When did Wests Tigers last beat Manly? How many wickets did Nathan Lyon take against India? Who was the Matildas' leading goal scorer in 2016? Sporting history is about context, for the reader and, sometimes, the writer. Reflecting on what happened some time ago gives resonance and insight to what just happened then. Example:

> It all began in 1993, when Vintage Crop and Drum Taps, also trained by Lord Huntingdon, arrived at Sandown at midnight. [Racing manager Les] Benton had an attack of nerves that was to last for weeks. What had he done? What if the knockers were right? What if the foreign horses turned out too slow? What if they didn't acclimatise?
>
> Drum Taps eventually went to Flemington for a fast gallop. He moved beautifully and Benton relaxed. One of these horses could win the Cup, he thought.
>
> Drum Taps didn't—that Flemington gallop jarred his legs—but Vintage Crop did. He came back in the drizzle looking like some invincible alien in a sheepskin noseband. Within an hour, the knockers were back. They had been saying the imports would be too slow; now they were saying they were too fast, and it wasn't fair.

Carlyon, 1997, p. 16

A fresh insight

For a feature to work best, it should communicate something new about a sporting situation. This can (ideally) be new information about, for example, the details of the sudden sacking of a soccer team's manager, or it could be a fresh reflection from an athlete on their approach to training. It could even be just sitting in a different spot in the venue, rather than alongside your colleagues in the press box, to get a fresh perspective. Whatever you choose, there has to be a compelling reason for a reader to engage with the story. Example:

> They [Cathy Freeman's closest friends] tell me about the mental delete button which she uses to block any input which might disturb her internal attention to the singular sensation of running. She employs the erase switch in different ways, from ignoring political controversies, or the performances of her rivals, to her legendary capacity to curl up and sleep ... What she does retain are vivid images and emotions about occasions, and these are the rich lodes I become privileged to discover.
>
> McGregor, 1999, p. 8

A strong narrative drive

While a strong narrative is characteristic of many features, it is more common in good sports features because the chronology of competition can provide a useful framework to house the story. Not only that, but the natural drama of a contest adds the kind of emotional hook that can bring your feature to life. The temptation is to utilise that drama and dial it up several notches to help give your feature more energy. Resist the temptation. Let the drama play out at its own speed. Your narrative doesn't need to be overwrought, turbo-charged or kick-started more than once. Often it's enough to let the rhythm of the sportsperson's story dictate the narrative. For example, a footballer's rehabilitation from serious injury can be bookended in your feature by the time of the injury and the start of the next football season. Those months in between become the basis for telling the story of the player's rehabilitation and his hopes for the coming season. In other examples, the narrative can be pushed along by the sportsperson themselves and their determination to realise their goals. Example:

> At 26 [Mark] Webber is far too focussed on his ambition to be bothered with such trifles as girls and toys. He's racing for a new team this year, and there is a razor-sharp competitive edge to be maintained. He wants to win, he wants to win bad, and nothing is going to get in the way.
>
> Chenery, 2003, p. 22

Key ingredients: conclusion

Of course, the truly outstanding sports feature will exceed this basic formula by the strength of its information and storytelling. But for most journalists undertaking a sports feature, the basic craft of all feature writing still applies: you have to work within limitations of time and space.

The premium challenge for sports feature writers is to see beyond the basic formula of who won and who lost, and tell the whole story of why and how such small human dramas came to shape the result and the broader sporting landscape. As English sportswriter Rob Steen explains it, covering sport is 'less about memorising results than analysing people' (Steen, 2008). In all of feature writing activity, it is the area of sports features that offers the most opportunity for journalists to work with material and personalities that—treated with the appropriate amount of scepticism (not cynicism), emotion (not romance or sentimentality) and insight (not glibness or faux intellectualism)—can amount to a story worth telling and, most importantly, worth reading.

Summary

o   Sport is a popular area of interest for many Australians, and sports features will always have an interested audience.

o   There are several traps for sportswriters to avoid:
    a   being too much of a fan
    b   failing to treat young sports people with respect and compassion
    c   writing in clichés (or reporting others' clichés)
    d   putting opinion before facts
    e   only blaming administrators for a sport's failings
    f   losing perspective on sport's importance.

o   Good sports features can have up to eight possible components: a sense of place; a sense of competition; an element of an epiphany; a sense of excellence (or ordinariness); a sense of action; a sense of history; a fresh insight; and, finally, a strong narrative drive.

o   Sports feature writing is about the drama behind the result or the event, not the result itself.

Questions

1   What are the advantages of writing about a sport that you play or know a lot about?
2   What are the disadvantages?
3   Why is sport important to readers?
4   What is a vital part of the sports feature and why is it important to spend time getting it right?

Activities

1   Find out what happened when Tracey Menzies coached Ian Thorpe. Then think about how you would start a feature on Menzies all these years later.
2   Sit down with your favourite sportswriter's most recent article. Go through it and identify the clichés. Rephrase each cliché in your own words.

3 Think about a sport you have played. It could be underwater hockey, equestrian, lacrosse or table tennis. Try to remember a moment you were in action—running, jumping, diving. Now write it as it would have looked to an observer.

4 Revisit your favourite sports website. Pick three of your favourite writers, read their reports and blog posts, and try to work out who they support. How hard is it to pick their allegiances?

References and additional reading

Amy, P. (2008). 'Honour for cricket great', *Mordialloc Chelsea Leader*, 12 March.

Barnes, S. (2006). *The Meaning of Sport*, London: Short Books.

Baum, G. (1996). 'What goes into NOT getting out', *Good Weekend*, 21 December.

Bodey, M. (2011). 'Ten Questions: Mike Sheahan', *The Australian*, 5 December.

Carlyon, L. (1997). 'On Her Majesty's service', *The Sunday Age*, 19 October.

Chenery, S. (2003). 'Mark Webber: the fastest of the fast', *The Weekend Australian Magazine*, 22 February.

Demetriou, A. (2010). 'AFL: The Great Game', 9th Ideas and Society lecture, 5 August: www.latrobe.edu.au/news/ideas-and-society/the-great-game-afl

Frith, D. (2007). *Battle Renewed: The Ashes Regained 2006–07*, Sydney: ABC Books.

Halberstram, D. (ed.) (1999). *The Best American Sports Writing of the Century*, Boston: Houghton Mifflin.

Harms, J. (2003). *Play On*, Melbourne: Text.

Headon, D. (ed.) (2001). *The Best Ever Australian Sports Writing 2001*, Melbourne: Black Inc.

Hutchinson, G. (ed.) (2003). *The Best Australian Sports Writing 2003*, Melbourne: Black Inc.

Hutchinson, G. (ed.) (2004). *The Best Australian Sports Writing 2004*, Melbourne: Black Inc.

Jeffrey, N. (2004). 'In the deep end: swimming upstream', *The Weekend Australian Magazine*, 31 July.

Kervin, A. (1997). *Sports Writing*, London: A&C Black.

McGregor, A. (1999). *Cathy Freeman: A Journey Just Begun*, Sydney: Random House.

Powers, J. (1978). *The Coach: A Season with Ron Barassi*, Melbourne: Sphere.

Smith, E. (2008). *What Sport Tells Us about Life*, London: Viking.

Steen, R. (2008). *Sports Journalism: A Multimedia Primer*, London: Routledge.

Truss, L. (2010). *Get Her off the Pitch*, London: Fourth Estate.

Wooldridge, I. (2008). *Searching for Heroes: 50 years of sporting encounters*, London: Hodder

Yallop, R. (2004). 'Sitting pretty', *The Weekend Australian Magazine*, 29 May.

Case study

Michael Gleeson on the strange collision between a footballer and a tram

Publication details:

'Who gets hit by a tram?' *The Age*, 22 November 2008.

The author:

Michael Gleeson is a senior sports journalist with *The Age* in Melbourne. He has an arts degree from the University of Melbourne, and has worked as a crime reporter and chief of staff at the *Herald Sun*. He has written several successful books, including two titles about the Collingwood Football Club. He covers AFL for *The Age* and he is also the paper's athletics correspondent.

The story:

This story had two reasons for coming into being: one was that the story of Richmond footballer Graham Polak's freak collision with a tram had not really been told, and the second reason was that the Melbourne daily tabloid the *Herald Sun* had become embroiled in a controversy over trying to interview Polak soon after the footballer was released from hospital. Polak, as this story reveals, was still in a precarious physical and mental state, but his football club decided that if the story was going to be told, it would be told in its entirety.

Michael Gleeson only had Richmond and Polak's agreement to take part in the story. He identified and then spoke to as many of the other participants in the drama as he could. But he was also aware of the story's space constraints. He only had 1200 words—five sources, a decent chronology, and it doesn't leave much room for anyone to say anything. Every detail and every quote had to be explicit. There was no room for being obtuse, subtle or cute. There was, however, room for being empathetic and incisive.

It took Gleeson two weeks to research, interview and write the story around his other work. Medical specialists can be hard to pin down because of their intense workloads, but Gleeson persevered and finally spoke to Polak's neurosurgeon. Other voices were important because Gleeson did not want the feature to be just another interview with an injured footballer.

The injury was incurred in unique circumstances, and Polak's recollection of the event was incomplete. That too necessitated talking to others about their impressions and recollections of the night. So in addition to the medical staff, the ambulance driver, the club medical specialists, and Polak and his family, Gleeson also approached the tram driver—who declined to cooperate—and Polak's friends who were with him on the night. Some of them were still distressed by the episode and opted not to comment. Polak's girlfriend, Alyce, also had a part to play and helped prompt her partner when his memory let him down.

This was Gleeson's other challenge. 'I was surprised that Polak was as good as he was but even so, you still had to moderate the detail,' he says. So the story does not contain some of the memory lapses Polak endured in the first few weeks after the accident. 'It was really about the difficulty of balancing the expectations of the medical fraternity, the football club and Polak himself about his recovery,' Gleeson explains. Polak was keen to play, and while being physically active again was a good thing for Polak's general health, his capacity to deal with it—and any other collision—was an appropriate cause for concern for everyone.

Despite all of these factors, Polak defied the conventions of the injured sportsman driving himself aggressively through rehabilitation to ensure he was back competing as soon as possible, taking nearly thirteen months to return to the AFL. 'I was surprised at his lack of bitterness and anger. I would have expected some of that,' Gleeson said. '[But] Graham was refreshing in a way. He asked the question: Who gets hit by a tram? It made him more interesting because it was out of the ordinary.'

Not one to fall back on the trite observation about the accident providing the sportsman with a fresh perspective on the game, Gleeson understood that it was nonetheless true that the story inevitably reflected some of that life-and-death conundrum. And that helped give the feature a broader appeal. 'This was an issue beyond footy. And there are probably some people who read footy stories who probably need that perspective,' Gleeson said.

Gleeson decided that when it came to telling the story he would not try to simplify or fudge the specialist medical information. If he understood it, so would his readers, trusting *The Age*'s readership to stick with the story and at least try to come to terms with the medical terminology. One other element of the neurosurgeon's story bothered him a little: should he actually start the feature with the surgeon's recollection of seeing Polak being treated on the tram tracks?

Gleeson decided instead to go with the conventional chronology because it meant he could make best use of his material in the space he had. Backtracking and providing too much explanatory material could compromise how much space he had to actually tell the story. 'I just decided to go with Graham being hit by the tram—the action moment in writing terms—because it was also the simplest process,' Gleeson explained.

And the story itself needed no tricks. It was, as Gleeson noted later, a compelling set of ingredients for a Melbourne readership: the villain was the iconic Melbourne tram; it involved a footballer from one of the city's founding clubs; and it offered the promise of a remarkable recovery. However, although Polak eventually returned to senior football, his career was never the same and he retired in 2011. And this story provides many strong clues to that outcome.

Writing sample

Who gets hit by a tram?

By Michael Gleeson, *The Age*, **22 November 2008**

Even Graham Polak can't believe what happened to him on the fateful night. Michael Gleeson traces the extraordinary events surrounding the accident and the road to recovery.

GRAHAM Polak remembers the after-match function but not the match.

He remembers the water he drank at the MCG that night, but not the quick glass of wine he shared with Cleve Hughes before stepping out the door of his flat.

He saw the first tram but not the second. But he remembers neither.

His next memory is of Trent Croad and another mate, Murray Silver, standing before him in Epworth Hospital. It was weeks later. He had had dozens of conversations before that with teammates, family, and doctors in the hospital but he recollected little even immediately afterwards. This post-traumatic amnesia is to be expected when you get hit by a tram.

It was late on June 28 when Polak and Hughes jogged across the four lanes of Dandenong Road to the avenue of trees that divides the arterial road, planning to get to a taxi on the other side, where Jordan McMahon and his girlfriend were waiting. He didn't make it.

'Jordy reckons I was nearly across and I saw the one tram coming but by the time I saw the other one coming it was probably a bit too late and I started to run for it, apparently, and nearly got past it and it just clipped me on the side and smashed me. They think it was the rear-view mirror that hit me,' Polak said this week.

He was spun like a top. In an odd coincidence, walking past was a friend of his manager who was also trained in emergency first aid. He put Polak into the correct position and called an ambulance, which arrived within minutes, quickly followed by a MICA (intensive care) unit.

Polak was quickly given oxygen and put on a spine board and loaded into the back of the ambulance. But there was a hold-up in leaving the scene when a piece of machinery in the ambulance failed. En route to the Alfred, Polak was upset and agitated, kicking and tugging at his face-mask.

Fortunately, an intensive care ambulance with two trained staff was available that night, and they were able to do what a regular staffed ambulance could not and induce a coma there.

'We induced the coma in the ambulance because we wanted to protect his airway and by paralysing and sedating him with drugs it stops further movement and that protects the brain from further swelling,' MICA paramedic Mark Eddey said.

Moments earlier, driving in the opposite direction, was neurosurgeon John McMahon, who had finished work at the Alfred and saw Polak being treated on the tracks. He did not stop.

Despite being a brain surgeon he figures unless he has a scalpel and an operating theatre he is of no more use than any other bystander. But it would not take long for him to become involved.

He was phoned by the hospital's registrar to consult soon after arriving home.

TESTS confirmed Polak had sustained a severe brain injury. On a clinical scale of three to 15, in which 15 is normal and three is dead, Polak was a seven.

Within 15 minutes of arrival at hospital he had been given a CAT scan that revealed tiny petechial haemorrhages around the brain.

Effectively, surgeon McMahon felt, Polak had been hit and violently spun so that the brain had sloshed in his skull so aggressively that many of the neurones connecting the inner and outer parts of the brain had sheared. He did not have a skull fracture or a single large haemorrhage, so it was doubtful his head hit the tram or the ground.

'This is a global, very severe brain injury that people take months to years to recover from, and some do not recover and may end up in a nursing home,' McMahon said.

It was decided to put Polak in intensive care and closely observe him for brain swelling, but not to insert a monitor to the brain to test for swelling. Inserting this monitor would have seriously affected Polak's ability to play football again, but the decision not to insert it was a clinical one, not a footballing one.

The brain scan also revealed another haemorrhage in the right thalamus and internal capsule that McMahon feared could have caused weakness in his left side.

He has since not experienced this.

'He did far better than we would ever have expected of someone with petechial haemorrhages,' McMahon said.

'He is on the lucky end of the scale when we take into account his initial neurological condition. The initial thing was this guy is probably not going to die because he is moving his arms at the scene—that is a good sign— but with him he still had a severe head injury, he still had these petechial haemorrhages which could represent something quite bad for prognosis.'

LESS than a week after the accident, Polak was transferred to the Epworth Hospital. For weeks more he swam in a fog of post-traumatic amnesia. He was up and out of bed within days of his accident and had some awareness but was not cognisant of all around him. Richmond coach Terry Wallace came to visit and Polak began doing sit-ups in his hospital bed; others came and he knew to tell jokes to some and not others, but could not recall afterwards any who had been there.

'He was gradually waking from his coma. It's not like Hollywood where you wake up and you are pleasantly confused but you cannot remember your wife. It's a gradual process and not a very nice process,' Epworth physio Gavin Williams said.

Polak presumed he had been in a car accident. He asked about the other car, about his own car and would point to the gravel marks and bruising on his legs and say, 'Look at the exhaust burns,' his girlfriend Alyce said.

On another occasion he turned to Alyce and asked determinedly, 'How long was I trapped in the car?' as though pleading with her to break a secret.

He was told it was a tram, not a car. His mind was muddy but he could barely believe it. Even now he finds it difficult to consider.

'Who gets hit by a tram? I just thought it was silly getting hit by a tram—things that don't swerve or don't do anything, just go on straight lines, and I still got cleaned up by one. How stupid am I getting hit by one of those?' he laughed ruefully this week.

The process of rehabilitation under associate professor John Olver at the Epworth has been painstaking, slowly seeking to return Polak's balance and short-term memory, which remain the worst affected.

'They reckon it is going to get better in time, the memory is going to get better, the balance is going to get better, but, myself, I can't see it getting better. Because I can't feel it getting better so I don't know if it is. It probably is, but I can't tell. It is frustrating the shit out of me,' he said.

His proudest moment came when he was allowed to run again. Having been held back by Williams until he was certain his balance would cope, it was a tangible sign to Polak that he was advancing.

'Running was the most satisfying thing. To know that I am actually able to run again and didn't have disabilities or anything that would stop me from running was pleasing,' he said.

Measuring these baby steps of change, Polak was satisfied this week to be allowed to drive. Having sustained such a serious injury, including some impairment of vision in his left eye, he was finally recovered sufficiently to be re-tested and cleared by the TAC and doctors to resume driving. It was a moment to celebrate.

'Driving again was great because well, you know, you must be getting better, but I had been sitting at home all day and you can't go anywhere, you can't do anything, you can't drive anywhere. It was very frustrating,' he said.

He has not drunk alcohol since the incident and is banned by doctors from doing so until he hits the 12-month anniversary of the accident. It will be a moment deserving of a celebratory drink.

He harbours a desire to play senior football again, which is a worthy goal and one the doctors believe is achievable, even if it will take time. He still tires easily, especially later in the day and week, and has troubles with his short-term memory, even needing teammates at times to remind him of drills they have just been instructed to perform.

'I reckon footy is what drove me the most, seeing the boys coming in. Because it was boring, I would come back home here and sit by myself and I couldn't drive and I was bored to death, so I just wanted to get back to the club and be around them and involved,' he said.

'I have come a long way from where I was but I have a long way to go. I definitely want to get back to playing. When that is, I'm not sure ... I will work my way back through. I wouldn't want to go back into the senior team until I am physically well enough to play, or jeopardise someone else's spot in the side, and I don't want to be in and do stuff-all—I don't want them to lose because of me.'

Polak believes the injury has flipped his skills. Renowned for his ability to mark strongly, he is dropping easy chest marks, while his kicking has improved.

'My hands are still hopeless, my left side is a bit shaky, a bit more "unco" than usual. I was never that good on my left anyway, but my hands are the main thing that annoy me. I have been dropping sitters but they reckon that is nothing, it will improve. But it gets you down,' he said.

The plan now is to recommence full-contact training early next year. There is little concern that he would be at risk of a worse brain injury from another knock, rather, more concern that he not be put in that position until such time as his balance and judgement has returned to normal.

Said Professor Olver: 'There has got to be a certain amount of protection but at the same time people have to live life, and you don't wrap them up in cotton wool.'

16
Columns

'The columnist is writing for an audience and a deadline, not eternity.'

Phillip Adams, in Silvester, 1997 p. xi

Objectives

This chapter looks at the nature of column writing. It considers the motivation for writing a column, a unique activity that involves the exposure of personal ideas, feelings and beliefs. Priorities and methods for budding columnists are analysed, then contextualised, by considering a range of specialised columnists, whose work appears in print and online. The chapter covers the following topics:

o   the reasons for writing a column

o   how to write a column

o   types of columns and columnists

o   blogging

o   a Case study: Wendy Tuohy on wading into controversial topics and dealing with the consequences

o   a Writing sample: 'Rougher, harder, violent: how porn is warping the male mind', by Wendy Tuohy, *RendezView* website, published 24 July 2015.

Information, provocation and entertainment

There is one type of feature writing that is unrivalled for drama, insight, humour, controversy and low cunning: it is the column. Every publication has at least one columnist and usually several. Their columns can cover everything, including fashion, art, sport, politics, life skills and scientific facts. Columns are the epicentre of reader engagement with newspapers, websites and magazines; they provide the structure for readers to help identify and classify what they are reading. Columnists help readers recognise the publication: Miranda Devine is identified with *The Daily Telegraph* in Sydney, Andrew Bolt with the *Herald Sun* in Melbourne, and Janet Albrechtsen with *The Australian*.

The above columnists write about the broad political issues of the day. Other columnists focus on other things, such as Maggie Alderson, who writes about fashion in Fairfax's weekend magazines, or the columnists who write for the celeb Q&A in *Who* magazine. Columns in all of these publications are points of information, provocation and entertainment; these are qualities that distinguish the column from all the news and features around it.

Columns are a growth industry. Opinions on just about everything are considered by editors and publishers to be a vital way to engage an audience, especially younger readers. This trend has been amplified by the evolution of the internet, which has made the personal reflection—or at least the personal diary—a staple for bloggers.

The critical difference between writing a non-fiction story and a column is the 'perpendicular pronoun'. Columns are about the individual, the writer, what they think, experience and believe. The word 'I' might not appear at all, but the author is present in every phrase and argument. Thus columns are the antithesis of measured, considered, objective prose.

Columns, however, are a vital part of a publication. Former Fleet Street editor Brian MacArthur wrote:

> Good columnists set us up for the day, help to define our views, make us argue or agree with them and quarrel with friends and colleagues ... Or they utter thoughts we might agree with but are ashamed to own up to ... Or we read them because we can't stand them.
>
> MacArthur, 2004, p. 39

Why write a column?

There are very few areas of writing where the question of motivation needs such close examination as the column. We do not ask a feature writer why they write features; as a reader we can appreciate the appeal of longer, more detailed, more engaging stories. Nor do we ask a profile writer about their motives for sitting down with a celebrity and tracking their life and times: most people—interviewers and readers—find the famous, and the almost-famous, fascinating.

But columnists are different. They write to be heard. The column provides a platform from which a writer can speak with a megaphone or throw back the curtain to reveal an insight or perspective. The columnist wants to *compel* the reader to engage with them, and 'them' is the critical word here.

If you look at mainstream publications, most columns will contain a large photo byline of the writer and even some in-publication promotion, either pointing to the column or celebrating its presence. This tells us that the column is personal opinion, but it also lets the reader know that the columnist is a 'personality' in their own right; that they have moved from the dispassionate recorder of facts to the passionate commentator or the partial participant.

This distinction has been clear to numerous columnists over the years, including the American Hallam Walker Davis, who wrote:

> They [columns] contribute to the health and sanity of thinking ... The good reporter and good feature writer do not encourage us to enquire into things. Even the editorial writer does not often ask us to look on both sides. But the columnist is ever flipping things upside down and wrong side out and inviting us to look and laugh—and think, even.
>
> Silvester, 1997 p. xviii

Whether this observation is accurate could be debated by a team of columnists, but the sentiment is clear—columnists are, collectively, working in an environment where they are trying to persuade and convince the reader about the soundness of their argument or the universality of their insights.

This is a big task for anyone, and the columnist has to demonstrate faith in their views of human nature and a certainty in their understanding of the world. Ultimately, writers become columnists because they think that what they know and what they believe should be shared with others. This is a crusading act that not every writer feels comfortable with or aspires to, but for those writers who do believe, it is the finest expression of their ability.

How to write a column

The writer has to be sure of four things before starting to write a column:

- what they are going to say
- to whom they are going to say it
- how they are going to say it
- how often they are going to say it.

These four considerations go to the heart of the column—the argument, the style, the audience and the columnist's role—but as columns are of such variety, there is vast scope for addressing them.

What

The first consideration is the most challenging one for a columnist. Think about it for a moment: every writer has one, two or perhaps three areas or issues that they feel strongly enough about to want to write about. But if you set out to be a weekly columnist, you will have exhausted your range of topics within six weeks. How do you sustain the rage? How do you find a topic or develop an argument about something that doesn't really interest you? How do you stop writing the same column—or at least about the same topic—every week?

The tyranny of a weekly deadline can, over time, sap inspiration and motivation. Alternatively, what happens if you run out of the anecdotes that fuel a personal column? Or what if you write a home renovation column and you keep getting emails about re-plastering when you've already devoted three recent columns to the task?

These are perennial problems for columnists. Some columnists think ahead, but even then there are no guarantees. One of Adelaide's toughest columnists, Des Ryan, articulated his predicament: 'In the early days, panicking, I remember having 14 columns up my sleeve at one stage in case I suffered writer's block. Now I pretty much write as I go but the panic is always there hunched over my shoulder' (Ryan, 2003, p. 2)

Columnists also find ways to craft an argument from research. This is much easier for the political or current affairs columnist because there will usually be something to talk about in any given week. However, it can be a real challenge for those who write lifestyle columns. Charmian Clift, a fine Australian writer, also composed a regular column about life for the *Sydney Morning Herald* between 1964 and 1969. This is an excerpt from her column—on the topic of how she dealt with the lack of inspiration:

> It has been more than a year now that I have been writing these pieces every week. And this week, as every week, I have come smack bang up against a crisis. Annihilation even.

Because I know myself to be completely incapable of writing an article. This is the most terrible feeling, of panic and desolation, of terror, of the most awful loss.

I have compared notes with other writers about this chronic recurring paralysis of the talent and find that it is common.

I suppose that ought to help, but in the grip of the paralysis it doesn't seem to be of any consolation at all … I ought to take the washing in from the line. I ought to unpack the groceries. I ought to have a real archaeological exploration of the midden accumulating in the rooms of my children, since nobody has two socks of the same colour or underwear or student passes for buses or anything. I ought to give up smoking, but my doctor knew I had to write this article today and has given me a period of grace which lasts until I go to bed tonight. At least that gives me something to write about next week. What I should be doing, of course, is writing this article.

Clift, in Silvester, 1997, pp. 401–2

This is all very well for a writer who has the ability to turn the humdrum into something compelling, and who can make a virtue out of writer's block, but not every writer has that kind of gift. Columnists can respond to that challenge by becoming versatile and adaptable with their topic choices and the way they write. Alternatively, many of the big-name conservative columnists return to familiar themes, including the science of climate change, the shortcomings of the ABC or the blinkered view of progressive columnists in other media outlets. The progressive columnists, on the other hand, have their own pet subjects, which often include what conservative columnists have to say. But the goal linking both sides of the ideological divide is the need to have an audience. Online responses are the lifeblood of every columnist. Provoking fierce agreement or furious disagreement is what helps drive a columnist's profile. 'Reasonable' columnists have their place, but they are not going to provoke readers' reactions, simply because most people are reasonable and do not feel the need to tell others when they agree with them. This does not, however, mean that columnists need to manufacture synthetic indignation, although some feel the need to do so. Former Fairfax columnist Sally Loane spoke of a trend where controversy is valued above reason in the art of the column:

[T]here seems to be no place for people who have a pragmatic view … Now I used to write columns and I felt that I was neither a screecher for the right nor the left and I felt very vulnerable because of that. And I know other columnists too who don't have columns any more because they do not fall into that category of instantly creating controversy …

Loane, in Henderson, 2004, p. 34

While there might be an argument about how 'controversial' a columnist can be, there is certainly no tolerance for one who is boring. A boring column—one that neither informs nor entertains—is an instant turn-off for any reader. To avoid boring their readers, columnists need to build an argument and use powerful prose (Lee, 2004, p. 93). To achieve this, they should look at the breadth of a particular subject—the pros, cons, drawbacks and advantages. This needs an investment in research that supports both sides of the argument.

Good columnists present a sound argument, based on facts, for their position. Putting both sides of an argument does not disqualify the columnist from having an opinion. They need to assemble the arguments in a way that supports their opinion and their conclusion. They are in the business of trying to persuade readers who don't agree with them or those who are looking for more specific information about a topic.

Using the right kind of prose—often words that are categorical or declamatory, rather than qualifying or equivocal—reinforces the impact of an argument. For example, a columnist supporting the introduction of health warnings on wine casks about a safe level of alcohol consumption might claim 'the change was necessary to deal with the appalling spectacle of teenage drinking and adults making a poor example of themselves with their flagrant over-consumption of wine in most social circumstances'. Note the use of words such as 'necessary', 'appalling' and 'flagrant'. These are strong and emotive words that leave the reader in no doubt about the columnist's view.

Consider the alternative, written by someone who is not sure what they think about the topic and is therefore cautious about taking up a position. This could be aggravated by a lack of knowledge or an innate reservation about overstating their case: 'The introduction of such a warning may make a difference to a problem that some critics appear to think is rampant in certain sections of teenage society.' It sounds reasonable, but it is neither powerful nor persuasive. The sentence uses the words 'may', 'some' and 'appear'—words that equivocate.

Language is vital to the clear expression of an argument, but it is a challenge to achieve the correct balance between hyperbole and persuasion. Language must never take the argument hostage. The great turn-off for readers is to start a column and find that it is a rant about a particular topic, an opinion without facts, driven only by passion and prejudice. Readers need to feel confident that the columnist is at least trying to engage with the topic they are writing about. This is the responsible approach for the columnist to adopt. The right words, chosen carefully, will reinforce an argument.

To whom

Audience is a critical part of a columnist's appeal. Susie O'Brien, for example, writes about women and family issues in the *Herald Sun*. Her audience is especially mums, and she writes from the standpoint of an intelligent, working mother who empathises with other mums' predicaments. Her audience is not the same as that of Katherine Murphy in *The Guardian*, whose political column is a finely attuned reading of what has occurred, or what is occurring, in Canberra. Her audience is those who have a high degree of interest in, and appreciation of, politics, economics and the national debate.

On occasion, columnists can actually reach a new audience by writing outside their specialised area. Peter Bowers, one of the finest political journalists of his generation, once wrote a column about the number of odd socks he had collected in his sock draw. He claimed it was his most popular column.

How

This brings us to the third consideration—how a columnist makes their point. Many columnists have a straight-up-and-down style that suits the laying-out of facts and the shaping of an argument. But there are some, particularly lifestyle columnists, who favour a more conversational style. This is entirely appropriate for the subject matter. The column is meant to invite people into the columnist's world and give them an insight into a life. It would be inappropriate for a sports columnist, such as Patrick Smith in *The Australian*, to write his column in the style of *The Age's* fortnightly columnist novelist Anson Cameron. Similarly the inspired and occasionally anarchic tone of Cameron's column would be inappropriate for the economics commentator Ross Gittins, who writes a column for the *Sydney Morning Herald*. So the style of expression is an important consideration when preparing to write a column.

How often

The final consideration is crucial to understanding exactly what role the columnist occupies in the context of the publication in which their column appears. The difference between a weekly columnist and an expert who writes an infrequent column is the frequency of their writing. For example, Miranda Devine's twice-weekly column for News Ltd tabloids differs from the occasional opinion piece from defence analyst Hugh White in that one occurs weekly and the other only when the *Sydney Morning Herald* or *The Age's* opinion editor needs a column about defence. But White is effectively still writing a column; what distinguishes him from Devine is that he has expertise (and a reputation as a defence expert) to bring to a particular area. Devine might have areas of expertise, but she is not a specialist. The world is her patch, and she needs that broad scope to provide material for a weekly column. There are not sufficient weekly issues in defence to ensure that White has enough material for a weekly column.

So writers who want to be weekly columnists have to be confident that they have something to say every week. Occasional columnists need only to have something to say on infrequent occasions. Readers will turn to expert columnists because of their knowledge in their specialised areas. Readers will turn to weekly columnists because they want to know what the columnist thinks about a given issue. The distinction is vitally important in analysing the work of the current range of columnists.

Types of columns and columnists

Columnists can be categorised into the types of people you might find at any social gathering.

The shouters

These are the strident commentators who have something provocative to say about most things. Their enemy is usually complacency and the status quo. Think Miranda Devine, Andrew Bolt, Phillip Adams, Elizabeth Farrelly and Rita Panahi. They are usually identified with a particular world view (that is, left-wing or right-wing). Their relentless determination and the consistency of their view about a set of disparate issues, ranging from the fortunes of the prime minister (any incumbent) to immigration, guarantee they will have an audience.

They often appear to be perverse, but their perceived perversity helps drive reaction. And their newspapers try to expand their profile and the interaction with their audience by enabling the columnist to have a blog, where they can continue dialogue and debate. These columnists contain few surprises for the reasonable reader, who can easily anticipate the sense of outrage that often permeates their work, regardless of the topic.

The clue to a columnist's success often lies in the fact that they have worked out what the broad community view on a certain issue is and so they fulfil expectations by often taking up the contrary stance. Superficially, this might appear to be a cynical piece of posturing, but these columnists believe what they write. They believe their role is to ensure that the majority of people consider alternative arguments and different points of view. These columnists see themselves, therefore, as evidence of a healthy democracy. They want us to agree with them, but it doesn't matter to them if we don't. They just want to make sure their argument is heard, and they will use passionate language to ensure that this is the case.

The whisperers

Gossip columnists are those people who mutter behind their hands, 'Have you heard about ...?' They often rely on innuendo, anonymity of sources and implied trysts, suspected outcomes and speculated career moves. Think Annette Sharp. The gossip column culture in Australia is a pale imitation of the great diary column tradition of England's Fleet Street, or of the page six columns that appear in *The New York Post*. The difference is simple: Britain has an aristocracy and the United States has a culture of celebrity. Australia has neither the aristocrats nor the celebrities to make its gossip columns anything other than a mild expression of the social scandal that constantly simmers in the other societies.

Another difficulty for such columnists in Australia is that they are often constrained by legal considerations. As we discussed in Chapter 9, Australia's defamation laws are strict enough to inhibit speculation about criminal activity or sexual and financial transgressions among the rich and famous. The consequence for those readers searching for salacious gossip is obvious, but it is not a bad thing for those readers who have no interest in anyone's private life, other than their own.

There are variations on these columns. For instance, Melbourne's society columnist Lillian Frank, who was a celebrity socialite and fundraiser herself, was known for not saying anything nasty about anyone she featured in her weekly column in the *Herald Sun*, which was a remarkable achievement.

The sages

Then there are the experts, the big brains, the wise men and women who do not deal only in opinion but deliver mainly analysis, usually political. Think Laurie Oakes (formerly in *The Bulletin* and most recently in the News Corp Saturday papers, not in his incarnation at Channel 9), Paul Kelly, Michelle Grattan, Peter Hartcher and Michael Gordon. Readers, especially those interested in politics, turn to them for information, understanding and analysis, and sometimes for their ability to gauge how well a government or opposition is performing.

The important point about these columnists is that they have extensive experience in their area and a vast range of contacts to call on to help them negotiate their way through specialist topics or situations. These columnists have gravitas and credibility and, as such, their positions in the paper are revered.

The next group of sages are the special experts, those who can be wheeled out to write an opinion on a running story in a short time. This is a difficult task because it demands expertise and the journalistic ability to write to length (between 750 and 1000 words) and to deadline, usually within four to five hours. The expert has to have the time to write such a column and the capacity to render their expertise—whether it is in defence, drugs in sport, or rock music—accessible to a broad audience.

The gurus

These are the people readers turn to for specialised life advice. Think David Herbert on simple and tasty cooking, Susan Kurosawa on travel, and Debi Enker on television. They have skills and experience in the areas they write about. They are specialists who work in broad areas of human activity and interest.

These specialists can be subject to trends in consumer demand. For example, gardening experts are never out of style, but there was a time when every major publication had a relationships column. That is less common now, largely, it would seem, because of the existence of the 'average Joe/Jo' columnist.

The average Joe/Jo

These columnists set out to convince readers that they, like them, live a plain and ordinary life. Connection is the key word here—it is all about saying something unique about the mundane. This is sometimes contained in a column by a celebrity (think radio personalities Chrissie Swan and Fifi Box) or in a column written by someone who just feels they've got something to say about family life (think Nikki Gemmell). These columns are about voyeurism as therapy; that is, readers empathise with the columnist's predicament because it might echo their own situation. This type of column, too, can fall prey to fashion.

English columnist Zoe Heller noted some years ago that the 'girl column' had fallen out of favour as it became trapped in repetition and self-parody. Heller identified three kinds of girl columns during the genre's heyday:

- the good-humoured home-front column ('Mum, Johnny's stuck a marble up his nose')
- the comment piece built upon the feminist point of view ('When was the last time the Foreign Secretary changed a nappy?')
- the daffy girl piece ('Never try shaving your legs in a moving taxi')—think Helen Fielding of *Bridget Jones* fame.

Heller, 1999, pp. 10–11

Part of the problem with the average Joe/Jo columns is that there are a good number of readers who are openly hostile to reading about someone else's life on their favourite website. For every group of readers who find the travails of the daffy single (male or female) compelling, there are many readers who do not understand the fuss.

In truth, the columnist is often dramatising—and sometimes fictionalising—their own life. Drama is injected to add appeal and interest; fiction is added to protect the family or the innocent, or perhaps, in a few cases, to embellish the writer. Such options are not desirable for the shouters, the whisperers, the sages or the gurus. It would be anathema to them. But readers forgive the average Joe/Jo such manipulations in the interests of a good read, even though they can grow tired of such columns.

Bloggers

The internet has transformed many personal columns into a web log, or blog. Many of the mainstream columnists in metropolitan papers now have thriving blogs, driven by a vocal and loyal readership that switches seamlessly between print and online.

The range of blogs carrying column-style material has virtues and drawbacks. There is virtue in the fact that the number of published voices has increased significantly. However, the drawback is that few blogs demonstrate the rigour of research and writing that goes into the production of credible columns. The most telling example of this was the proliferation of blogs—and in particular, Facebook sites—during the 2016 US presidential election. There was a significant amount of online commentary that was demonstrably wrong and driven by a fierce partisan perspective that deliberately avoided the basic principles of fairness, research and balance. British analysis of far-right commentary during the presidential campaign identified a hub in Hungary that was home to a network of US-focused websites and Facebook groups that promoted Republican candidate Donald Trump and denigrated his Democrat rival Hillary Clinton (Townsend, 2017).

It emphasises the point that bloggers—and those who follow them—have a potential international audience far greater than a columnist working for an Australian newspaper or magazine can command. And unlike newspaper columnists, bloggers write (or post) when they have something to say, rather than having to meet a deadline or fill a hole on the opinion pages. Even so, the most established blogs are those published for internet magazines or publications (Simons, 2007, p. 221). Established is, of course, different to being influential. And it is feasible that the eruption of what could be dubbed 'toxic' blogging and 'fake news' that eddied through a number of websites in 2016 had an important role to play in the presidential campaign.

Summary

o Columns are about the columnists: what they think, how they live and who they know.

o Columnists write to be heard.

o Columnists need to think ahead.

o Columnists need to think about what they are going to say and to whom.

o Expert columnists write when they need (or are asked) to express their expert opinion.

o Most weekly columnists need to research a range of topics because they are not experts. They are usually generalists.

Questions

1 What are the four considerations for a columnist?
2 What helps advance the columnist's argument?
3 Find the blog of one of the 'shouters'. Read some of the reader responses and try to work out how you would reply to the favourable comments, and then the critical comments.

Activities

1 Pick two 'shouters' from the same publication published on different days. Consider their style and expression. Which columnist creates the more engaging and convincing case for you, the reader? How did they do that?
2 Think about the topic or issue that you know most or care most about. Go online and try to find a columnist (or blog) that writes about that subject. Critique the column: How would you improve it? Does it cover all you know? Did you learn something from it?
3 Find a columnist you disagree with. Now write a 750-word response, addressing each of the points they have made in one of their columns.

References and additional reading

Heller, Z. (1999). 'Girl columns', in S. Glover (ed.) *The Penguin Book of Journalism*, London: Penguin, pp. 10–17.

Henderson, G. (2004). 'Gerard Henderson's media watch', *The Sydney Institute Quarterly*, Issue 23, Vol. 8, No. 2, July.

Lee, C. (ed.) (2004). *Power Prose*, Melbourne: Hardie Grant.

MacArthur, B. (2004). 'Ego trips full of passion that set the tone for newspapers', *The Times*, 27 February.

Ryan, D. (2003). *The Messenger*, Adelaide: Wakefield Press.

Silvester, C. (ed.) (1997). *The Penguin Book of Columnists*, London: Penguin.

Simons, M. (2007). *The Contentmakers*, Melbourne: Penguin.

Townsend, M., (2017). 'Britain's extremist bloggers helping the "alt-right" go global, report finds,' *The Observer*, 12 February, https://www.theguardian.com/uk-news/2017/feb/11/how-britains-extremist-bloggers-helped-the-alt-right-go-global

Case study

Wendy Tuohy on tackling the hard subjects

Publication details:

'Rougher, harder, violent: how porn is warping the male mind', by Wendy Tuohy, *RendezView* website, published 24 July 2015, http://www.dailytelegraph.com.au/rendezview/rougher-harder-violent-how-porn-is-warping-the-male-mind/news-story/504698ce318f551052847f13ac678fd1.

The author:

Wendy Tuohy is a *Herald Sun* journalist, feature writer and columnist. Having started as a school-leaver cadet at *The Age* in the 1980s, Wendy has worked as a reporter and feature writer, section editor and news desk manager (deputy COS) in nearly 20 years at *The Age* and nearly 10 years at the *Herald Sun*. She is a fill-in host on ABC Radio Melbourne and appears regularly on Channel Nine's *Today Extra* and *A Current Affair*, and ABC TV's *News Breakfast* program, as a news commentator.

The story:

I wrote my piece 'Rougher, harder, more violent' for the News Ltd online comment site *RendezView* after seeing the youth sexuality educator Maree Crabbe present research at a VicHealth forum on preventing violence against women. It was clear to me from the statistics and findings from local and international research as outlined by Maree that many parents and non (current) porn-users probably had little to no idea what is common in contemporary 'adult' videos.

As the topics I write comment articles about are mostly focused on issues impacting on women and girls, this subject stood out to me as something about which many people have outdated ideas. Few people who do not watch contemporary porn have a good understanding of what is commonly considered 'run of the mill' treatment of women. Many parents think of 'porn' as the kind of racy *Playboy* stuff they saw in their own adolescence, and having listened to Maree I realised that many probably have no idea about what their children are seeing—even if they don't go looking for it—or how to talk to children about what they see.

While I'm not against porn globally, and have written about the 'Make Love Not Porn' movement (consensual home-made porn that doesn't involve seriously demeaning acts performed on women by multiple men while the woman is restrained, for example), I was disturbed by what I heard at Maree's presentation; that quite high levels of violence against women are considered normal is extremely concerning. I've revisited Maree as a source of information about adolescent mental and sexual health several times since this event.

My aim with this piece was to get some of the stand-out statistics out there to the wider audience and make them think about what is healthy: that 88 per cent of scenes in the most popular porn include physical aggression such as gagging, choking and slapping of women. That women were slapped in 75 per cent of those scenes etc. I then wanted to try to engage people in questioning if we take it for granted now that porn has become very violent in nature towards women, and whether this was really OK, especially for young people learning about sex via porn (as statistics show many do).

While some columnists can make a very convincing argument even if they don't necessarily 'believe' the argument they are making, this is not one of my skills and I write exclusively about stances I authentically feel matter. I have three kids 18 and under at the time of writing and this subject does matter to me. However I always try, as I did in this article, to 'bring people along' and bring them around to seeing my argument rather than hectoring them.

I took a persuasive approach with this piece: starting with the strong expert statistics alerting people to things they may not know, but should know to my mind, and then backed it up with grassroots statements from the porn actor 'Anthony Hardwood'—whose comments about porn once being about 'lovey-dovey sex' but now being about 'destroying' a woman I considered very powerful. The fact he is making a living from porn, so could have defended it exactly as it is being made, but chose to express honest concerns about how porn treats women now stood out to me as a stronger way to support my argument than a generalisation by me. I then used some research from Relationships Australia (an expert body on relationships research)—timely material from visiting sex-positive 'porn disruptor' Cindy Gallop.

One of the strongest ways there is to scaffold a stance in an opinion piece, to my mind, is to let other people with more knowledge and expertise speak facts they have researched or proven, rather than to make blanket statements as a third party (writer/observer). Every time I write an opinion piece I look first for expert opinion to give ballast and credibility.

I always try to get at least three, but preferably four or five other references into an opinion column to reinforce my own stance and illustrate that there is an actual issue here, I am not making it up!

Though I make a big effort to lend my articles weight by citing other evidence, as a female columnist working on a platform with a very wide, mass audience—many of whom do not comment, but those who do being frequently aggressive in their tone—I am always ready for negative responses.

Some readers of our platforms have concluded I am a 'feminazi' and react to every one of my pieces in very strong, negative and personal language. For a younger woman writer this would very likely be a very confronting experience, but I am now quite used to this, and while I don't chase the angry comments I don't shy away from subjects out of concern they will come.

Over the years I've moved through the following stages: shocked that people are so furious when a woman dares say something (in moderate language) that they don't like, then keen to engage with commenters to try to persuade them I have what I consider the greater good at heart and hope they can understand that, to no longer engaging with the nastiest men who comment on my articles and finally to no longer reading them at all.

I don't want to self-censor in order to allay potential personal criticism; I think that would be extremely harmful to my credibility as someone ready to say things even if a proportion of the readership will definitely attack me for doing so. Though some of the language I have read in comments made towards me previously has been clearly chosen to try to intimidate me or shut me up (or shut me down) I've realised the loudest commenters attacking me are also right across our platforms attacking women writers generally. This was very liberating as I realised that to try to bring them on board or make myself better understood by them was futile, so don't waste time trying.

I never avoid a subject out of fear but I know I will need to definitely avoid comments on anything I write on the following topics: women's right to choose, the gender pay gap, workforce equality generally, sexual harassment (even straight-out statistical reports of it that I may comment on are treated as fabricated and slanted/biased against men) and family violence.

I do not believe it would be easier for younger columnists, even those raised on social media and used to the often gloves-off tone, to deal with some of the things said commonly in comments on opinion pieces written by women. I think they, and we all, need to make sure we are as OK as we think we are—sometimes a comment will cut through the static and make you feel authentically terrible for a minute.

The best possible advice though, and three words that have completely freed me from anxiety about what may be said to me or about me were offered to me by another columnist: consider the source.

Is the source of something really vile and personal, said with little to no reference to the actual article and aimed solely at hurting you—possibly just for the sake of it—really worth taking seriously? Usually, the answer is no.

Writing sample

Rougher, harder, violent: how porn is warping the male mind

By Wendy Tuohy, *RendezView* website, 24 July 2015

Rougher, harder, more violent: even those who fancy porn as legitimate entertainment are being urged to understand rapidly escalating aggression towards women in mainstream porn makes it a violence issue that can't be ignored.

Statistics around how violence towards women has become the most commonly viewed porn are alarming: according to Australian adolescent sexuality expert and researcher Maree Crabbe, recent analysis of the 'most popular' porn found 88 per cent of scenes included physical aggression such as gagging, choking and slapping.

In 94 per cent of those scenes the aggression was directed towards women. Women were slapped in 75 per cent of those scenes. There was verbal aggression in 48 per cent of scenes.

For a glimpse of how much popular porn has changed in the last decade, try this quote from LA-based porn actor Anthony Hardwood (interviewed for Crabbe's recent Australian documentary *Love and Sex in the Age of Porn*).

Hardwood told the film-makers he had seen porn change dramatically since his beginnings in 1997 when it simply involved 'making love on a bed', and confirmed what Crabbe had discovered elsewhere—that rougher 'Gonzo' porn had left the fringe and replaced old-school stylised porn sex.

'You know when I started it was like very lovey dovey sex, not tough like Gonzo,' says Hardwood.

'After three years they wanted to get more energy, more rough, they do like one girl with you know like four guys and they just take over and destroy her.'

Little by little, slapping women around and 'destroying' them sexually has come to be normalised in sex entertainment. Ironically, Relationships Australia warned this week that intimacy in one in five Australian relationships is being impacted by internet porn consumption.

The national counselling service found readily accessible online porn is leading to a breakdown of trust and an erosion of intimacy in about 21 per cent of all relationships and pornography consumption is also increasingly being cited as a reason for marriage breakdowns.

Crabbe's warning about the extreme nature of, and normalised violence in, most mainstream porn also coincides with the speaking tour of Australia by Cindy Gallop, former advertising guru and now self-described 'porn disruptor' and founder of a movement to try to promote healthy porn, the #realworldsex website MakeLoveNotPorn.

Her startup, MakeLoveNotPorn.tv, prides itself on being 'of the people, by the people, and for the people who believe that the sex we have in our everyday life is the hottest sex there is'.

Users submit their 'real world sex' videos, and also rent other people's in what is hoped to be a satisfying transaction for all involved.

Gallop's world of more democratic porn intersected with Maree Crabbe's research-based warnings about the content of industrial porn when Crabbe phoned ABC radio recently during a long interview given by Gallop.

Unfortunately Gallop did not have time to address the serious issues raised by Crabbe's statistics around the promotion of violence against women in mainstream porn—the porn whose standards Gallop is attempting to disrupt.

However she had earlier described the rise of Gonzo porn as 'driven by a bunch of guys seriously scared they're not making money, doing what the other guys are doing who are making money', thinking 'that's what's making money that's what we will do'.

Crabbe's concern that extreme (now normalised) porn is where the money is should worry all who hope to reduce violence against women in and outside the home: not only has porn become the main sex educator of adolescents according to many health experts, degradation of women is stock in trade of the stuff that sells.

As Crabbe told VicHealth's audience of anti-violence policy influencers: 'For all its professed diversity, mainstream porn tends to communicate messages of male aggression and female sexual subservience.

'Often times it eroticises the degradation of women and male brutality.'

She said the influence of pornography means girls are increasingly being asked—or expected—to follow that script in real life, even if it's not what they want or is painful or degrading.

Denying the prevalence of porn (whose use accounts for 30 per cent of internet traffic and a global industry making $25 billion a year) is useless. It's here to stay and for many it's a completely routine part of life.

But if he's getting off on slapping and abusing her, and she thinks she must act like it's OK, then people we have issues.

17

Long-form Writing: Creative Non-fiction

'You're gonna be a great writer someday, Gordie. You might even write about us guys if you ever get hard-up for material.'

from *Stand by Me* by Raynold Gideon & Bruce A. Evans (1986) (screenplay), based on the novel by Stephen King

Objectives

As you have made your way through the first chapters of this book, you've been given the tools you need to write a great feature article. But what if you have found a story that won't be confined to a few hundred or a couple of thousand words? Then you need to move into the world of creative non-fiction and write a book. This chapter covers:

o   the world of books

o   the market

o   understanding creative non-fiction

o   publication styles

o   features versus books: similarities and differences

o   a Case study: Lee Gutkind, the godfather of creative non-fiction

o   a Writing sample: *Almost Human: Making Robots Think* (Chapter 1) by Lee Gutkind, 2006.

Going the distance

The term 'creative non-fiction' has been mentioned more than a few times in this book. It refers to a genre of writing with its roots in literary or New Journalism, and covers publication styles as diverse as memoir, feature article and biography. Creative non-fiction involves writing about true events using techniques normally associated with fiction writing, such as crafting dialogue, scenes and detailed descriptions of character and place. It sometimes goes by the name 'narrative non-fiction'. But although there may be some novelistic or artistic flair in the storytelling, the 'creative' in creative non-fiction is not a pejorative term: it is just another way of reflecting the means of telling a story. In the internet era, the phrase 'long form' has become more common, to capture the distinction between the short and ephemeral information on the Web with the more substantial and textured long-form information. This has particular connections to the multimedia storytelling we discussed in Chapter 1. But the fundamental approaches—and the end results—are all the same. We are, in Matthew Ricketson's phrase, 'telling true stories' (Ricketson, 2014). Famous writers who have done this at length include Gay Talese, Truman Capote, Susanna Kaysen, Bill Bryson, Mark Bowden and Susan Orlean (Blair, 2007). Some of their work appeared in magazines, while others pursued the book path. While there are fewer opportunities for long features (beyond 1500 words) to appear in mainstream media because publications just don't have the advertising-supported space any more, there are some wonderful opportunities to write longer pieces for a range of websites or turn a great idea into a book. The techniques for both a 3000-word feature and a non-fiction book are similar: they both demand a determination to peel back the layers that a basic news report or short feature can rarely achieve. Long-form journalism, narrative non-fiction, creative non-fiction—whatever you choose to call it—burrows in to a topic, an issue or an individual. It is about revealing depths. The reader embarks on it knowing they are getting something that will not only inform them, but probably challenge their thinking. 'Because narrative non-fiction dives deep into the grey areas of human experience and because it makes such a powerful impact on readers it necessarily prompts complex and knotty issues,' Ricketson writes (2014, p. 235). And that means the writer needs to be on top of their material, confident in how they use it, and observe the obligations attached to journalism's priority to deal in verifiable information.

While you can use the techniques of creative non-fiction in your feature articles, this genre of writing is particularly suited to book-length journalism. This chapter will reveal the opportunities book publishing presents, and advise how you can equip yourself with the tools for writing creative non-fiction. It will also discuss what styles of writing you might like to employ.

The market

They say that within every journalist there is a book (or at least the desire to write one). If you are among the many people who want to see their name emblazoned on the front cover of a best-seller, your journalistic skills have prepared you well for the journey. While many people want to write the great Australian novel, it is the great Australian non-fiction book that is the most likely to be published. In 2015, for example, 45 per cent of books bought by Australians were non-fiction, compared to 24 per cent fiction and 30 per cent children's books, the industry monitor Nielsen Bookscan found (Wilson, 2016). Putting aside the cookbooks, gardening tomes and self-help bibles, there is a sizeable market for compelling creative non-fiction.

Nikki Gemmell is a successful Australian novelist who started her writing career in journalism. Her novels include *Cleave*, *Lovesong* and *The Bride Stripped Bare*. Gemmell has also written creative non-fiction and she acknowledges the opportunities provided by mixing non-fiction with book-length writing: 'I think there is an even bigger market for creative non-fiction than fiction now, it certainly seems to be the buzz in the publishing world' (Gemmell, in Blair 2007).

Gemmell's speculation appears to be correct. In the United States, non-fiction is outselling fiction by around 100 million books a year. Michael Coffey, Executive Managing Editor of *Publishers Weekly*, said, 'Fiction seems to have lost a lot of authority in the culture. People now look more toward true stories as something that justifies the expense of their time' (Kloberdanz et al., 2006, p. 52).

The non-fiction boom is not just in overseas markets, but also in Australia where authors such as Robert Drewe, Helen Garner, Rob Mundle, Peter FitzSimons, David Hunt and Sophie Cunningham tell Australian stories. As New Journalism founder Tom Wolfe (2005) said, 'The publishers are crying out for these books [creative non-fiction] because this form is never going to be out of style.'

Understanding creative non-fiction

'Creative non-fiction' is a term that sets one group of non-fiction books apart from the others. In the publishing world, creative non-fiction books are those that are narrative in form (literary journalism, memoir, biography etc.) rather than purely informative (cookbooks, how-to books, encyclopaedias, instruction manuals etc.).

You can tell you are reading creative non-fiction when it is almost indistinguishable from a novel—the only difference being that the non-fiction work is completely factual.

In creative non-fiction books you'll notice that the writer's point of view is often used (especially in literary journalism and memoir). Creative non-fiction writers will also use a descriptive narrative structure. This means their story will generally have a beginning, middle and end, and be structured for theme and interest, rather than by what information is most important. These writers also borrow language and literary devices from fiction writers to ensure their work is interesting and enjoyable to read.

In creative non-fiction you'll also discover characters that readers can visualise and empathise with—you should have a real emotional response to the people described in these books (after all, it is often only because you care about the characters that you'll bother finishing a book). This differs from many feature stories, where people are sometimes used only as sources of information, rather than for who they are. You'll also see that writers will include large portions of dialogue—conversations between two or more characters—rather than just the odd quote here and there.

An important element of many creative non-fiction books is that they provide an explanation of *why* something happened (rather than just describing *what* happened). Writers will examine all the factors that culminated in a situation and try to make sense of it for the readers.

Finally, what creative non-fiction writers strive to do is to tell an engaging story while telling the truth. The story may read like a novel, but it cannot and must not ever fabricate, change or embellish anything. If you are writing non-fiction, you must not lie to your readers—it is completely unethical. Apart from finding that your conscience is keeping you awake at night, if you make up parts of your story you will probably get caught—even if you fabricate just the tiniest detail. The last thing you want is to work your way to the top of the best-seller list, become the toast of the literary world, be interviewed by Oprah and then be exposed as a fraud. This is what happened to James Frey, author of *A Million Little Pieces*. When the lies and exaggerations in his books were revealed, Frey was publicly humiliated.

Publication styles

There is a wide range of publication styles for creative non-fiction—too many to list here. But three common styles you'll find at almost any bookshop are literary journalism, memoir and biography.

Literary journalism

Books that fall into this category usually have a journalistic feel, but they are also engaging, character-based and written using the techniques of the fiction writer. They will also usually try to explain not just how something occurred, but why.

Literary journalism covers travel writing, true crime, war coverage, social commentary and many other topics of narrative-based non-fiction. Examples of books of literary journalism include *In Cold Blood* by Truman Capote, *Joe Cinque's Consolation* by Helen Garner, and *Black Hawk Down* by Mark Bowden.

Memoir

This publication style is all about you. In a memoir you detail your life, or sections of it, for your readers. Memoir is all about baring your soul, your deepest and darkest secrets, your successes and your failures, your family and your friends (which sometimes means you could lose a couple of mates once they've read your book). The real difference between memoir and literary journalism is that memoir focuses on you and how you experienced an event, rather than on the event itself. Examples of memoirs are *Girl Interrupted* by Susanna Kaysen, *The Life and Times of the Thunderbolt Kid: A Memoir* by Bill Bryson and *Almost French* by Sarah Turnbull.

Biography

This is really just one long, detailed profile piece. The same rules apply, only more so. You need to truly understand the person you are writing about. You must visit the places where they lived, speak to the people they knew, go through their old correspondence, and research every facet of their existence. Essentially, you need to eat, sleep and breathe the life of the person you are writing about. This means you need access to this person (if they are still alive; their relatives and friends if they are deceased) and their world. You will find unauthorised biographies of celebrities on the shelves, but it is rare that these books reach any real understanding of the person—it is very difficult to accurately portray someone if you only have access to what others have written about them and to people who aren't part of the celebrity's inner circle. Examples of biographies are *Schulz and Peanuts: A Biography* by David Michaelis, *Paul Jennings* by Matthew Ricketson and *The Rise and Rise of Kerry Packer* by Paul Barry.

Features versus books: similarities and differences

Now that you know there is a marketplace for non-fiction books and are aware of the different styles of creative non-fiction, how do you get started? The first thing you need to understand is that you already have all the skills you need; it's just a matter of pushing them in a slightly different direction.

Ideas

So you want to write a book, but you don't have an idea yet? You'll find that the same techniques you use for finding feature stories also work for book-length writing. The only real difference is that you'll need to find a story that will last for somewhere between 60,000 and 200,000 words. This means you need to come up with an idea that has depth, conflict and detail. You also need an idea that excites you. Writing a book can sometimes take a year or two, or even longer. You need a story that will keep you interested for all that time (and that will keep your readers interested from the first page until the last). Sometimes that will mean engaging with a range of interview subjects, just like a piece of journalism but with more time spent on talking to each subject about their own lives and the events surrounding the time when they intersect with the larger story you're writing about. If you are writing a historical book —a piece of social history, for example, such as the biography of a feminist in Australia during the 1960s—you will need to find the relevant documents, whether it is newspaper coverage, state archives or the person's correspondence in the National Library of Australia so that you can learn more about who she talked to, who she knew and the social circumstances of the time.

All writers need to read. To publish in newspapers, you need to read newspapers. To publish in magazines, you need to read magazines. Strangely enough, if you want to write a creative non-fiction book, you will have to read a few of these books. Find a publication style that appeals to you (perhaps literary journalism or memoir is your passion) and read as much as you can. You'll begin to see how much information you need to write an entire book, which ideas really work and what falls flat.

Also, research the authors of books you have enjoyed. You'll find that many writers have websites that detail their work and often will describe how they discovered the story that became their book. You can also look for articles on your favourite authors or books on the internet, either through basic searches or by using news databases like Factiva.

Finally, look at your own life. Everyone has a story to tell—maybe you have experienced something others would be interested in hearing about, or maybe the lives of your parents, grandparents or friends are rich sources of book material. Whether you are 18 or 80, you have the potential to write a book and the pages can be ripped from your own experiences.

Research

The research techniques you have learned in this book will be as useful to you in writing book-length non-fiction as they are in your career as a feature writer. Edward Southorn is a newspaper journalist who went on to write a creative non-fiction book: *You Should've Been Here Yesterday: Tales from Surfing Mythology*. Through his journey into this new field, he found that no matter what style or genre he was writing in, he had to be vigilant with research: 'I think both of them [journalism and creative non-fiction] require you to not be lazy and to get out there and do the bloody work and find all the info' (Southorn, in Blair, 2007). He says he uses the tools he learned in his creative non-fiction in his journalism and vice-versa: 'I think they're very complementary. You have to make sure what you put down there is right and if you make any claims you have to be able to back them up with a solid point of view' (Southorn, in Blair, 2007).

Approach

The way you should approach writing a book or a feature article is almost identical. You think about your readers and your topic, do your research, conduct interviews, create a thematic structure, utilise literary devices and write a well-crafted story. The only major difference is the word-count.

Two Walkley Award-winning feature writers who have published numerous best-selling creative non-fiction books are Helen Garner and Hugh Lunn. They agree that you can approach these two publication styles in the same way. Garner (in Blair, 2007) explains that no matter what you are writing, 'You just go in there, poke your nose around, see what you can find and then write it down in the most interesting way you can.' Lunn also sees no differences:

> What I think when I sit down to write a feature is that I have to tell people something they
> didn't know before. And that's what I think about when I sit down to write a book and that's the
> only thing I think about.
>
> Lunn, in Blair, 2007

Structure

When you structure your book, you think along the same lines as you do for a feature article. You match the theme with anecdotes, quotes, facts and description, and you create the most interesting structure possible.

In the following quote, Hugh Lunn reminds us that to produce interesting stories you must not just rely on a chronological structure or other simple order of events:

> The people who can't write and can't write memoirs say stuff like 'I went to primary school and
> then I went to play cricket and then I went to secondary school and then I passed my exams and
> then I went to university' and that's how they write. But what I'm trying to do is avoid that and
> recapture a time and capture some interesting characters.
>
> Lunn, in Blair, 2007

For example, Lunn's book *Over the Top with Jim* (1999) is structured around his relationship with school friend James Egoroff, rather than other, perhaps closer, relationships. This is because this friendship reflected the themes and images wound into the story.

Many creative non-fiction books rely on a narrative structure. The term 'narrative' comes from the Latin *narrar*—to tell the particulars of an event—and really means storytelling. The director of the Nieman Narrative Program at Harvard University, Mark Kramer, describes narrative succinctly and comprehensively:

> At a minimum, narrative denotes writing with (A) set scenes, (B) characters, (C) action that
> unfolds over time, (D) the interpretable voice of a teller—a narrator with a somewhat discern-
> able personality—and (E) some sense of relationship to the reader, viewer or listener, which, all
> arrayed, (F) lead the audience toward a point, realisation or destination.

The thing to remember is that you are trying to transport your reader to the place and time of your story—and to do this you will need to develop a structure (whether that be narrative or thematic) that entices the reader into this other world.

Writer's point of view

Creative non-fiction often stands apart from many feature articles in its use of the fiction-writing technique of first-person point of view (though, as we discussed in chapters 5 and 6, some features are also written in the first person). Point of view 'is the presentation of a particular scene through the eyes of one or more characters. It is the writer's device for opening up a character to the reader' (Forrest, 1997, p. 22). In the case of creative non-fiction, the use of the first-person point of view is the writer's way of channelling the story through their own perceptions.

Donna Lee Brien, the head of the School of Arts & Creative Enterprise at Central Queensland University in Rockhampton, says using this technique will encourage people to read your work:

> I think it is quite true to say about all creative non-fiction that the first person point of view of the 'I' is either totally explicit or totally implicit … and that's another one of my reasons why readers really like creative non-fiction.

Brien, in Blair, 2007

Brien also points out that it is the use of this personal point of view that lends credibility to creative non-fiction. She states that, unlike some journalism that carries no byline, or some historical writing where the author writes as if omnipotent, the work of creative non-fiction writers lays bare their biases and the limits of their understanding:

> And some of that more pure non-fiction is almost written as if it's universal, even though it's written by one person and analysed by one person it's almost like 'this is what's happened, and this is what everyone would think happened'. Whereas the creative non-fiction writer really says 'this is what I think' … without pretending. And with the acceptance of all the individual subjectivity that would therefore inform that.

Brien, in Blair, 2007

So don't be afraid to tell your story in a book, or to explain how you uncovered someone else's.

Character

In fiction, characters are created from the imagination and rendered on the page so that they are as 'real' to the reader as possible. In a non-fiction book, even though the characters are already real people, your job is not dissimilar to that of your fiction-writing colleagues (though you never make anything up).

Unlike traditional hard-news reporters (and even some feature writers), the creative non-fiction writer does not simply mention someone's name and their title, report what they said and then move on to the next piece of information. In creative non-fiction, the writer must help the reader to understand who the person is, what they look like, sound like and how they interact with other people.

As with fiction, a reader of creative non-fiction must be able to have an emotional reaction to the characters that populate a story; the people they read about are not simply there to add an extra piece of information or expert testimony on a particular subject. Journalist and author Rebecca Skloot says there are no tales without characters to populate them: 'To me, any time you write about characters you are writing about personal and private things ... characters are key when you write creative non-fiction' (Skloot, in Blair, 2007). So remember: when you sit down to write a book, you can't just quote a source; you must slip on the shoes of the novelist and reveal to your reader exactly *who* is talking.

Dialogue and quotes

Part of developing characters is using their voices to reveal their personalities. In Chapter 6 we discussed the differences between the types of quotes. You'll find that in books you will use very few paraphrased quotes and instead include swathes of dialogue.

When you provide dialogue for your readers, you are letting them feel as if they are there, listening in to the conversation. You also allow them to really 'hear' the way the characters talk. Consider the following excerpt from Truman Capote's *In Cold Blood* (1966). This was one of the first novel-length works of creative non-fiction and has since been the subject of four films. As part of his research for the book, Capote spent countless hours interviewing his subjects. From these interviews he was able recreate the chilling scenes that have made this book famous. In one chapter, Capote describes two killers in a supermarket buying supplies, including cord to tie up their victims:

> They discussed how many yards of it they required. The question irritated Dick, for it was part of a greater quandary, and he could not, despite the alleged perfection of his over-all design, be certain of the answer. Eventually, he said, 'Christ, how should I know?'
>
> 'You damn well better.'
>
> Dick tried. 'There's him. Her. The kid and the girl. And maybe the other two. But it's Saturday. They might have guests. Let's count on eight, or even twelve. The only *sure* thing is every one of them has got to go.'
>
> 'Seems like a lot of it. To be so sure about.'
>
> 'Ain't that what I promised you, honey—plenty of hair on them-those walls?'
>
> Perry shrugged. 'Then we'd better buy the whole roll.'
>
> Capote, 1966

This small piece of dialogue provides a real insight into *who* these men are. Imagine how much less you'd know if Capote had simply paraphrased the conversation instead.

Also, remember that you want your readers to feel as if they are on a journey—the same way they feel when they're reading a novel, watching a film, or even (with any luck) when they experience life. To do this you need to include complete conversations between characters—after all, humans don't speak in quotes; we have discussions with other people, and the way they speak to us changes the way we speak and what we say.

Truth

As discussed earlier, it is imperative to remember that just because you are writing a book and using fiction-writing techniques, this doesn't mean you can make up any part of what you write.

Nikki Gemmell is adamant that her non-fiction work must be 100 per cent reliable, factual and as close to the truth as possible: 'I feel like creative non-fiction is just like my radio days: it's non-fiction so it has to be the truth.' Gemmell's commitment to the truth means she carries a notebook wherever she goes:

> I am constantly writing things down, that's one thing radio journalism taught me—to be a good observer and to be constantly recording observations and conversation scraps. I did that as a cadet journalist when I was 22 and I still do it now as a fiction writer, just as much as I always have. And that always ends up in my creative non-fiction and my fiction and everything.
>
> Gemmell, in Blair, 2007

Gemmell says that it is important to record the truth 'rigorously', to use what she calls 'old-fashioned' techniques—like recording conversations. Gemmell is adamant that the creativity comes when pen is put to paper, not before. 'You have to have a solid basis of the truth as in "this is exactly what happened and this is exactly what he said". Otherwise you can get into enormous trouble' (Gemmell, in Blair, 2007).

Of course, if you are writing a memoir of your life, you may not recall absolutely, exactly how you felt at your fifth birthday party, but you will have a pretty fair idea. You will also talk to your parents and others who attended the festivities to check that their memories of the event are in line with yours. Essentially, you will do everything possible to make sure you are giving your readers the facts. And if you are really not sure about something, don't be afraid to explain that in the book.

Summary

o   There is a market out there for your non-fiction book—go ahead and start writing!

o   Creative non-fiction is a genre of writing that gives readers the facts, while entertaining them with the techniques of the fiction writer.

o   There are many publication styles to choose from, including literary journalism, memoir and biography.

o   You have the tools to write a book; just take your feature-writing skills to the next step.

o   Always, always, always tell the truth. Fudging the facts, making up dialogue or creating characters means you are writing fiction, not non-fiction.

Questions

1   What are some benefits to writing a creative non-fiction book instead of a novel?
2   What are the key similarities between book-length creative non-fiction and feature stories?

Activities

1 Head to the book shop or library and pick up three creative non-fiction books. Read them and ask yourself why they made it to the shelves. What is it about the stories in these books and the writing styles that make them work?

2 Start thinking about ideas for your non-fiction book. Write a list of stories you tell people about your childhood, or about more recent history. Add to the list some similar anecdotes you have been told by your family and friends. Assess these stories for their potential to be expanded into a book.

References and additional reading

Blair, M. (2007). 'Putting the storytelling back into stories: Creative non-fiction in tertiary journalism education', PhD thesis, Bond University, Gold Coast, Qld: http://epublications.bond.edu.au/theses/blair.

Capote, T. (1966). *In Cold Blood: A True Account of a Multiple Murder and its Consequences*, New York: Random House.

Forrest, C.V. (1997). 'On publishing', *Lambda Book Report*, 6(5).

Grenville, K. (1990). *The Writing Book: A Workbook for Fiction Writers*, Sydney: Allen & Unwin.

Gutkind, L. (1974). *Bike Fever*, New York: Avon.

Gutkind, L. (1990). *Many Sleepless Nights: The World of Organ Transplantation*, Pittsburgh: University of Pittsburgh Press.

Gutkind, L. (1998). 'Style and substance', *Creative Nonfiction*, 4(10), p. 1.

Gutkind, L. (2006). *Almost Human: Making Robots Think*, New York: W.W. Norton & Co.

Kloberdanz, K., Lofaro, L., Sachs, A. & Maag, C. (2006). 'The trouble with memoirs', *TIME*, 23 January.

Lunn, H. (1999). *Over the Top with Jim*, St Lucia, Qld: University of Queensland Press.

Ricketson, M. (2014). *Telling True Stories: Navigating the Challenges of Writing Narrative Non-fiction*, Crows Nest, NSW; Allen & Unwin

Scanlan, C. (2003). 'Breaking into creative nonfiction, part 1: the basics', The Poynter Institute: https://www.poynter.org/2003/breaking-into-creative-nonfiction-part-1-the.../10048/

Wilson, A. (2016). 'The state of the Australian book market': www.postprepress.com.au/the-state-of-the-australian-book-market/October 5

Wolcott, J. (1997). 'Me, myself and I', *Vanity Fair*, October, pp. 89–93.

Wolfe, T. (2005). 'Setting, psychology and mommy in narrative journalism', keynote address, Nieman Conference on Narrative Journalism, Boston, 2 December.

Woo, W.F. (2000). 'Just write what happened', *Nieman Reports*, 54(3).

Online resources

Australian Bureau of Statistics (2001) *Book Publishers, Australia 1999–2000*, Canberra: ABS: www.ausstats.abs.gov.au/Ausstats/subscriber.nsf/0/8A384B3A937390A9CA256AA300061D9E/$File/13630_1999-2000.pdf

Australian Bureau of Statistics (2002) *Book Publishers, Australia 2000–01*, Canberra: ABS: www.ausstats.abs.gov.au/Ausstats/subscriber.nsf/0/59899DFD59E30E02CA256C3700039FC7/$File/13630_2000-2001.pdf

Australian Bureau of Statistics (2003) *Book Publishers, Australia 2001–02*, Canberra: ABS: www.ausstats.abs.gov.au/Ausstats/subscriber.nsf/0/238CA09838ACA522CA256D9F00048C9A/$File/13630_2001-02.pdf

Australian Bureau of Statistics (2004) *Book Publishers, Australia 2002–03*, Canberra: ABS: www.ausstats.abs.gov.au/Ausstats/subscriber.nsf/0/EB755F67E0A2635FCA256EE50078A693/$File/13630_2002-03.pdf

Australian Bureau of Statistics (2005) *Book Publishers, Australia 2003–04*, Canberra: ABS: www.ausstats.abs.gov.au/Ausstats/subscriber.nsf/0/5D65642E28A86ADCCA25705F0075012E/$File/13630_2003-04.pdf

Creative Nonfiction: www.creativenonfiction.org

Factiva: www.factiva.com

Case study

Lee Gutkind, the godfather of creative non-fiction

Publication details:

Almost Human: Making Robots Think, New York: W.W. Norton & Co., 2006.

The author:

Lee Gutkind has been credited by *Harper's Magazine* as the founder of the creative non-fiction movement. He has received numerous awards and honours, including an Honorary Doctorate in Letters from Chatham College in the United States, the Steve Allen Individual Award from United Mental Health Inc., the Meritorious Service Award from the American Council on Transplantation and the Howard Blakeslee Award from the American Heart Association for 'outstanding journalism'. Gutkind has also received a National Endowment of the Arts Creative Writing Fellowship. He has written long and short works of fiction and non-fiction, including textbooks, and has frequently worked as an editor. Gutkind is Professor of English at the University of Pittsburgh.

The story:

Lee Gutkind takes us into the world of robotics. He transports us to a place full of whizzing gears, flashing lights and passionate roboticists who, toiling to all hours alongside boxes of cold pizza, bring science fiction into reality.

Gutkind has been called the 'godfather' of creative non-fiction (Wolcott, 1997). He is one of the world's leading experts on this genre of writing, so it's no surprise he has written more than a few examples of both short and book-length work. But, like the rest of us, Gutkind had to start somewhere. His first book was *Bike Fever*, which catalogued his travels on the back of a motorbike. Since that book, Gutkind has looked further afield for his story ideas.

To find an idea that will sustain thousands of words, Gutkind suggests you take a leaf out of the environmentalist's book. Think globally and act locally: 'Find a subject to which you have easy access, but one that is as important and relevant in Australia as in Indonesia or Iowa. It should have a universal chord. *Almost Human* and *Many Sleepless Nights* take place in my home town. Robots and organ transplantation trigger worldwide interest. They are intriguing on a number of different levels.'

Once you have your idea, the next step is research. Gutkind explains that his research techniques are fairly simple, but in-depth: 'I read everything I can on the subject, talk to as many people as possible and find a way to hang out, to be a fly on the wall with the person about whom or in the place about which I am writing, in order to capture the behind-the-scenes real-life aspect of the story and subject.'

In fact, Gutkind explains that there is no need to be too anxious when you are embarking on a book; your experience with journalism has prepared you well. You'll only need more time and more determination: 'Researching and writing a book is like working on a feature article times one thousand. You actually do the same work, but instead of it taking three days it takes three years.'

As part of your journey from feature to creative non-fiction, Gutkind explains that your greatest challenge will be transporting your reader from their lounge room to the world you have created in your book: 'The challenge is always the same. Researching the facts, gathering information is relatively easy. Meshing facts with scene and narrative—that is what is difficult. And figuring out how to focus or narrow the concentration of facts—you can't "shotgun" the information.' Instead, you will need to understand the theme of your work and slowly reveal that to your readers.

As time progresses you will find that while you will still use those tried-and-tested research and interview skills you have learned in this book, your understanding of your craft will evolve. Gutkind explains that as his career has developed, so has his confidence in his abilities and his knowledge of what works and what doesn't. 'I am much more conscious of my message now than I was before. I am more aware of and respectful of the power of the written word.'

Gutkind cautions that while writing a book is an amazing experience it should only be embarked upon if you have a vision and a mission, 'Something you want to show, share and say to your reader. You should want to make readers think more clearly about your subject. Creative non-fiction evokes dramatic reality in a way that traditional journalism could never equal.'

Finally, Gutkind has one piece of advice as you step on your road to creative non-fiction: 'Don't be so anxious to be published. Take your time and make certain you are doing the best work possible and that you will be proud of the work, looking back in one or two decades. Today, I feel as if I can stand behind *Bike Fever*. It still works for my readers and for me. Don't compromise quality.'

Writing sample

Almost Human: Making Robots Think (Chapter 1)

By Lee Gutkind, published in New York by W.W. Norton & Co., 2006

Wild ride to base camp

Francisco Calderon, the Chilean student and translator whom everyone calls 'Finch', is waiting for us at the entrance to the tiny airport in Iquique. Of my travelling companions, Alan Waggoner and Paul Tompkins are veterans of previous Atacama expeditions, while Dora Jonak and I are viewing this eerie landscape for the first time. Jonak and Tompkins are from the Robotics Institute at Carnegie Mellon University in Pittsburgh while Waggoner directs the Molecular Biosensor and Imaging Center (MBIC) at Carnegie Mellon.

The Atacama Desert stretches from the Peruvian border south in a narrow band 600 miles into northern Chile. With its dazzling white salt flats and vast expanses of rusty-red emptiness, the Atacama is the driest place on Earth, a place climatologists call absolute desert. Death Valley in California and the Gobi Desert in Mongolia get anywhere from three to six times more moisture annually than the Atacama. Obviously, there are very few living organisms in this desert, which makes the Atacama an ideal analog to Mars. Seeking life on Mars is an ongoing obsession of many of the scientists and software engineers at Carnegie Mellon and the National Aeronautics and Space Administration (NASA), a frequent partner.

We pile our bags into the bed of the double cab Toyota HiLux pickup, a sturdier version of the Toyota Tacoma we use in the United States. The HiLux, an Action Utility Vehicle (AUV) according to Toyota, is aptly named because of its capacity to endure constant, violent, and aggressive abuse. They are perfect for the terrain and also for the crazed, explosive spirit with which the roboticists drive when unleashed in the wilds with a vehicle built for battering. The programmers' frustration of sitting behind a computer and writing and struggling endlessly with code is released in this desert—with passion. Soon, we are rocketing out onto this sun-scorched plain.

The road from the airport into the desert is smooth, and the terrain is flat and red, with white mis-shapen clumps of salt dotting the landscape to the west where we are headed. They look like gigantic white fat globules, glittering, almost oozing, in the sun. We can see the distant bejeweled reflection of the ocean off to one side, a rather disconcerting sight, considering the barrenness of the landscape surrounding us. Although it does not form rain, the moisture contained in the thick dense fog from the ocean seeping above the mountains allows some organisms to survive. We will be seeking those organisms at Salar Grande, the location of our base camp, less than an hour away. Iquique—the name comes from the Aymara (a native Andean ethnic group) word that translates to *'laziness'*—is a tourist stop popular for its surf and beaches and its architecture. There's also a bustling commercial port area to service the copper and salt unearthed from mines in the desert.

The road we're on ends after a high-speed half-hour of full-throttle straightaway driving. Finch—so called because he resembles the character of the same name in the movie *American Pie*—skids to a stop in front of the security gate of the salt mine, the Compania Minera Punta de Lobos, the biggest open cast mine of common salt in the world. Swarthy, curly haired, and slender, Finch jumps out of the truck, places a flashing yellow light on top of the cab, and releases a high-flying antenna, which has been secured against the cab, with a red flag at its tip. This is to make us as visible as possible to avoid dangerous collisions with the gigantic tractor-trailer salt trucks, which commute from the mine to the port where the salt ships are loaded for transport, to spots around the world for refining.

At this point, leaving the mine and the ocean behind us, the smooth road peters out and in its place is a rutted washboard rock-and-dirt right-of-way that has not been maintained for many years, if ever. There's a single deep set of tire tracks seared into the landscape and extending into a red, dust-swirling infinity. 'Hang on,' Finch says in his heavily accented English, turning to look at us, and smiling. 'To minimize brain damage, I have to drive like a bat out of hell. We will soar over the bumps.'

This then is our brief introduction to the most harrowing and frenzied aspect of desert life during field operations, called OPS: Driving with a roboticist. The HiLux has a roll bar, I am happy to note.

A few weeks later, one of these trucks, rocketing down this road at breakneck speed while racing with another in the pitch dark dead of night, would flip over, somersaulting its occupants, breaking windows and collapsing metal. Luckily, the young roboticists in the cab will survive without too many scratches.

Today, ten minutes of wild, bumping, swerving, backbreaking, jaw-crunching, roller-coasting later, with our backs aching and our knees bruised, we are all about to puke our guts out, when, at an invisible marker, Finch suddenly takes a wild turn right, skids on the salt-laden sand like a downhill skier, and streaks up a steep hillside in an explosion of red dust. The base camp is on the top of the hill.

Zoe is on the periphery as we pull in. It is wide and low to the ground, sitting on thick mountain bike tires. A flat row of shiny solar panels energizes a row of batteries below the panels. Three high-resolution digital cameras gawk into the bright sun atop a scrawny crane-like neck. It reminds me of an ice cream cart at a carnival—or a self-propelled flatbed railroad car. Zoe's watching as we stumble out of the truck. Or at least Zoe *seems* to be watching. We don't know at the time that Zoe can't see. Or, to put it more precisely, Zoe can see, technically; but what Zoe sees isn't exactly what is there—a fact that makes the prospects for a successful OPS very tenuous.

Part C

Reviews

Introduction

'Criticism at its best elicits a response of "that's what I think, but I'd have never have thought it like that"... Critics criticise so that everybody else can get on with enjoying themselves. We are civilisation's traffic wardens.'

A.A. Gill, 2007, p. xiv

In that horrible old cliché, 'everyone's a critic'. As an old British actor observed: 'A member of the audience, if he's worth anything at all, when he gets home after a performance, will criticise the entertainment he has seen. It is the nature of things that he should...' (Richardson in Rigg, 1987, p. 10). It is a sentiment that could not be more true in the internet age: everything we eat, drink, watch, read, listen to, drive, or piece of equipment we use to do the washing or to send a text is evaluated, analysed and critiqued. Then it's shared, among friends, or sometimes, beyond that immediate circle. In such an environment, you could be forgiven for thinking that the paid critic or reviewer is actually becoming redundant. Nothing could be further from the truth—in fact, the vast number of consumables (from food to whitegoods) actually means that we need advice, and we need someone to guide us through the maze of choices we confront every day. Years ago, there was just tap water—now there's spring water, filter water and sparkling water to name just three. Beer drinkers in Australia used to be identified by their state-brewed tipple—Queenslanders went for XXXX, Tasmanians for Cascade or Boags (depending on which part of the state you came from), South Australians for West End or Coopers. Not any more: the proliferation of smaller breweries and craft beers has meant there are so many more beers to choose from. But how do you know what to choose? What's going to be right for you?

The late British food (and TV) critic A.A. Gill understood the difference between what the critic does and what everyone else experiences, whether it's a restaurant meal, a play, a book or a TV show. 'For most people, the enjoyment is enough; pleasure doesn't need explaining,' Gill wrote. 'There is something odd, something obsessive, something a touch neurotic about wanting to be a critic, wanting to pull the legs off delicate bits of fun' (Gill, 2007, p. xiii). It might be odd and neurotic, but reviewers are an integral part of the broader feature writing fraternity, largely because it takes rare skill to write a review that does actually explain pleasure. Just think about how difficult it is to describe the way your favourite food makes you feel, the anticipation you get when you see it on the plate and perhaps even the disappointment you notice when you've eaten it. Not easy is it? And try to communicate that to thousands of strangers who know nothing about your tastes.

Often though it is the stinging observation from a reviewer that stays with us and convinces us that we don't want to buy that video game, drink that coffee or see that show. Would you have bothered to see this piece of theatre, when the lead actor was described this way? 'Never has anyone been so much at sea since Columbus. He cried when he should have laughed, clowned when he should have been serious, and generally had everything back to front, including his guitar in the second act, and his lady-friend's favours in the third' (Rigg, 1987, p. 27). Or go to this restaurant: 'It's like the function room your sister was married in 16 years ago ... I'm trying hard to think of someone I'd recommended it to. I just can't' (Lethlean, 2016). Or this movie: 'This is indeed the movie skeezy (OK) grandfathers have been waiting since retirement for: a rancid filth-test about a rotten old widower desperate to knock boots with willing women aged approximately five decades younger ASAP' (Paatsch, 2016).

All of the reviews were written by professional reviewers—there is a barbed wit at work, but fundamentally a deep understanding of the theatre, the restaurant and the film gleaned from years of doing the job. Being an enthusiast—loving coffee or the *Fast and Furious* movie franchise—is not enough to qualify as a reviewer, because you won't know much outside your particular areas of taste. Reviewers have to experience a lot— good, bad and indifferent—along the way. And each of those experiences helps shape their critical faculties and the review that follows. But because they are fundamentally involved in a subjective exercise, they will polarise their audiences—reviewers have their fans, those who agree with the reviewers' perspective, gleaned over years of reading their reviews and coming to trust their critique. Think about your own experience— there's probably a reviewer you seek out because they've been right in the past, and you've agreed with them about the coffee at the corner deli, or the latest Xbox game. It takes time to build that trust—and the credibility that goes with it. That's why reviewing is such a difficult task and one reserved for the talented specialists in the feature-writing stable.

In the chapters that follow you'll see what it takes to write reviews across a range of areas, including food and drink, travel, theatre, music, books, art, interiors, technology, games and motor vehicles.

References

Gill, A.A (2007). *Table Talk – Sweet and Sour, Salt and Bitter*, London: Phoenix.
Lethlean, J. (2016). 'Hill of Grace: Adelaide Oval', *The Weekend Australian* magazine, 20 February.
Paatsch, L. (2016). '*Dirty Grandpa* marks career low for Robert De Niro', *The Herald Sun*, 27 January.
Rigg, D. (1987). *No Turn Unstoned – The worst ever theatrical reviews,* London: Phoenix.
http://www.theaustralian.com.au/life/food-wine/restaurants/hill-of-grace-adelaide-oval-restaurant-
    review/news-story/5349ebb200ac7623fdc2395aef041eb8

18
Travel

'A traveler without observation is a bird without wings.'

Moslih Eddin Saadi

Objectives

The burgeoning shelves of books, the magazines, newspaper liftouts, television shows, and the countless blogsites about travel to exotic places, cater to the dreams and passions many of us hold dear. This chapter provides tips to equip you to write about destinations near and far. In fairness, however, it should not be read in isolation. It should be read in conjunction with the following two chapters on food and drink as they go hand in hand. Specifically, this chapter discusses:

o   travel writing

o   tips on what to include in your reviews

o   some of the issues to be wary of

o   some of the ethical issues to consider.

Introduction

People travel for different reasons, including for business and pleasure. Their destinations will range from domestic (within their home country) to international. Some people travel alone, or with their partners. Others will travel in family groups. Invariably, travellers will have different budgets and expectations of what they will see and do when they arrive at a particular destination. Some travellers will dream of flying first class, being met at their destination by a liveried chauffeur and whisked off to a five-star resort where they'll be pampered by a personal chef and butler. Others will be happy to throw a backpack over their shoulder and head off into the unknown. The majority will fit somewhere in between. While they might be attracted by luxury hotels and the reclining beds in first-class cabins, the reality is that they will travel cattle class and stay in family-friendly budget or mid-tier accommodation.

Understand your market

The first thing a travel writer needs to understand is their market. Ask yourself the question: For whom am I writing this story? Are you pitching your story at the wealthy young executive who wants to impress their partner and is not concerned about cost? Or are you writing for the parents who have been scrimping and saving for years to take their children on a special holiday before they leave home? Or perhaps this story is aimed at the recent retiree who is financially comfortable but cautious about over-spending because their children live interstate or overseas and they want to be able to visit them on a regular basis. Is it seeking to capture the imagination of young singles who are planning a backpacking trip once they have finished university and before they commit themselves to a job and a mortgage? Or is it pitched at the business traveller who wants some brief information about a destination they'll be passing through? These questions are all pertinent and will influence the destinations you focus on, as well as the quality of accommodation you review, the activities and the travel options you suggest.

Choosing the destination

The first task is to choose the destination to be written about. Often this decision is made by your editor and will depend on the requirements of the paper, magazine or program you are working for. In some cases this decision is determined, in part at least, by the demographics of the audience. Linked to this is advertising. Sometimes the stories are linked directly to the interests of companies that advertise in the publications where the stories will appear. Often a feature will contain a kicker line at the end that says that the journalist was a guest of the resort, airline or perhaps travel agency. Such a qualifier is significant because it provides important advice to the reader or viewer, namely that the journalist's views may have been influenced by the fact that they were a guest of the company identified and that readers or viewers should take that into account when deciding whether they will visit the place or not.

This raises potential ethical issues. For example, was the journalist entirely honest in their report? If there was something about the trip that they did not like, did they include it in the story, or did they choose not to report on it rather than bring it to the attention of their audience?

When choosing the destination to write about, it is important to remember that most travel plans seem to be determined by three factors:

- the purpose of the trip
- the cost
- the time available.

Purpose

The first of these factors is critical and will ultimately impact on the second and third. Business trips generally involve tighter time frames than those taken for leisure. Often the key considerations for business people are 1) getting to a destination as quickly and as comfortably as possible; 2) knowing that the hotel is comfortable and provides them with the facilities they need to conduct their business; and 3) having a list of recommended restaurants where they can entertain or just escape to wind down. Generally, business people will have little time to play tourist, but if they do, they will want to know where to go and how to get there without too much inconvenience.

This is not to say that you should ignore the business market. Business people take holidays and often have higher disposable incomes than the average holidaymaker, and may therefore have different demands—and expectations. They may be prepared to pay more for something a little more exotic. They may want personal staff, access to a private beach, or even a personal shopping guide. Things that might interest them while they're on holiday may not fit comfortably into a business agenda, but that doesn't mean you shouldn't write about them. Your task is to tempt them.

Generally, all holidaymakers will be looking for things to do, irrespective of their budget. What they're interested in may vary considerably. Families with children, for example, will tend to look for destinations that offer recreational options, such as theme parks, beaches or pools. Older people may be more interested in less energetic pursuits (art galleries, museums, theatres, restaurants, wineries and clubs). But you can't assume they're not interested in recreational pursuits too (many older Australians roam the world playing golf and bowls, and fishing and bushwalking). Equally, many younger families will avoid the beach, preferring cultural pursuits, or even a shopping binge. The clue is to include as much detail as you possibly can to cater for the variety of interests you'll undoubtedly encounter among your readers and viewers.

Cost

Cost can impact on all aspects of the trip: how to get there, where to stay (caravan park or camping ground, hostel or hotel), how much to spend on a daily basis (How expensive are the attractions?). Cost can also determine the place someone visits (Is there an entrance fee and are there family discounts?) and how long they can afford to be away. Budget is probably more of an issue for the family than for the business person who is travelling on a company expense account. But it is worth remembering that even those with corporate credit cards usually have to operate within limits.

Time

There is another important dimension that the writer needs to take into account, irrespective of whether the destination is domestic or international—time. How much time are your travellers likely to have? This will vary considerably, depending on their circumstances. Some people may have less than 24 hours to spend, stopping over on their way to another destination. Others will have a few days. The more fortunate may have weeks or longer. Your task—if you are seeking to convince them to make a particular country, city or town part of their itinerary—is to paint a picture of the destination that will convince them to include it or exclude it from their travel plans. You need to be honest. Don't say a place has enough attractions to keep them running from morning to night for a week, when most people would see and do all they wanted in 48 hours and spend the remainder of the week waiting for their flight home.

Generally speaking, travel writers will seek to provide a mix of domestic and international stories. The former could include stories about destinations outside of the reader's home state. State-based publications or programs will probably focus on local destinations—that is, those that are within easy distance of the target market.

While interstate travel is likely to involve planes or trains (particularly if the travellers are time-dependent), intrastate travel will frequently involve motor vehicles, or other, slower forms of transport, such as bicycles, or even boats. Remember, people are looking for different experiences. This is what you're looking for as a writer: the points of difference between one town and another, one city and another, one country and another. Remember too that trips don't need to involve overnight stays. Some of the most interesting destinations may well be within a few hours by car of home base.

The differences between different countries are often easy to identify and write about. Many writers paint a picture of a particular country by focusing on the culture, language and history. The history of cities, particularly in exotic overseas destinations, can also provide a starting point for a travelogue. But what about a small town? Sometimes small towns have their own stories: famous people, historic events, or even architectural highlights that attract visitors. Occasionally the attraction is more recent in origin: the establishment of a signature event (such as the Birdsville Race Day or the Todd River Derby in Alice Springs), the creation of a wine trail (Tamar Valley in Tasmania; Hunter Valley in New South Wales; Yarra Valley in Victoria; Barossa Valley in South Australia; Margaret River or Swan Valley in Western Australia) or craft markets. All attract tourists and have spin-off benefits for other tourism operators in the surrounding region (restaurants, accommodation, markets etc.).

Travel reviews are built around a number of questions (see Box 18.1).

Box 18.1   Travel review checklist

1 Domestic

- How do you get there?
- What are the travel options—plane, car, boat, train—and costs?
- How far is the destination from the major population centres?
- How long does it take to get there? If the trip is by car, how good are the roads? Are the roads accessible by two-wheel drive, or do you need a four-wheel drive? Is the road trailer-friendly or caravan-friendly? Are there petrol and food stops?

When you get there:

- What is the range of accommodation (caravan parks or camping grounds; different standard hotels or motels)? Is the accommodation children-friendly or pet-friendly? Are there eco-tourism options?
- What are the accommodation costs?

Activities:

- What are the attractions—recreational, cultural, social?

Best times to travel:

- What are the best months to visit a particular destination? What can influence this decision (weather, pests)?

2 International

As for domestic, but with the following additional considerations:

Political:

- Are there any risks of unrest?
- Is the destination a known terrorist target?
- What does the Federal Government's Smart Traveller website recommend? (See <www.smartraveller.gov.au>. This site contains travel advisories and a host of other information that can help travellers and travel writers.)

Cultural/social:

- What is the local language?
- To what extent is English spoken?
- Are there religious considerations you should be aware of (clothes, relationships, language)?
- Anything else that travellers should be aware of?

Medical:

- What inoculations, if any, are required? (See the Smart Traveller website.)
- Are there any possible health risks (from food, water, stonefish, mosquitoes etc.)?
- What precautions should be taken to prevent illness?
- Is there any advice about seeking medical assistance in the event of an accident? Is a hospital stay covered by an agreement between the Australian Government and the host country?

Food:

- Is it safe to eat food prepared at street stalls?
- Is it appropriate to eat uncooked food?
- What are the restaurants like?
- What should people expect to pay for food?

Money:

- What is the local currency?
- What are the exchange rates?
- Is it possible to use credit cards?

Visas etc.:

- Are visas necessary?
- Do you pay arrival or departure tax?
- What are you allowed to bring in/take out of the country?
- Are there restrictions on taking out 'culturally valuable' goods?
- What are local attitudes towards drugs (prescription or illegal)?

Other factors:

- Provide readers/viewers with websites they can access before heading off.
- Don't forget to give people an idea of costs (of sightseeing, food, accommodation, transport etc.) so that they can budget.

Summary

- Good reviewers seek to live the experience.
- Good travel reviewers try to cater for both the adventurous and the timid.
- Good writing about leisure pursuits convinces people that they have made the right decision to visit a particular destination, restaurant or winery, that they should consider doing so or—more dramatically—that they should bypass it.
- Travel writing needs more space than restaurant or wine reviews as travel reviews tend to be wide-ranging, covering cultural highlights, tourist must-dos, accommodation and food.

Questions

1 What are the key elements travel writers should include in their reviews?
2 What ethical and legal considerations should travel writers be aware of?

Activities

1 Select an international destination you would like to visit (or perhaps have visited). Visit a local travel agent (or go online) and ask for the information that would enable you to write with greater authority or knowledge about the destination (including how to get there, the quality of accommodation, types of restaurants etc.). Using the guidelines in Box 18.1, write a travel story that highlights the strengths and weaknesses of the destination.
2 Visit a local tourist attraction and write a story about it (don't forget to include information about how long it takes to get there, entry fees, whether it is wheelchair-friendly etc.).

Online resources

Smart Traveller: www.smartraveller.gov.au
Tourism Australia: www.tourism.australia.com

19

Food

'Food critics are very powerful people … They've become so sort of farcical that they're now a parody of themselves and so people aren't taking them as seriously as they were 10 years ago.'

Gordon Ramsay, celebrity chef, in Meager, 2008

Objectives

Remember the song 'Food, Glorious Food', in the hit musical, *Oliver*? It is a powerful song, sung by the young boys of the workhouse while receiving their daily bowl of gruel from Mr Bumble, the master, conscious of the fact that in the next room the overweight members of the Board of Governors were feasting. The song closes with the following words:

Why should we be fated to do
Nothing but brood on food
Magical food,
Wonderful food
Marvellous food,
Beautiful food,
Food, glorious food, glorious food

If only these urchins could take the place of a restaurant reviewer or food critic, they would truly understand the meaning of the last five lines, beginning with the words: 'magical food …'. Restaurant reviewers are generally fortunate in that they are able to dine at the best restaurants. That's not always possible, sometimes they are disappointed by the quality of the food, the size of the portions, or the service. But generally speaking they get to eat out regularly and in style, and in so doing, give meaning to the words sung by Oliver Twist and his colleagues in the workhouse. Welcome to the world of the restaurant reviewer.

In this chapter we provide you with tips to help you to espouse the virtues of fabulous eateries and to discuss those you'd recommend people avoid. Specifically, this chapter discusses:

o   restaurants
o   legal and ethical concerns.

Introduction

As we discussed in chapter 18, people travel for many and varied reasons, one of the most popular being to experience a different culture. For many travellers, food is a central theme and consequently there has been an enormous growth in restaurant reviews for domestic, national and international restaurants. Many people will travel simply to eat at a particular restaurant. For example, during his younger days, one of the authors and a group of friends occasionally negotiated the back roads of northern Tasmania to eat at a very popular restaurant called Gossips. The trip was approximately 40 kms each way, but the restaurant's reputation was such that many people were prepared to make the trip, although only after having booked a table, as the restaurant was always full. There are many restaurants like this, both in Australia and overseas. They survive by word-of-mouth recommendations.

This is where the role of the restaurant reviewer can be influential, although it is not just the professional reviewer who can help influence people's attitudes to food. You only need to think about the number of television programs dedicated to food. Some are competitions between amateurs, others feature amateurs competing against professionals, or professionals competing against their peers. Some are travelogues with food the central theme: the host or a guest preparing dishes using local ingredients. Some involve chefs preparing meals on a step-by-step basis, encouraging people at home to do the same. Others involve chefs seeking to reinvigorate tired or failing restaurants. All rate highly, both on free TV and pay-to-view channels, such is the allure of food.

Restaurants

Australia has some of the best restaurants in the world, and some of our successful chefs and restaurateurs are now having an influence elsewhere. While this may be largely due to the restaurateurs who have been prepared to take a gamble and invest in an unpredictable industry, some of the credit must also go to the reviewers who, over time, have tempted the tastebuds of Australians.

These days there are any number of 'instant' reviewers—those who take images of the food with their phone and post it immediately on Facebook. While many of those diners who post such material have probably eaten in many restaurants, it doesn't make them professional food or restaurant reviewers. That takes a deep understanding of food, its preparation, its source and the trends that shape the dining experience.

One of the challenges facing restaurant reviewers is choice: Which restaurants should they choose to write about? While it is tempting to focus on the silver-service restaurants, the reality is that most prospective diners pitch their sights a little lower. Expensive restaurants are fine for special occasions, but for regular meals out most people are looking for something a little different. Thus, reviewers have to work across the various categories of restaurant.

Restaurant reviews are built around a number of questions (see Box 19.1).

Box 19.1   Restaurant review checklist

1 To what extent does the restaurant meet its stated aims?

2 How good is:

   a   the food?

   b   the service?

   c   the ambience?

3 Obviously there are a number of sub-questions:

   a   How well is the food prepared and presented?

   b   Is the price reasonable?

   c   Is the service timely?

   d   Are the staff polite and well trained? Do they understand the menu and can they talk knowledgeably about it?

   e   Does the wine service match the food service (both in quality of the wine list and the knowledge of the waiter entrusted with selling it)?

   f   Are you given sufficient time to enjoy the meal or are you under constant pressure to eat and leave?

   g   Does it take bookings or is it a case of turn up at the door and try your luck?

The food

Nowadays there are a number of elements to this. The first has to do with the menu. How comprehensive is it? How many choices do you have in each course? How broad is that choice? Does it cater for people who have allergies or food intolerances (to nuts, gluten, seafood, lactose, soy, wheat, etc.)? What about people who have particular dietary requirements (vegetarian, vegan, raw vegan, macrobiotic; see <bighospitality. co.uk> website for an explanation of these terms)? Are there off-menu options for people who have particular dietary requirements?

Linked to this is the question of quantity. Remember the reference to Oliver Twist earlier in the chapter. There is another song in the musical where Oliver is conned into approaching Mr Bumble, the master of the workhouse, and asking for another helping. His request: 'Please, sir, I want some more,' caused great consternation among the workhouse staff and governors and resulted in him being banished. This is rarely a problem for reviewers, although occasionally they will complain that the helpings were less than adequate.

The second element deals with food presentation. Nowadays, this is significant. Remember the television food shows? Food presentation is a key element when food is judged. The same applies to food featured in magazines, on websites, and in newspaper supplements. Before the camera is directed at the meal, a trained stylist has probably spent considerable time ensuring that the food looks magical, to return to the theme of the 'Food, Glorious Food' lyrics. The contestants in the television shows will have spent a great deal of time before the show, looking through magazines and websites for inspiration. The same applies to restaurants. One of the authors was in Canberra recently. He was dining at a small restaurant that was changing its menu. Each of the new dishes was being professionally styled and photographed. This process contained a double benefit: (1) the images could be used for promotional purposes; and (2) it meant that kitchen staff had a clear idea as to how each meal should look when it was presented to customers. The goal: to make people want to eat the food.

Obviously the visual effect is important, but at the end of the day, the experience is in the eating. This is the third element. Food must look good, but it must also be well prepared. It must appeal to two of our senses: smell and taste. Both are critical, and work in combination. Something can smell terrific, but is it well cooked (and to your instructions)? For example, was the meat rare, as requested, or was it well done? Was the chicken under-cooked? Did the scallops taste like bullets? In the case of food that is prepared, rather than cooked, smell and texture become the critical elements. Do the ingredients work well together? Or do they clash? If they clash, what is the cause? Is it one of the major ingredients, or a minor element? Would removing it materially impact on the meal?

Service

For many people, this is just as important as the quality of the food served. It begins with the greeting: do you feel welcome, or are you treated as if you are an inconvenience? Are you shown to your table, the chairs pulled out for you, and napkins placed in your lap? Or are you pointed in the vague direction of an empty table? Has the table been cleaned, or does it contain a pile of empty dishes and half-eaten meals? How long does it take for the menu to arrive? Are you offered a pre-dinner drink?

There is a second element to this: how knowledgeable is the waiter? We touched on this indirectly when we talked about the menu. It is important that staff have a working knowledge of the menu. For example, we discussed the scope of the menu, including its capacity to cater for people with a range of dietary requirements. Staff should know which dishes are inappropriate for people with particular allergies. Equally, they should have a working knowledge of the menu. For example, how are particular dishes prepared? What does that herb from South America with an interesting name taste like? Which meal would they select if asked to choose between the slow cooked pork belly and the sautéed scallops? What is the fish of the day? What vegetables are served with the main courses? If they don't have this information at their finger-tips, they are failing in their job.

They should also be prepared to acknowledge when they—or the restaurant—are wrong. For example, one of the writers was eating at a well-known seafood restaurant a couple of years ago with a group of friends, one of whom was a cray-fisherman from Tasmania. The restaurant offered 'Tasmanian crayfish', which he ordered. When the crayfish was served, however, he informed the waiter that the crayfish was not Tasmanian, but South Australian, as there were distinctive physical differences between the two which, as a fisherman, he could identify. Rather than apologise, the waiter was prepared to challenge him on that point, despite the guest revealing his credentials, and those of another guest whose father was also a Tasmanian cray-fisherman.

Finally, front-of-house staff should also be prepared to recommend wines to accompany a particular dish. In silver service restaurants, this is the responsibility of the sommelier. But few mid-tier restaurants can afford to employ such people, and rely on their waiting staff to provide such services. Often, a restaurant will try to get around this by having a consultant sommelier match wines with dishes. These matches are then indicated on the menu.

Ambience

The ambience of a restaurant is often the most difficult to quantify (or write about). For example, a fantastic meal by one of the world's most revered chefs would probably be memorable even if served in a tent. But sometimes the setting can be the difference between a meal you rave about and one that is simply passable. For example, Gossips restaurant (mentioned previously) was in an old farmhouse. It was nothing special, a little dilapidated in fact, but the rustic nature of the building added to the appeal. In fact, there are a large number of small historic cottages throughout Australia that have been turned into highly regarded restaurants. While the food and wine they serve have contributed to their reputations, much of the reason for their success is due to other factors, including location, atmosphere and the skills of the floor staff. Thus, reviewers should always consider a range of factors when writing a restaurant review, including all of those already discussed.

Remember, reviews must be contextual. Don't criticise a restaurant for not being of five-star standard when it is pitched at the family market. Equally, don't criticise the ambience if that is not a stated feature of the restaurant.

Legal issues

As indicated earlier, restaurant reviews can provide a number of traps for the unwary. This has been highlighted on a number of occasions, including in 1984 when John Fairfax and Sons was sued for defamation over a review written by Leo Schofield and published in the *Sydney Morning Herald*. The action was taken by the owners of the Blue Angel Restaurant because of Schofield's comments about the way the lobster was prepared. He allegedly described the lobster as 'cooked until every drop of juice and joy in the thing had been successfully eliminated, leaving a charred husk of a shell containing meat that might have been albino walrus' (Pearson, 2004, p. 201).

Schofield also allegedly made a number of comments about other seafood, including garlic prawns and lemon sole. The owners argued, successfully, that Schofield had described them and their staff as incompetent and inhumane. Schofield and the *Sydney Morning Herald* claimed a fair comment defence, which was rejected by the judge, who found in favour of the plaintiffs and awarded $100,000 in damages, an enormous amount in those days.

In 2003 the *Sydney Morning Herald* and its then restaurant critic Matthew Evans were sued over a review of Sydney restaurant Coco. Evans had allegedly twice eaten at the restaurant. He rated the restaurant nine out of twenty, describing it as 'expensive, with many unpalatable flavours, a menu flawed in concept and execution, and good and bad service' and 'the best thing was the view' (Dilanchian, 2007). The restaurant owners lost at the initial trial, but won an appeal to the Supreme Court and a subsequent appeal to the High Court, which sent the matter back to the New South Wales Court of Appeal. That judgment provoked an interesting debate among media outlets, particularly in relation to the role of juries in defamation actions (see Albrechtsen, 2007). The case was not ultimately finalised until 2011, when the case went again before the New South Wales Court of Appeal, which found in favour of the restaurant owners. The case is complex, and has its roots in the fact that there were two restaurants on site—Coco (upstairs) and Roco (downstairs). Evans, while mentioning this fact, and indicating that his review was of the upmarket Coco, named the restaurant as Coco Roco. (For a full discussion of the facts and the judgments, see Ackland, 2005; Ackland, 2011; George, 2011.)

There are a number of lessons here for restaurant reviewers. The first is to be fair. Remember that while we are allowed to be critical, we need to be able to defend our comments if the restaurant owners take umbrage at what we have said. It is fine to say that the food was overcooked, bland or overpriced. It is also reasonable to say that service was slow, and that the cutlery or crockery wasn't sparkling clean. But don't go over the top. It is possible to tell people that you were dissatisfied without defaming everyone associated with the restaurant.

Other considerations

There are a number of strategies you should consider when embarking on a career as a restaurant reviewer. The first is to try to retain your anonymity. While it is flattering to be identified as a well-known restaurant reviewer, reviews should ideally be conducted under normal conditions. If the restaurant knows you are a reviewer when you ring to book a table, they will tend to pay you more attention than they would an average patron. This means that the quality of service—including food—may be of a higher standard than that received by the customers sitting at adjacent tables. Because of this, your review may be skewed—that is, influenced by the special attention received. Also, pay for your meals. That way, you are in no way beholden to the restaurant. You shouldn't feel obliged to be nice when describing a dining experience you didn't enjoy.

Summary

- Good food writing is a pleasure to read. The great writers tease people, in effect saying to them: 'Why aren't you here, enjoying this wonderful food or wine?'
- Great writing will tempt people to ring up the restaurant and book a table, or call up their local wine supplier and order a few bottles of the latest vintage.

o   Great food and wine writers can effectively act as salespeople, but they can also undermine a restaurant or winery's reputation.

Questions

1   What are restaurant reviewers looking for when evaluating a new restaurant?
2   What ethical and legal considerations should restaurant writers be aware of?
3   What does the finding in the Coco case say about the obligations facing restaurant reviewers? Do these same constraints apply to reviewers more broadly?

Activities

1   Choose a restaurant you enjoy and visit it with a partner, friend or group of people. Order a range of dishes and share them, writing notes about what you like or dislike about the food (and other aspects of the experience, including the ambience, quality of service, quality of cooking, presentation and cost).
2   Go online and have a look at some of the reviews by the late UK reviewer A.A. Gill. In particular read his review of the French restaurant L'Ami Louis in Paris, which appeared in *Vanity Fair* in April 2011. Would Gill's review be published in Australian newspapers? What, if anything, would prevent it from being published? <http://www.vanityfair.com/style/2011/04/lami-louis-201104>

References and additional reading

Ackland, R. (2005). 'Food critic saved by a gut feeling—the jury's', *Sydney Morning Herald*, 10 June: www.smh.com.au/news/Opinion/Food-critic-saved-by-a-gut-feeling—the-jurys/2005/06/09/1118123958123.html

Ackland, R. (2011). 'When judges judge critics, the result can taste a bit like reflux', *Sydney Morning Herald*, 2 December: www.smh.com.au/opinion/society-and-culture/when-judges-judge-critics-the-results-can-taste-a-bit-like-reflux-20111201-1o94p.html>

Albrechtsen, J. (2007). 'Judicial hubris makes messy meal of our rights', *The Australian*, 20 June: www.theaustralian.news.com.au/story/0,20867,21934311-32522,00.html

Dilanchian, N. (2007). 'The cooks, the critics, the restaurant proprietors and their court cases', *Sydney Morning Herald*, 27 June: www.dilanchian.com.au/index.php?option=com_content&view=article&id=306:the-cooks-the-critics-the-restaurant-proprietors-and-their-court-cases&catid=23:ip&Itemid=114

George, P. (2011). 'Aggrieved Coco Roco owners make Fairfax media reviewer pay', *The Australian*, 5 December: www.theaustralian.com.au/media/opinion/aggrieved-coco-roco-owners-make-reviewer-pay/story-e6frg99o-1226213573537

Meager, D. (2008). 'So you think you can swear', *The Weekend Australian Magazine*, 17–18 May.

Oliver, the lyrics: http://www.metrolyrics.com/food-glorious-food-lyrics-oliver.html

Pearson, M. (2004). *The Journalist's Guide to Media Law*, 2nd edn, Sydney: Allen & Unwin.

Online resources

The Australian Bureau of Statistics is a useful reference for journalists, as it has a great deal of information covering the wine, restaurant and hospitality sectors: www.abs.gov.au

Big Hospitality: http://www.bighospitality.co.uk/Features/Dietary-requirements/Dietary-requirements-Everything-you-need-to-know

Good Food: http://www.goodfood.com.au/eat-out/good-food-guides/the-sydney-morning-herald-2017-good-food-guide-hatted-restaurants-20160901-gr6of2

Slow Food: www.slowfood.com

Smart Traveller: www.smartraveller.gov.au

20
Drink

'If food is the body of good living, wine is its soul.'

Clifton Fadiman

'Wine is the drink of the gods, milk the drink of babies, tea the drink of women, and water the drink of beasts.'

John Stuart Blackie

'I drink coffee because I need it, and wine because I deserve it.'

Anonymous

Objectives

Let's face it, we drink a lot. Everyone drinks a lot. It's not just alcohol; for some of us it might be tea, coffee, milk, juice or water. For most of us, a meal—no matter how well prepared—is one-dimensional without the appropriate liquid accompaniment. In fact, many of us don't require food to enjoy a drink; it is a pleasure by itself. In this chapter we look at our fascination with drink, and how to write knowledgeably about the various kinds. Specifically, this chapter discusses:

o   beer and cider

o   wine

o   coffee and tea.

Liquid refreshments

Australians are fortunate in that our climate is conducive to producing great beer, wine, cider and spirits. Perhaps it is due to the quality of our water, which is considered so good that it is now being bottled for drinking, despite the fact that our tap water is second to none. Figures released by the Australian Bureau of Statistics show that in 2010–11 Australia's vineyards produced 1.56 million tonnes of grapes. Domestic wine sales totalled 463.9 million litres, with a further 746.6 million litres of wine exported (ABS, 2012). In recent years Australians have also been treated to a wider range of wines (catering to different tastes and budgets). From 2008–13 wine consumption was fairly consistent at 29 litres per person. While beer consumption in Australia has declined in recent years (from 108 litres per person in 2008 to 93 litres in 2013), there is a new market emerging. That is the craft beer and cider market, along with locally grown spirits (did you know, for example, that Australian whisky and vodka are being exported to Ireland and

Russia respectively, the home of such beverages?). A study conducted by Roy Morgan showed that in 2015 27 per cent of Australians (5.3 million) drank bottled water in the preceding seven days, up from 4.9 million the preceding year. On top of that, Australians are heavy coffee drinkers (on average consuming 9.8 cups per week). While this is down slightly over the decade, it is very high and when linked to tea drinking (50 per cent of Australians will have at least one cup of tea in a week), highlights the fact that Australians also like a hot brew. But it is not just any brew. Australians are becoming increasingly particular about what they drink, whether it is alcohol, tea, coffee or water, hence the growth of reviewing in these areas.

Beer

As we have indicated, in the last few years boutique industries have developed around beer, spirits and liqueurs. It used to be that the beer you chose to drink was proof of where you hailed from: Tooheys and Reschs in Sydney, XXXX in Brisbane, West End (and Coopers) in Adelaide, Melbourne Bitter, Victoria Bitter and Carlton Draught in Melbourne, Boags and Cascade in, respectively, northern and southern Tasmania. But geography is meaningless for beer drinkers these days. The proliferation of beers means that there is a huge market for advice and guidance on what beers are out there and if they are any good.

If you are serious about writing in this area, we suggest that you talk to the brewers/makers. There are some terrific stories that are yet to be told about why people are moving into this market segment and challenging the dominance of the large-scale brewers.

It is also a good idea to go online and download some of the tasting sheets. For example, beerology produces a tasting sheet that highlights the various elements judges are looking for (see Online resources). This is a useful starting point and begins with six categories, most of which are relatively straightforward. Within each category there are a number of sub-categories that utilise a nine-point scale (see Box 20.1).

Box 20.1   A beer taster's checklist

1 Appearance:

- Colour (a colour swatch is provided)
- Clarity (brilliant ... dull ... cloudy)
- Head (poor ... good ... persistent)

2 Aroma:

- Intensity (faint ... strong)
  - Malt aroma (grain, bread, sweet, toast, nut, caramel, toffee, chocolate, coffee)
  - Hops aroma (earth, floral, herbal, spice, resin, citrus)
  - Other (fruit, skunk, corn, chemical)

- Balance (sweet … sharp)
- Impression (off … neutral … nice)

3 Flavour:

- Intensity (faint … strong)
  - Malt flavour (grain, bread, sweet, toast, nut, caramel, toffee, chocolate, coffee)
  - Hops flavour (earth, floral, herbal, spice, resin, citrus)
  - Other (fruit, skunk, corn, chemical)
- Balance (sweet … bitter)
- Impression (off … neutral … nice)

4 Mouth Feel:

- Body (light … medium … full)
- Sensation (creamy, slick, drying, warming, puckering, astringent, chalky, mouth-coating, prickly)
- Carbonation

5 Finish:

- Length (short … medium … long)
- Intensity (faint … strong)
- Balance (sweet … bitter)

6 General impression:

- Craftsmanship (boring … excellent)
- Freshness (off … stale … fresh)
- Personal taste (disliked … liked)

This is a very useful guide and is one most Australian beer drinkers could relate to, even the options under the aroma and flavour sub-categories, with the possible exception of 'skunk'. The others make sense. Online there are a number of other judging templates that probably require greater experience to work through (see, for example <http://www.bjcp.org/docs/SCP_BeerScoreSheet.pdf>). Remember, that in writing about beer you are catering to a diverse market, particularly in the case of craft beer, and that should be reflected in your writing style. Make sure your writing is accessible, and don't be pretentious, as is often the case with wine writing. At the end of the review, it is a good idea to include the following information:

- Who the beer was produced by (is it a large-scale-producer or a craft beer?)
- How much does it cost?

- Where can it be purchased?
- What food you believe it could be paired with if served during a meal.

Cider and perry

The approach adopted when judging cider (apple) and perry (pear) is not too dissimilar. Again, there are some useful judging score sheets online. These provide a good introduction to the language judges use when judging this increasingly popular drink. For example, have a look at the Cider Australia score sheet (see link under Online resources). Judging is calculated out of 100 points, with medals being awarded in the following categories:

Box 20.2   Meeting the criteria for a medal

Gold	92.5 – 100 points	Outstanding
Silver	85 – 92 points	Excellent
Bronze	77.5 – 84.5 points	Very good

For the following discussion, we'll rely on the standards produced by Cider Australia. There are a number of standard styles for cider and perry, including New World, Traditional, Speciality, and Intensified or distilled. Within the New World and Traditional styles, there are four categories, including Dry, Medium, Sweet and Method Traditional (Disgorged). The new world and traditional ciders and perries are judged according to four criteria, as detailed in Box 20.3:

1 Aroma/flavour;

2 Appearance;

3 Mouth feel; and

4 Overall impression.

Box 20.3   Judging cider and perry

Aroma/flavour:

This will depend on the style of cider or perry.

New World Cider: medium to high acidity. Should be refreshing, but not harsh.

Traditional Cider: Some fermentation, which will give it a distinctive taste (reminiscent of farmyard, spice, smoke). Considered desirable, but shouldn't overpower the senses.

New World Perry: Pear character is present. Similar to a young white wine, but no obvious bitterness present

Traditional Perry: No obvious fruit. Similar to a young white wine. May be slightly bitter. For example, sweeter types have a stronger aroma, with dry ciders showing wine-like qualities. The combination of sugar and acidity should produce a refreshing character.

Colour:

New World Cider: Clear to brilliant, pale to yellow in colour

Traditional Cider: Cloudy to brilliant. Medium yellow to amber

New World Perry: Lightly cloudy to clear; generally pale in colour

Traditional Perry: Lightly cloudy to clear; generally pale in colour

Mouth Feel:

New World Cider: Medium body

Traditional Cider: Medium to full

New World Perry: Full. Low to moderate tannin levels

Traditional Perry: Full. Low to moderate tannin levels

Overall impression:

New World Cider: Refreshing (not too bland, watery or austere to the taste).

Traditional Cider: Complex flavours, balanced, long finish. Refreshing (as per above).

New World Perry: Mild, medium to medium sweet. Rarely dry. Still or lightly sparkling only. Mousy, ropey, oily flavours are frowned upon.

Traditional Perry (as per New World Perry, but possibility of some tannin): Some dry perries can taste sweet.

Judging the speciality styles is more complex, so we'll leave that up to you. If you want to head down this path, have a look at the online judging templates.

Wine

Because of the nature of our wine-growing industry, wine writers face challenges similar to those faced by restaurant reviewers. Wine reviewers too must cover the market. Consequently, most reviewers focus on the premium and mid-range wines and, particularly, the new releases; although in some instances it is appropriate to focus on the bottom end, for example when writing for a student audience.

Wine writing is a highly specialised field. Wines are judged according to a scale (there are a number of scales used, ranging from stars to points). If you read wine reviews in magazines, newspapers or online, you will see that different reviewers prefer different scales. However, in essence, wine judging involves three senses: smell, sight and taste. While the application of these may appear relatively straightforward, the reality is that wine judging is a complex science. It relies on a combination of factors, including knowledge of the wine-making process and the difference between the different grape varieties, and knowing which sense to favour when making an interpretation of a particular wine.

Of the three senses involved in judging wine, sight is probably the easiest to apply. The other two are more complex and can produce some very interesting descriptions of wine.

The following checklist provides a summary of the qualities and characteristics wine reviewers look for.

Box 20.4   Wine review checklist

Appearance

Is the wine clear, or does it appear cloudy? Good wines will have a clear or transparent appearance. Wine writers will often use the term 'clarity' when describing the appearance of a wine. Outstanding wines should be transparent. Older wines may show a little cloudiness, particularly if there is sediment in the bottle. If the wine is cloudy, the reviewer should ask: Why?

Colour

Reviewers will often use the terms 'dark', 'medium' or 'light' to describe the colour of a wine. However, this really depends on the style of wine. Pinots, for example, are lighter in colour than full-bodied reds, such as cabernet sauvignons. White wines are by their nature light in colour, although they can vary, and range from a deep golden (such as a dessert wine) to a very pale young riesling. Colour can be a good indicator of a wine's health. Red wines become paler as they age, while white wines turn a darker colour. Wine judges will hold a glass of wine up to the light to gain a clear idea of its colour. It is virtually impossible to judge the colour of reds while they are in the bottle.

Bouquet and aroma

This is one of the most challenging parts of the wine-judging process. You'll notice that wine judges will swish the wine around in the tasting glass, allowing it to aerate. They then place their nose into the mouth of the glass and inhale. What are they seeking, you ask? They're trying to detect all of the aromas that combine to make a great wine. Wine judges will write down each of the aromas they are able to discern.

Taste

The 'nose' of the wine (its smell) will often give you a pretty clear idea of what to expect once you taste it. For example, you may be able to detect that the wine is off (it has been exposed to the air or may be suffering from cork taint, although this is not a problem with most wines today, given the move to synthetic corks or screw-top bottles). Sometimes, you can't tell by nosing the wine, and occasionally a wine that smells off will impress when it has been decanted and allowed to breathe.

The real test, however, comes when you taste the wine. Again, it is important that you swirl the wine around the glass to aerate it. Take a sip and swish it around in your mouth so that it touches all parts of your tongue. What can you taste? Generally speaking, you will be able to detect variations that, hopefully, will reflect the bouquets or aromas you identified when nosing the wine. Some of these may be sweet; others might be sour or even bitter. You might also pick up some new tastes that weren't detectable earlier.

Sweetness is generally determined by the sugar content. Dessert wines, for example, tend to be very sweet. Many can be described as syrupy. Rieslings and chardonnays are often described as crisp or dry. How crisp depends on the level of acidity. White wines tend to be more acidic than reds. When discussing reds, reviewers will often refer to the tannins. This comes from the skins, seeds and even stalks of the grapes. So-called 'big reds' display considerable quantities of tannin. However, they should not leave an excessively bitter taste in the mouth.

Balance

To what extent is the wine balanced? Do the various elements discussed earlier produce a wine that is enjoyable?

Finish

What do you think after drinking a wine? What tastes remain? And for how long? Does the wine have a short finish or a long finish? That is, how long do the tastes linger?

What would you recommend the wine be served with?

Is it suited to game, fish, chicken, curry, cheese, pasta or dessert? Different wines suit different dishes. The task of a wine writer or sommelier is to match the wine with food that will complement it.

Tea and coffee

While Australians have always enjoyed a cup of tea or coffee, it has only been in recent years that we've become focused on the quality of the product. This is particularly so in the case of coffee, where there has been huge growth in job opportunities for baristas (the people who make coffee), coffee roasters (those who roast our favourite blends) and 'cuppers' (those who judge the coffee). There is also an art to tea-making, as centuries of Japanese and Chinese history reveal, although this is not reflected in the demand for tea, as is the case with coffee. Because of that we'll conclude this chapter by looking at what is involved in reviewing coffee.

Coffee tasting is similar to tasting wine, beer, cider, spirits, even water. The taste elements combine with the aroma to produce what we know as the flavour. Even the tasting process is similar to that of other beverages, as it involves a 'slurp'. The slurp helps to infuse the coffee with oxygen, and in so doing helps release the flavours (much as we see in wine and beer tasting, or even spirits for that matter). The rest of the process is quite similar too. According to at least one coffee judge, the process is similar to a six-part waltz (smell, slurp, swirl, swish, savour and swallow). Let's look at each of these quickly (see Box 20.5).

Box 20.5   Tea and coffee checklist

1   Smell: This is the first stage. Is it a welcoming smell? Are you trying to absorb the different aromas the coffee imparts? It is similar to the nosing involved in wine tasting.

2   Slurp: Apparently this helps to atomise the coffee and release the flavours.

3   Swirl: Wine, beer and spirit drinkers swish the drink around in their mouths so that the flavours hit different parts of the tongue and palate. Coffee drinking is the same.

4   Swish: If you swish it between your teeth you get a sense of how thick it is.

5   Savour: Enjoy the coffee while it is in your mouth, contemplating the taste combinations.

6   Swallow: After you've swallowed, think about the tastes that remain. How do they compare with the initial tastes and aromas you detected? Some judges will suggest that you block your nose the first time you sip your coffee, so that the tastes you detect on your tongue are not overwhelmed by the aroma. Let your nose play a role in subsequent mouthfuls and draw comparisons between the taste combinations you detect the more of the cup you consume.

Summary

o   Good reviewers seek to live the experience and share it with their reader or viewer.

o   Good writing is a pleasure to read. The great writers tease people, in effect saying to them: 'Why aren't you here, enjoying this wonderful coffee, beer, wine or cider?'

o   Great writing will tempt people to call up their local wine supplier and order a few bottles of the latest vintage.

o   Great reviewers can act as salespeople, but they can also undermine a reputation, be that of a winery, brewery, coffee roaster or even distillery.

Questions

1   What are the key elements wine writers should include in their reviews?
2   Do these differ in any significant ways to what brewers or coffee cuppers are looking for?
3   What ethical and legal considerations should such writers be aware of?

Activities

1   Select your favourite tipple and write a review of it, based on the tasting notes provided by the producer. You should be able to obtain these either online or from the outlet where you purchased the drink. Don't forget to mention its price and how many awards it has won.

2   After you have finished your review, go online and see if it has been reviewed by another person. How does your review compare with the online version? What did they include that you omitted? What did you include that they did not cover?

3   Go online and see if you can find the judging criteria for a range of other beverages (tea, water, spirits). How do these differ from the criteria adopted for wine, beer, cider, perry or coffee?

References and additional reading

Australian Bureau of Statistics (2012). *Australian Wine and Grape Industry*, 2010–2011, cat. no. 1329.0, Canberra: ABS: www.abs.gov.au/ausstats/abs@.nsf/Latestproducts/1329.0Main%20Features22010-2011?opendocument&tabname=Summary&prodno=1329.0&issue=2010-2011&num=&view=

Online resources

The Australian Bureau of Statistics is a useful reference for journalists, as it has a great deal of information covering the wine, restaurant and hospitality sectors: www.abs.gov.au

ABS 4307.0.55.001 'Apparent consumption of alcohol, Australia, 2012-13 (released 4 April 2014): http://www.abs.gov.au/ausstats/abs@.nsf/Lookup/4307.0.55.001main+features42012-13

Australian Food News, March 12, 2014. 'Average Australian coffee consumption drops, but café visits continue to grow, research': http://www.ausfoodnews.com.au/2014/03/12/average-australian-coffee-consumption-drops-but-cafe-visits-continue-to-grow-research.html

Australian Society of Viticulture and Oenology: http://www.asvo.com.au/wp-content/uploads/2016/01/ASVO-2015-BPR.pdf

beerology: http://beerology.ca/wp-content/uploads/2011/09/Beerology_Tasting.pdf

Cider Australia: http://www.cideraustralia.org.au/wp-content/uploads/2015/09/Cider-Australia-2015-Styleguide-Official.pdf>; <http://www.bjcp.org/docs/SCP_CiderScoreSheet.pdf

cleanskins.com: Wine terminology/glossary of wine terms: www.cleanskins.com/wine_terminology.html

Coffee Judge: http://coffee-judge.com/tasting_coffee_17.html

Cognac Knowledge: http://www.cognac-knowledge.com/cognac-review-and-tasting-notes

Dan Murphy's A-Z of wine terms: https://www.danmurphys.com.au/liquor-library/wine/more-about-wine/wine-glossary

DrinkSkool: http://drinkskool.com/lesson-seven-tasting-spirits-and-cocktails

Fischer, T., Judging spirits: https://www.youtube.com/watch?v=Buu1RYwknBA

Hypebeast: https://hypebeast.com/2016/10/water-sommelier-video

Master of Malt Guides: https://www.masterofmalt.com/guides/how-to-taste-whisky

Roy Morgan Research, 19 April 2016. 'Bottled water consumption booming': http://www.roymorgan.com/findings/6763-bottled-water-consumption-booming-201604190004

Roy Morgan Research, 29 August 2016. 'The tea party: Australians love a cuppa': http://www.roymorgan.com/findings/6937-tea-party-australians-love-a-cuppa-201608290942

The Wineanorak's glossary of wine terms: www.wineanorak.com/glossary/glossary.htm

Wine Australia: www.wineaustralia.com

21

Television, Film, Video Games and Books

'Creativity is allowing yourself to make mistakes. Art is knowing which ones to keep.'

Scott Adams, American cartoonist, n.d.

Objectives

In this chapter we:

o discuss writing reviews for film, television, video games and books

o provide tip sheets that will help you produce reviews in each of these fields

o consider the ethical and legal issues that might impact on this style of reviewing.

Television

This is a good starting point for people who think they would like to be reviewers because there is an enormous variety of programs available, and they can be accessed cheaply, or at no cost. You just need to sit back, relax, turn on the box and start watching. Television reviewing is a little different from theatre or live concert reviewing in the sense that while there are a large number of genres, most people feel comfortable talking about all of them. It is an area where you don't have to be an expert. But you need to remember that it can be time-consuming and you will have to watch a lot of material that you don't like because your tastes may be contrary to others'. Popular programs are invariably reviewed in the mainstream media—if you don't like reality TV, sport and soaps, then perhaps TV reviewing is not for you. Alternatively, if you only watch *Game of Thrones* and think nothing else on the small screen gets close to it, you shouldn't be doing the job either. You need to have eclectic tastes, and be genuinely interested in what it takes to make television to really be a good TV reviewer.

In the space of one night, you can switch from a news and current affairs program, to a comedy, documentary, movie-length drama, game show, DIY, soap opera or a sporting event. Depending on the genre, our review can potentially be informed by Tim Maddock's theatre reviewing guidelines in Chapter 22. But if you don't find these helpful, then the following should provide you with enough information to help you decide what to include and what to leave out. Just bear in mind that the first episode of a particular series may—or may not—be compelling and watchable. A laudatory first episode does not guarantee a coherent and engaging series. But as a TV reviewer the networks will probably only send you the preview 'reels' of the first and perhaps second episode of a series. The series may change for the worse—or the better—as it goes along. It's always good for a reviewer to revisit an over-hyped series that has caught viewers' attention with uniformly good reviews—the quality may not last. Or it may even improve.

Here's our list of what to look for:

1 Is it a new show, a revamped show, or a new season of an established show? Who is producing/directing it? What experience do they have? What other programs have they been associated with? Were they successful or big-time flops?

2 Who are the headline actors? Is this a role (or type of role) they've played before? Based on the previews you've seen, do they produce commanding performances, or do they appear out of their depth? This is particularly relevant when playing a well-known personality and was highlighted in reviews of the Paul Hogan mini series that aired on Channel 7 in early 2017. The reviewers were critical of a number of aspects, including the fact that the actor who played Paul Hogan, Josh Lawson, was 'a parody approximation of him'. The term 'parody' was used by a number of reviewers (see Schipp, 2016; Eriksen, 2016; Buckmaster, 2016). According to Debbie Schipp in a news.com.au review:

> In TV, looks are everything. So if you're going to play an Aussie icon like Hoges, who made his name on TV, you're going to have to look like the bloke.
>
> In Seven's miniseries, you can't get past the wig. The look is all wrong: halfway between Donald Trump's and the plastic smoothness of a Ken doll.
>
> Lawson's face isn't craggy enough. Hoges' facial tics are there, the cadence of his laconic drawl is there but, somehow, Hoges is not.

3 What about the supporting cast? Do they make up for a poor performance from the lead characters? Or do they add to the disappointment?

4 In the case of a drama (say a murder mystery), is the plot plausible? Is it sufficiently complex to keep you guessing, or have you worked out who the murderer was five minutes into the one-hour show?

5 In the case of a documentary, how accurate is the information being provided? In some programs, say a David Attenborough wildlife series, or a nature series with Professor Brian Cox, the evidence tends to speak for itself, but what about a series produced by a lesser known production house featuring a little known presenter?

6 In the case of reality programs (*The Amazing Race, The Block, Master Chef, My Kitchen Rules* etc.) where is the focus? Is it on the tasks the contestants have to perform in order to win, or is it on the intrigue and personality clashes that appear so central to these shows?

7 In game shows, think about the concept. Does it work? Is it based on a show already successful elsewhere? How does the host engage with the contestants?

8 Consider who the show is pitched at. Is it young children, teenagers, adults, or the whole family?

9 Identify and talk about both strengths and weaknesses. Perhaps even draw comparisons with other similar themed shows.

Movies

In many respects, this is similar to television reviewing, although sometimes you get the benefit of leaving home and sitting in a theatre to watch the latest release, rather than sitting back in the loungeroom with your family. Doing this—that is sitting in a theatre full of strangers—can add a separate dimension to the experience. Whereas the reaction of your family and friends is likely to be predictable, that of a group of strangers is not. Therefore, when you're reviewing a new release, don't just focus on the movie itself, also pause to consider the reactions of those people seated around you in the theatre. Are they commenting? If so, what are they saying? Is it positive or negative? Are they restless? Are they sitting as if glued to their seats? Do they jump or cry out at scary scenes?

Movie reviewing is a vital role: Australians regularly report that their most frequent cultural pursuit is going to see a film. And with the proliferation of movies—and the vast suburban multiplexes in Australian cities—every piece of advice about what's on and what it's like will help patrons make an informed choice. Bear in mind that sometimes the movie reviewer's words can be redundant. There are a number of movie advertisements that just provide the star rating, rather than any quoted critique. But even so, the movie reviewer has to be clear about their reasoning for giving a film two stars or five.

Sometimes it is easier to review a standalone film, than it is to critique one that had its beginnings in a very popular novel, or even television series. For example, if the film is based on a well-known book, how do the two compare? Did the film belabour parts of the book that you felt were unimportant, while skipping over bits you wanted to see more fully developed? Did the film stray too far from the original plot? Was the director able to capture the nuances in plot or character that made the book so memorable?

If there is no book version with which to draw comparisons, your task is easier. But still you need to think about character and plot. You need to ask: Is there a storyline? Is it convincing? Is it too contrived? Too slow? What are the characters like? How well did individual actors perform? Do the special effects work? Are they innovative or tired? What about the costumes, are they authentic, clever, quirky? How does the film compare with other similar films you've seen? How does it compare with other films by the same writer, producer, director? Take the Mad Max or Stars Wars series: Is there continuity between one instalment and the next? Is there a disconnect? Is this deliberate? Was the last instalment just one too many? Who is the film likely to appeal to? You might not have enjoyed it, but would it appeal to your younger siblings, or even to your parents or grandparents? What rating would you give it?

Video games

This is another area where young journalists, including journalism students, are creating a niche for themselves as reviewers. Okay, so what do you need to be a good games reviewer?

1 You need to be a gamer. You need to understand what makes a good game and what makes a poor one. You can't write a fair review if you've only had a cursory look at a game. To do it justice, you need to play it from start to finish. That means playing through each of the levels.

2 Then ask yourself the question: 'what did I like/dislike?'

3 Most reviews are built around a number of elements, including:

    a Graphics (the production of pictorial images, usually in the form of animation)

    b Music (background, scene setting etc.)

    c Cinematics (giving life to the pictorial images)

    d Story (plot, storyline)

    e Content (what themes does it contain: violence, sex scenes, language, fantasy etc?) In Australia, computer games, like films, are classified according to their content. Three of the classifications (G, PG and M) are advisory, while two (MA 15+ and R 18+) are restricted. For details of the classifications, see <http://www.classification.gov.au/Guidelines/Pages/Guidelines.aspx>.

    f Controls (devices used to provide input to a game, PC/console)

    g Gameplay (the way a game is played).

Have a think about each of these elements. Which were strong? Which were weak? For example, were the characters clunky and slow moving? How difficult was it to work your way through each level? What skill levels were required? Was the storyline convincing? Did it need further development? Was the classification realistic given the content? Does it present good value for money? In the case of upgraded editions, do they dramatically build upon the earlier editions? Do they resolve technical issues with the earlier versions? Are there any unique features that stand out? Do the controllers work as they should?

One of the issues worth considering is what an older audience will make of the game. In recent years, some of the violence and depictions of women in some video games have provoked debates among older Australians that such brutal storylines are not appropriate for younger users. This is a debate that cannot really be resolved but the astute games reviewer will flag such concerns and warn gamers that a particular product may well become the focus of some attention from non-gaming quarters.

Think about the language you employ when writing your review. Remember that gamers have a language that is unique to their craft. You need to adopt that language, while making sure that newcomers can understand what you're talking about. Finally, remember to include video clips or screen shots to illustrate your review. Make sure that legally you are allowed to do so. Try to find material that is available under a Creative Commons licence, or available through the company's website. If in doubt, contact their PR department or company, asking for permission to use particular video or sound grabs for your review. If you need to resize images or screenshots so that you can insert them into your web blog, use one of the software programs such as Pixlr.com.

Books

In some respects, a book review is like a TV, movie, video game, or even a music review. There are certain critical elements that you are looking for. Book reviewing can be divided into two distinct types: fiction and non-fiction. Non-fiction book reviews can be the preserve of specialists—people who work in a particular discipline, or are experts in the topic of the book under review. For example, historians are often asked to review books that deal with major events; journalists or political scientists will review books on recent political events or biographies by recently retired politicians; self-help books on health care or diet are often reviewed by medical practitioners, nutritionists or psychologists. Fiction, on the other hand, is often reviewed by other published writers, or people with a degree in creative writing or English literature. We will look briefly at what is involved in reviewing both non-fiction and fiction.

Non-fiction

Non-fiction can cover a range of areas, including sport, politics, cooking, wine, travel, finance, health and even collecting. It can also include memoir and biography. When reviewing non-fiction it is important to have either a strong understanding of the subject matter being written about or a willingness to research the topic covered by your review. For example, memoir is an enormously popular form of writing, particularly when it involves well-known public figures (such as actors, politicians and sportspeople). So too is the unauthorised biography. While memoirs and biographies can provide an important insight into an individual's life, they can also involve a not-too-subtle rewriting of history, or even selective amnesia in the case of autobiographies.

People writing their memoirs need to understand that their interpretation of history might be critically reviewed by others who were also involved. For example, journalist and former Liberal staffer Nikki Savva released a book in 2016 that contained a series of sharp observations about former Liberal Prime Minister Tony Abbott and the nature of his relationship with his female chief of staff, Peta Credlin. Savva claimed that there was a deep dysfunction at the heart of Abbott's government, which could be traced to the problematic issues between Abbott and Credlin. While Savva pointed out there was nothing improper in the relationship, she did not contact Abbott or Credlin for a response to the material she had collected, on the record and on background, from a range of political sources. Savva claimed that Abbott and Credlin had their own platforms from which to respond and that she didn't need to seek out their views on her allegations. This right-of-reply issue became a feature of discussions about the book's approach and content. Sharp reviewers—which included former politicians—made it plain they didn't agree with Sava's approach.

Equally, readers should not be misled. There have been a number of instances in recent years in which writers have deliberately sought to mislead their readers, including *A Million Little Pieces* by US author James Frey in 2005 (allegedly a memoir, but large parts were exposed as having been made up), *The Hitler Diaries* (published by Stern in 1983), Clifford Irving's 1972 *Autobiography of Howard Hughes* (for which Irving was paid an advance of nearly US$800,000 by McGraw Hill), Norma Khouri's *Forbidden Love* (2003) and Helen Demidenko's *The Hand that Signed the Paper* (1994).

Fiction

Having a degree in creative writing suggests that you understand the technicalities of such writing, including plot, character development and language. This means that you should be able to identify the strengths and weaknesses in the book being reviewed. But you need to be careful when discussing another person's work, particularly if you have not had an opportunity to discuss the book with them. In fact one of the strengths of a great review (either laudatory or critical of the work in question) is the provision of information that comes from knowing the author or at least talking to them.

One of the traps reviewers fall into is assuming that they know what the author was seeking to achieve. Remember, it is almost impossible to get inside the author's head, so don't presume you know. It is possible to comment on plot and character development, and obviously you would begin by asking yourself questions along the lines of: Does the book work? Does it immediately capture one's attention and entice you to keep reading? If not, what are its failings? Are the characters poorly developed?

Dr Shady Cosgrove, an Associate Professor in creative writing at the University of Wollongong, was a finalist in the 2007 Vogel Prize for young writers. She is the author of *She Played Elvis* (2009) and *What the Ground Can't Hold* (2013). Cosgrove believes there are a number of critical questions that reviewers need to consider. These are outlined in Box 21.1.

Box 21.1   Literature review checklist

- Sound structure: How is the 'data' in the novel ordered? How are the chapters structured and do they operate together to support the larger structure of the novel?

- Characterisation: Do the characters undergo a change or follow a character arc? Are they different at the end of the novel from how they are at the beginning? Do we believe the characters? Are they compelling and original?

- Is there synergy between form and content? That is, do the narrative strategies employed serve to support the subject matter and vice-versa? Does the novel address themes that illuminate the 'human condition'?

- Use of language: Does the novel use language in beautiful and innovative ways? Are the descriptions free of cliché?

- Is the point-of-view (POV) schema clear and consistent? (See Chapter 7.)

- Is the novel grounded with a strong sense of setting?

- Are the narrative strategies integrated with one another? That is, does the POV inform the narrating voice? Does the plot inform the structure?

- Is the passing of time handled clearly?

- Is the plot gripping? Do we care what happens next? Is the author strategic in ordering the plot points?

- Is symbolism and added layering present without being stifling? Is it thoughtful without being pretentious?

Shady Cosgrove

Losing the plot

A good review recaps a story but doesn't give the conclusion away. This was one of the great challenges many reviewers faced when writing about the last book in the *Harry Potter* series, where there was a great expectation that at least one of the major characters would die. How do you convince potential readers to buy the book but not spoil the surprise for them?

One way for you to spoil the surprise—be it a review of a book, movie, film or play—is to focus on the plot. Reviewers need to tread a fine line between teasing their readers or listeners with elements of the plot and spilling the beans and telling them everything that happened, when it happened and how. Remember, you need to engage your readers, listeners or viewers. If you think it is a great story, then tell them so, but don't tell them so much about the plot that they don't need to read the book, attend the performance or see the film.

To do this effectively, you need to understand not only the subject of your review, but also the audience you are writing for. This is the critical point: you are writing *for* a group of people who have not yet had the opportunity to hear the CD, see the movie, play the game, or read the book. They are seeking guidance from you—the expert. For that reason, they do not want to be spoken *at*. They don't want to be tortured with pompous writing. They want your writing to be as fresh and exciting as the book you are raving about. Remember too that readers and listeners want your view—if you are considered an expert, they will even seek it out—but it may be only one of a number they canvass.

Summary

o   Television, movies, video games and books all provide reviewing opportunities for young journalists.

o   The key to successful reviewing is a capacity to engage the reader, viewer or prospective participant without giving too much away. You need to entice them with promises of what is to come, without providing so much information that they know what the outcome is.

o   Good reviews are built around language, although in the case of movies, television and even video games, it is a good idea to include a short clip or even screen shot that highlights the strengths or weaknesses of what it is you are reviewing.

Questions

1   What are the similarities and differences between film and television reviews?
2   What are the key elements to look out for when reviewing a video game?
3   What should you look out for when reviewing a book? How does reviewing a non-fiction book differ from the review of a novel?

Activities

1   Watch an episode of a popular television program. Write a review (400–500 words), pointing to the strengths and weaknesses of the show, and explain why people should watch or ignore it.
2   Select your favourite video game and write a review of it, highlighting the elements you like and those you feel need further development. Discuss how it is an improvement on, or worse than, other similar games (or earlier versions of the same game)

3   Write a review of a recent release movie you have seen (200–300 words). Go online and have a look at other reviews of the same movie. How do they differ (from each other and from your review)? Do you believe these differences are justified? Why?

4   Select a book you have recently read. Write a brief review, but be careful not to spoil the experience for someone who is yet to read it.

References and additional reading

Buckmaster, L. (2016). 'Hoges review – biopic bombs badly as Josh Lawson parodies Paul Hogan instead of playing him', *The Guardian*, 13 February: https://www.theguardian.com/tv-and-radio/2017/feb/13/hoges-review-biopic-bombs-badly-as-josh-lawson-parodies-paul-hogan-instead-of-playing-him

Cosgrove, S. (2009). *She Played Elvis*, Sydney: Allen & Unwin.

Cosgrove, S. (2013). *What the Ground Can't Hold*, Sydney: Picador Australia.

Eriksen, D. (2016). 'That's not Hoges! Seven miscasts Aussie legend', *New Daily*, 29 November.

Schipp, D. February 10, 2016. 'The big problem with the Paul Hogan miniseries', News.com.au: http://www.news.com.au/entertainment/tv/tv-shows/the-big-problem-with-the-paul-hogan-miniseries/news-story/cd1d47330abdc611fba585bacb2bc986

Online Resources

The Hollywood Reporter: http://www.hollywoodreporter.com/topic/tv-reviews
Metacritic: http://www.metacritic.com/tv

22
Music and Theatre

'Movies will make you famous; Television will make you rich; But theatre will make you good.'

Terrence Mann, n.d.

'Ultimately one has to pity these poor souls who know every secret about writing, directing, designing, producing, and acting but are stuck in those miserable day jobs writing reviews. Will somebody help them, please?'

David Ives, n.d.

Objectives

In this chapter we discuss:

o   how to write music reviews

o   how to produce theatre reviews

o   some of the ethical and legal traps associated with music and theatre reviews.

Much of the advice we give in this chapter is provided by industry professionals—people who have considerable experience not only producing particular forms of work, but also reviewing the work of others. You'll see from the tip sheets they provide, that in many respects what they are looking for is quite similar across the disciplines. For example, the term 'plot' can be used when discussing novels, theatre, drama in its various forms, video games, or even opera; so too can the term 'characterisation'. Characters are key to all of these and more; it's just that they might be employed differently across the various genres, depending on the technology through which they are delivered (video game versus movie, versus novel etc).

So, in reading this chapter (as well as the previous one, for that matter) we suggest that you look at the suggested treatment of each of these genres with a view to seeing how the advice can be utilised in other forms of review.

Music

Most people love music. That's evidenced by the number of people you see walking around with earphones on, listening to their favourite band, singer or album. It is also confirmed by the large numbers who spend hundreds of dollars to attend a musical performance, often in unfavourable weather. Music reviews can take a number of different forms. In the 1980s, the authors worked with a journalist who was passionate about music. This wasn't his major job—he was actually a senior sports sub-editor—but through his love of music he'd developed a relationship with the major music companies that meant he would receive an advance copy of nearly every vinyl album released into Australia (both EP and LP). At one stage he had two rooms of his house filled floor to ceiling with albums, all of which he had reviewed for various newspapers and magazines around Australia.

These reviews were not particularly detailed; some would only cover four or five paragraphs. But they were widely read because he was considered knowledgeable by readers, and he was fair. He would highlight the strengths and weaknesses of the album and the tracks it contained.

Like many reviewers, he tended to specialise. He focused on the music styles he liked. This is important from an ethical perspective. If you don't like a particular style of music, don't write about it because your prejudices will likely shine through. However, this doesn't apply to bad examples of music within a genre you do like. If you don't like a particular album, say so. But don't only state that you don't like it. Tell your readers and viewers why you think it is flawed.

Reviewing a digital download of an album is quite different to reviewing a live musical performance. You'd expect all the bugs to have been removed from the album, but this is not necessarily the case with a live performance. A number of unknowns can impact on your experience, including injury or illness to the performer, technical problems with equipment, including power outages, and problems with the venue itself, including poor acoustics, unruly patrons, weather etc. All of these can impact on your experience and thus on the type of review you write.

Ethical considerations

As a reviewer, you need to be aware of the impact that a negative review can have on a performer. If the artist or performer is well established in their career, a poor or mediocre performance is not likely to have too much of an impact. However, if the performer has had a number of poor performances while on a nationwide tour (turning up late or drunk, for example), then a negative review might start to impact on ticket or album sales. This was the case with 1980s music icon, Meatloaf, who was lambasted for his performance at the 2011 AFL grand final. When Meatloaf's latest album, ironically named 'Braver than we Are', was released in Australia in 2016, it sold just 334 copies in its first week. Today, fans are speaking not just with their wallets, but also in the courts. In August 2016 Australian singer Sia was sued for $2.1 million by fans following a concert in Israel (for reviews of the concert, see the *Guardian* Australia 2016).

While both Meatloaf and Sia were well established in their careers, negative reviews can destroy the careers of hopeful performers, as the lyrics of the song 'Mr Tanner' by the well-known American singer–songwriter Harry Chapin reveal. In the song, Chapin wrote about a small-town dry cleaner whose friends believed he could be a professional singer, and encouraged him to try his luck in New York. The man took their advice, booking a concert hall in New York where he made his debut:

[sung:]

The evening came, he took the stage, his face set in a smile.
And in the half filled hall the critics sat watching on the aisle.
But the concert was a blur to him, spatters of applause.
He did not know how well he sang; he only heard the flaws.
But the critics were concise; it only took four lines.
But no one could accuse them of being over kind.

[spoken:]

Mr Martin Tanner, Baritone, of Dayton, Ohio made his town hall debut last night. He came well prepared, but unfortunately his presentation was not up to contemporary professional standards. His voice lacks the range of tonal color necessary to make it consistently interesting.

[sung:]

Full time consideration of another endeavor might be in order.

<http://harrychapin.com/music/tanner.shtml>

The song continues to record how Mr Tanner, his dreams of a professional singing career shattered, returned to his home town, where he never sang publicly again. According to Chapin's wife, this particular song was inspired by the singer's own experiences with reviewers.

Clearly there is a difference between reviews of so-called popular music, and performances by classical performers, whether soloists, or members of a touring symphony orchestra, chamber orchestra or smaller collection of artists and instruments. To review classical music or opera does require a different set of skills— and employs a different set of criteria—than those employed when reviewing more contemporary music. The differences are highlighted in the following checklist produced by Associate Professor David Vance— an accomplished pianist, critic and former lecturer in music at the University of Wollongong—in Box 22.1.

Box 22.1 Music review checklist

One might consider the following contextual questions before the process of criticism begins:

- Is the work performed familiar to me?
- Have I heard previous performances?
- Is the style familiar, even if the work is not? Though I can't say I know every one of Vivaldi's concertos, for example, I am thoroughly familiar with the idiom of his instrumental writing.
- Is this a premiere performance of a new work?
- What are the appropriate models/comparisons for a new work?
- Is the performance part of some festive/memorial occasion?
- How does occasion influence reception?
- Is the performer a celebrity? What bearing might this celebrity status have on me and on the audience?

Let the music begin ...

I suppose the first question I want to ask about a performance is: Did it engage me and sustain my attention? If so, why? If not, why not? What did the performance have or lack? What did it communicate and how? Was my ability to engage impaired by fatigue after a heavy day at the office, a headache or some other minor ailment? Remember, the critic, like the performer, is human.

I might consider the following specific details for critical comment: the quality of sound, the interpretative skills and the technical facility of the performer, intonation, tempi and dynamics, precision of rhythm and ensemble, phrasing, diction (if a vocal work), breath control (particularly, but not exclusively, with singers, since all music, as a form of speech, needs to breathe).

I might also remark on various musicological aspects of the music as a way of 'placing' the performance, for example, interpretative approaches, including so-called authenticity, performance history, whether the musical architecture (the plan or overall structure of the piece) is made apparent etc.

I will also look for some image or metaphor arising in the music or performance on which to build my critical commentary. This is not always possible, or easy, but it can make for more lively writing.

Ultimately, I will try to comment on the artistry of the performer, in whatever way that elusive word might be defined for that particular artist—but the artist's ability to communicate and engage is central. Does the performance offer some illumination about the human condition—do I hear/find something I had not noticed before, or do I recognise a feeling or experience, expressed poetically in sound?

David Vance

Clearly Vance's love is for classical music and opera, but many of the questions he poses can apply equally to an Adele or DJ Snake concert. In a simplified form, the list of questions you might ask yourself are:

1   Is this vintage Adele? Did she sing her standard repertoire of songs? Were they to the high standard you would expect? If not, why? Was her voice flat/off-key? Did she appear tired or disengaged? How did she interact with the audience? How long did she sing for?

2   Were there any special effects? What were the costumes like?

3   Who were the support artists? How good were they? Were they better than Adele? If so, why?

4   What was the venue like? What were the crowds like, in terms of numbers? Did they get value for money? Could everyone see or hear the artist, or did those patrons in the cheaper seats have problems because of their distance from the stage?

5   Were there any disturbances/interruptions? What was the cause? Was it crowd behaviour, an isolated incident such as a fan jumping up on stage, the star or a band member collapsing, the show late starting?

6   How could the concert have been improved? Would you attend another performance or are they past their best? What did other patrons think?

Summary

o   Music reviewing is a popular form of journalism.

o   However, there are clear differences between reviewing albums and live performances. While the former is all about the music, which is produced in a controlled environment, in the latter case, there are a number of other variables that must be taken into account, including the venue, costumes, the artist's capacity or willingness to engage with their audience, their choice of songs, how long they sang for and, of course, technical features such as sound quality.

o   As with all forms of reviewing, fairness should be the overriding feature of any music review. If you like the album or performance, say so. If you didn't like it, say so. But either way, tell your readers or listeners why it was so good, or fell short of your expectations. Remember, if you are writing for a popular magazine, television show, or website at the start of a national tour, your review could, potentially, impact on the success of the tour.

Theatre

There are clear parallels between reviewing music and theatre. Theatre, like a concert, is live and thus subject to everything that can beset a live event. In Box 22.2, Tim Maddock, a senior lecturer in drama at the University of Wollongong, discusses what he looks for when reviewing a play.

Box 22.2   Theatre review checklist

The process of critiquing a production begins when you first hear about it, and the expectations you might have will condition your actual experience.

A number of things create an expectation: knowledge of a director's work, a company or a writer, publicity materials, posters, interviews in the media and talking to people who have seen the work.

Sometimes a work comes as part of a festival, and our expectations are conditioned, in part, by our respect for the curatorial skills of the artistic director and by any fore-knowledge of the company or the director's body of work.

Walking into the theatre, we are taking in the signs in order to have a reasoned expectation.

Some directors will mess with the conventions to create alertness to the coming event or to 'teach' the audience how to enter their work.

Once one has assessed whether it is to be a night of challenges or a comforting ritual, the process of judging the work on its merits begins.

If the reviewer is acting in a professional capacity, then there is an obligation to draw the reader's attention to the piece's achievements by its own terms. For example, if it is a conventional text-based play, then the critic could talk about how skilfully the director has used time and space, how insightful are his or her interpretations, whether the actors are alive on stage and whether this is an exciting performance. And to what degree are the feelings of the audience engaged or their intellects stimulated?

If the work is a classic, then the critic could consider what has been done to renew our experience of it.

One will be aware of the combination of elements, stage design, costume, lights and sound design, and whether these elements work with the body of the actor and the words to create a cohesive (while possibly dislocated and dislocating) language.

Having said this, it is possible to come away from an event acknowledging the skills of all who participated yet wearing a huge yawn.

Depending on whether you require theatre to reassure you in your comforting certainties or to shake and capsize your certainties, you will be asking different things from the performance.

The immense power of the theatre lies in its being a place of speculation, a place to worry and wear at the boundaries of thought and action.

A checklist might read like this:

- Did the work puzzle, appal, challenge, infiltrate, capsize, transgress, re-alienate or estrange me?
- Above all, did it speak to me?
- Did it move me?
- Am I still worrying away at it weeks, years later?

The very best theatre changes what we think possible in theatre and extends the possibilities of self.

Tim Maddock

The checklists provided by Maddock and Vance point to an important difference between reviewing theatre, ballet, opera and classical music on the one hand, and reviewing contemporary music on the other. There is a technical element in the case of the former that is not necessary in the case of a contemporary music review. Yes, they need to be technically solid, but the level of sophistication is not as great (on the whole) as is the case with a theatre performance, or discussion of a ballet, opera, or performance by a world-renowned chamber orchestra or symphony orchestra.

The reality is that most reviewers working in this area have a background in the discipline they are reviewing, perhaps as a writer, director, producer or actor, in the case of theatre, as a dancer or choreographer in the case of ballet, or as a singer or classically trained musician in the case of opera or orchestral performances. Some may even have university qualifications in these fields. That's not to say that you shouldn't aspire to producing such reviews if you have a strong interest in one of these areas. Rather, it might be a good idea to start with amateur theatre.

Amateur theatre

While professional theatre reviewing can be a complex, perhaps even daunting, occupation and therefore tends to be the preserve of people with specialised training, young journalists are often asked to review amateur performances. These pose many of the challenges listed by Maddock, with a couple of extras thrown in.

Remember that amateur performers do not aspire to, or have not quite reached, the level of competence assumed by professional performers. Because of this, you need to be a little more forgiving when reviewing a performance of the local drama society. It would be unfair, for example, to compare a locally produced performance of *Fiddler on the Roof*, which features amateur performers and has been cobbled together on a shoestring budget, with a fully funded version you saw a few years back on Broadway that featured box office names—unless of course you feel that the local version was of such a high standard as to warrant comparison with the professionally produced version. But don't draw comparisons simply to highlight the inadequacies of the local production.

Local newspapers, in particular, provide reviews of such performances to highlight the achievements of local people, not to denigrate them. The last thing you—or your editor—want is an inbox full of hate mail from the parents or family of those you have criticised. Equally, you need to remember that the performance is being put on by amateurs and, like their professional counterparts, they rely on positive reviews to attract people through the door. Cut them a break, even if you weren't particularly enthralled with the production. And try to familiarise yourself with the script before you attend the performance (a relatively straightforward task in the case of well-established performances, though more difficult in the case of a new work).

Summary

o While theatre reviewing tends to be the preserve of people who have a background in performance, there are opportunities for keen young journalists to break into the field.

o This can often be achieved by starting off with amateur theatre, often musical theatre, which enables the reviewer to develop skills across a range of genres.

o If working in this area, it is important, however, to consider the consequences of any review you might produce. Before hitting the publish button, ask yourself the fairness question: Is what I am saying reasonable in the circumstances? And, have I justified my comments?

Questions

1 What are the key differences between an album review and a review of a live performance?
2 To what extent do you believe Harry Chapin's song, 'Mr Tanner', highlights the fact that reviews can be brutal, perhaps even ill-conceived?
3 What should a reviewer be aware of when reviewing amateur theatre compared with professionally produced and directed theatre?

Activities

1 Select a music CD or theatre performance you have listened to or watched recently. Write a review of it, using the criteria outlined in the guidelines developed by David Vance or Tim Maddock.

2 Write a comparison of a live performance by an artist you admire and one of their albums. Which do you believe is better? Why?

3 Go online and locate a series of professionally written reviews of a favourite musician or theatre production. Explain how the reviews differ and which ones you believe are more accurate.

References and additional reading

Harry Chapin:

http://harrychapin.com/music/tanner.shtml

Guardian Australia (2016). https://www.theguardian.com/music/2016/aug/18/sia-lawsuit-israel-banter-concerts-stage-live-music

Sia lawsuit:

1 http://www.digitalmusicnews.com/2016/08/18/fans-sue-sua-for-short-and-poor-performance/

2 https://www.theguardian.com/music/2016/aug/18/sia-lawsuit-israel-banter-concerts-stage-live-music

3 http://www.independent.co.uk/arts-entertainment/music/news/sia-hit-by-lawsuit-from-fans-wanting-refunds-for-lacklustre-gig-a7196916.html

23

Visual and Decorative Arts

'I was an awful critic. I operated on the assumption that there was an absolute scale of values against which art could be measured. I didn't trust my own subjective responses.'

Tom Stoppard, dramatist, n.d.

Objectives

As we indicated in the previous chapter, covering the dramatic arts is considered difficult, particularly if the writer does not have a background in a particular discipline. The same could also be said of the visual and decorative arts. But again, this is not to say that you can't do it. Like all good journalism, the key is preparation and a willingness to seek answers to the questions you ask, because the chances are that your readers or viewers will ask those same questions. In this chapter we focus on:

o   the visual arts
o   the decorative arts.

Introduction

Visual and decorative artists traditionally work in a range of different media, including, but not limited to, paint, charcoal, ink, wood, metal, ceramics, textiles and plastic. Some work exclusively in one medium, while others combine them. For example, furniture, ceramics, textiles and jewellery are considered decorative arts, although the former is often discussed in the context of interior design (see Chapter 24), whereas textiles and ceramics are situated within the visual arts. Jewellery sits alone as a fashion accessory. For the purposes of this chapter, we're going to discuss them together, given that they are often the basis of exhibitions in their own right. Having said that, there is a key difference between so-called 'fine art' on the one hand and 'decorative art' on the other, with the latter being considered useful, as well as aesthetically pleasing. There is another element to this: not all furniture qualifies as 'decorative art'. Mass-produced furniture is excluded; the field is limited to pieces produced by artist-craftspeople, generally one-offs, or small-scale runs that are essentially hand-made.

In recent times, the definition of 'visual art' has been challenged by exhibitions that have included bodily excretions and animal parts. These latest ventures have offended some traditionalists, but excited others who believe art can be broadly interpreted.

Unconventional artists who have established high-profile careers by adopting unique approaches include Andy Warhol, whose paintings of Campbell's soup cans can fetch millions of dollars; Christo, who has wrapped major monuments in polyethylene fabric, plastic and rope; the photographer Spencer Tunick, who shoots large-scale outdoor nude scenes (for example, 18,000 nudes in Mexico City in 2007; 1200 nudes floating in the Dead Sea (2011, 2016); 3200 blue nudes in Hull (2016; see Online resources later in this chapter); and artists such as Damien Hirst, who features dissected animals in his art (see, for example, *The Physical Impossibility of Death in the Mind of Someone Living*, 1991) and Andres Serrano, whose work includes body fluids (for example, the controversial 1989 photograph *Piss Christ*, which featured a plastic crucifix in a bottle of the artist's urine).

The last three artists have all enjoyed notoriety, Tunick for the fact that his work often breaks local laws, and because participants are told at the last minute where the shoot will take place so that authorities cannot prevent the event. Hirst and Serrano have been criticised for the nature of their work. Serrano's *Piss Christ* was, not surprisingly, condemned as blasphemous by some church groups when it appeared (Casey, 2004). A recent addition to this group is Tasmanian patron of the arts David Walsh, who has received mixed reviews for his multimillion-dollar collection of art housed at Mona (the Museum of Old and New Art), a purpose-built gallery and museum at Berriedale on Hobart's foreshore. One of the controversial centrepieces is a portrait by Chris Ofili titled *The Holy Virgin Mary* (1996). Another is the *Cloaca* machine produced by Belgian artist Wim Delvoye—a working model of the human digestive system, which turns food into faeces. (For details of these and other works at Mona, see Lohrey, 2011 and the Mona website: <http://mona.net.au>).

One thing is clear: our appreciation of art is subjective. We see that every year when Australia's major art prizes are judged (see, for example, debates over the Archibald Prize, and the Doug Moran National Portrait Prize winners). But that helps to attract crowds to exhibitions, and has enabled Australian museums and art galleries to develop magnificent collections that date back centuries; in many instances, well before Australia was settled.

In this chapter, the checklist is provided by Emeritus Professor Diana Wood Conroy, now retired, but formerly of the University of Wollongong's Visual Arts Program. Professor Conroy is herself an artist of note, combining her training in archaeology with a love of weaving tapestries.

Box 23.1 Visual arts review checklist

- Comment first on the main impact of the show. What visual languages are used in the exhibition?
- Who are the artists? Give dates of birth, places of birth, if possible, and the context of how the exhibition originated. What is the theme?
- Discuss medium, scale, tone, colour and composition.
- Discuss content and style—have other visual styles been appropriated or collaged in these works?

- Relate the work to other artists or to an art period (past or present).
- If possible, use a quote from the artist—the artist's voice is always vital.
- Describe one or two pieces, focusing on visual languages and content. Include at least one image in your review, fully referenced (title, artist, dimensions, date, provenance and medium).
- Think of ideas of difference, hybridity, diaspora and migration.
- Does text appear in the exhibition? Which language is central?
- Are issues of power coming through in the visual languages or in the content? (For example, certain media—painting, film—may be more 'powerful' than others, such as ceramics, textiles.)
- Is the gallery space itself important in constructing meaning in the works? Is it brilliantly lit or dim, low or high, crowded or empty? Does it remind you of a church or a supermarket, or is it neutral?

Don't forget

- What is the name of the gallery, the place and date?
- Who is the curator of the exhibition?
- Relate your final comment to your opening image of the main impact of the show.

Diana Wood Conroy

Let's have a look at some of these. As Professor Wood Conway's checklist reveals, much of her focus is technical in nature. Your artistic talents may have been limited to secondary school dabbles in oils or acrylics. You may even have attempted some lino cuts, or managed to produce a small sculpture or bowl that did not explode in the school kiln. Despite this, you've been sent along by your chief of staff or editor to cover a touring exhibition or perhaps an exhibition by an up-and-coming artist. If you're covering the exhibition for television, you'll really only have a minute, perhaps 90 seconds on a slow news day, to capture the essence of the show. And you'll do that by talking briefly to the artist or the curator of the exhibition and to marry this with some footage of the pieces on display. That will be all you can achieve in the limited time available.

However, if you have been assigned a page or a double spread in the arts section of the newspaper, or given space on a website, you need to think closely about how you will cover the exhibition. To start off, you need to think about your audience: are they generalists or specialists? If they are generalists, then you won't need to provide too much technical information (the focus will be on telling them what they could potentially gain from attending. However, if you are writing for a knowledgeable audience, you will be seeking to provide them with information they might not already know.

This is where your preliminary research becomes important. You need to go online (or to the library's collection of art history books) and find out as much as you can about the artist. Consider the following questions: who is featured? Are they contemporary artists, or from an earlier period (what is that period)? Are they internationally renowned (for example an old master), or a highly regarded Australian artist? If they come from an earlier period, what can you find out about the style of work? Who were the artist's contemporaries? Were they considered a leader or a disciple? Is there anything in their background that might interest your readers or listeners? Did they have multiple wives or mistresses, did they have a problem with alcohol or drugs, were they run out of town for failing to pay their debts, did they have a wealthy patron? How did they become interested in art? Were they a precocious young talent, or did they grow into their art slowly? Did they move from one field to another (for example, from painting to sculpture), or did they work across a range of different media?

Once you have conducted this preliminary research you are better placed to then talk to the artist (if they are alive) or to the curator (the person who has put the exhibition together), if they are not. You might want to ask them the questions that led your preliminary research. They may have a different take from that which appears online or in the books. If you have an opportunity to interview the artist, ask them about their work: why do they paint in a particular style, or work in a particular medium? Who or what influenced that decision? What underpins their work: is it a social or political conscience, events in their own life, or that of a friend? Is there a constant theme? To what extent has their focus and style changed over time?

In the case of an up-and-coming artist, you might ask about how they deal with the attention they're now receiving. This might be positive attention, but equally it could be negative, as was the case with the street artist Banksy before he became famous. Street art has become hugely popular in the past decade or so, and yet in the minds of many there is no difference between it and graffiti. In fact in the UK in 2008 a number of street artists were jailed, one for two years, for defacing public property that cost £1 million to clean up (see the *Independent* link at the end of the chapter). The question is now being asked, however, should street art be subjected to the same academic criticism as fine art? (See Artfuldodgy in Online resources.)

The curator might provide a different perspective to that of the artist. While the artist can talk about their motivation or inspiration, and their preferences for one medium over another, or even discuss why they focus on large canvases, or even triptychs over miniatures, the curator is more likely to address the exhibition (and individual pieces of art) from an academic perspective. Ideally, you should talk to both.

Furniture

To date in this chapter, we've tended to focus on art that adorns walls, with occasional mentions of sculpture. We now want to turn our attention to artisan furniture. Australia has a strong tradition of producing outstanding furniture makers. While we don't have the schools or styles that were identified with particular craftsmen (such as Chippendale or Morris in the UK), or styles (Arts and Crafts and Shaker to give just two examples from the US), early craftsmen did draw from the work of contemporaries in the UK, US and France, while others made do with what was available (the famous Tasmanian rustic chairmaker Jimmy Possum being a case in point). In an Australian context, the modern era began in the 1980s when people began to appreciate the outstanding work that was being commissioned for new buildings such as Parliament House in Canberra. This provided a much-needed fillip and effectively kick-started an industry that is showcased around the world today. Initially the furniture being produced was predominantly timber-based, but nowadays craftsmen and women are working in a wide range of materials, including steel, aluminium, glass and plastics.

Artisan furniture is relatively easy to review, although as with art, we shouldn't try and impose our views on our readers or viewers. There are a number of key issues to think about when reviewing furniture.

The first is design. Does it work? Do the different elements (in the case of steel combined with timber or another medium) work together aesthetically? Linked to this is practicality: What is its purpose? Does it achieve that goal? This is the old form versus function conundrum. In the case of some pieces, for example, chairs, standard questions are: 'Would you sit on it, or avoid it for fear of breaking it?' 'Is it comfortable?' 'Can I sit on it for two or three hours, in the case of a dining chair?' In the case of a dining table, the follow-up question is: 'How high is it?' 'Can a standard dining chair fit under it?' These questions can be applied to other forms of chairs and tables/desks.

The second question has to do with quality. What is the quality of the workmanship? In the case of timber furniture, you could ask: does it feature hand-cut dovetails and other joints, or are they machine-made? How well do they fit? Are the fasteners visible or concealed? How well do the drawers and doors fit? Do the top and sides sit flat or are they cupped or bowed? Are there glue lines visible? How well finished is the piece? Does it feel smooth to the touch, or should it have been further sanded before and between coats?

In the case of steel or furniture made from a combination of materials, you could look at the quality of the welding. Is it smooth, or rough? Does it display splatter? How well has it been finished? What coating has been applied? Does this work with the other elements?

Obviously, you need to go beyond the pieces on display to talk to the artist and/or curator of the show. The questions asked of them will provide the background readers or viewers are looking for.

Again the questions can be simply listed:

- Who is the maker/designer?
- Where do they come from?
- How long have they been making furniture?
- How did they become involved?
- What influences them: are they inspired by a particular period/maker?
- Do they allow the timber/steel/glass/synthetic/other material to speak for itself?

As with the earlier visual arts review, you need to include the following information in your review:

1 Where the exhibition is being held (address)
2 How long it is open for (dates and daily opening times)
3 Whether there is an entry fee and how much it is
4 Whether the pieces are on sale (and a price range).

Summary

o Writing reviews covering the arts is a challenging but rewarding experience.

o Writing such reviews is invariably a subjective process.

o However, reviewers need to recognise that the principal tenet guiding their approach should be fairness. If you don't like a particular exhibition, say so. But in so doing, make sure you explain *why* you don't like it. If there are good elements that help to offset the bad, make sure you let your viewers or readers know.

o At the end of the day, people will be seeking your guidance as to whether they should spend their money attending an exhibition.

Questions

1 What are the key elements to be considered when reviewing an exhibition of visual or decorative art?

2 To what extent should a reviewer's personal opinions (say an aversion to public displays of nudity in the case of a Spencer Tunick exhibition) influence their approach to the exhibition and how they couch their review?

3 What is the difference between visual and decorative art? If you were reviewing an exhibition of jewellery, what questions would you ask the designer?

Activities

1 Go to <www.supertouchart.com/2007/07/21/techniquethe-making-of-damien-hirsts-diamond-skull> or select an online photograph of Damian Hirst's diamond-encrusted skull *For the Love of God*, which is reputedly the most expensive piece of art in the world. Write a description of the skull as if you had been invited to its unveiling.

2 Using either *Piss Christ* or *Madonna and Child* as examples, write a piece explaining how Andres Serrano challenges popular orthodoxy with his work. You can draw on other reviews or commentaries, although you must acknowledge the work of other people.

3 Visit a local art/furniture gallery and write a review of a current exhibition. Remember to include artists' details and to interview the gallery owner and/or curator of the exhibition. If possible, see if you can also include comments from the artist/s.

References and additional reading

Akbar, A. (2008). Graffiti: Street Art or Crime? *Independent*. Accessed from http://www.independent. co.uk/arts-entertainment/art/features/graffiti-street-art-ndash-or-crime-868736.html

Casey, D. (2004). 'Sacrifice, *Piss Christ* and liberal excess', *Arts and Opinion*, 3(3).

Lohrey, A. (2011). 'High priest: David Walsh and Tasmania's Museum of Old and New Art', *The Monthly*, January: www.themonthly.com.au/arts-letters-amanda-lohrey-high-priest-david-walsh-and-tasmania-s-museum-old-and-new-art-2918

Online resources

Artfuldodgy: http://www.artfuldodgy.com/blog/street-critique-is-it-time-we-extended-art-criticism-to-street-art

Mona (the Museum of Old and New Art): http://mona.net.au

Spencer Tunick (Mexico, 2007): http://www.reuters.com/article/us-mexico-tunick-idUSN0626494920070506

Spencer Tunick (Hull, 2016): https://news.artnet.com/art-world/spencer-tunick-naked-crowd-hull-549758

Spencer Tunick (Dead Sea 2016): https://vimeo.com/182457714

Spencer Tunick (Dead Sea, 2016: https://news.artnet.com/art-world/spencer-tunick-revisits-dead-sea-installation-626669

24

Interiors and Makeovers

'A room should never allow the eye to settle in one place. It should smile at you and create fantasy.'

Juan Montoya, n.d.

Objectives

In this chapter we're talking about interiors, including makeovers and even large-scale renovations. We're not talking about knock-downs and rebuilds, or external projects, such as decks, patios and courtyards, even though these are very popular and feature heavily on the DIY television shows, websites, magazines and newspapers. Rather, we'll talk about some of the pros and cons of writing about interiors, including:

o   why this is a popular form of journalism

o   the skills required

o   some of the issues to think about when writing about interiors

o   your responsibilities as a journalist.

Introduction

Why interiors? The reality is that buying a house or apartment is the biggest single purchase most people will make in their lives. And even for those who can't afford, or choose not to buy, their own house or apartment, the prospect of turning where they live into a 'home' that reveals their personality is very strong.

We've also included this chapter in the revamped book because of the important role that real estate plays in the media advertising market, and of the opportunities this has subsequently created for journalists. Most journalists are familiar with the term 'rivers of gold'. This refers to the highly profitable advertising streams that newspapers and magazines enjoyed before the internet came along and obnoxious start-ups began to jockey for, and win, a share of the advertising dollar.

Today, real estate, and its various spin-offs, including interior design and DIY home renovations, has spawned a huge market. Have a think about some of the long-running shows that you see on television (including *The Block, Renovation Rescue, Better Homes and Gardens, Renovation Australia* and *Grand Designs*). These shows all cater to the wishes of people to both showcase their skills, and to turn their houses and apartments into homes they are proud of. In doing so, they are sharing tips and providing inspiration for other would-be renovators.

It's not just television shows that are catering to this market sector. It is newspapers, magazines and websites as well. You only need to walk into a newsagent and scan the shelves to see how many magazines are devoted to home renovation, building or interior and exterior design. Some of these are exclusively Australian, such as the *Better Homes and Gardens* magazine, which is a spin-off of the popular television show of the same name. Others are international (or locally adapted versions of an international publication, such as the *Grand Designs Australia* magazine). A great many of these shows and magazines also have companion websites that provide readers and viewers with additional information.

If you watch these shows, access the websites or flick through the magazines, you'll find that they are driven by advertising. For example, Bunnings Warehouse chain features heavily in the *Better Homes and Gardens* program and magazine. The support of the Mitre 10 Hardware Group was critical to the success of *The Block*, as were Reece Plumbing, Beaumont Tiles and Beacon Lighting. It has been estimated that the major advertisers paid $3 million each to partner with the show (News.com.au, 2014).

Creating a niche for yourself

The popularity of home renovation and interior design has created significant opportunities for journalists to provide stories for established publications, programs and websites, as well as to branch out on their own. For example, during his early years as a journalist, one of the authors saw an opportunity to do some freelance work for *House and Garden*, one of Australia's best-known magazines. He realised that the magazine often ran features on historic homes, but never of historic Tasmanian homes. Working in Tasmania at the time, and knowing that the state possessed a number of beautiful old Georgian, Victorian and Federation homesteads, he pitched a series of stories to the magazine.

The editor said that he was welcome to submit a story, but the magazine would not commit to it until they'd seen it. Knowing that the articles published in *House and Garden* were built around photographs, rather than text, he enlisted the work of a photographer friend who had the equipment required to take high quality transparencies. After gaining permission to profile one of Tasmania's oldest historic homes, and conducting the research required to understand its history, they completed the assignment and submitted it to *House and Garden*.

House and Garden loved the article and over the years, the author and his photographer submitted a number of articles for publication. All were used, some even reappearing in the magazine's annual, which was effectively a compendium of its best pieces published that year. This is a good example of seeing an opportunity and seizing it.

Where do you start?

You don't need to be a qualified interior designer, or even architect to write on this topic. You do, however, need to have a good sense of style, and you need to be able to tap into the latest trends. According to Karen

Watts Perkins, who is both a designer and journalist, there are a number of skills required if you want to succeed in this field, including:

1   The ability to write well;

2   A willingness to learn; and

3   An interest in the field.

Let's look at these individually.

The ability to write well

This is a given, although it is worth noting, as we point out with the historic homes example earlier, that the ability to write well is not as important as the capacity to take powerful photographs and, increasingly, video and audio. Remember that your work may appear on multiple platforms and you need to be able to cater for their individual needs. For example, if you are writing for a hard-copy newspaper or magazine, you will focus on photographs and text. But if you're producing a story for a television or online audience then you can include video and audio. The use of video broadens your scope. For example, whereas a photograph will only capture part of a room, with a video camera you can do a 360-degree walk around, showing the whole room in one go.

The ability to take powerful photographs also involves the capacity to frame those photographs so that the room is not cluttered. Have a think about the central elements in a room. Are there too many objects in sight? Would the photograph or video benefit if some of the lesser items are removed or placed elsewhere?

With interior photography it is important that the lighting is correct. This is a complex area—one that involves considerable skills and thought. We don't profess to be expert photographers or videographers. However there are a number of excellent online sites that provide some very helpful tips on lighting and product placement. For example, Mike Kelley (2012) says that he takes a number of factors into account when composing an interior shot, including 'interior light levels, exterior light levels, the amount of flash that we want to use [and] color temperature.' Kelley's advice is important and his article (see link at the end of the chapter) is worth reading, because it provides a step-by-step approach to lighting and framing interiors. Another good example is provided by Tony Roslund (2014). There is nothing worse than photographs or video of an interior that show objects half in light and half out of light, or where you can see the flash flaring off a polished surface, or a face in a mirror.

Likewise, the room and objects in it need to retain their perspective. Editors get cranky if they receive photographs that distort the shape of a room or object. Interiors photography is an art form in which you need to be able to maintain the perspective of the items you are featuring. You must understand how to use your camera and tripod in combination so these flaws don't appear in your photographs.

Audio can also be a powerful tool. It can add to a written piece or work as a standalone, or complement to a slide show or video. Audio is a particularly powerful medium if the journalist has a particular element of a story that they want to highlight. For example, one of the historic homes covered for *House and Garden* was attacked by bushrangers. The family that owned the property was aware of this story and advised the writer. While he included that little snippet in his feature, it would have lent itself to a more personalised account via audio where there was greater capacity to explore the episode in more detail than was the case with print space. The same applies to a house that may have been home to an important person in Australian history (for example, see the *Restoration Australia* program on Emmaville, a cottage linked to Banjo Paterson (ABC, 2017), or a building that had an interesting history (perhaps as a well-known factory, or store, before being converted into residential accommodation).

Even though journalists are increasingly tapping into these technologies, they rarely stand alone. Good interior design writing relies on explanation. Yes, you can provide photographs and video of rooms or houses showing the latest trends, but these can be meaningless unless you can explain or interpret them in words for your readers, viewers or listeners. As we discuss later in the chapter, the writing that accompanies the visuals must be light and bright. If you are using technical language, break it down in a way that an ordinary reader or viewer will understand. If you're explaining how to do something, break the process down into easy steps.

A willingness to learn

This is where a willingness to learn (Karen Watts Perkins's second criterion) becomes important. There are several elements to this. One is basic to journalism. It is a willingness to do any research required to be able to tackle a story and do it justice. This was highlighted with the *House and Garden* articles. The writer had always had an interest in architecture, particularly period architecture. He'd also had an interest in antique— mainly Georgian and Victorian—furniture. This meant that he could comfortably write about the building and furniture styles. But the features weren't just about the furniture, or the crockery and cutlery that adorned the extension dining table. Just as important were the architectural features (the doors, skirtings, architraves, cornices and windows, as well as the colour schemes). He had to do considerable research to make sure that the terminology was correct, to avoid being inundated by architects, antique collectors and history buffs railing that he'd confused Georgian with Colonial, or Federation with Edwardian. This links directly to Watts Perkins's third criterion.

Be interested in the field you're writing about

This applies to all forms of feature writing. But it is particularly relevant to interiors writing where you not only need to be knowledgeable, but you should also be interested in the field. While the two generally go hand in hand, it is possible to have one without the other. To be knowledgeable you need to do the research and know where to find the information. Much of this can be located online. But to be genuinely interested in the topic, you need to do more: you need to talk to the experts, go to the trade shows, and talk to the manufacturers.

With interiors writing you're selling a dream. You're encouraging people to think about what might be feasible in their own home or apartment. That's why light and bright writing is important. And in the majority of cases, you're also trying to convince them that such makeovers can be achieved on a budget that is within their reach, so don't deceive your audience. Don't say that something is achievable for a few dollars and/or a weekend of labour by a relatively competent DIYer, when you know that realistically it will cost thousands of dollars and probably require a team of professionals to pull off.

Sometimes, however, you get to write pieces on interiors that you know are well beyond the budgets of your readers or viewers, but you write them anyway, because people just like to share someone else's dream. And let's face it, while most of your readers or viewers won't necessarily be able to afford the whole makeover, there might be one or two elements that they can use (or adapt) when it comes to their own project.

This is the thing about writing on interiors (or even exteriors for that matter). People often begin to look for ideas well before they start the actual project, sometimes years before. Many people cut articles or photographs out of magazines and paste them into an 'ideas book', which they then call upon when the time arrives to start the project (be it a room, a whole house makeover, or even a new house).

Of course there can be problems with this approach: fashions change so quickly that if someone chooses a tile, paint colour or carpet three years before they start a project, then chances are when they actually get around to ordering them, they are either out of fashion, or no longer available. But that doesn't really matter. It is about generating ideas and convincing people that what they are proposing is feasible. One of the critical things about interiors writing is that it is generally focused on the here and now.

It tends to highlight the new trends, or what the experts believe the trends will be in the year (or season) ahead. There are exceptions to that, of course; for example, when talking about the interiors of heritage-listed homes. But generally, these represent a very small segment of the market. Most of what the market focuses on is new. If you go online, for example, and do a search for interior design tips, you'll get plenty of hits. You'll also notice that:

- the tips change quickly (often they are seasonal); and
- while the various sites and magazines seem to agree broadly on what is in vogue and what is not, they can differ widely when it comes to the specifics.

Who determines what the trends will be? Is it the interior designers? Is it the journalists and their editors? Is it the manufacturers? We suspect they all have a role to play, although design trends are probably a bit like the latest clothing fashions: they are largely determined by the manufacturers. And, if the interior designers and journalists like them then they'll probably promote them.

But if they don't like them—or they like another product more—then they'll probably favour the one they prefer over the one they don't and this can have serious ramifications for the manufacturer whose product is not getting the free air-play or exposure. Yes, they can pay for an ad to appear in a popular magazine or TV show, but normally they like to couple that with favourable editorial coverage. They'd hardly pay for an ad that sits beside a rave review of a competitor's product (which might also involve a promotional price as well for readers of the magazine, or the first 100 people to ring an SMS number).

This is where the ethical dilemmas can start to appear for the journalist, or perhaps more broadly the editor/producer who is responsible for the positioning of advertisements in the publication, website or program. The journalist has to be fair about reviewing products, remembering that just because they like or dislike a product doesn't mean that everyone else will hold the same view. Fairness means writing in a balanced way, pointing out what you see as the strengths or flaws of a product, while giving consumers room to make up their own minds.

Types of stories

As a journalist, interior design stories can take a number of different forms. There are the typical stories about makeovers (rooms, apartments, houses), there are profiles on people (and companies) working within a particular sector. For example, magazines that produce a dedicated issue on kitchen or bathroom makeovers will frequently profile some of the best-known and up-and-coming names working in that sector. Sometimes companies will pay to be included in such issues, calculating that the cost involved will be rewarded through the sales such involvement generates (as is the case with the companies that advertise on *The Block* etc.).

There are also articles on new product releases (paints, floor coverings, window furnishings, handles, lighting, benchtops, whitegoods, furniture etc.). These might be relatively short pieces (a couple of hundred words plus a photograph), or they might be part of an integrated article (a much larger piece with multiple photographs or video that takes a number of new products and has an interior designer work them into a room). Both types of article are important, because while the first might draw a potential purchaser's attention to a new item, it is the second—longer—piece that helps them visualise how it could potentially fit into their kitchen, bedroom, bathroom or loungeroom.

Box 24.1   Tips for writing about buildings (both interiors and exteriors)

1   Start by doing your research:
  - Is the building new or old?
  - What is the dominant architectural style?
  - Has it been renovated/adapted over the years?
  - Does it have links to someone who is important, interesting or notorious?
  - What can you find out about them to help structure your article?

2   Are you writing about the whole building (inside and out, including the grounds) or are you focusing on one part of it, for example a kitchen or bathroom makeover?

3   Who are the key people involved (the architect, the builder, interior decorator, landscape designer, clients)?
  - What have they sought to achieve with the makeover/build/rebuild?
  - Have they achieved it?

4   What are the strengths of the project?
  - Use of materials?
  - Environmental impact?
  - The use of light/shade?
  - View?

- A clever use of space?
- Sympathy to historic origins?

5   What are the weaknesses (as above, but also the following considerations)?
- Small, crowded rooms?
- Poor workmanship?
- A mismatch of colours?
- Building materials that don't go together?
- Poor lighting?
- Furniture, floor, wall and window coverings that clash?
- Appliances that don't fit the brief (trying to meet a budget shortfall by buying cheap kitchen whitegoods, lights, tap fittings etc.)?

Summary

o   Remember when writing about interiors you don't have to reinvent the wheel. As a journalist working in this area you will be inundated with promotional material about new products. But that shouldn't be your only source of inspiration. See what other people are writing about. It may be that your audience would be interested in a similarly themed article, program, or special edition. You might be able to take a different angle, and feature different products. You might want to specialise on top end products or makeovers, or, if that has been done, focus on mid-range or lower-end products. Interior design is highly individualistic. That is, what one person loves, another may hate.

o   And while we tend to be trend followers rather than trendsetters when it comes to design (think about all the box-style houses that are being built at the moment), we often look for something that appeals to us when embarking on a design project.

o   So, don't impose your views on your readers, listeners or viewers. You can tell them what is in fashion and what's not. You can tell them what goes with what. But at the end of the day, you shouldn't tell them what they must do, or what they shouldn't do.

Questions

1   Why is writing about interiors—or real estate for that matter—so important to journalism?
2   Why shouldn't journalists seek to tell their audience what they must do when it comes to interior design?
3   Name six types of stories you could write if working in this area.

Activities

1   Select a house or apartment you are familiar with (it might be your family home, a friend's place, or even your university accommodation). Write a 400–500 word review of it, detailing its best and worst features, and indicating how it could be improved by a makeover. Supply at least three photographs, or a short video clip with your profile.

2   Go online and locate as much promotional material as you can on a product that has just been released. It might be a new line of whitegoods, or range of furniture. Provide a 300-word profile on the product.

3   Select two magazines and two websites. Write a comparison of their treatment of a similar topic, looking at writing style, use of photographs/video and content. Which do you believe is the most effective and why?

References and additional reading

Australian Broadcasting Commission (2017). *Restoration Australia*, Episode 5: Emmaville. Accessed from: http://www.abc.net.au/tv/programs/restoration-australia/

Kelley, M. (2012). 'The anatomy of a luxury interior': https://fstoppers.com/strobe-light/bts-anatomy-luxury-interior-shot-3127

News.com.au (2014). http://www.news.com.au/finance/business/brands-such-as-mitre-10-the-good-guys-suzuki-and-iselect-were-the-real-winners-of-the-block-fans-v-faves/news-story/681ccb6b94898f7f00404c45e9999169

Roslund, T. (2014). 'How to quickly light and composite architectural interiors': https://fstoppers.com/architecture/how-quickly-light-and-composite-architectural-interiors-50492

25
Technology

'Any sufficiently advanced technology is indistinguishable from magic.'

Arthur C. Clarke, science fiction author, n.d.

'All of the biggest technological inventions created by man—the airplane, the automobile, the computer—says little about his intelligence, but speaks volumes about his laziness.'

Mark Kennedy, American politician, n.d.

Objectives

Irrespective of whether you agree with the views of Clarke or Kennedy, quoted above, the reality is that nowadays people are consumed by technology. Whether that involves the latest techno-gadget, mobile phone, computer, tablet, stereo system or television, people appear willing to spend to acquire. Those looking to buy tend to seek information that provides them with the justification to buy one make or model over another. Much of the information is developed by PR companies for the manufacturers, but a great deal, including often the most useful information for would-be purchasers, is produced by independent reviewers, be they writing for newspapers, magazines, online publication, or even working for one of an increasing number of radio and television programs that are devoted to, or have segments on, product reviews.

Why is so much space devoted to technology in the media? In part because as consumers we're infatuated with them; and secondly because we don't think that we can live without them. This is highlighted by the following statistics. Nearly 80 per cent of Australians own a smartphone, and six in 10 people own multiple devices (Deloittes, 2016). For the media, this represents a great money-making opportunity. In this chapter we cover:

o   how to write technology reviews

o   how to support your reviews visually

o   some of the ethical issues to consider.

Introduction

As indicated above, Australians seem to be obsessed by technology. Virtually all homes have televisions, and internet access is considered a 'must have' by most families, along with iPods, iPads, mobile phones and digital cameras. The technological revolution has, within one generation, replaced vinyl records with cassette tapes, which were quickly superseded by CDs. Today, we're all going digital and tapes (both audio and audio-visual) are virtually a thing of the past. How do we keep up? Or should we?

Despite the cost of new technology, many people believe they must have the latest gadgets, and this lust has created new opportunities for writers. We don't profess to be experts in the area of technology, computers and gadgets—in fact we've been known to turn to our children for advice. But we do recognise that opportunities exist for writers who can tap into the wants and needs of readers, listeners and viewers.

The task for reviewers in this area is made relatively easy by the fact that manufacturers want exposure for their products. If you are an established commentator on new technologies and have a column, multiple columns or even a combination of columns and regular slots on radio or television, then manufacturers will bombard you with material and samples. You will be asked to try out everything. Some of these inventions will become the next 'must have', as demand is driven by comments, reviews and advertising campaigns. A good example is 'Digital life', a column by John Davidson that runs online during the week and in the weekend edition of *The Australian Financial Review*. Davidson provides a no-nonsense insight into the products he reviews, mixing praise with criticism and a smattering of humour.

'Digital life' is only one of a number of publications or sites that review new products as, or even before, they hit the shops. Others include *Technology Review* <www.technologyreview.com>, CNET <www.cnet.com.au>, ZEDNet <www.zdnet.com/reviews>, Switched On Technology <www.news.com.au/technology> and PC & Tech Authority <www.pcauthority.com.au>.

Some of the reviews on these sites are written by so-called tech heads, but the majority are produced by journalists who have a technological bent. Again, there are considerable opportunities in this area. It is just a case of targeting what you want to write about and then identifying potential publications or websites that cover these products. You might even decide that no one is doing what you'd like to do, thereby creating an opportunity for you to establish a new website or magazine dedicated to a particular type of technology review.

Remember, the key to successful reviews is to write accessibly. Write a review that provides enough technical information for those who are so inclined, while not ignoring the fact that the majority of potential consumers are probably not that interested in the hi-tech specs. They are primarily interested in knowing if the product will do what the manufacturers claim, if it is good value for money and if it can be repaired if it breaks down inside the warranty period. It is also a good idea to try to infuse a little humour—even a personal anecdote, if relevant—into your writing. Bear in mind that your job is to engage with your audience and, to do that, you need to understand who is reading your work or listening to you.

Box 25.1   Critical tips for writing tech reviews

1 Understand your product. There are a number of aspects to this. Try to access information the manufacturer has prepared. This can include technical manuals and public relations material. Hopefully this will be accessible online, but if it is not, contact the company directly, tell them who

you are and the name of the website/program/publication you're writing for. If you're lucky (or have a sufficiently high profile as a reviewer) they may offer to provide you with a review sample of the product. If the product has already been released, have a look at what other reviewers are saying about it (read widely, go online, listen to what other people, reviewers and consumers alike, are saying). Are they generally positive or negative? Is there a common complaint, or feature that has been singled out for praise?

2   It is difficult to review a product if you can't test-drive it. It doesn't matter whether it is software, the latest smartphone or tablet, audio system, or television, you can't reasonably talk about it unless you have had a chance to review it first-hand. As we've discussed elsewhere in this book, it is often difficult for new reviewers or start-up publications and websites to obtain pre-release copies of a product. Remember, the companies and the PR agencies working for them want maximum exposure, so they're likely to hand out the freebies to those reviewers, publications and sites that can prove they have a solid audience (and that those people are in the market to purchase the product they're hoping to sell). That's why companies such as Bauer (the publisher of more than 60 magazine titles in Australia) tend to conduct considerable market research to help them understand what their audience is interested in.

3   If you are unable to obtain a free sample, don't despair. You have a couple of options:

a   you could borrow a friend's (this might be an option in the case of a new smartphone, camera, etc.). If it is a television or sound system, they might let you check it out at their place.

b   you could purchase the product itself

c   you can go into a local store and see if they stock it. You might be able to convince a helpful salesperson to take you through its features. Alternatively, you might be able to spend enough time playing with it yourself to develop a relatively clear impression of its strengths and weaknesses.

Generally tech reviews, like motoring reviews, are conducted over days, weeks or even months, depending on the complexity of the product. So if you've only been granted brief access to a product, you need to say so, as this will limit the type of review that you can produce, and may influence any audience reactions to your review.

4   In conducting your review, there are a number of things you need to look out for, particularly if the product being reviewed is an updated model of a product that has been around for a while, or if it is a newcomer to an already established market (for example, the new generation of smartphones that are seeking to compete with the iPhone). In this case, the first question to ask yourself is: (a) how does the new edition or newcomer differ from the previous edition or competitors? Is it larger or smaller, thinner, or bulkier? How does it fit in your hand? Is it easy to navigate, or has the manufacturer added a new level of complexity that makes accessing your messages or contacts more difficult? Is the camera better or worse? In what ways? Are there more apps? How does it talk to other devices you might want to pair it with? Can you use your old charger, or earphones? Is your music collection transferable? Does it appear more robust, or is the screen/case likely to shatter if accidentally knocked off your desk, or dropped while you're walking along taking a selfie? Finally, ask yourself, how unique is the product? Does it do what

the company claims in the advertising blurb? Will it stand out from the competition? Is the price reasonable? If not, why not? Is there a warranty? How long is the warranty period and how does it compare with the competition?

5   Before writing up your review or recording your vlog, you need to have a clear idea of who will read or listen to your piece. Ask yourself the question: are they likely to be technically knowledgeable, or are they just interested in buying a product that will do a particular task (or series of tasks)? This will help determine what information you provide, and how you present it. If you're writing for a technically knowledgeable audience, then you can include more details about the specifications. But if you're writing for a generalist audience, you would tone this information down, focusing instead on the everyday features, such as, in the case of a new television, picture clarity, whether it has live wind-back features, the capacity to record programs etc.).

6   Ideally, technology reviews should contain some visuals. A photograph is the most obvious starting point. Increasingly, however, video has become an important feature of such reviews, and is often coupled with audio. While photography is static, video can provide viewers with an opportunity to see a product being used. It might even include a 'how to' section, covering set up, or even some of the advanced features. Finally, it is a good idea to include a fact box that summarises specifications, including recommended retail price, as this is often the determining factor for many purchasers.

7   While technology reviews are often standalone, that is they feature one product, it is a good idea to produce comparisons of a number of products that compete in a particular market segment. Remember, consumers often draw comparisons between different products before making a decision to buy. If you have a reputation for doing that leg-work for them, you will attract increasing numbers of readers, viewers or listeners to your publication or website. Again, the task is relatively straightforward: ask yourself the questions you would consider when purchasing a particular product. List the differences, highlighting what you see as the relative strengths and weaknesses, again using a fact box, so that the information is conveniently summarised.

Ethical considerations

While we deal with ethical issues in more detail in Chapter 8, there are a number of questions that are particularly relevant to the topics we've discussed in this chapter. They are:

1   how do you deal with information that paints a product in a negative light? And

2   should you reveal to your audience that you have been provided with a product free of charge, or have travelled to the launch of a product as the guest of a particular company?

The second of these is probably easier to answer than the first. All major media organisations have (or should have) a code of conduct that requires journalists, among other things, to state when they have received hospitality paid for by a company whose product they are reviewing, or even received a gift from a company. In fact, a number of Australian media organisations will not allow their journalists to travel as the guest of a company whose product they are reviewing: if the media organisation believes the story is worthwhile, it will cover the costs itself. Other companies require their journalists to forfeit all 'gifts' they receive. The ABC in Tasmania, for example, wraps these gifts and places them under its Giving Tree. These are then distributed to needy people at Christmas each year.

As we reveal in Chapter 18 when discussing travel journalism, a number of media organisations require their journalist to include a kicker line in their story along the lines of: 'Joe Bloggs travelled to Japan to inspect facilities for the 2020 Olympic Games as a guest of the Japan–Australia Alliance.' Ideally, this same requirement should apply to tech reviews. Why? Because having this knowledge might influence how the audience responds to the review. We're not saying that journalists shouldn't accept freebies. However, it is worth pointing out that readers or listeners might be less willing to accept everything said in the review if they knew that the journalist had been wined and dined by the host company, or had received the product free of charge. This is particularly the case if a product is later found to be defective.

This brings us to the first question raised earlier, namely, should reviewers highlight a product's deficiencies if they find them. Our response is yes. If you find fault with a product, say so. But there is a rider: you need to be fair. Most tech reviews will point to the strengths and weaknesses of a product (often summarised in a pros and cons box). Generally, reviews focus on a product's strengths before turning to the negatives. But sometimes, the negatives overwhelm the positives, as Samsung found out recently when its Galaxy 7 Note was withdrawn from the market after bursting into flames, causing it to be banned by a number of airlines around the world. Samsung's version of the phablet, as some reviewers call the larger style smartphones, was widely praised in early reviews, as the following comment reveals: 'The Galaxy Note 7 is the pinnacle of Samsung's design and is the culmination of everything the company's learned since ditching faux-leather and plastic disguised as metal.' The full review is available at Trusted Reviews (see References). However, Samsung was forced into the biggest product recall in history when faulty batteries caused the phones to burst into flames. In this situation, the reviews turned from positive to negative, not because the reviewers didn't like the original concept, but because of the risks associated with them, something that Samsung acknowledged.

Summary

o Reviewing is one of the most enjoyable areas of journalism. To be given access to a latest-model techno gadget for a couple of days, weeks or months can be great for the reviewer. If you love the product, however, giving it up may be difficult.

o As with other forms of reviewing, you do need to consider the consequences of your comments. Will it cause a product to be unfairly shunned by prospective purchasers?

Questions

1 To what extent has advertising influenced the growth of the technology reviews sector?
2 What are the primary issues a technology reviewer should consider when writing a product review?
3 Are there any ethical considerations that apply to technology reviews?
4 How would you have covered the Samsung recall if you'd been a technology reviewer who had previously praised the Galaxy Note 7?

Activities

1 Write a review of your favourite piece of technology (mobile phone, iPod etc.) and compare it with other similar products owned by at least two friends. How do the different products compare in terms of price, capacity, robustness etc.?
2 Go online and find a number of professionally written reviews of the product you reviewed above. How do they compare with the review you produced?
3 Locate two technology websites. Write a comparison of how they review new releases. Which approach do you prefer and why?

References and additional reading

CNET Australia: www.cnet.com.au

Switched on Technology: news.com.au—technology: www.news.com.au/technology

PC&Tech Authority: www.pcauthority.com.au

Technology Review: www.technologyreview.com

Trusted Reviews: http://www.trustedreviews.com/
samsung-galaxy-note-7-review#U3fQLedOPyTgKzWe.99

ZEDNet: www.zdnet.com/reviews

Online resources

Deloittes (2016): http://landing.deloitte.com.au/rs/761-IBL-328/images/Media_Consumer_Survey_
Report.pdf

26
Motor Vehicles

'I will build a motor car for the great multitude ... constructed of the best materials, by the best men to be hired, after the simplest designs that modern engineering can devise ... so low in price that no man making a good salary will be unable to own one.'

Henry Ford, n.d.

'We at BMW do not build cars as consumer objects, just to drive from A to B. We build mobile works of art.'

Chris Bangle, designer, n.d.

Objectives

A great deal has changed in the nearly 100 years between Henry Ford's comment above and that of Chris Bangle. In that time, Ford's dream of accessibility has been realised, but motor vehicle technology has morphed from the simple to the highly complex, with computers replacing traditional mechanics' tool kits in many of the tasks associated with building and maintaining motor vehicles. In this chapter we cover motor vehicle reviews. While we focus on motor cars, much of what we say could equally apply to motor bikes, motor homes, caravans, boats and other forms of transport.

In this chapter we cover:

o   how to write motor vehicle reviews

o   how to support your reviews through the use of video, photography and audio

o   some of the ethical issues to consider.

Motor vehicle reviews

Introduction

Historically, motor vehicle advertising, along with real estate advertising, has been a cash cow for the media. With motor vehicles the second most significant purchase most people make, outside of a home or apartment, its importance as a media revenue source is not surprising. According to the ABS, in 2016 there were 18.4 million registered motor vehicles in Australia, a 2 per cent increase on the previous year (ABS, 2016). That includes motor cars, commercial vehicles, motor bikes and campervans. Not bad for a country of just 24 million people (ABS, 2016). According to Price Waterhouse Coopers (PWC) in the 2016 financial year motor vehicle advertising accounted for 17 per cent of the $6.8 billion online advertising market $1.16b (IAB Australia, 2016).

Media organisations recognise this, with whole publications, websites and newspaper sections dedicated to motoring, both during the week and at weekends. For example, Australia's two largest newspaper groups, News Ltd and Fairfax, both devote considerable resources—both online and hard copy—to motoring. The popularity of motor vehicles has also led to something of a boom in specialist magazines, including both print and soft copy versions. For example, a scan of the *Press Reader* site in February 2017 showed 15 publications covering a range of interests, including new vehicles, classic cars, racing cars, off-road vehicles and even a specialist magazine on in-car entertainment (<http://www.pressreader.com.ezproxy. sl.nsw.gov.au/catalog/magazines/australia>). On top of that, there are specialist magazines catering for people interested in caravanning, trucks, buses, motor bikes, industrial and farming equipment or boats. This does not even include the large number of online sites that cater to these and other interests.

Many of the magazines have companion websites, and some, such as Bauer's *Whichcar* (<https:// www.whichcar.com.au>), draw from reviews published in three of its magazines—*Wheels*, *Motor* and *4x4 Australia*. What this means is that prospective purchasers can find information on the vehicles they're interested in test-driving, without having to venture into the showroom. It is only when they're narrowed the options down to an achievable shortlist that prospective buyers venture out to test drive the product for themselves. Before they do that, however, they've spent countless hours online, or skimming through newspapers and magazines, reading and listening to what the so-called 'experts' have to say.

Format

If you look through the large number of newspapers, magazines and websites devoted to motor vehicle reviews, you will notice that they all follow a fairly similar format, which can be summarised under the following headings: 1) price, 2) performance, 3) safety, 4) comfort and 5) environmental features. Price is obviously a key factor (see ABS, Social Trends study, 2013). It will determine whether Australians can genuinely afford to buy a particular vehicle, or simply read about it, hoping that one day they might enjoy a financial windfall that turns their dream into reality.

Because of this, it is unusual for newspapers (with the possible exception of the *Australian Financial Review*), to run full-scale features on higher-end vehicles, such as the $3.9 million Aston Martin AM-RB 00, due for release in 2018, or the various European super cars that will cost the average Australian more than 10 years' salary (in pre-tax dollars). The majority of reviews, therefore, tend to be pitched at the low to middle end of the market, although there are some exceptions. For example, in early 2017, Motoring.com.au ran a review of the yet to be released BMW M760i limousine, which was due to arrive in Australia in mid-2017 at a price of $420,000 plus on-road costs. In recent times, many reviewers have sought to draw comparisons between different vehicles in the same market niche, rather than write about just one new release. For example, in October 2016, the same website published a direct comparison between the Renault Koleos and Hyundai Tucson (Matthews, 7 October). A month later, the Tucson was compared with the Volkswagen Tiguan (Armstrong, 16 November). The benefit of working on an online site is that the reviewers can use audio and video to complement the traditional written review.

In talking about performance, motoring writers tend to pitch their comments at male readers and listeners. For example, in his review of the E63 AMG estate, Toby Hagon described its performance in the following terms: 'The new 5.5 litre V8 is the mightiest AMG engine yet. A new design and the addition of twin turbochargers means it manages a blend of sledgehammer-like torque delivery and prodigious higher-rev power that ensures phenomenal acceleration' (Hagon, 2012). He went on to talk about the optional performance pack that offers even more for those drivers who are not satisfied with the fact that in standard configuration it is 'quicker than any large wagon deserves to be'.

Discussions of safety features are often directed at women or families. In the case of the Mercedes, the inclusion of 11 airbags, stability and traction control were all mentioned, and reinforced through the following statement: 'nineteen inch tyres grip the bitumen like a limpet and make for superb cornering ability' (Hagon, 2012).

Like safety, comfort is often pitched at female purchasers. There is often a hard sell on space and features such as rear DVD players, sound systems and the like, particularly in vehicles categorised as family movers (for example, have a look at the Hyundai comparisons discussed above).

Finally, environmental features have become a major selling point, with emphasis on hybrids and smart technology vehicles: those that produce low CO_2 emissions and are economical in their fuel use. The AMG review covered the latter with the following comment: 'The AMG can also be frugal—to a point. Claimed consumption is just 10.1 litres per 100 kilometres, although it is not difficult to double that if you get enthusiastic' (Hagon, 2012).

Motoring journalism provides considerable opportunities for aspiring writers. Before applying for an internship or traineeship at one of these publications, it is important to understand not only who they write for (their audience), but critically how they write. To do this, you should read the magazine and try to emulate the house writing style. You will see that all the magazines have a slightly different style that may be reflected in the type of reviews they do, the language employed, the use of photographs, video and audio, etc. Of course, if you are unsuccessful when pitching a story at the established magazines or websites, think about setting up your own blog. It might take you a while to build up enough rapport with dealers who will let you borrow one of their vehicles for a test run, but perseverance is the key here. Start small, start local and see how you go. If you produce good work, then you might just develop a niche for yourself. For example, you might start with second-hand cars, some you review yourself, others reviewed by people who own a particular vehicle. You could quickly build a website that becomes a must-read for mums and dads who are looking out for a first car for their son or daughter. This could potentially feed into the various magazines run by the various state-based motoring organisations, like the NRMA in NSW, or RACV in Victoria.

Box 26.1 Critical tips for writing motoring reviews:

1 Motoring reviews can't be carried out by armchair critics, including watchers of the BBC's iconic *Top Gear* program. To write an effective review, you need to get behind the wheel of the car, boat or bike for yourself and see how it performs. There are a number of elements that need to be included in an effective review, including:

a *The type of vehicle.* Is it a sedan, hatch, family wagon, SUV, ute? This is particularly relevant when you are conducting comparisons of vehicles. There is no point comparing a ute with an SUV, or a small station wagon with an open top tourer, or even a million dollar Mercedes Maybach sedan with a $2000 Series 1 Land Rover produced in the late 1940s or 1950s. You must compare like with like. People who look at comparisons are doing so because they want a realistic choice, as the discussion above which talks about how the Hyundai Tucson was compared with the Volkswagen Tiguan and Renault Koleos, reveals. One of the key comparisons between these vehicles was price.

b *Price.* This is obviously a key factor. It will determine whether someone can genuinely afford a particular motor vehicle or not. They might dream about buying a $400,000 Lamborghini, but with five children know that a $30,000 or $40,000 people mover is more realistic. Significantly some websites will have repayment calculators on their web pages, thereby allowing people to do a quick calculation on how much a vehicle will cost them each week, fortnight or month in repayments. These calculators also enable them to draw comparisons between cars in their wish list.

c *Performance.* Some prospective drivers want to know how quickly a vehicle will go from 0—100kph, and what its top speed is, even though Australian speed limits prevent drivers in all states bar the Northern Territory from even remotely challenging their car's top-end performance. But there are other factors as well that will enter their calculations, including its towing capacity (in the case of people who own a boat, caravan or trailer), its torque, or whether it is a manual or automatic.

d *Safety.* In Australia, all motor vehicles have an ANCAP safety rating, in which vehicles are rated from one to five stars based on supervised crash tests. The howsafeisyourcar.com.au website distinguishes between crash avoidance, crash protection and driver features. It identifies 30 features that could improve the safety of modern motor vehicles (see <http://howsafeisyourcar. com.au/Safety-Features/>). It is important to identify which of these features the car under review possesses, and how its ANCAP rating compares to other vehicles in the same category.

e *Comfort.* There are a number of elements to this. How comfortable are the seats? How much leg room (and head room) is there? Will an average-sized person struggle to get in or out of the vehicle, or position themselves in the driver's seat?

f *Interior fitout.* What are the seating configurations? Are they realistic? What fabrics are used on the seats? How effective is the air-conditioning and/or heating? What other mod cons are included (arm and head rests, drink holders, stereo system, seat-back DVD players, bluetooth connectivity etc.)? What is the quality of the fitout like? Is it high end, or cheap looking (given the price point they're pitching at car at)? What are the sound levels like? Can you hear any squeaks and rattles? Do you need to turn the stereo on high to hear it?

g   *External features.* These vary across the different types of motor vehicle. Four-wheel drives, for example, tend to have far more optional features than standard vehicles (bull bars, tow bars, different size wheels and tyres, roof racks, chequer plate wing tips etc.).

h   *Environmental features.* Does it meet the latest emissions standards? What is the fuel economy (around town versus on the open road)? Does it come in an electric or hybrid option? If not, is such a model planned and when is its anticipated release date?

i   *Luggage space.* Can it fit a pram, a couple of sets of golf clubs, or the family's 10-year-old Great Dane with hip dysplasia?

j   *Did you enjoy driving it?* If so, say why. If not, indicate what you think the issues are. Run a pros and cons table. Say what helps it stand out from the pack, or why it gets lost among its competitors.

k   Remember to include plenty of photos, both internal and external, and if you have the capacity, run some video of the test drive.

Ethical considerations

What happens if you don't like the motor vehicle and think that it is a dud? Should you abandon your review, or should you leave out the negatives? In some respects this is a tough question, although it shouldn't be as you have an obligation to your readers, viewers or listeners to say it as you see it. Against that, however, you also have an obligation to the manufacturer to be fair. Remember our discussion in chapters 8 and 9 when we talk about our ethical and legal obligations. As writers we do need to be careful. We need to ask ourselves, how serious are the faults that we identify? Are they sufficiently serious that the occupants' lives could be placed at risk (remember the recall of more than 50 million Takata airbags between 2015 and early 2017 after a number of people were injured in separate incidents worldwide)? Or are they just annoying (rattles and squeaks, unappealing colour combinations, or poor interior fitouts)?

A good example is the media's treatment of Volvo's crash avoidance technology in 2010. Australian journalists were provided with a first-hand demonstration of the technology in Europe. However journalists produced negative reports when the technology, which employs radar sensors and a camera to avoid pedestrians, hit a crash test dummy in three out of 12 runs. In another example, motoring writers were critical of the new Lexus hybrid, the CT200h hatchback, with one writer describing the noise inside the cabin as 'headache inducing'. Both of these incidents are different to the situation facing Volkswagen which, in late 2016 and early 2017, was facing penalties totalling billions of dollars for manipulating emissions controls in approximately 11 million diesel-powered motor vehicles during laboratory testing.

The decision to deceive consumers was a conscious one, although there is still debate as to who within the company knew about the decision, whereas in the case of the Lexus, the product was released in good faith, with engineers believing that it would meet sound-proofing requirements. In these situations, we should ask ourselves a number of questions: What impact will a negative review have on the company? Will it destroy its reputation and drive it into bankruptcy? This is a potentially valid question in the case of Volkswagen and even the Takata Airbags. Was the Volkswagen decision life-threatening? Probably not, although it was designed to deceive people who were genuinely conscious about pollution. As the Takata recall reveals (see the link at the end of this chapter), people did die and/or were injured because of the airbags, but we don't know whether the company was aware of the faults. Nor should we be so critical of the Lexus decision because it was a pre-release showcase for journalists, highlighting some of the technological advancements the company was working on. Thus, before being unduly critical of a company or a product, you need to consider the context.

There is a separate ethical question—one that we've touched on in other chapters: should you reveal to your readers or viewers that you have been provided free access to the motor vehicle you've been reviewing? Or that you've been flown business class (or even first class) to an exotic destination by the manufacturer and put up at a five-star hotel, while being wined and dined in silver service restaurants? The reality is, however, that most media organisations could not afford to self-fund the costs of attending such launches. Motoring journalists are constantly on the go, and the costs associated with such travel are astronomical. But that doesn't mean that they shouldn't advise their readers and viewers of this fact, as is generally the case with travel writing. For an insider's take on this, have a read of motoring writer Alborz Fallah's well-crafted piece in CarAdvice.com.au. Although, that doesn't eliminate the fact that readers or listeners might be less willing to accept everything said in the review if they knew that the journalist had been wined and dined by the host company.

The legal considerations are less problematic, although still worth bearing in mind. You can't defame a company, despite the damage a negative review will cause to its reputation. You can, however, defame individuals who work for a company, particularly if they are identified by name. You also need to be careful that even if you don't name people, your comments might identify them and therefore give them cause to consider legal action. But, as with the ethical considerations, this shouldn't be an issue if you consider what you write or say before you publish.

Summary

- o Motor vehicle reviewing is a rewarding form of journalism, one that can take journalists to exotic places to test-drive the latest vehicles.

- o While much of what appears in a review is templated, this is one of its strengths, as it helps people to draw comparisons between various options, and to make clear decisions.

- o Despite this, motoring writers, like reviewers generally, have obligations to potentially competing interests, in this case the manufacturer and the consumer. They also have obligations to distributors, who could also be affected by a poor review. For example, a poor review of a new model vehicle could cause a local distributor to lay off sales and workshop staff.

o Therefore, you do need to consider the consequences of your comments. Will it cause a product to be unfairly shunned by prospective purchasers? Are your criticisms justified?

Questions

1 Why is it that motor vehicles are considered the second most important purchase most people make in their lifetimes?
2 In what ways have changes in car affordability affected our attitudes towards motor vehicles?
3 What are the major ethical questions confronting the motor vehicle reviewer?

Activities

1 Write a review of your own car under the heading 'Bombs I would buy or avoid'. Provide a history of the car (type, model, year, how many owners, whether it has been in an accident etc.). Then focus on issues such as comfort, reliability, performance, cost of repairs and whether it would meet current safety and environmental concerns. Finally, give an honest appraisal of whether you would purchase it again.
2 Go online and find three websites that review the same make and model of motor vehicle. Compare the reviews. Why is one better than the others? What information does it contain that the others do not include? What photographic or video treatment do the various sites provide?
3 See if you can locate a copy of the NRMA's motoring magazine. How does it differ from other motoring magazines you have read? What are the most important/interesting aspects of the magazine?

References and additional reading

ABS, *see* Australian Bureau of Statistics

ACCC (2016). 'Takata Product Recall': https://www.productsafety.gov.au/news/takata-airbag-recalls-affecting-australian-consumers

Armstrong, N. (2016). http://www.motoring.com.au/volkswagen-tiguan-v-hyundai-tucson-2016-comparison-104611/

Australian Bureau of Statistics (2013). 'Australian social trends. Report No. 4102.0.: http://www.abs.gov.au/AUSSTATS/abs@.nsf/Lookup/4102.0Main+Features40July+2013

Australian Bureau of Statistics (2016, January). 'Motor vehicle census-Australia. Report no. 9309.0. Accessed from http://www.abs.gov.au/ausstats/abs@.nsf/mf/9309.0

Australian Bureau of Statistics (2016 Census). http://www.abs.gov.au/websitedbs/censushome.nsf/home/2016

Matthews, A. (2016). 'The new Renault Koleos features improved style and packaging, but can it knock Hyundai's Tucson off the perch?' http://www.motoring.com.au/hyundai-tucson-v-renault-koleos-2016-comparison-104149/

Fallah, A. (2014). 'The truth about automotive journalism': http://www.caradvice.com.au/296577/the-truth-about-automotive-journalism/

Hagon, T. (2012). 'Road test: Mercedes-Benz E63 AMG Estate', *Sydney Morning Herald, Drive Life* magazine, 10 February.

Online resources

Australian Muscle Car: www.musclecarmag.com.au

CarAdvice.com.au: http://www.caradvice.com.au/

CNET Australia: www.cnet.com.au

GoAuto.com.au: www.goauto.com.au

IAB Australia (2016). 'Online advertising spend in Australia reaches record $6.8 billion in 2016 financial year': http://www.campaignbrief.com/2016/08/online-advertising-spend-in-au.html

motoring.com.au: www.motoring.com.au

Online Motor Vehicle Advertising (2016). http://www.campaignbrief.com/2016/08/online-advertising-spend-in-au.html

roadtester: www.roadtester.com.au

Street Machine: http://streetmachinemag.typepad.com

Wheels Magazine: http://motoring.ninemsn.com.au/wheelsmag

Index